Contents

AFRICA
DEVELOPMENT
INDICATORS
2007

DATE DUE

THE WORLD BANK

To order *Africa Development Indicators 2007*, *The Little Data Book on Africa 2007*, and the Africa Development Indicators 2007—Multiple User CD-ROM, please visit the publications web site at www.worldbank.org/publications.

For more information about *Africa Development Indicators* and its companion products, please visit our web site at www.worldbank.org/africa. You can email us at ADI@worldbank.org.

Cover design by Communications Development Incorporated.

Photo credits: front cover, Eric Miller/World Bank; back cover, large top inset, Eric Miller/World Bank; bottom, left to right: Arne Hoel/World Bank, Arne Hoel/World Bank, M.Hallahan/Sumitomo Chemical - Olyset® Net, Arne Hoel/World Bank, Arne Hoel/World Bank.

ISBN: 978-0-8213-7283-8
e-ISBN: 978-0-8213-7284-5
DOI: 10.1596/978-0-8213-7283-8
SKU: 17283

Part IV. Household welfare

Foreword

Something decidedly new is on the horizon in Africa, something that began in the mid-1990s. Many African economies appear to have turned the corner and moved to a path of faster and steadier economic growth. Their performance in 1995–2005 reverses the collapses in 1975–85 and the stagnations in 1985–95. And for the first time in three decades, they are growing in tandem with the rest of the world. Average growth in the Sub-Saharan economies was 5.4 percent in 2005 and 2006, and the consensus projections are that growth will remain strong. Leading the way are the oil and mineral exporters, thanks to high prices. But 18 nonmineral economies, with 36 percent of Sub-Saharan Africa's people, have also been doing well.

Is this the outcome of good luck or good policy? Luck certainly has been a factor. Global economic growth has been fairly steady over the last 10 years, trade has expanded rapidly, and foreign direct investment has rocketed. But policies in many Sub-Saharan countries have also been getting better. Inflation, budget deficits, exchange rates, and foreign debt payments are more manageable. Economies are more open to trade and private enterprise. Governance is also on the mend, with more democracies and more assaults on corruption. Yes, some luck, but policy improvements have also made a difference.

Better economic policy and performance will also be at the core of improving African's well-being. More than 40 percent of the people in Sub-Saharan Africa still live on less than $1 a day, life expectancy gains have stalled in some countries and retreated in others, and poor health and poor schooling hold back improvements in people's productivity—and the chances of meeting the Millennium Development Goals. That is why

it is essential to spread economic growth to all of Africa and so essential to sustain it, by avoiding the collapses that have erased past gains.

This year's *Africa Development Indicators* essay explores the patterns of growth in Sub-Saharan Africa over the past three decades. It finds that the volatility of growth—an outcome of conflict, governance, and world commodity prices—has been greater than in any other region. Volatility has dampened expectations and investments—and has obscured some periods of good performance for some countries. The essay shows that pickups in growth were seldom sustained—indeed, that they were often followed by ferocious declines, and hence, Africa's flat economic performance over 1975–2005.

The essay shows that avoiding economic declines is as important as promoting growth. Indeed, it may be more important for the poor, who gain less during the growth pickups and suffer more during the declines. The essay discusses a key question for economic policymakers in Africa: how best to sustain pickups in growth and its benefits.

Africa Development Indicators 2007 is the latest annual report from the World Bank on social and economic conditions across the continent. Along with this book, *The Little Data Book on Africa 2007*, and the Africa Development Indicators 2007 CD-ROM, the Africa Development Indicators suite of products now has a new member: Africa Development Indicators Online.

With demand increasing for information to monitor the African Action Plan, Poverty Reduction Strategy Papers, national development programs, and the Millennium Development Goals and with access to electronic media widening in Africa, the Africa Development Indicators products are expected to continue evolving with the goal of offering the most relevant information to monitor development progress. This will allow us to assess the magnitude of problems and challenges faced and measure progress in a feasible way. Better statistics are of great value, and this still remains a great challenge for Africa.

Africa Development Indicators Online, available by subscription, contains the most comprehensive database on Africa, covering more than 1,000 indicators on economics, human development, private sector development, governance, and aid, with time series for many indicators going back to 1965. The indicators were assembled from a variety of sources to present a broad picture of development across Africa. The Microsoft Windows™–based format permits users to search and retrieve data in spreadsheet form, create maps and charts, and import them into other popular software programs for study or presentation. Africa Development Indicators Online also brings the *Africa Development Indicators 2007* essay, *The Little Data Book on Africa 2007*, country-at-a-glance tables, technical boxes, and country analyses from *African Economic Outlook 2007*.

The Africa Development Indicators suite of products is designed to provide all those interested in Africa with a set of indicators to monitor development outcomes in the region and is an important reference tool for those who want a better understanding of the economic and social developments occurring in Africa.

It is my hope that the Africa Development Indicators products will contribute to the way countries, development partners, analysts, academics, and the general public understand and design development policies in Africa.

John Page
Chief Economist, Africa Region

Acknowledgments

Africa Development Indicators 2007 was produced by the Office of the Chief Economist for the Africa Region and the Operational Quality and Knowledge Services Group.

Jorge Arbache and Rose Mungai were the managers of this book and its companions, Africa Development Indicators Online, Africa Development Indicators 2007—Multiple User CD-ROM, and *The Little Data Book on Africa 2007*. The core team of *Africa Development Indicators 2007* included Mpho Chinyolo, Francoise Genouille, Jane K. Njuguna, Joan Pandit, and Christophe Rockmore. The work was carried out under the general guidance and supervision of John Page, chief economist for the Africa Region.

The Development Data Group of the Development Economics Vice Presidency—including Mehdi Akhlaghi, Abdolreza Farivari, Richard Fix, Shelley Lai Fu, Shahin Outadi, William C. Prince, Atsushi Shimo, and Malarvizhi Veerappan—collaborated in the production of the Africa Development Indicators 2007—Multiple User CD-ROM, and *The Little Data Book on Africa 2007*.

The boxes in the technical notes benefited from contributions from Edward Al-Hussainy, Thorsten Beck, Francisco Galrão Carneiro, Punam Chuhan-Pole, Kene Ezemenari, Nevin Fahmy, Giuseppe Iarossi, Emily Gosse Kallaur, Caterina Ruggeri Laderchi, Sonia Plaza, Quentin Wodon, and Yutaka Yoshino.

Many colleagues from the Office of the Chief Economist and other units have made valuable contributions, including Gozde Isik, Ann Karasanyi, Vijdan Korman, Lebohang Lijane, Sergio Margulis, Kenneth Omondi, Xiao Ye, and Vildan Verbeek-Demiraydin.

Communications Development Incorporated provided overall design direction, editing, and layout, led by Bruce Ross-Larson, Meta de Coquereaumont, and Christopher Trott. Elaine Wilson created the graphics and laid out the book. Dohatec New Media prepared the navigation structure and interface design of the Africa Development Indicators Online.

Staff from External Affairs, including Richard Crabbe, Valentina Kalk, Malika Khek, Mario Trubiano, and Stuart Tucker, oversaw publication and dissemination of the book and its companions. Aby Toure, from the Africa External Affairs Group (AFREX), also helped disseminate Africa Development Indicators products.

Spreading and sustaining growth in Africa

Something decidedly new is on the horizon in Africa, something that began in the mid-1990s. Many African economies appear to have turned the corner and moved to a path of faster and steadier economic growth. Their performance over 1995–2005 reverses the collapses over 1975–85 and the stagnations over 1985–95. And for the first time in three decades, African economies are growing with the rest of the world. Average growth in the Sub-Saharan economies was 5.4 percent in 2005 and 2006. The consensus projection is 5.3 percent for 2007 and 5.4 percent for 2008. Leading the way: the oil and mineral exporters, thanks to high prices. But 18 non-mineral economies, with more than a third of the Sub-Saharan African people, have also been doing well.

Is this the outcome of good luck or good policy? Luck certainly has been a factor. Global economic growth has been fairly steady over the last 10 years—at 3.2 percent. Global trade has expanded at 40 percent a year. And foreign direct investment rocketed from 1.15 percent of world GDP in 1995 to more than 2.23 percent in 2005, with private equity funds scouring the globe for new opportunities. Emerging stock markets have also been burgeoning, thanks to global investors searching for high returns.

But policies in many Sub-Saharan countries have also been getting better. Inflation, budget deficits, exchange rates, and foreign debt payments are more manageable. Economies are more open to trade and private enterprise. Governance is also on the mend, with more democracies and more assaults on corruption. The conclusion: yes, some luck, but policy improvements have also made a difference.

Better economic policy and performance will be at the core of continuing to improve Africans' well-being. About 41 percent of Sub-Saharan Africa's people live on less than $1 a day. Because of AIDS, tuberculosis, malaria, and other diseases, improvements in life expectancy have stalled in some countries, retreated in a few others. And despite substantial progress in primary enrollments, educational outcomes are not improving as quickly as they might. Poor health and poor schooling naturally hold back improvements in people's productivity—and the chances of meeting the Millennium Development Goals. That is why it is so essential to spread economic growth to all of Africa and so essential to sustain it, by avoiding the collapses that have erased past gains.

This essay explores the patterns of growth in Sub-Saharan Africa over the past 30 years. It finds that the volatility of growth—a product of conflict, governance, and world commodity prices—has been greater than in any other region. That volatility has dampened expectations and investments—and has obscured some periods of good performance for some countries. The analysis here finds that pickups in growth were seldom sustained—indeed, that they were often followed by ferocious declines. Hence, Africa's flat economic performance over 1975–2005. Where an economy started in 1975 is pretty much where it ended in 2005. The reason: when things go well they do not last, and when they go wrong they go very wrong.

So, avoiding a decline from 2 percent GDP growth to –3 percent is as important as going from 2 percent to 7 percent. Indeed, it may be more important for poor people, who gain much less during growth pickups and suffer much more during the declines. The question for economic policymakers in Africa, then, is how best to sustain the pickups in growth. The answer: avoid the crushing declines.

Growing in tandem with the rest of the world

Since the mid-1990s average incomes in Africa have been rising in tandem with those in other regions. Despite an unanticipated oil shock, growth has remained good. Average growth in 2005 was 5.5 percent; it is estimated at 5.3 percent in 2006 and projected to be 5.3 percent in 2007. More than a third of Africans now live in countries that have grown at more than 4 percent a year for 10 years.

A group of diversified sustained growers has begun to emerge, and natural resources have gained new importance. In 2005 growth varied substantially, from –5.3 percent to 20.6 percent, and eight countries were near or above the 7 percent threshold needed to sustain poverty reduction. Along this continuum of growth performance three broad country types are emerging: slow-growth economies (36.7 percent of Africa's population), which include many conflict or post-conflict countries; diversified, sustained-growth economies (35.6 percent of Africa's population), which have grown at more than 4 percent a year for at least 10 years; and oil exporters (27.7 percent of Africa's population) (table 1).

Most of the successful growing economies share some characteristics. They integrate more with the world economy through trade, especially exports. Their investment and productivity are on the rise. And their institutions are getting better. What do recent data reveal about these aspects of growth in Africa (figures 1–9)?

Investment and efficiency

Africa's growth deficit is the product of low productivity and low investment. Growth accounting shows that physical capital per worker has grown less than 0.5 percent a year, half the world average. Capital shrank between 1990 and 2003, mirroring low capital investment. But the contribution of human capital to growth has kept pace with the rest of the world, mainly a result of rising average years of schooling. Indeed, the main culprit in Africa's disappointing growth is total factor productivity, negative since the 1960s and –0.4 percent between 1990 and 2003 (Bosworth and Collins 2003).

New evidence indicates improvement in these areas. Some improvements in the growth of output per worker in Africa were registered in recent years, and the contribution of total factor productivity dominated this recovery (Berthelemy and Soderling 2001).

Overall, investment increased between 2000 and 2006, from 16.8 percent of GDP to 19.5 percent. Sustained-growth countries have aggregate efficiency on par with India's and Vietnam's, and they are approaching these countries in investment. For the slow growers, by contrast, efficiency and investment were lower.

The aggregate productivity numbers are supported by firm studies (Eifert, Gelb, and Ramachandran 2005). Recent research shows that efficient African enterprises can compete with Chinese and Indian firms in factory floor costs (figure 10). They become less competitive, though, due to higher indirect business costs, including infrastructure (figures 11 and 12). In China indirect costs are about 8 percent of total costs, but in African countries they are 18–35 percent.

| Table 1 | African GDP growth rates, by country type, 1996–2005 |

Slow-growth economies GDP growth less than 4 percent a year (36.7 percent of population)		Diversified, sustained-growth economies GDP growth 4 percent a year or more (35.6 percent of population)		Oil exporters (27.7 percent of population)	
Country	GDP growth (percent)	Country	GDP growth (percent)	Country	GDP growth (percent)
Zambia	3.80	Mozambique	8.3	Equatorial Guinea	30.8
Guinea	3.70	Rwanda	7.6	Chad	9.0
Niger	3.50	São Tomé and Principe	7.1	Angola	8.5
Malawi	3.30	Botswana	6.7	Sudan	6.3
Mauritania	3.30	Uganda	6.1	Nigeria	4.3
Togo	3.30	Cape Verde	5.8	Congo, Rep.	3.4
Madagascar	3.20	Mali	5.8	Gabon	1.1
Lesotho	3.00	Tanzania	5.3		
Kenya	2.90	Ethiopia	5.2		
Eritrea	2.41	Sierra Leone	5.2		
Seychelles	2.30	Burkina Faso	5.0		
Comoros	2.13	Mauritius	4.8		
Central African Republic	0.85	Ghana	4.7		
Guinea-Bissau	0.47	Benin	4.6		
Burundi	0.43	Senegal	4.5		
Congo, Dem. Rep.	0.08	Cameroon	4.2		
Zimbabwe	–2.20	Gambia, The	4.2		
		Namibia	4.0		

Note: GDP growth rates are compound annual averages.
Source: World Bank Development Data Platform.

Trade

African exports have been growing over the last few years, most dramatically for the oil exporters, but for the non-oil-producers as well (table 2). Exports rose from $182 billion in 2004 to $230 billion in 2005, and 38 countries increased their exports, with pockets of nontraditional exports (such as clothing from Lesotho, Madagascar, and Mauritius). Rwanda, by helping farmers connect to buyers of high-quality coffee, boosted its coffee exports to the United States by 166 percent in 2005—driving its impressive growth. In Ghana thousands of employees process U.S. health insurance claims around the clock, and many customers in France do not realize that they are dealing with call centers in Senegal. In Kenya exports of cut flowers more than doubled between 2000 and 2005 to rank second among its exports, after tea. While these trends are encouraging, growth rates for non-oil-exporters are not yet high enough to constitute an export push.

Policies and governance

A central lesson of Africa's growth experience is that "policy and governance matter a great deal" (Ndulu and others 2007, p. 42). Africa today enjoys better growth prospects because its leaders have undertaken major reforms over the past 10 years. In 2006 Africa's best Country Policy and Institutional Assessment (CPIA) ratings were in macroeconomic management and trade policy. Over 1999–2006 average scores from the CPIA rose year on year, and the number of African countries with scores at or above the international "good performance" threshold of 3.5 on a scale of 1 to 6 increased from 5 to 15. The average African CPIA score in 1995 was 2.80. By 2006 it had risen to 3.2, and 27 of 36 countries evaluated in both years had improved their scores.[1]

Recent data from *Global Monitoring Report 2007* (World Bank 2007b) provide some evidence of better governance. Measures of bureaucratic capabilities and the quality of checks and balances institutions improved in six African countries (The Gambia, Ghana, Kenya, Madagascar, Senegal, and Tanzania). And three of the seven countries worldwide showing improved governance in a balanced manner over the last decade were in Africa. However, four countries suffered large declines in governance indicators (Central African Republic, Côte d'Ivoire, Eritrea, and Zimbabwe). In mid-2007 there were still 5 civil wars, much fewer than the 16 that existed in the late 1990s.

Doing more business

In the 2006/07 Doing Business indicators, the average rank of African countries was 136 among 178 countries (table 3). Four countries had ranks in the top third—Mauritius 32, South Africa 35, Namibia 43, and Botswana 51. Kenya rose to 72, and Ghana to 87. But all the others had ranks of 90 or higher.

Before 2005 African countries were slow to reform, but the pace has picked up in the last two years. Presidential investors' councils or similar bodies are active in seven countries, among them Mozambique, Rwanda, and Tanzania. Benchmarking through the World Bank's Doing Business surveys and Investment Climate Assessments has proven very useful in focusing high-level attention on the business environment.

Forty-six Sub-Saharan countries introduced at least one business environment reform in the past year, and Ghana and Kenya were among the top 10 reformers in the world in 2006/07. Eleven African countries introduced reforms to reduce the time and cost needed to start a business. For example,

Table 2	African export growth rates, by country type, 2003–06 (percent)			
Country group	**2003**	**2004**	**2005**	**2006**
All countries	8.2	12.9	14.1	11.3
Oil exporters	16.7	21.6	19.2	13.5
Non-oil-producers	4.5	7.6	5.7	7.1

Source: International Monetary Fund data.

Table 3	Average ease of doing business rank, by region, 2006/07
Region	**2006**
East Asia & Pacific	76
Europe & Central Asia	77
Latin America & the Caribbean	87
Middle East & North Africa	96
South Asia	107
Sub-Saharan Africa	136

Note: A lower rank is better.
Source: World Bank 2007a.

Figure 1 — African per capita income is now increasing in tandem with other developing countries

Annual change in real GDP per capita (%)

- **Developing countries**
- Developing countries, excluding China and India
- Sub-Saharan Africa
- High-income countries

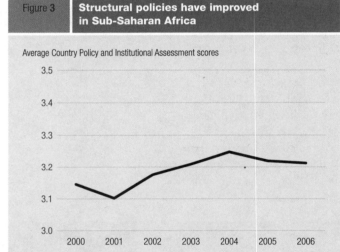

Source: World Bank Development Data Platform.

Figure 2 — Macroeconomic management has improved

Inflation, 2000–06 (percent)

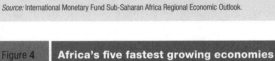

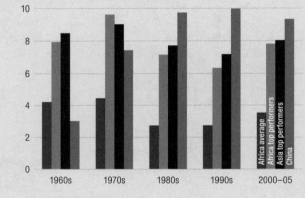

Oil-exporting countries
Sub-Saharan Africa
Oil-importing countries

Source: International Monetary Fund Sub-Saharan Africa Regional Economic Outlook.

Figure 3 — Structural policies have improved in Sub-Saharan Africa

Average Country Policy and Institutional Assessment scores

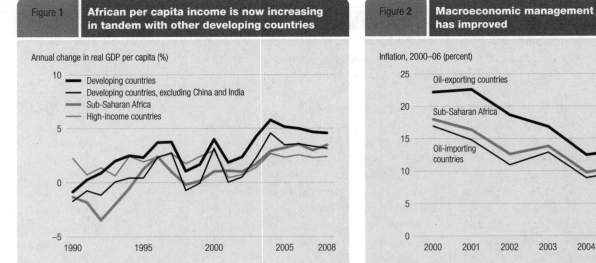

Source: World Bank 2006.

Figure 4 — Africa's five fastest growing economies stack up well with Asia . . .

Average annual GDP growth, by decade (percent)

Africa average
Africa top performers
Asia top performers
China

1960s 1970s 1980s 1990s 2000–05

Source: World Bank Development Data Platform.

Figure 5 — . . . but high population growth takes its toll on per capita income

Average annual GDP per capita growth, by decade (percent)

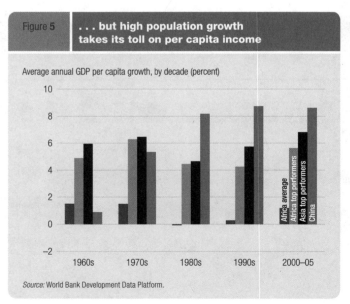

Africa average
Africa top performers
Asia top performers
China

1960s 1970s 1980s 1990s 2000–05

Source: World Bank Development Data Platform.

Figure 6 — Africa's best performers are on a par with India and Vietnam

Percent

Incremental output-capital ratio (percent)
Investment (percent of GDP)

Africa, sustained growth countries
Africa, slow growth countries
Africa, little or no growth countries
India
Vietnam

Source: World Bank Development Data Platform.

Figure 7

Exports are important . . .

Nonoil exports as share of GDP, by region (percent)

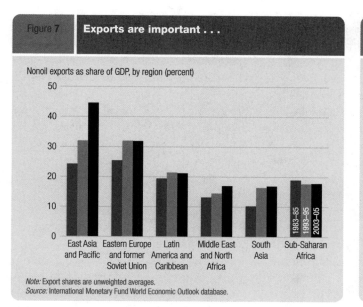

Note: Export shares are unweighted averages.
Source: International Monetary Fund World Economic Outlook database.

Figure 8

. . . but are growing slowly . . .

Average annual growth in exports, by decade (percent)

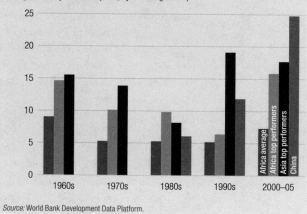

Source: World Bank Development Data Platform.

Figure 9

. . . and are declining in importance for Africa's top performers

Exports as a share of GDP (percent)

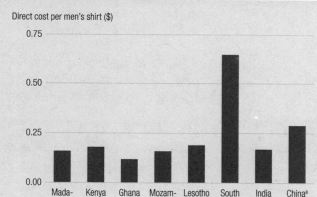

Source: World Bank Development Data Platform.

Figure 10

Factory floor costs in Sub-Saharan Africa compare well with those in China and India

Direct cost per men's shirt ($)

a. For factories in an export processing zone.
Source: World Bank Development Data Platform.

Figure 11

The overall cost structures of firms show that indirect costs are much higher in Africa

Share of total costs (percent)   ■ Material ■ Labor ■ Capital ■ Indirect

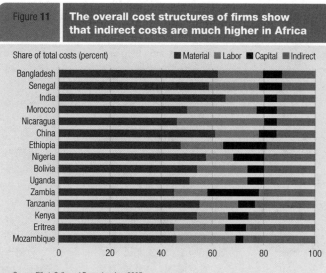

Source: Eifert, Gelb, and Ramachandran 2005.

Figure 12

And net productivity is much lower than "factory floor" (gross) productivity due to high costs of doing business

Total factor productivity (China = 1)

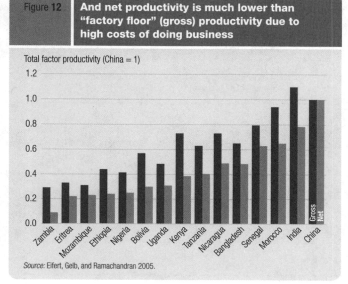

Source: Eifert, Gelb, and Ramachandran 2005.

Burkina Faso created a one-stop shop for business entry, cutting required procedures from 12 to 8 and time from 45 days to 34.

Although financial depth remains low in Africa, signs of recovery are encouraging. Real private sector credit as a share of GDP in low-income African countries has turned the corner, reaching almost 13 percent in 2005, about a third higher than its low point in 1996.

Africa's success in restoring growth is beginning, however, to reveal some emerging constraints to future growth. Infrastructure across the continent is under stress. Skills to build and sustain competitive enterprises are lacking. And the many small and landlocked economies face unique challenges that can be addressed only through effective regional integration. African agriculture—long neglected—may also emerge as a constraint to growth in some economies and as the sector for sharing the benefits of growth broadly in others.

Closing the infrastructure gap

Sub-Saharan Africa lags at least 20 percentage points behind the average for International Development Association countries on almost all major infrastructure measures.[2] In addition, the quality of service is low, supplies are unreliable, and disruptions are frequent and unpredictable—all pushing up production costs, a critical impediment for investors (table 4). There are also large inequities in access to household infrastructure services, with coverage rates in rural areas lagging behind those in urban areas. The region's unmet infrastructure needs are estimated at $22 billion a year (5 percent of GDP), plus another $17 billion for operations and maintenance.

Recent progress is encouraging. Except roads, indicators of infrastructure access rose between the 1990s and the 2000s (table 5). The Africa Partnership Forum reported steady improvements in effectively using existing infrastructure and in increasing public investments. Countries are also undertaking regulatory and policy reforms, especially in water, telecommunications, and transport (Africa Partnership Forum 2006b). Twenty of the largest African countries have or are formulating reform agendas for water and sanitation.

Compared with other regions, Africa has been slow to mobilize the private sector for the provision and financing of infrastructure. The Infrastructure Consortium reports that private sector interest has gradually spread. There is an upward trend in private sector provision and management of infrastructure, which stood at $6 billion in 2006, up from $4 billion in 2004. Most private flows (84 percent) go to telecommunications and energy. Concessions have now been awarded to operate and rehabilitate many African ports and railways and some power distribution enterprises, but financial commitments by the concessionaire companies are often small. This reflects both the value of the management improvements that the concessionaire is expected to bring and the limited scale and profitability of the enterprises taken over. An important facilitator in some cases has been the insurance instruments developed over the past 15 years by such bodies as the U.S. Overseas Private Investment Corporation and the Multilateral Investment Guarantee Agency and by the World Bank's Partial Risk Guarantee offerings.

Table 4	Impact of unreliable infrastructure services on the productive sector		
Service problem		Sub-Saharan Africa	Developing countries
Electricity			
Delay in obtaining electricity connection (days)		79.9	27.5
Electrical outages (days per year)		90.9	28.7
Value of lost output due to electrical outages (percent of turnover)		6.1	4.4
Firms maintaining own generation equipment (percent of total)		47.5	31.8
Telecommunications			
Delay in obtaining telephone line (days)		96.6	43.0
Telephone outages (days per year)		28.1	9.1

Note: Data for Sub-Saharan Africa are for 6 countries; data for developing countries are for 55 countries.
Source: World Bank Investment Climate Assessments.

Table 5	Improvements in African infrastructure access			
Service		1990s	2000s	Percent change
Telephones (per 1,000 people)		21	90	328.6
Improved water (percent of households)		55	65	18.1
Improved sanitation (percent of households)		31	37	19.3
Grid electricity (percent of households)		16	23	43.8

Source: World Bank 2006.

There has been significant progress in information and communication technology. Access to communications services has increased dramatically over the past three years, with the proportion of the population (excluding South Africa) living under the mobile telephone footprint rising from 3 percent in 1999 to 50 percent in 2006. This has been matched by an equally rapid increase in the use of communications services. By the end of 2006 there were 123 million mobile subscribers. Average penetration rates in the region doubled between 2004 and 2006 to reach 16 percent.

Building skills for competitiveness and growth

The enrollment trends in secondary and tertiary education are positive, though completion rates and quality remain low. The secondary gross enrollment rate rose from a regional average of 24 percent in 1999 to 31 percent in 2004. Still, only 30 percent of each age cohort completes junior secondary school and 12 percent senior secondary. There is also considerable variation. Botswana, Cape Verde, Mauritius, Namibia, Seychelles, and South Africa enroll more than 80 percent of the relevant population in junior secondary schools, while Burundi, Burkina Faso, Central African Republic, Niger, and Rwanda enroll less than 20 percent. Access to tertiary education has been increasing at 15 percent a year across the region, but coverage remains the lowest in the world, less than 5 percent of the relevant age population. Gender parity in secondary education is improving, with women making up more than 40 percent of enrollments in most countries (up from 20–30 percent 10 years ago).

Over the past two years African policymakers and development partners have placed greater emphasis on postprimary education and primary school completion. National policies are being reoriented toward better tertiary education in Botswana, The Gambia, Kenya, Nigeria, Rwanda, Tanzania, and Uganda. Private secondary education and training are expanding, and public-private partnerships are emerging. Previously neglected issues—such as labor market links among curricula, science and technology capacities, and research performance—are emerging in public discussions. And private options are increasing.

Integrating the region's economies

The small size of African economies and the fact that many countries are landlocked call for regional approaches to common problems: infrastructure in trade corridors, common institutional and legal frameworks (customs administration, competition policy, regulation of common property resources such as fisheries), and transborder solutions to regional health issues.

African leaders are more aware of the benefits of regional approaches, especially in matters related to trade and infrastructure. The New Partnership for Africa's Development has adopted regional integration as one of its core objectives, and the African Union is leading efforts to rationalize regional economic communities. Most countries in Africa are party to multiple treaties or conventions addressing joint development and management of shared water resources (including navigation and fisheries), hydropower, trade corridors, irrigation, and flood control. Progress has been most notable in regional infrastructure, particularly regional power pools (in West and Southern Africa) and in launching customs unions (West, East, and Southern Africa). Progress on regional infrastructure is slowed by the technical complexity of multicountry projects and the time required for decisions by multiple governments. There is less progress in regional approaches to education and in systematically addressing regional health issues.

Making agriculture more productive

Sustained growth that reduces rural poverty will require that more countries achieve 5 percent annual growth in agricultural value added. While growth in agricultural value added has been strong since 2000, averaging 4.6 percent in 2004, too little of it has come from higher productivity or yields.[3] While land productivity is increasing in 38 of 46 countries, only 6 have a rate of increase of 5 percent or more.[4] Labor productivity is increasing in 29 countries, with 10 achieving increases of 3 percent a year or higher.[5]

Productivity growth will require an expansion of area irrigated, as well as better performance of rainfed agriculture. But less than 4 percent of cultivated land is irrigated. Because of the long lead time before investments are completed and operational, this proportion changed little in the past 18 months. Improvements in management of soil fertility have been slow, as has the adoption of better seeds. Spending for agricultural research and technology remains low, although it is starting to increase along with overall spending on agricultural programs in the region (Africa Partnership Forum 2006a). On a positive note there has been an increase in the use of water management techniques (water harvesting, reduced tillage).

Why growth is so important: meeting the Millennium Development Goals to reduce poverty and improve social outcomes

Human development outcomes are improving across the region, and progress toward the Millennium Development Goals is picking up. In 1990, 47 percent of Africans lived in poverty. In 2004, 41 percent did, and on present trends 37 percent will in 2015. Gross primary school enrollment rates rose from 79 percent in 1999 to 92 percent in 2004. Health outcomes are more varied but are also improving in many countries. In 2005 eight countries were near or above the 7 percent threshold needed to sustain poverty reduction.

Good economic growth and sustained efforts by governments and their development partners have accelerated progress on the Millennium Development Goals. Although Sub-Saharan Africa is one of two regions not expected to reach most of the Millennium Development Goals by 2015 (the other is South Asia), there is substantial variation among countries in both the level of attainment of the goals and the pace of progress. Mauritius has met four goals. Botswana has met three and will likely meet one more. And South Africa has met three. Among other countries nine will meet two goals, and 13 will meet at least one. But despite better progress—especially in education, malaria, and HIV/AIDS—23 African countries are not likely to meet any of the Millennium Development Goals.

Education

Between 1990 and 2004 the average literacy rate (in the 29 countries for which data are available) rose from 54 percent to 62 percent, while the range improved from 11–81 percent to 26–87 percent. This convergence is the result of rising primary school enrollments. Regionwide gross enrollment rose from 79 percent in 1999 to 92 percent in 2004. Some 87 percent of Africans live in countries where the average enrollment rate is above 75 percent, and fewer than 2 percent live in countries where the rate is below 50 percent. Six of the seven top countries worldwide in boosting primary completion rates (by more than 10 percent a year between 2000 and 2005) are in Africa (Benin, Guinea, Madagascar, Mozambique, Niger, and Rwanda). There have not been comparable improvements in secondary and tertiary education. While East Asian countries increased secondary enrollment rates by 21 percentage points and tertiary enrollment rates by 12 percentage points over 12 years, Africa raised its secondary rates by only 7 percentage points and its tertiary rates by 1 percentage point.

Health

Between 1990 and 2005 life expectancy at birth in Sub-Saharan Africa declined from 49.2 years to 47.1. Although life expectancy increased in 25 countries by an average of eight years, it declined in 21 more populous countries by an average of four years. HIV/AIDS, malaria, and armed conflict have contributed to these falling life expectancies. Progress against malaria, tuberculosis, and HIV/AIDS is mixed but showing some positive signs. The spread of AIDS has slowed in Africa, but the continent still bears the brunt of the epidemic. Rapid increases in tuberculosis infections in Africa are linked to the greater likelihood of tuberculosis appearing from latent infections among HIV carriers. Malaria remains Africa's leading killer of children under age 5, but a strong new global partnership has formed to address the disease.

There is evidence that outcomes are improving for some of the other health Millennium Development Goals. Progress in addressing child mortality has been slow worldwide, but there are promising signs in Africa. The share of children ages 12–23 months immunized against measles went from 57 percent in 1990 to 64 percent in 2005. Some 70 percent of Africans now live in countries where under-five mortality has dropped to 100–200 per 1,000 live births, while only 16 percent live in countries with rates above 200. Eritrea, despite a per capita income of only $190, cut child mortality in half between 1990 and 2005. Substantial work is still needed for countries to meet the Millennium Development Goal of reducing the rate by two-thirds by 2015.

Can growth be spread and sustained? Yes, if the past is not prologue

Africa today is thus very different from the Africa of the early 1990s, when it was coming out of the declines after the first two oil price shocks and the stagnation of the adjustment years. Whether it can stay different will depend on whether it can spread and sustain growth. To find out what that might take, this section looks at the patterns of long-term growth in Sub-Saharan Africa, using the most recent purchasing power parity data for 45 countries (Arbache and Page 2007a).

Country patterns

Sub-Saharan GDP per capita increased only modestly between 1975 and 2005 (figure 13). The average GDP per capita of most countries in 2005 closely mirrors that in 1975, reflecting inertia, stratification, and initial conditions in economic output (figure 14). Countries that started poor, stayed poor, and those that started richer, stayed richer—with few exceptions. Botswana and Namibia saw their GDP per capita shoot up, and Eritrea and Mozambique saw theirs tumble. Accompanying Africa's slow growth is considerable instability in countries. The GDP per capita of countries varied wildly, as did the volatility of growth (figure 15). Volatility hit countries at different incomes (Botswana and Malawi) and on different long-term paths (Cape Verde, Comoros, and South Africa).

With poorer countries growing more slowly, the gap between their incomes and those of richer countries widened. The richest 10 percent of countries had 10.5 times the GDP per capita of the poorest 10 percent in 1975 and 18.5 times that in 2005. So even with country growth rates now converging, Africa has become more unequal across countries. The polarization of richer and poorer countries appears to

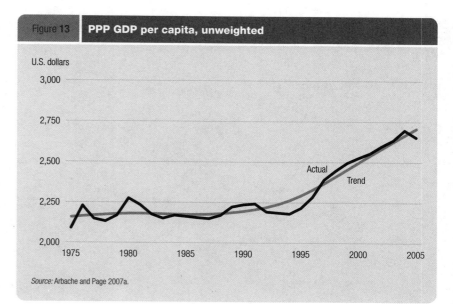

Figure 13   **PPP GDP per capita, unweighted**

Source: Arbache and Page 2007a.

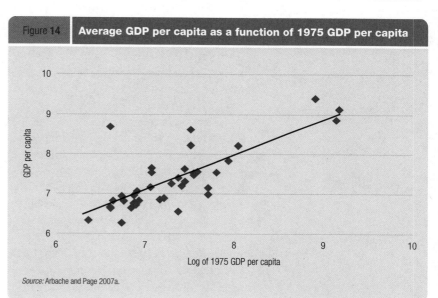

Figure 14   **Average GDP per capita as a function of 1975 GDP per capita**

Source: Arbache and Page 2007a.

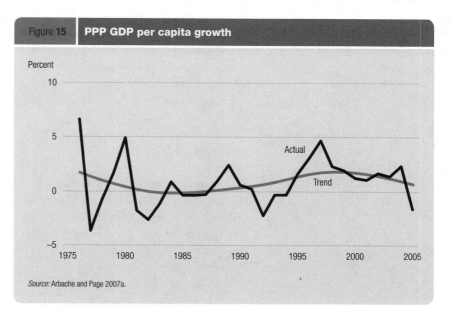

Figure 15   **PPP GDP per capita growth**

Source: Arbache and Page 2007a.

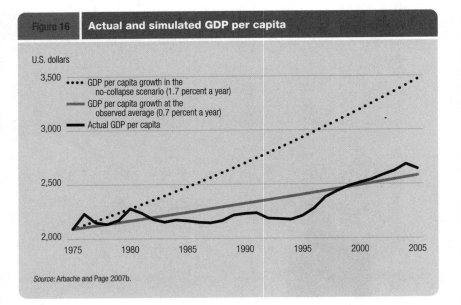

Figure 16 Actual and simulated GDP per capita

U.S. dollars

- •••• GDP per capita growth in the no-collapse scenario (1.7 percent a year)
- —— GDP per capita growth at the observed average (0.7 percent a year)
- —— Actual GDP per capita

Source: Arbache and Page 2007b.

have increased over 1985–95, when many countries plunged into conflict. Emerging as regional stars are Botswana, Cape Verde, Gabon, Mauritius, Namibia, Seychelles, and South Africa, with 9 percent of the region's people but 45 percent of its GDP.

How did countries fare in income per capita relative to South Africa, the region's largest economy (now 38 percent of the region's total GDP)? Nineteen improved, 13 stayed put, and 11 saw steep declines. The mineral exporters Botswana, Cape Verde, and Equatorial Guinea registered among the strongest improvements. But Angola, Chad, and Nigeria stayed put, showing that mineral resources do not always determine success.

This all suggests that African countries experience similar economic cycles, in an environment of interdependence, contagion, and other regional spillovers. Among the channels for the cross-country similarities in GDP per capita and productivity are worker remittances, temporary migration, and regional conflicts. Consider Chad and Sudan, Liberia and Sierra Leone, and the Democratic Republic of Congo and its neighbors.

Volatility matters little for growth

Slow output growth and high volatility are the defining characteristics of the long-run pattern of Sub-Saharan growth just described. But does high volatility mean slow growth? Not necessarily—or not directly.

Recent work finds a negative but not statistically significant relationship between volatility and growth and between volatility and GDP per capita. That could be because policy and structural characteristics were not properly taken into account. It could also be that African economies are so stuck in their long-run ruts that short-term volatility cannot divert them. Or it could be that volatility and poor growth performance are both symptoms of institutionally weak societies and so are not independent (Acemoglu, Johnson, and Robinson 2003). In this view, policies are tools for the groups in power to reap rents and stay in power, adding to the difficulty of dealing with political and economic shocks, leading to more political and economic instability.

Because long-run growth in Africa was both low and volatile, it is a challenge to identify periods of sustained growth or decline. In 1975–85 Africa suffered two oil shocks, a plunge in commodity prices, and the eruption of conflict. In 1985–95 it introduced structural reforms that brought austerity to many countries. In 1995–2005 it began to recover. But the economic trajectories for individual countries were far from linear. The volatility of growth, just discussed, bears little relation to the long-run performance of an economy.

Though volatility itself may matter little for the overall rate of economic growth—and per capita income—for a typical African country, it may nevertheless indicate that growth spurts are offset by growth collapses. Some of these growth accelerations and decelerations may be due to pure bad luck: commodity prices rise and then fall. But others may be due to policy choices by governments. Looking at the underlying characteristics of growth accelerations and decelerations might thus provide some insights into how to sustain the spurts and avoid the collapses (Arbache and Page 2007b).

Sustaining the good times and avoiding the bad are what matter

The accelerations and decelerations on a country's economic path—the good times and the bad—show that African countries experienced several episodes of growth over 1975–2005. But they have also saw a comparable number of collapses, offsetting most of the growth. If Africa could have avoided the collapses, it would have grown at 1.7 percent a year per capita, not 0.7 percent. A percentage point might seem small, but it would have added 30 percent to the region's GDP (figure 16). So avoiding the collapses is a major economic challenge in Africa.

What constitutes good times for a given country? Four conditions. First, the four-year forward moving average of GDP per capita growth minus the country's four-year backward moving average is greater than zero for a given year. Second, the four-year forward moving average of growth is above the country's long-run trend. Third, the four-year forward moving average of GDP per capita exceeds the four-year backward average. Fourth, the first three conditions are satisfied for at least three years in a row followed by the three subsequent years after the last year that satisfies the first three conditions. And what constitutes the bad? The opposites of the first three conditions for the good.

Consider Tanzania. The first condition was met for the high growth years 1995–2005 (figure 17). But all four conditions were met for 1998–2005, which thus qualify as good times. The years just before that were a recovery from recession.

Now consider Senegal. It contracted during the bad times of 1998–2004, when the average rate of decline was –1.4 percent, well below the trend of 0.35 percent (figure 18). Then it grew at 1.75 percent during the good times of 1994–2001, not great but more than three points better than before.

And now South Africa. It contracted at –1.9 percent during 1982–87 and at –1.5 percent during 1989–94, below the trend of 0.1 percent (figure 19). Then during the good times of 1999–2005 GDP per capita growth rebounded to 2 percent.

Africa the region grew by 3.6 percent a year during good times and shrank by –2.7 percent during the bad. Most of the good times were in 1995–2005, and most of the bad in the preceding two decades. In 1975–85 the bad times were 3.5 times more frequent than the good, and in 1985–95, 0.7 times more frequent.

For many countries there is no substantial difference in the unconditional probability of good times or bad, canceling the benefits of growth (table 6). But for oil exporters and resource-rich countries, the good and bad times are well above the mean,

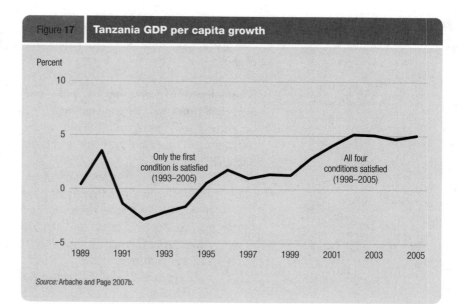

Figure 17 Tanzania GDP per capita growth

Percent

Only the first condition is satisfied (1993–2005)

All four conditions satisfied (1998–2005)

Source: Arbache and Page 2007b.

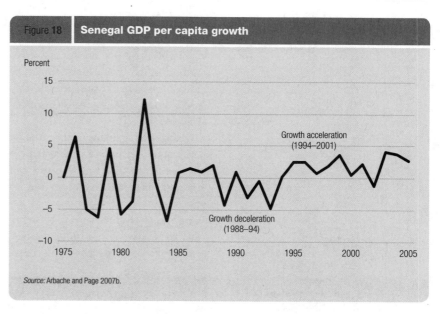

Figure 18 Senegal GDP per capita growth

Percent

Growth acceleration (1994–2001)

Growth deceleration (1988–94)

Source: Arbache and Page 2007b.

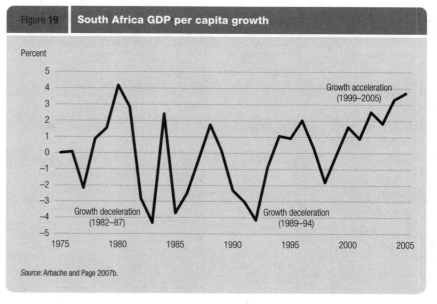

Figure 19 South Africa GDP per capita growth

Percent

Growth acceleration (1999–2005)

Growth deceleration (1982–87)

Growth deceleration (1989–94)

Source: Arbache and Page 2007b.

and for conflict countries the probability of bad times is substantially higher than that of good.

What happens in good times and bad—and in normal times, neither good nor bad?

Countries see numerous differences between normal times and good and bad times (table 7):

- Saving and investment (and especially foreign direct investment) are higher in good times than in normal times—and much lower in bad times. And countries with higher savings and investment have more good times and fewer bad times. So, growth swings seem associated with changes in economic fundamentals.
- Domestic consumption is lower in good times than in normal times, probably because more resources are going to investment. But it is also lower in bad times, probably because households have less purchasing power.
- The share of agriculture in the economy is higher in bad times, as people return to the land. The share of industry is somewhat larger in good times.
- Countries that rely less on agriculture have more good times, probably because they are more diversified and less exposed to insects, drought, other natural disasters, and swings in the prices for agricultural products.
- Inflation is higher in bad times.
- Trade is substantially lower in bad times, with imports dropping sharply.
- The real effective exchange rate is more competitive in good times, but substantially less in bad. It depreciates in the good, appreciates in the bad.
- Official development assistance per capita is higher in good times, far lower in bad, as is official development assistance as a percentage of GDP. So, official development assistance is procyclical, reinforcing the importance of predictable aid for sustained growth.
- Life expectancy is lower in bad times.
- Infant mortality and child mortality are significantly higher in bad times (box 1).
- Primary school completion rates are significantly lower in bad times.
- The Country Policy and Institutional Assessment score drops in bad times, and countries with lower scores tend to experience more bad times. Countries that have more good times also have more voice and accountability. All governance indicators get worse during bad times. There is thus a close relationship between governance and growth, but it is far more relevant for understanding the bad times than the good.

Country differences

Countries with a high probability of good times tend to have faster growth and a lower probability of bad times—while countries with a high probability of bad times tend to have slow growth. This may sound obvious, but the wide gap between growth rates during good times and bad times is most important. True, volatility is at play, but the gap also suggests that countries have the capability and resilience to grow when internal and external economic conditions and institutions favor them. The gaps tend to be wide for countries

Table 6	Frequency of growth acceleration and deceleration, by country category, 1975–2005			
	Growth acceleration		Growth deceleration	
Country category	Frequency (country-years)	Above or below all countries mean	Frequency (country-years)	Above or below all countries mean
All countries mean	0.25		0.22	
Coastal	0.26	Above	0.22	Equal
Landlocked	0.23	Below	0.22	Equal
Coastal without resources	0.24	Below	0.23	Above
Landlocked without resources	0.22	Below	0.22	Equal
Oil exporters	0.29	Above	0.23	Above
Non–oil exporters	0.24	Below	0.22	Equal
Resource countries	0.30	Above	0.21	Below
Nonresource countries	0.23	Below	0.23	Above
Major conflict	0.16	Below	0.17	Below
Minor conflict	0.19	Below	0.32	Above

Source: Arbache and Page 2007b.

During normal times the average infant mortality rate across Sub-Saharan Africa is 86.2 per 1,000. During good times, the ratio falls slightly to 84.2, which is not statistically different. But there is a major increase of infant mortality to 114.1 during the bad times. This evidence is illustrated by the kernel density distribution. During normal or accelerating times the kernel is right skewed (figures 1 and 2). But during decelerating times the kernel curve is clearly skewed to the left, and a second peak emerges, representing the countries experiencing much worse infant mortality levels (figure 3).

Among the countries in the second peak are Malawi and Mali in 1980, both of whose infant mortality rate was 176. Remarkably, as growth accelerated these countries experienced substantially lower figures: 115 in 1995 for Malawi and 124 in 2000 for Mali. Other countries in the second peak include Angola in 1990 and 1995, Niger in 1985 and 1990, and Sierra Leone in 1985, 1990, and 1995. These examples highlight the asymmetric relationship between growth acceleration and deceleration and social indicators, suggesting that growth volatility does matter and is marginally more important for the poor than growth acceleration.

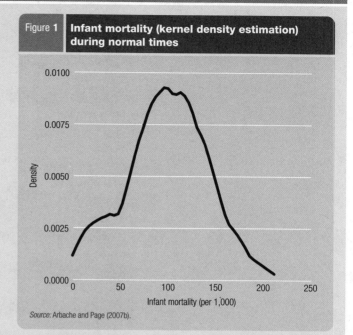

Figure 1   **Infant mortality (kernel density estimation) during normal times**

Source: Arbache and Page (2007b).

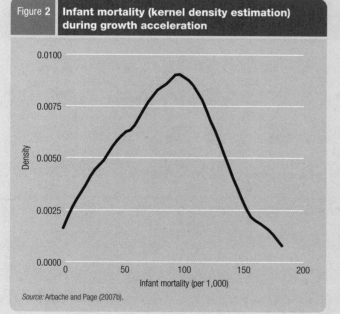

Figure 2   **Infant mortality (kernel density estimation) during growth acceleration**

Source: Arbache and Page (2007b).

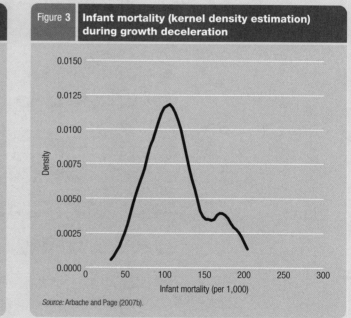

Figure 3   **Infant mortality (kernel density estimation) during growth deceleration**

Source: Arbache and Page (2007b).

in conflict and for countries rich in resources and thus exposed to commodity price volatility. But they are also wide for landlocked, resource-poor countries (such as Ethiopia and Mali).

What appears to increase the odds for good times? Higher savings. More foreign direct investment. A more competitive exchange rate. And what might reduce those odds? Higher government spending and major conflicts.

What appears to increase the odds for bad times? Inflation and minor conflicts. And what might reduce those odds? Higher savings, more domestic investment, more foreign investment, and more trade.

So, policies to sustain the good times and hold the bad at bay should increase savings, investment, and trade; attract foreign investment; and reduce conflict. Contributing to this are a friendlier business environment, stronger institutions, and better

Table 7 | Difference between sample averages, 1975–2005

Variable	Normal times	Growth acceleration		Growth deceleration	
		Mean	t-test	Mean	t-test
Savings (percent of GDP)	11.4	15.3	*	7.09	*
Investments (percent of GDP)	20.0	23.1	*	15.5	*
Private sector investment (percent of GDP)	12.2	13.8	*	9.17	*
Foreign direct investments net flow (percent of GDP)	2.51	4.2	*	0.72	*
Consumption (percent of GDP)	93.4	88.8	*	89.7	*
Agriculture value added (percent of GDP)	29.8	28.5		31.9	*
Industry value added (percent of GDP)	25.3	27.0	**	24.5	
Service value added (percent of GDP)	44.9	44.4		43.5	
Consumer price index (percent)	27.2	15.2		184.7	*
GDP deflator (percent)	26.9	16.7		175	*
Public debt (percent of GNI)	87.3	112.3	*	115.7	*
Government consumption (percent of GDP)	17.2	16.0	**	15.2	*
Trade (percent of GDP)	74.7	76.2		58.7	*
Exports (percent of GDP)	30.1	31.6		26.5	*
Imports (percent of GDP)	44.6	44.4		32.5	*
Real effective exchange rate (2000=100)	130.2	115.1	*	186.4	*
Terms of trade (2000=100)	109.5	102.2	*	114.5	
Current account (percent of GDP)	−5.96	−5.83		−6.03	
ODA (percent of GDP)	14.2	13.8		12.1	**
ODA per capita ($)	57.3	69.5	*	41.8	*
Life expectancy (years)	50.8	51.3		48.2	*
Dependency ratio	0.93	0.91	**	0.93	
Under-five mortality (per 1,000)	150.4	145.8		188.7	*
Infant mortality (per 1,000 live births)	86.2	84.2		114.1	*
Primary completion rate (percent of relevant age group)	53.2	52.7		40.9	*
Country Policy and Institutional Assessment (1 low to 6 high)	3.17	3.2		2.75	*
Voice and accountability (−2.5 low to 2.5 high)	−0.65	−0.45	*	−1.08	*
Political stability (−2.5 low to 2.5 high)	−0.47	−0.45		−1.07	*
Government effectiveness (−2.5 low to 2.5 high)	−0.65	−0.58		−1.03	*
Regulatory quality (−2.5 low to 2.5 high)	−0.61	−0.49		−0.97	*
Rule of law (−2.5 low to 2.5 high)	−0.62	−0.65		−1.14	*
Control of corruption (−2.5 low to 2.5 high)	−0.55	−0.57		−0.92	*
Minor conflict (frequency)	0.09	0.08		0.16	*
Major conflict (frequency)	0.12	0.05	*	0.07	*

* indicates test that the mean is not equal to the value for normal times, significant at the 5 percent level.
** indicates that the mean is not equal to the value for normal times, significant at the 10 percent level.
Source: Arbache and Page 2007b.

governance. And more trade can stave off collapses in growth. But these are generalizations. Only country case work can provide a more accurate view.

So, is Africa's recent growth likely to last?

Per capita incomes in Africa grew at 1.9 percent a year during 1995–2005, up from −0.1 percent over 1975–95, with growth shared by countries with very different

characteristics and accompanied by better fiscal performance and better governance. But driving that growth was the high demand for minerals and particularly for oil. Resource-rich countries grew at 3.4 percent a year, oil-exporting countries at 4.5 percent, and non-oil-exporting countries at 1.3 percent. And the unconditional probability of an episode of good times was 55 percent for the resource-rich countries, 49 percent for the

Table 8	Difference between sample averages, 1985–94 and 1995–2005								
	All countries			**Resource rich**			**Non–resource rich**		
Variable	1995–2005	1985–94	t-test	1995–2005	1985–94	t-test	1995–2005	1985–94	t-test
Savings (percent of GDP)	12.05	11.44		14.85	9.31	*	10.88	12.42	**
Investments (percent of GDP)	20.94	19.32	*	25.06	19.04	*	19.19	19.44	
Private sector investment (percent of GDP)	12.51	10.88	*	15.43	11.81	*	11.23	10.49	
Foreign direct investments net flow (percent of GDP)	4.95	1.48	*	8.22	1.69	*	3.63	1.40	*
Consumption (percent of GDP)	91.12	92.45		79.90	85.87	*	95.85	95.19	
Trade (percent of GDP)	76.58	67.29	*	85.77	75.29	*	72.73	63.82	*
Exports (percent of GDP)	32.27	27.71	*	40.32	34.73	*	28.86	24.67	*
Imports (percent of GDP)	44.27	39.57	*	45.25	40.55	**	43.86	39.15	*
Real effective exchange rate (2000=100)	103.52	138.32	*	109.18	145.54	*	100.06	134.38	*
Terms of trade (2000=100)	102.40	106.98	*	104.53	113.65	**	101.63	104.45	
Current account (percent of GDP)	−5.58	−5.18		−3.71	−5.22		−6.43	−5.16	**
Consumer price index (percent)	33.98	112.52		77.81	56.45		16.98	133.11	
GDP deflator (percent)	42.85	106.63		71.73	54.40		30.46	129.07	
Public debt (present value, percent of GNI)	128.41	115.16	**	163.61	146.79		114.53	101.90	**
Government consumption (percent of GDP)	15.48	17.13	*	16.44	20.52	*	15.12	15.64	

* indicates that 1985–94 and 1995–2005 values are not equal, significant at the 5 percent level.
** indicates that 1985–94 and 1995–2005 values are not equal, significant at the 10 percent level.
Source: Arbache 2007.

oil-exporting countries, and 36 percent for the non-oil-exporting countries.

If growth is now more likely to last, the economic fundamentals should be stronger in 1995–2005 than they were in 1985–95. Investments in recent good times were slightly higher, but foreign direct investment and trade were significantly higher. The exchange rate was more competitive, but the terms of trade slightly less favorable. Government consumption was down slightly. And with investment basically at the same level, productivity should have increased substantially. Indeed, productivity has been one of the biggest factors behind Africa's recent growth (Ndulu and others 2007).

For resource-rich countries savings and investments and most notably foreign investment increased in the last decade, while consumption fell (table 8). The exchange rate became more competitive, and the current account improved.

For the other countries savings fell and investments remained at the same level, while current account and public debt worsened. But the exchange rate was more competitive, and trade increased.

How does Africa stand up to other developing regions? Its GDP growth is on par only with slow-growing Latin America and the Caribbean, a third that in South Asia, and a fifth that in East Asia and Pacific. Savings and investment were well below those in all other regions. Foreign direct investment compared well, but it was concentrated in oil and minerals in only a few countries. Trade also compared well, but again it was highly concentrated and dependent on few sectors. Consumption was higher, reflecting the low propensity to save. And inflation and government consumption were higher.

The upshot? Africa's economic fundamentals on average are not much better after a decade of growth. Favoring that growth was certainly better trade conditions, but not significantly more savings and capital accumulation. Statistically it cannot be said that growth is more likely to last than it was a decade ago. It remains vulnerable to lower demand for oil and metals and to other outside shocks. What can be done to reduce that vulnerability?

Be sure to avoid the bad times while pursuing the good

To spread and sustain growth in Africa, the evidence here points to three key objectives: avoiding collapses in growth, accelerating productivity growth, and increasing private investment. This can be accomplished by increasing the number and variety of firms and farms that can compete in the global economy. For the coastal economies this implies pushing exports, and for the landlocked, increasing their connectivity to regional and global markets through deeper regional integration. These in turn require adopting the four sets of policies proposed in *Challenges of African Growth* (Ndulu and others 2007), published this year by the World Bank's Africa Region.

- *Improving the investment climate* requires reducing indirect costs to firms, with energy and transportation topping the list of major impediments. It also requires reducing and mitigating risks, particularly those relating to crime, property security, political instability, and macroeconomic instability. Although individual countries are the focal point of action, their efforts could be pooled to coordinate policy, promote investment, improve security, and increase connectivity.

- *Improving infrastructure* is essential to reducing the transaction costs in producing goods and services. Transportation and energy make up the largest part of indirect costs for businesses, weighing heavily on the competitiveness of firms in most African countries. The focus would be on reducing the high costs associated with the remoteness of landlocked countries to facilitate their trade with neighbors and the rest of the world. Again, there will be a clear need to look beyond country borders and adopt a regional approach to coordinating cross-border infrastructure investment, maintenance, management, and use to lower costs (power pooling is an example).

- *Spurring innovation* will require investment in information technology and skill formation (higher education) to enhance productivity and competitiveness. The potential comparative advantage of low wages in Africa is too often nullified by low productivity. Surveys of investors show that labor is not cheap where productivity is low. Information and communication technologies can be the main driver of productivity growth. And there is strong empirical evidence showing that investment in information and communication technologies and in higher education boosts competitiveness, making both key parts of the growth agenda. African countries can make a huge leap forward over antiquated technology by exploiting the technological advantages of information and communication technologies as late starters.

- *Building institutional capacity* will underpin the first three. The World Bank's Investment Climate Assessment surveys and analysis for *World Development Report* 2005 (World Bank 2004) spotlight costs associated with contract enforcement difficulties, crime, corruption, and regulation as among those weighing most heavily on the profitability of enterprises. The main focus here would be to strengthen the capacity of relevant public institutions for protecting property rights and the scrutiny of, and accountability for, public action.

Action on these four fronts can accelerate growth in Africa and help countries break out of the boom-bust-stagnate cycles. The patterns described in this essay provide a guide for public policy, not a formula for success. Each country faces its own challenges and opportunities, and each country has to work within its own historical and geographical resources and constraints. Sustained faster growth in Africa is possible, if Africa's economies can meet the challenges of avoiding growth collapses, raising productivity, and boosting private investment.

Notes

1. CPIA scores in the two years are not strictly comparable because of changes in the composition of the index. They are sufficiently comparable, however, to show meaningful trends.

2. An important exception is the penetration of fixed-line and mobile telephones, where Sub-Saharan Africa leads low-income countries by as much as 13 percent. The largest gaps are for rural roads (29 percentage points) and electricity (21 percentage points).

3. Growth in Angola, Burkina Faso, Cape Verde, Republic of Congo, Eritrea, Ethiopia, Ghana, Mauritius, Mozambique, Nigeria, and Tanzania has been through an expansion of cropped area.

4. Five-year moving average based on 2001–05.

5. Five-year moving average based on 2000–04.

References

Acemoglu, D., S. Johnson, and J. Robinson. 2003. "Institutional Causes, Macroeconomic Symptoms: Volatility, Crises and Growth." *Journal of Monetary Economics* 50: 49–123.

Africa Partnership Forum. 2006a. "Progress Report: Agriculture." Moscow.

————. 2006b. "Progress Report: Infrastructure." Moscow.

Arbache, J.S. 2007. "Is the Recent African Growth Robust?" World Bank, Washington, D.C.

Arbache, J.S., and J. Page. 2007a. "Patterns of Long Term Growth in Sub-Saharan Africa." World Bank, Washington, D.C. [http://ssrn.com/abstract=1014133].

————. 2007b. "More Growth or Fewer Collapses? A New Look at Long-Run Growth in Sub-Saharan Africa." World Bank, Washington, D.C.

Berthelemy, Jean-Claude, and Ludvig Soderling. 2001. "The Role of Capital Accumulation, Adjustment and Structural Change for Economic Take-Off: Empirical Evidence from African Growth Episodes." *World Development* 29 (2): 323–43.

Bosworth, B.P., and S.M. Collins. 2003. "The Empirics of Growth: An Update." Brookings Papers on Economic Activity 2. Washington, D.C.

Eifert, Benn, Alan Gelb, and Vijaya Ramachandran. 2005. "Business Environment and Comparative Advantage in Africa: Evidence from the Investment Climate Data." CGD Working Paper 56. Center for Global Development, Washington, D.C.

Ndulu, B.J., L. Chakraborti, L. Lijane, V. Ramachandran, and J. Wolgin. 2007. *Challenges of African Growth: Opportunities, Constraints, and Strategic Directions.* Washington, D.C.: World Bank.

World Bank. 2004. *World Development Report 2005: A Better Investment Climate for Everyone.* Washington, D.C.

————. 2006. *Africa Development Indicators 2006.* Washington, D.C.

————. 2007a. *Doing Business 2008.* Washington, D.C.

————. 2007b. *Global Monitoring Report 2007: Confronting the Challenge of Gender Equality and Fragile States.* Washington, D.C.

Indicator tables

Table 1.1 Basic indicators

	Population (millions) 2005	Land area (thousands of sq km) 2005	GNI per capita Constant 2000 prices Dollars[a] 2005	GNI per capita Constant 2000 prices Average annual growth (%) 2000–05	Life expectancy at birth (years) 2005	Under-five mortality rate (per 1,000) 2005	Gini coefficient 2000–05[b]	Adult literacy rate (% of ages 15 and older) Male 2000–05[b]	Adult literacy rate (% of ages 15 and older) Female 2000–05[b]	Total net official development assistance per capita (current $) 2005
SUB–SAHARAN AFRICA	743.7	23,619	572	2.1	46.7	163	..	..	..	41.3
Excluding South Africa	696.8	22,405	380	2.4	46.6	166	..	..	..	43.0
Excl. S. Africa & Nigeria	565.3	21,494	362	2.1	47.2	160	..	..	..	41.7
Angola	15.9	1,247	937	6.9	41.4	260	..	82.9	54.2	27.7
Benin	8.4	111	323	0.6	55.0	150	36.5	47.9	23.3	41.4
Botswana	1.8	567	4,559	5.5	35.0	120	..	80.4	81.8	40.2
Burkina Faso	13.2	274	260	2.3	48.5	191	39.5	31.4	16.6	49.9
Burundi	7.5	26	105	–0.9	44.6	190	..	67.3	52.2	48.4
Cameroon	16.3	465	739	1.8	46.1	149	44.6	77.0	59.8	25.4
Cape Verde	0.5	4	1,343	2.2	70.7	35	..	87.8	75.5	316.9
Central African Republic	4.0	623	227	–2.7	39.4	193	..	64.8	33.5	23.6
Chad	9.7	1,259	286	12.0	44.0	208	..	40.8	12.8	39.0
Comoros	0.6	2	386	0.5	62.6	71	..	..	..	42.0
Congo, Dem. Rep.	57.5	2,267	91	1.5	44.0	205	..	80.9	54.1	31.8
Congo, Rep.	4.0	342	994	0.9	52.8	108	..	90.5	79.0	362.3
Côte d'Ivoire	18.2	318	564	–2.1	46.2	195	44.6	60.8	38.6	6.6
Djibouti	0.8	23	798	0.8	53.4	133	..	..	..	99.1
Equatorial Guinea	0.5	28	7,533	20.4	42.3	205	..	93.4	80.5	77.5
Eritrea	4.4	101	172	–0.9	54.9	78	..	..	..	80.7
Ethiopia	71.3	1,000	146	2.6	42.7	127	30.0	50.0	22.8	27.2
Gabon	1.4	258	3,991	–0.1	53.8	91	..	88.5	79.7	38.9
Gambia, The	1.5	10	335	0.8	56.8	137	..	..	..	38.3
Ghana	22.1	228	288	2.8	57.5	112	..	66.4	49.8	50.6
Guinea	9.4	246	385	0.7	54.1	160	38.6	42.6	18.1	19.4
Guinea-Bissau	1.6	28	135	–3.5	45.1	200	..	..	..	49.9
Kenya	34.3	569	442	1.1	49.0	120	..	77.7	70.2	22.4
Lesotho	1.8	30	547	2.9	35.2	132	..	73.7	90.3	38.3
Liberia	3.3	96	135	–8.0	42.5	235	..	58.3	45.7	71.9
Madagascar	18.6	582	233	–0.8	55.8	119	47.5	76.5	65.3	49.9
Malawi	12.9	94	154	1.2	40.5	125	39.0	..	..	44.7
Mali	13.5	1,220	244	2.8	48.6	218	40.1	32.7	15.9	51.1
Mauritania	3.1	1,025	429	1.0	53.7	125	39.0	59.5	43.4	62.0
Mauritius	1.2	2	4,404	3.0	73.0	15	..	88.2	80.5	25.7
Mozambique	19.8	784	288	6.2	41.8	145	47.3	..	..	65.0
Namibia	2.0	823	2,096	3.3	46.9	62	..	86.8	83.5	60.7
Niger	14.0	1,267	158	0.2	44.9	256	..	42.9	15.1	36.9
Nigeria	131.5	911	456	3.4	43.8	194	43.7	78.2	60.1	48.9
Rwanda	9.0	25	260	2.7	44.1	203	46.8	71.4	59.8	63.7
São Tomé and Principe	0.2	1	..	..	63.5	118	..	92.2	77.9	203.8
Senegal	11.7	193	503	2.1	56.5	119	41.3	51.1	29.2	59.1
Seychelles	0.1	0	6,666	–2.9	..	13	..	91.4	92.3	222.6
Sierra Leone	5.5	72	217	9.1	41.4	282	..	46.7	24.2	62.1
Somalia	8.2	627	..	..	47.7	225	..	..	..	28.7
South Africa	46.9	1,214	3,429	2.6	47.7	68	57.8	..	..	14.9
Sudan	36.2	2,376	462	4.1	56.7	90	..	71.1	51.8	50.5
Swaziland	1.1	17	1,381	0.9	41.5	160	50.4	80.9	78.3	40.7
Tanzania	38.3	884	325	4.5	46.3	122	34.6	77.5	62.2	39.3
Togo	6.1	54	241	–0.3	55.1	139	..	68.7	38.5	14.1
Uganda	28.8	197	270	2.0	50.0	136	45.7	76.8	57.7	41.6
Zambia	11.7	743	351	3.0	38.4	182	50.8	..	..	81.0
Zimbabwe	13.0	387	432	–6.3	37.3	132	..	92.7	86.2	28.3
NORTH AFRICA	152.9	5,738	1,928	2.2	71.1	35	..	..	..	15.4
Algeria	32.9	2,382	2,121	3.6	71.7	39	..	..	..	11.3
Egypt, Arab Rep.	74.0	995	1,617	1.7	70.5	33	34.4	..	..	12.5
Libya	5.9	1,760	6,904	0.7	74.4	19	..	..	..	4.2
Morocco	30.2	446	1,356	2.5	70.4	40	..	..	..	21.6
Tunisia	10.0	155	2,412	3.5	73.5	24	39.8	..	..	37.5
ALL AFRICA	896.6	29,358	803	2.0	50.8	149	..	..	..	36.8

a. Calculated by the *World Bank Atlas* method.
b. Data are for the most recent year available during the period specified.

Table 2.1 Gross domestic product, nominal

	Current prices ($ millions)									Annual average		
	1980	1990	1999	2000	2001	2002	2003	2004	2005[a]	1980–89	1990–99	2000–05
SUB-SAHARAN AFRICA	276,257	301,252	329,679	341,510	334,953	350,017	435,171	533,192	629,793	262,128	317,316	437,439
Excluding South Africa	197,076	189,368	196,523	208,697	216,614	239,369	268,614	316,786	387,869	171,678	183,302	272,991
Excl. S. Africa & Nigeria	129,295	160,961	161,753	162,643	168,541	192,629	210,239	244,390	290,629	135,084	153,325	211,512
Angola	..	10,260	6,155	9,129	8,936	11,432	13,956	19,775	32,811	7,560	7,042	16,007
Benin	1,405	1,845	2,387	2,255	2,372	2,807	3,558	4,047	4,288	1,318	2,005	3,221
Botswana	1,061	3,792	5,623	6,177	6,033	5,933	8,280	9,823	10,445	1,576	4,595	7,782
Burkina Faso	1,929	3,120	2,811	2,601	2,814	3,203	4,182	5,139	5,698	2,002	2,629	3,939
Burundi	920	1,132	808	709	662	628	595	665	800	1,065	979	677
Cameroon	6,741	11,152	10,487	10,075	9,598	10,880	13,622	15,775	16,875	9,159	10,616	12,804
Cape Verde	..	339	583	531	550	616	797	925	999	265	448	737
Central African Republic	797	1,488	1,051	953	968	1,046	1,195	1,307	1,369	929	1,177	1,140
Chad	1,033	1,739	1,537	1,383	1,712	1,994	2,728	4,420	5,896	1,068	1,602	3,022
Comoros	124	250	223	202	220	251	325	362	387	144	233	291
Congo, Dem. Rep.	14,395	9,350	4,711	4,306	4,692	5,548	5,673	6,570	7,104	10,028	7,161	5,649
Congo, Rep.	1,706	2,799	2,354	3,220	2,794	3,020	3,564	4,343	5,971	2,106	2,343	3,819
Côte d'Ivoire	10,175	10,796	12,556	10,425	10,554	11,482	13,734	15,475	16,055	8,609	11,200	12,954
Djibouti	..	452	536	551	572	591	628	666	709	380	490	620
Equatorial Guinea	..	132	872	1,254	1,737	2,166	2,966	4,899	7,520	108	294	3,424
Eritrea	..	..	689	634	671	631	584	635	970	..	609	687
Ethiopia	..	12,083	7,638	7,903	7,888	7,429	8,030	9,485	11,373	9,256	9,521	8,685
Gabon	4,279	5,952	4,663	5,068	4,713	4,932	6,055	7,178	8,666	3,676	5,064	6,102
Gambia, The	241	317	432	421	418	370	367	401	461	225	374	406
Ghana	4,445	5,886	7,710	4,972	5,313	6,157	7,624	8,872	10,720	4,692	6,576	7,276
Guinea	6,685	2,667	3,461	3,112	3,039	3,208	3,624	4,047	3,327	6,892	3,403	3,393
Guinea-Bissau	111	244	224	216	199	201	235	270	301	156	242	237
Kenya	7,265	8,591	12,896	12,705	12,984	12,915	14,639	16,143	19,193	7,069	9,906	14,763
Lesotho	432	615	904	853	752	687	1,039	1,319	1,457	412	843	1,018
Liberia	954	384	442	561	543	559	410	460	529	935	264	510
Madagascar	4,042	3,081	3,717	3,878	4,530	4,397	5,474	4,364	5,040	3,124	3,326	4,614
Malawi	1,238	1,881	1,776	1,744	1,717	1,935	1,765	1,903	2,076	1,256	1,901	1,856
Mali	1,787	2,421	2,570	2,423	2,630	3,343	4,362	4,874	5,305	1,609	2,486	3,823
Mauritania	709	1,020	1,195	1,081	1,122	1,150	1,285	1,548	1,837	806	1,286	1,337
Mauritius	1,154	2,383	4,259	4,469	4,539	4,549	5,248	6,064	6,290	1,387	3,563	5,193
Mozambique	3,526	2,463	3,985	3,778	3,697	4,092	4,789	5,904	6,823	3,375	2,766	4,847
Namibia	2,169	2,350	3,386	3,414	3,216	3,122	4,473	5,712	6,185	1,859	3,119	4,354
Niger	2,509	2,481	2,018	1,798	1,945	2,171	2,731	2,942	3,398	2,000	2,013	2,498
Nigeria	64,202	28,473	34,776	45,984	48,000	46,711	58,294	72,271	97,018	35,577	30,007	61,380
Rwanda	1,163	2,584	1,931	1,811	1,703	1,732	1,684	1,835	2,154	1,761	1,771	1,820
São Tomé and Principe	..	..	..	..	77	92	99	107	113	..	..	98
Senegal	3,503	5,717	5,151	4,692	4,878	5,334	6,815	7,947	8,600	3,736	5,172	6,378
Seychelles	147	369	623	615	619	698	706	700	723	197	494	677
Sierra Leone	1,101	650	664	634	806	936	990	1,072	1,193	963	779	938
Somalia	604	917	..	..	..	..	..	*	..	855	917	..
South Africa	80,710	112,014	133,184	132,878	118,479	110,882	166,654	216,443	242,059	90,894	134,008	164,566
Sudan	7,617	13,167	10,682	12,366	13,362	14,976	17,780	21,690	27,895	12,478	9,659	18,012
Swaziland	543	882	1,377	1,389	1,260	1,192	1,907	2,382	2,613	552	1,186	1,790
Tanzania	..	4,259	8,638	9,079	9,441	9,758	10,283	11,351	12,586	4,760	5,904	10,417
Togo	1,136	1,628	1,576	1,329	1,328	1,476	1,759	2,061	2,109	1,021	1,458	1,677
Uganda	1,245	4,304	5,999	5,926	5,681	5,836	6,250	6,817	8,725	3,611	4,835	6,539
Zambia	3,884	3,288	3,131	3,238	3,637	3,697	4,327	5,423	7,270	3,171	3,350	4,599
Zimbabwe	6,679	8,784	5,964	7,399	10,257	21,897	7,397	4,712	3,418	7,204	7,375	9,180
NORTH AFRICA	131,760	172,192	225,883	241,901	236,696	221,239	243,570	272,517	313,443	141,535	186,168	254,895
Algeria	42,345	62,045	48,641	54,790	55,181	57,053	68,019	85,014	101,786	53,750	48,197	70,307
Egypt, Arab Rep.	22,913	43,130	90,711	99,839	97,632	87,851	82,924	78,845	89,686	31,646	60,220	89,463
Libya	35,545	28,905	30,484	34,495	29,994	19,195	23,822	30,498	41,667	27,793	29,592	29,945
Morocco	18,821	25,821	35,249	33,334	33,901	36,093	43,813	50,031	51,621	16,987	31,337	41,466
Tunisia	8,743	12,291	20,799	19,443	19,988	21,047	24,992	28,129	28,683	8,923	16,823	23,714
ALL AFRICA	406,816	473,347	555,533	583,400	571,637	571,185	678,581	805,454	942,916	403,308	503,383	692,196

a. Provisional.

Table 2.2   Gross domestic product, real

	Constant prices (2000 $ millions)									Average annual growth (%)		
	1980	1990	1999	2000	2001	2002	2003	2004	2005[a]	1980–89	1990–99	2000–05
SUB-SAHARAN AFRICA	227,290	273,322	330,095	341,510	354,095	366,236	381,357	402,405	425,186	1.8	2.4	4.4
Excluding South Africa	131,907	162,389	202,585	208,697	217,658	224,762	235,686	249,509	264,506	2.2	2.6	4.8
Excl. S. Africa & Nigeria	99,676	127,371	158,898	162,643	170,180	176,555	182,302	192,868	204,410	2.6	2.7	4.5
Angola	6,746	8,464	8,862	9,129	9,416	10,780	11,137	12,383	14,935	3.5	1.0	9.9
Benin	1,084	1,412	2,131	2,255	2,368	2,474	2,571	2,650	2,727	2.7	4.7	3.9
Botswana	1,208	3,394	5,707	6,177	6,500	6,866	7,290	7,740	8,046	10.9	5.6	5.6
Burkina Faso	1,263	1,750	2,560	2,601	2,754	2,875	3,062	3,205	3,433	3.9	4.1	5.6
Burundi	559	865	715	709	724	756	747	783	790	4.5	-3.2	2.2
Cameroon	6,339	8,793	9,669	10,075	10,530	10,952	11,393	11,815	12,057	4.5	1.3	3.7
Cape Verde	..	303	498	531	552	577	613	608	681	6.3	5.9	4.7
Central African Republic	730	809	931	953	967	959	886	898	918	1.6	1.8	-1.4
Chad	664	1,104	1,395	1,383	1,544	1,675	1,922	2,568	2,789	6.7	2.3	15.9
Comoros	136	181	200	202	209	217	223	222	232	2.9	1.2	2.6
Congo, Dem. Rep.	7,016	7,659	4,625	4,306	4,215	4,362	4,614	4,921	5,239	2.1	-5.0	4.4
Congo, Rep.	1,746	2,796	2,992	3,220	3,342	3,503	3,563	3,691	3,975	3.8	0.8	4.0
Côte d'Ivoire	7,706	8,274	10,787	10,425	10,436	10,266	10,095	10,261	10,230	0.7	3.5	-0.5
Djibouti	..	660	549	551	563	577	596	614	633	..	-2.3	2.9
Equatorial Guinea	..	207	1,105	1,254	2,035	2,411	2,694	3,549	3,793	..	20.7	23.2
Eritrea	..	..	729	634	692	697	739	753	757	..	7.9	3.5
Ethiopia	..	6,292	7,461	7,903	8,513	8,618	8,315	9,407	10,367	2.0	3.3	4.7
Gabon	3,594	4,298	5,165	5,068	5,176	5,162	5,290	5,361	5,523	0.5	2.9	1.6
Gambia, The	213	305	399	421	445	431	461	484	509	3.5	2.7	3.7
Ghana	2,637	3,263	4,795	4,972	5,171	5,404	5,685	6,003	6,357	2.6	4.3	5.1
Guinea	1,539	2,088	3,055	3,112	3,236	3,372	3,413	3,505	3,621	3.0	4.4	2.9
Guinea-Bissau	115	186	200	215	216	201	202	206	213	3.8	1.4	-0.5
Kenya	7,087	10,557	12,630	12,705	13,188	13,261	13,657	14,319	15,152	4.1	2.2	3.4
Lesotho	392	602	832	853	868	893	917	954	982	4.1	4.3	2.9
Liberia	1,391	433	446	561	577	599	411	422	444	-3.3	0.2	-6.8
Madagascar	3,099	3,266	3,701	3,878	4,111	3,590	3,941	4,149	4,339	0.8	1.7	2.0
Malawi	1,000	1,243	1,716	1,744	1,657	1,704	1,808	1,936	1,990	2.4	3.8	3.4
Mali	1,536	1,630	2,347	2,422	2,716	2,828	3,039	3,105	3,294	0.5	3.9	5.9
Mauritania	693	816	1,062	1,081	1,112	1,125	1,188	1,249	1,317	1.9	2.9	4.0
Mauritius	1,518	2,679	4,296	4,469	4,718	4,846	5,000	5,235	5,475	5.9	5.3	4.0
Mozambique	2,245	2,279	3,706	3,778	4,273	4,621	4,987	5,361	5,695	-0.9	5.7	8.4
Namibia	2,002	2,263	3,298	3,414	3,495	3,729	3,858	4,088	4,258	1.1	4.0	4.7
Niger	1,523	1,507	1,824	1,798	1,926	1,984	2,071	2,059	2,199	-0.4	2.4	3.6
Nigeria	31,452	34,978	43,628	45,984	47,409	48,143	53,292	56,543	59,992	0.8	2.4	5.8
Rwanda	1,457	1,782	1,709	1,811	1,933	2,114	2,134	2,218	2,351	2.5	-1.6	5.1
São Tomé and Principe	..	..	..	..	..	..	..	..	..	..	..	..
Senegal	2,683	3,463	4,546	4,692	4,907	4,939	5,268	5,562	5,866	2.7	2.8	4.5
Seychelles	290	393	587	615	601	609	573	557	563	3.1	4.5	-2.1
Sierra Leone	935	1,021	610	634	749	954	1,043	1,120	1,201	0.5	-5.4	13.7
Somalia	..	..	..	..	..	..	..	..	..	..	..	..
South Africa	95,503	110,945	127,577	132,878	136,512	141,549	145,761	152,996	160,793	1.4	2.0	3.9
Sudan	5,555	7,100	11,611	12,366	13,120	13,960	14,742	15,509	16,749	2.4	5.3	6.1
Swaziland	554	1,024	1,361	1,389	1,411	1,452	1,494	1,526	1,562	6.5	3.3	2.5
Tanzania	..	6,801	8,639	9,079	9,646	10,345	10,931	11,667	12,461	..	2.7	6.5
Togo	964	1,071	1,340	1,329	1,327	1,382	1,419	1,461	1,480	1.5	3.6	2.5
Uganda	..	3,077	5,610	5,926	6,219	6,613	6,926	7,306	7,786	2.3	7.2	5.6
Zambia	2,730	3,028	3,126	3,238	3,396	3,508	3,688	3,887	4,090	1.0	0.2	4.7
Zimbabwe	4,376	6,734	8,034	7,399	7,199	6,883	6,167	5,933	5,618	3.3	2.7	-5.7
NORTH AFRICA	126,904	176,633	234,042	241,901	251,458	260,036	269,560	282,196	294,925	3.4	3.2	4.0
Algeria	35,291	46,367	53,611	54,790	56,215	58,857	62,918	66,190	69,698	2.9	1.7	5.2
Egypt, Arab Rep.	38,503	65,574	94,738	99,839	103,357	106,649	109,964	114,559	119,714	5.5	4.3	3.6
Libya	14,354	..	34,104	34,495	36,053	37,228	36,204	38,014	40,409	-7.0	..	2.7
Morocco	18,308	26,717	33,018	33,334	35,433	36,563	38,582	40,220	40,910	4.2	2.4	4.3
Tunisia	8,622	12,237	18,571	19,443	20,401	20,738	21,891	23,213	24,194	3.2	4.6	4.5
ALL AFRICA	356,401	451,457	564,126	583,400	605,543	626,261	650,902	684,580	720,082	2.4	2.7	4.3

a. Provisional.

Table **2.3** Gross domestic product growth

	1980	1990	1999	2000	2001	2002	2003	2004	2005a	1980–89	1990–99	2000–05
						Annual growth (%)					Annual average	
SUB-SAHARAN AFRICA	4.2	1.1	2.6	3.5	3.7	3.4	4.1	5.5	5.7	2.2	2.0	4.3
Excluding South Africa	2.1	2.1	2.7	3.0	4.3	3.3	4.9	5.9	6.0	2.1	2.5	4.6
Excl. S. Africa & Nigeria	1.2	0.5	3.2	2.4	4.6	3.7	3.3	5.8	6.0	2.6	2.3	4.3
Angola	..	–0.3	3.2	3.0	3.1	14.5	3.3	11.2	20.6	2.7	1.0	9.3
Benin	6.8	3.2	4.7	5.8	5.0	4.5	3.9	3.1	2.9	3.1	4.5	4.2
Botswana	12.0	6.8	7.2	8.2	5.2	5.6	6.2	6.2	4.0	11.5	6.1	5.9
Burkina Faso	0.8	–1.5	6.7	1.6	5.9	4.4	6.5	4.6	7.1	3.6	3.8	5.0
Burundi	1.0	3.5	–1.0	–0.9	2.1	4.4	–1.2	4.8	0.9	4.3	–1.4	1.7
Cameroon	–2.0	–6.1	4.4	4.2	4.5	4.0	4.0	3.7	2.0	4.0	0.4	3.7
Cape Verde	..	0.7	8.6	6.6	3.8	4.6	6.2	–0.7	11.9	6.4	5.2	5.4
Central African Republic	–4.5	–2.1	3.6	2.3	1.5	–0.8	–7.6	1.3	2.2	0.9	1.3	–0.2
Chad	–6.0	–4.2	–0.7	–0.9	11.7	8.5	14.7	33.6	8.6	5.4	2.2	12.7
Comoros	..	5.1	2.9	0.9	3.3	4.1	2.5	–0.2	4.2	2.7	1.6	2.5
Congo, Dem. Rep.	2.2	–6.6	–4.3	–6.9	–2.1	3.5	5.8	6.6	6.5	1.8	–5.5	2.2
Congo, Rep.	17.6	1.0	–2.6	7.6	3.8	4.8	1.7	3.6	7.7	6.8	0.8	4.9
Côte d'Ivoire	–11.0	–1.1	1.6	–3.3	0.1	–1.6	–1.7	1.6	–0.3	–0.2	2.6	–0.9
Djibouti	..	..	2.2	0.4	2.0	2.6	3.2	3.0	3.2	..	–2.0	2.4
Equatorial Guinea	..	3.3	41.4	13.5	62.2	18.5	11.7	31.7	6.9	0.9	20.2	24.1
Eritrea	..	..	0.0	–13.1	9.2	0.7	6.1	1.9	0.5	..	8.1	0.9
Ethiopia	..	2.0	6.0	5.9	7.7	1.2	–3.5	13.1	10.2	2.1	2.2	5.8
Gabon	2.6	5.2	–8.9	–1.9	2.1	–0.3	2.5	1.3	3.0	1.9	2.5	1.1
Gambia, The	6.3	3.6	6.4	5.5	5.8	–3.2	7.0	5.1	5.0	3.9	3.1	4.2
Ghana	0.5	3.3	4.4	3.7	4.0	4.5	5.2	5.6	5.9	2.0	4.3	4.8
Guinea	2.6	4.3	4.7	1.9	4.0	4.2	1.2	2.7	3.3	2.9	4.3	2.9
Guinea-Bissau	–16.0	6.1	7.8	7.5	0.2	–7.1	0.6	2.2	3.5	2.9	2.0	1.2
Kenya	5.6	4.2	2.3	0.6	3.8	0.6	3.0	4.9	5.8	4.2	2.2	3.1
Lesotho	–2.7	6.4	0.2	2.6	1.8	2.9	2.7	4.0	2.9	3.6	4.0	2.8
Liberia	–4.1	–51.0	22.9	25.7	2.9	3.7	–31.3	2.6	5.3	–4.5	1.2	1.5
Madagascar	0.8	3.1	4.7	4.8	6.0	–12.7	9.8	5.3	4.6	0.4	1.6	3.0
Malawi	0.4	5.7	3.0	1.6	–5.0	2.9	6.1	7.1	2.8	1.7	4.1	2.6
Mali	–4.3	–1.9	6.7	3.2	12.1	4.2	7.4	2.2	6.1	0.6	3.6	5.9
Mauritania	3.4	–1.8	6.7	1.9	2.9	1.1	5.6	5.2	5.4	2.2	2.6	3.7
Mauritius	..	5.8	5.8	4.0	5.6	2.7	3.2	4.7	4.6	5.9	5.4	4.1
Mozambique	..	1.0	7.5	1.9	13.1	8.2	7.9	7.5	6.2	0.4	5.2	7.5
Namibia	..	2.5	3.4	3.5	2.4	6.7	3.5	6.0	4.2	1.1	4.1	4.4
Niger	–2.2	–1.3	–0.6	–1.4	7.1	3.0	4.4	–0.6	6.8	0.0	1.9	3.2
Nigeria	4.2	8.2	1.1	5.4	3.1	1.5	10.7	6.1	6.1	0.9	3.1	5.5
Rwanda	9.0	–2.4	7.6	6.0	6.7	9.4	0.9	4.0	6.0	3.2	2.1	5.5
São Tomé and Principe	..	..	..	..	..	..	..	..	..	..	..	..
Senegal	–0.4	–0.7	6.3	3.2	4.6	0.7	6.7	5.6	5.5	2.7	2.7	4.4
Seychelles	–4.2	7.0	1.9	4.8	–2.2	1.3	–5.9	–2.9	1.2	2.1	4.9	–0.6
Sierra Leone	4.8	3.4	–8.1	3.8	18.1	27.5	9.3	7.4	7.3	1.1	–4.3	12.2
Somalia	..	..	..	..	..	..	..	..	..	..	..	..
South Africa	6.6	–0.3	2.4	4.2	2.7	3.7	3.0	5.0	5.1	2.2	1.4	3.9
Sudan	1.5	–5.5	6.3	6.5	6.1	6.4	5.6	5.2	8.0	3.4	4.5	6.3
Swaziland	12.4	8.6	3.5	2.0	1.6	2.9	2.9	2.1	2.3	6.8	3.8	2.3
Tanzania	..	7.0	3.5	5.1	6.2	7.2	5.7	6.7	6.8	3.8	3.1	6.3
Togo	14.6	–0.2	2.5	–0.8	–0.2	4.1	2.7	3.0	1.2	2.6	2.6	1.7
Uganda	..	6.5	8.1	5.6	4.9	6.3	4.7	5.5	6.6	3.0	6.9	5.6
Zambia	3.0	–0.5	2.2	3.6	4.9	3.3	5.1	5.4	5.2	1.4	0.4	4.6
Zimbabwe	14.4	7.0	–3.6	–7.9	–2.7	–4.4	–10.4	–3.8	–5.3	5.2	2.6	–5.8
NORTH AFRICA	4.6	4.0	4.3	3.4	4.0	3.4	3.7	4.7	4.5	3.4	3.3	3.9
Algeria	0.8	0.8	3.2	2.2	2.6	4.7	6.9	5.2	5.3	2.8	1.6	4.5
Egypt, Arab Rep.	10.0	5.7	6.1	5.4	3.5	3.2	3.1	4.2	4.5	5.9	4.3	4.0
Libya	0.6	..	..	1.1	4.5	3.3	–2.8	5.0	6.3	–6.4	..	2.9
Morocco	3.6	4.0	–0.1	1.0	6.3	3.2	5.5	4.2	1.7	3.9	2.7	3.7
Tunisia	7.4	7.9	6.1	4.7	4.9	1.7	5.6	6.0	4.2	3.6	5.1	4.5
ALL AFRICA	4.4	2.1	3.2	3.4	3.8	3.4	3.9	5.2	5.2	2.6	2.5	4.2

a. Provisional.

Table 2.4 Gross domestic product per capita, real

	Constant prices (2000 $)									Average annual growth (%)		
	1980	1990	1999	2000	2001	2002	2003	2004	2005[a]	1980–89	1990–99	2000–05
SUB-SAHARAN AFRICA	590	531	510	515	521	527	536	553	572	−1.1	−0.2	2.1
Excluding South Africa	369	339	335	337	343	346	354	366	380	−0.8	0.0	2.4
Excl. S. Africa & Nigeria	345	327	325	324	331	335	338	349	362	−0.4	0.1	2.1
Angola	861	804	656	660	662	737	740	799	937	0.5	−1.8	6.9
Benin	292	273	305	313	319	323	325	324	323	−0.7	1.3	0.6
Botswana	1,152	2,376	3,288	3,522	3,681	3,877	4,115	4,375	4,559	7.5	3.3	5.5
Burkina Faso	192	205	233	230	237	239	247	250	260	1.3	1.2	2.3
Burundi	135	153	112	109	109	111	106	108	105	1.1	−4.4	−0.9
Cameroon	724	755	664	678	695	709	724	737	739	1.6	−1.2	1.8
Cape Verde	..	852	1,132	1,179	1,196	1,221	1,267	1,229	1,343	4.1	3.4	2.2
Central African Republic	314	270	251	252	252	247	225	225	227	−1.0	−0.6	−2.7
Chad	143	182	176	168	182	190	210	272	286	3.9	−0.8	12.0
Comoros	405	416	378	374	378	386	387	378	386	0.3	−1.0	0.5
Congo, Dem. Rep.	251	203	95	86	82	83	85	88	91	−0.8	−7.7	1.5
Congo, Rep.	969	1,126	899	937	942	958	945	951	994	0.6	−2.5	0.9
Côte d'Ivoire	924	654	658	623	612	592	574	574	564	−3.5	0.6	−2.1
Djibouti	..	1,183	792	771	767	770	779	788	798	..	−4.5	0.8
Equatorial Guinea	..	588	2,521	2,794	4,428	5,128	5,598	7,210	7,533	..	17.8	20.4
Eritrea	..	..	213	178	187	180	182	178	172	..	6.2	−0.9
Ethiopia	..	123	119	123	129	128	121	135	146	−1.0	1.1	2.6
Gabon	5,162	4,490	4,150	3,984	3,990	3,911	3,944	3,935	3,991	−2.7	−0.1	−0.1
Gambia, The	327	326	313	320	328	308	321	328	335	−0.2	−0.8	0.8
Ghana	233	211	247	250	255	260	268	277	288	−0.6	1.7	2.8
Guinea	321	336	370	369	376	383	379	381	385	0.5	1.2	0.7
Guinea-Bissau	144	183	151	158	154	138	135	134	135	1.4	−1.6	−3.5
Kenya	435	451	421	414	421	414	417	428	442	1.1	−0.6	1.1
Lesotho	303	378	469	477	483	496	510	531	547	1.8	3.0	2.9
Liberia	745	203	153	183	183	187	128	130	135	−4.9	−3.3	−8.0
Madagascar	342	271	235	239	247	209	224	229	233	−2.0	−1.3	−0.8
Malawi	162	131	153	151	141	141	147	154	154	−1.9	2.0	1.2
Mali	220	183	207	208	226	229	239	237	244	−1.9	1.2	2.8
Mauritania	431	402	413	409	408	401	411	419	429	−0.5	0.3	1.0
Mauritius	1,572	2,535	3,656	3,766	3,932	4,004	4,089	4,245	4,404	4.9	4.0	3.0
Mozambique	186	170	211	211	234	247	262	276	288	−1.9	2.5	6.2
Namibia	2,029	1,619	1,780	1,802	1,811	1,902	1,943	2,035	2,096	−2.3	0.8	3.3
Niger	246	178	160	153	158	157	159	153	158	−3.4	−0.9	0.2
Nigeria	460	386	380	391	394	391	423	439	456	−2.0	−0.3	3.4
Rwanda	280	251	228	226	231	245	244	250	260	−1.2	−1.7	2.7
São Tomé and Principe	..	..	..	..	..	..	..	..	..	..	..	..
Senegal	450	434	451	454	463	455	474	489	503	−0.3	0.2	2.1
Seychelles	4,507	5,614	7,294	7,579	7,405	7,277	6,922	6,654	6,666	2.3	2.9	−2.9
Sierra Leone	289	250	140	141	160	195	204	210	217	−1.9	−6.0	9.1
Somalia	..	..	..	..	..	..	..	..	..	..	..	..
South Africa	3,463	3,152	2,972	3,020	3,046	3,123	3,180	3,300	3,429	−1.2	−0.3	2.6
Sudan	278	272	361	376	391	408	423	437	462	−0.4	2.8	4.1
Swaziland	981	1,330	1,335	1,329	1,321	1,334	1,352	1,363	1,381	3.3	0.1	0.9
Tanzania	..	259	254	261	272	286	296	310	325	..	−0.2	4.5
Togo	346	270	258	248	240	243	243	244	241	−2.1	0.5	−0.3
Uganda	..	173	238	244	248	255	258	263	270	−1.3	3.9	2.0
Zambia	451	361	298	303	311	316	327	339	351	−2.3	−2.2	3.0
Zimbabwe	599	637	644	588	567	538	479	459	432	−0.5	0.8	−6.3
NORTH AFRICA	1,389	1,505	1,693	1,722	1,762	1,792	1,829	1,875	1,928	0.8	1.4	2.2
Algeria	1,876	1,833	1,785	1,799	1,818	1,876	1,975	2,046	2,121	−0.1	−0.3	3.6
Egypt, Arab Rep.	878	1,178	1,435	1,484	1,507	1,526	1,543	1,577	1,617	2.9	2.3	1.7
Libya	4,717	..	6,555	6,501	6,662	6,745	6,432	6,623	6,904	−10.6	..	0.7
Morocco	950	1,117	1,200	1,197	1,258	1,284	1,339	1,349	1,356	2.0	0.8	2.5
Tunisia	1,351	1,501	1,964	2,033	2,109	2,120	2,225	2,337	2,412	0.6	2.9	3.5
ALL AFRICA	748	714	718	726	736	745	758	780	803	−0.5	0.2	2.0

a. Provisional.

Table 2.5

Gross domestic product per capita growth

	Annual growth (%)									Annual average		
	1980	1990	1999	2000	2001	2002	2003	2004	2005[a]	1980–89	1990–99	2000–05
SUB–SAHARAN AFRICA	**1.1**	**–1.7**	**0.1**	**0.9**	**1.3**	**1.1**	**1.8**	**3.2**	**3.3**	**–0.8**	**–0.6**	**1.9**
Excluding South Africa	–1.0	–0.8	0.2	0.5	1.8	0.8	2.4	3.4	3.6	–0.9	–0.2	2.1
Excl. S. Africa & Nigeria	–1.9	–2.4	0.6	–0.1	2.1	1.3	0.8	3.3	3.5	–0.5	–0.3	1.8
Angola	..	–3.0	0.9	0.5	0.4	11.3	0.4	8.0	17.2	–0.3	–1.7	6.3
Benin	3.5	–0.3	1.7	2.7	1.8	1.2	0.6	–0.2	–0.3	–0.2	1.1	1.0
Botswana	8.2	3.9	5.7	7.1	4.5	5.3	6.1	6.3	4.2	8.0	3.7	5.6
Burkina Faso	–1.3	–4.4	3.8	–1.3	2.7	1.1	3.1	1.4	3.8	1.1	0.9	1.8
Burundi	–1.9	1.0	–2.1	–2.5	–0.2	1.6	–4.3	1.3	–2.7	1.0	–2.8	–1.1
Cameroon	–4.8	–8.8	2.2	2.1	2.4	2.0	2.1	1.8	0.3	1.1	–2.1	1.8
Cape Verde	..	–1.6	6.1	4.1	1.4	2.2	3.7	–3.0	9.3	4.2	2.8	3.0
Central African Republic	–7.0	–4.4	1.7	0.6	0.0	–2.1	–8.8	0.0	0.9	–1.6	–1.1	–1.6
Chad	–8.0	–7.0	–3.8	–4.1	7.9	4.7	10.7	29.2	5.2	2.7	–0.8	8.9
Comoros	..	2.4	0.7	–1.2	1.2	2.0	0.3	–2.3	2.1	0.1	–0.6	0.3
Congo, Dem. Rep.	–0.9	–9.7	–6.1	–8.9	–4.5	0.7	2.8	3.5	3.3	–1.2	–8.2	–0.5
Congo, Rep.	14.0	–2.2	–5.7	4.2	0.6	1.6	–1.3	0.6	4.6	3.5	–2.4	1.7
Côte d'Ivoire	–15.1	–4.4	–0.8	–5.4	–1.8	–3.2	–3.2	0.1	–1.9	–4.4	–0.3	–2.5
Djibouti	..	..	–1.3	–2.6	–0.5	0.3	1.2	1.1	1.4	..	–4.3	0.2
Equatorial Guinea	..	1.4	38.1	10.8	58.5	15.8	9.2	28.8	4.5	–1.6	17.4	21.3
Eritrea	..	..	–3.3	–16.3	4.8	–3.7	1.4	–2.4	–3.4	..	6.4	–3.3
Ethiopia	..	–1.7	3.5	3.4	5.3	–0.9	–5.5	11.0	8.2	–0.9	–0.1	3.6
Gabon	–0.5	1.8	–11.1	–4.0	0.2	–2.0	0.8	–0.2	1.4	–1.3	–0.5	–0.6
Gambia, The	2.9	–0.3	3.0	2.2	2.6	–6.1	3.9	2.3	2.3	0.3	–0.4	1.2
Ghana	–2.0	0.5	2.1	1.4	1.7	2.2	3.0	3.4	3.8	–1.1	1.6	2.6
Guinea	–0.1	0.8	2.6	–0.2	1.8	1.9	–1.0	0.5	1.1	0.4	1.1	0.7
Guinea-Bissau	–18.8	3.1	4.9	4.5	–2.7	–9.8	–2.4	–0.8	0.5	0.4	–1.0	–1.8
Kenya	1.7	0.8	0.0	–1.6	1.6	–1.6	0.8	2.6	3.4	0.5	–0.6	0.9
Lesotho	–5.2	5.0	–0.8	1.8	1.3	2.6	2.7	4.2	3.1	1.3	2.7	2.6
Liberia	–7.2	–50.5	14.2	19.3	–0.2	2.2	–31.6	2.0	3.9	–6.2	–3.2	–0.7
Madagascar	–2.0	0.2	1.6	1.7	3.0	–15.1	6.8	2.4	1.8	–2.4	–1.3	0.1
Malawi	–2.6	1.7	0.2	–1.1	–7.3	0.5	3.8	4.8	0.6	–2.4	2.0	0.2
Mali	–6.5	–4.3	3.8	0.3	8.9	1.1	4.3	–0.8	3.0	–1.8	0.9	2.8
Mauritania	0.9	–4.0	3.7	–1.1	–0.1	–1.9	2.5	2.1	2.4	–0.2	0.0	0.6
Mauritius	..	5.0	4.5	3.0	4.4	1.8	2.1	3.8	3.7	4.9	4.2	3.2
Mozambique	..	–0.3	5.2	–0.2	10.7	6.0	5.8	5.4	4.3	–0.6	2.4	5.3
Namibia	..	–1.8	0.8	1.2	0.5	5.0	2.1	4.7	3.0	–2.3	0.8	2.8
Niger	–5.2	–4.3	–3.9	–4.7	3.5	–0.5	0.9	–3.9	3.3	–3.0	–1.4	–0.2
Nigeria	1.2	5.1	–1.3	2.9	0.7	–0.7	8.3	3.8	3.8	–1.9	0.4	3.1
Rwanda	5.5	–2.1	–1.8	–1.0	2.2	6.5	–0.7	2.5	4.2	–0.3	1.2	2.3
São Tomé and Principe	..	..	..	..	..	..	..	..	..	..	..	..
Senegal	–3.0	–3.5	3.7	0.7	2.1	–1.7	4.1	3.1	3.0	–0.2	0.0	1.9
Seychelles	–5.4	6.1	–0.1	3.9	–2.3	–1.7	–4.9	–3.9	0.2	1.2	3.3	–1.4
Sierra Leone	2.9	1.6	–10.2	0.8	13.8	22.0	4.4	3.0	3.6	–1.2	–5.2	7.9
Somalia	..	..	..	..	..	..	..	..	..	..	..	..
South Africa	4.2	–2.3	–0.1	1.6	0.9	2.5	1.8	3.8	3.9	–0.3	–0.8	2.4
Sudan	–1.7	–7.5	4.0	4.3	4.0	4.4	3.7	3.2	5.9	0.6	2.1	4.2
Swaziland	9.0	5.2	0.6	–0.4	–0.6	1.0	1.3	0.8	1.3	3.6	0.6	0.6
Tanzania	..	3.5	1.3	2.9	4.1	5.1	3.6	4.7	4.9	0.4	0.2	4.2
Togo	11.1	–3.1	–1.1	–4.0	–3.1	1.3	0.0	0.4	–1.3	–0.9	–0.4	–1.1
Uganda	..	2.7	4.8	2.4	1.6	2.8	1.2	1.9	2.9	–0.6	3.5	2.1
Zambia	–0.3	–3.4	0.0	1.5	2.9	1.5	3.4	3.7	3.5	–1.8	–2.1	2.7
Zimbabwe	10.5	3.8	–4.7	–8.8	–3.5	–5.1	–10.9	–4.3	–5.8	1.4	0.6	–6.4
NORTH AFRICA	**1.9**	**1.7**	**2.6**	**1.7**	**2.3**	**1.7**	**2.0**	**2.5**	**2.8**	**0.8**	**1.4**	**2.2**
Algeria	–2.5	–1.7	1.8	0.8	1.1	3.1	5.3	3.6	3.7	–0.3	–0.4	2.9
Egypt, Arab Rep.	7.5	3.5	4.1	3.4	1.6	1.2	1.1	2.2	2.5	3.4	2.4	2.0
Libya	–3.9	..	..	–0.8	2.5	1.2	–4.6	3.0	4.2	–10.1	..	0.9
Morocco	1.1	1.9	–1.2	–0.2	5.1	2.0	4.3	0.7	0.6	1.6	1.1	2.1
Tunisia	4.6	5.4	4.7	3.5	3.7	0.5	4.9	5.1	3.2	1.0	3.3	3.5
ALL AFRICA	**1.3**	**–0.6**	**0.8**	**1.1**	**1.5**	**1.2**	**1.7**	**2.9**	**3.0**	**–0.3**	**0.0**	**1.9**

a. Provisional.

Table 2.6 Gross national income, nominal

	Current prices ($ millions)									Annual average		
	1980	1990	1999	2000	2001	2002	2003	2004	2005[a]	1980–89	1990–99	2000–05
SUB-SAHARAN AFRICA	**260,874**	**285,278**	**317,118**	**323,171**	**318,330**	**332,091**	**412,296**	**502,686**	**593,441**	**247,283**	**303,929**	**413,669**
Excluding South Africa	185,300	177,754	187,157	193,501	203,711	224,208	250,318	290,574	356,330	160,445	173,028	253,107
Excl. S. Africa & Nigeria	120,229	152,246	153,861	153,199	159,542	183,398	199,806	229,656	271,336	125,148	145,460	199,490
Angola	..	8,214	4,717	7,449	7,375	9,791	12,230	17,295	28,736	6,696	5,269	13,813
Benin	1,402	1,806	2,372	2,243	2,351	2,781	3,515	4,006	4,259	1,298	1,971	3,192
Botswana	1,028	3,686	5,361	5,826	5,896	5,235	7,564	8,796	9,633	1,461	4,551	7,158
Burkina Faso	1,924	3,113	2,806	2,596	2,808	3,202	4,181	5,139	5,695	1,994	2,622	3,937
Burundi	922	1,117	797	723	650	614	577	646	780	1,051	967	665
Cameroon	5,618	10,674	10,019	9,413	9,179	10,207	13,097	15,374	16,413	8,774	10,032	12,280
Cape Verde	..	340	575	520	544	605	781	907	966	264	444	720
Central African Republic	800	1,465	1,038	937	957	1,039	1,191	1,303	1,367	917	1,159	1,132
Chad	1,038	1,721	1,535	1,366	1,689	1,934	2,270	3,725	4,867	1,069	1,593	2,642
Comoros	124	249	223	202	221	250	323	360	385	144	233	290
Congo, Dem. Rep.	13,899	8,581	4,317	3,918	4,280	5,250	5,485	6,276	6,760	9,482	6,630	5,328
Congo, Rep.	1,544	2,324	1,645	2,275	1,960	2,201	2,679	3,247	4,456	1,961	1,779	2,803
Côte d'Ivoire	9,680	9,209	11,743	9,723	9,920	10,802	13,014	14,711	15,237	7,875	10,136	12,235
Djibouti	..	..	548	567	585	606	679	731	776	..	510	657
Equatorial Guinea	..	124	417	884	753	1,321	1,296	1,868	3,562	101	225	1,614
Eritrea	..	..	686	634	668	625	574	620	962	..	678	681
Ethiopia	..	12,016	7,586	7,843	7,836	7,389	7,964	9,421	11,338	9,221	9,449	8,632
Gabon	3,856	5,336	4,094	4,289	4,084	4,453	5,342	5,971	6,678	3,393	4,439	5,136
Gambia, The	237	291	411	400	395	347	348	381	446	218	363	386
Ghana	4,426	5,774	7,546	4,825	5,205	6,028	7,459	8,674	10,533	4,621	6,447	7,121
Guinea	..	2,518	3,377	3,035	2,947	3,170	3,585	3,987	3,279	2,051	3,290	3,334
Guinea-Bissau	105	233	210	203	183	193	225	258	289	153	227	225
Kenya	7,039	8,224	12,723	12,575	12,836	12,793	14,473	16,013	19,084	6,831	9,622	14,629
Lesotho	695	1,022	1,149	1,072	927	848	1,287	1,620	1,761	727	1,198	1,253
Liberia	930	..	334	389	403	453	350	373	416	807	306	397
Madagascar	4,024	2,958	3,675	3,807	4,470	4,326	5,394	4,285	4,962	3,012	3,203	4,541
Malawi	1,138	1,837	1,734	1,707	1,683	1,890	1,723	1,858	2,033	1,190	1,858	1,816
Mali	1,768	2,405	2,526	2,392	2,464	3,103	4,203	4,679	5,073	1,539	2,457	3,652
Mauritania	672	1,076	1,216	1,092	1,089	1,276	1,343	1,613	1,901	795	1,269	1,386
Mauritius	1,130	2,363	4,235	4,434	4,551	4,541	5,246	6,028	6,285	1,346	3,547	5,181
Mozambique	3,550	2,320	3,777	3,546	3,393	3,919	4,592	5,564	6,409	3,292	2,588	4,570
Namibia	1,818	2,388	3,368	3,447	3,215	3,156	4,702	5,787	6,158	1,672	3,182	4,411
Niger	2,476	2,423	1,999	1,782	1,930	2,146	2,718	3,039	3,397	1,958	1,980	2,502
Nigeria	61,079	25,585	33,300	40,256	44,107	40,806	50,468	60,847	84,820	34,111	27,609	53,551
Rwanda	1,165	2,572	1,920	1,796	1,680	1,713	1,653	1,800	2,128	1,758	1,761	1,795
São Tomé and Principe	..	..	..	..	..	..	..	..	..	..	..	..
Senegal	3,403	5,520	5,058	4,601	4,800	5,232	6,710	7,856	8,527	3,589	5,041	6,288
Seychelles	142	355	598	583	601	630	663	667	678	188	480	637
Sierra Leone	1,071	580	639	614	780	906	963	1,039	1,162	928	721	911
Somalia	603	835	..	..	..	..	..	..	..	818	835	..
South Africa	77,378	107,746	129,975	129,704	114,742	108,093	162,044	212,092	237,179	87,304	130,899	160,642
Sudan	7,508	12,395	9,372	10,479	11,919	13,749	16,446	20,043	25,984	12,026	8,695	16,437
Swaziland	548	941	1,465	1,423	1,362	1,190	1,903	2,402	2,633	575	1,260	1,819
Tanzania	..	4,072	8,543	8,959	9,356	9,579	10,135	11,153	12,383	4,580	5,760	10,261
Togo	1,096	1,598	1,538	1,300	1,298	1,454	1,736	2,033	2,091	979	1,425	1,652
Uganda	1,237	4,227	5,985	5,819	5,571	5,719	6,127	6,678	8,557	3,571	4,787	6,412
Zambia	3,594	3,008	2,975	3,080	3,469	3,542	4,179	4,999	6,804	2,881	3,100	4,345
Zimbabwe	6,610	8,494	5,718	7,145	9,919	21,651	7,207	4,503	3,220	7,010	7,070	8,941
NORTH AFRICA	**122,344**	**159,989**	**222,024**	**235,207**	**235,468**	**229,591**	**248,356**	**276,347**	**317,215**	**130,760**	**175,938**	**257,031**
Algeria	41,147	59,955	46,351	52,080	53,491	54,823	65,319	81,414	96,706	52,260	46,075	67,305
Egypt, Arab Rep.	21,453	42,025	91,923	100,838	98,496	88,763	83,006	78,757	89,532	29,927	60,225	89,899
Libya	35,480		..	..	..	..	24,357	30,253	41,385	27,588	..	31,998
Morocco	18,402	24,835	34,263	32,462	33,068	35,355	43,024	49,354	51,312	16,320	30,201	40,763
Tunisia	8,450	11,882	19,940	18,526	19,077	20,096	23,957	26,895	27,176	8,559	16,024	22,621
ALL AFRICA	**384,281**	**448,967**	**539,712**	**558,248**	**553,368**	**562,511**	**664,599**	**784,210**	**916,892**	**380,575**	**483,338**	**673,304**

a. Provisional.

Table 2.7

Gross national income, real

	Constant prices (2000 $ millions)									Average annual growth (%)		
	1980	1990	1999	2000	2001	2002	2003	2004	2005[a]	1980–89	1990–99	2000–05
SUB-SAHARAN AFRICA	227,290	273,322	330,095	341,510	354,095	366,236	381,357	402,405	425,186	1.8	2.4	4.4
Excluding South Africa	131,907	162,389	202,585	208,697	217,658	224,762	235,686	249,509	264,506	2.2	2.6	4.8
Excl. S. Africa & Nigeria	99,676	127,371	158,898	162,643	170,180	176,555	182,302	192,868	204,410	2.6	2.7	4.5
Angola	6,746	8,464	8,862	9,129	9,416	10,780	11,137	12,383	14,935	3.5	1	9.9
Benin	1,084	1,412	2,131	2,255	2,368	2,474	2,571	2,650	2,727	2.7	4.7	3.9
Botswana	1,208	3,394	5,707	6,177	6,500	6,866	7,290	7,740	8,046	10.9	5.6	5.6
Burkina Faso	1,263	1,750	2,560	2,601	2,754	2,875	3,062	3,205	3,433	3.9	4.1	5.6
Burundi	559	865	715	709	724	756	747	783	790	4.5	–3.2	2.2
Cameroon	6,339	8,793	9,669	10,075	10,530	10,952	11,393	11,815	12,057	4.5	1.3	3.7
Cape Verde	..	303	498	531	552	577	613	608	681	6.3	5.9	4.7
Central African Republic	730	809	931	953	967	959	886	898	918	1.6	1.8	–1.4
Chad	664	1,104	1,395	1,383	1,544	1,675	1,922	2,568	2,789	6.7	2.3	15.9
Comoros	136	181	200	202	209	217	223	222	232	2.9	1.2	2.6
Congo, Dem. Rep.	7,016	7,659	4,625	4,306	4,215	4,362	4,614	4,921	5,239	2.1	–5	4.4
Congo, Rep.	1,746	2,796	2,992	3,220	3,342	3,503	3,563	3,691	3,975	3.8	0.8	4
Côte d'Ivoire	7,706	8,274	10,787	10,425	10,436	10,266	10,095	10,261	10,230	0.7	3.5	–0.5
Djibouti	..	660	549	551	563	577	596	614	633	..	–2.3	2.9
Equatorial Guinea	..	207	1,105	1,254	2,035	2,411	2,694	3,549	3,793	..	20.7	23.2
Eritrea	..	..	729	634	692	697	739	753	757	..	7.9	3.5
Ethiopia	..	6,292	7,461	7,903	8,513	8,618	8,315	9,407	10,367	2	3.3	4.7
Gabon	3,594	4,298	5,165	5,068	5,176	5,162	5,290	5,361	5,523	0.5	2.9	1.6
Gambia, The	213	305	399	421	445	431	461	484	509	3.5	2.7	3.7
Ghana	2,637	3,263	4,795	4,972	5,171	5,404	5,685	6,003	6,357	2.6	4.3	5.1
Guinea	1,539	2,088	3,055	3,112	3,236	3,372	3,413	3,505	3,621	3	4.4	2.9
Guinea-Bissau	115	186	200	215	216	201	202	206	213	3.8	1.4	–0.5
Kenya	7,087	10,557	12,630	12,705	13,188	13,261	13,657	14,319	15,152	4.1	2.2	3.4
Lesotho	392	602	832	853	868	893	917	954	982	4.1	4.3	2.9
Liberia	1,391	433	446	561	577	599	411	422	444	–3.3	0.2	–6.8
Madagascar	3,099	3,266	3,701	3,878	4,111	3,590	3,941	4,149	4,339	0.8	1.7	2
Malawi	1,000	1,243	1,716	1,744	1,657	1,704	1,808	1,936	1,990	2.4	3.8	3.4
Mali	1,536	1,630	2,347	2,422	2,716	2,828	3,039	3,105	3,294	0.5	3.9	5.9
Mauritania	693	816	1,062	1,081	1,112	1,125	1,188	1,249	1,317	1.9	2.9	4
Mauritius	1,518	2,679	4,296	4,469	4,718	4,846	5,000	5,235	5,475	5.9	5.3	4
Mozambique	2,245	2,279	3,706	3,778	4,273	4,621	4,987	5,361	5,695	–0.9	5.7	8.4
Namibia	2,002	2,263	3,298	3,414	3,495	3,729	3,858	4,088	4,258	1.1	4	4.7
Niger	1,523	1,507	1,824	1,798	1,926	1,984	2,071	2,059	2,199	–0.4	2.4	3.6
Nigeria	31,452	34,978	43,628	45,984	47,409	48,143	53,292	56,543	59,992	0.8	2.4	5.8
Rwanda	1,457	1,782	1,709	1,811	1,933	2,114	2,134	2,218	2,351	2.5	–1.6	5.1
São Tomé and Principe	..	..	..	..	..	..	..	..	..	..	..	..
Senegal	2,683	3,463	4,546	4,692	4,907	4,939	5,268	5,562	5,866	2.7	2.8	4.5
Seychelles	290	393	587	615	601	609	573	557	563	3.1	4.5	–2.1
Sierra Leone	935	1,021	610	634	749	954	1,043	1,120	1,201	0.5	–5.4	13.7
Somalia	..	..	..	..	..	..	..	..	..	..	..	..
South Africa	95,503	110,945	127,577	132,878	136,512	141,549	145,761	152,996	160,793	1.4	2	3.9
Sudan	5,555	7,100	11,611	12,366	13,120	13,960	14,742	15,509	16,749	2.4	5.3	6.1
Swaziland	554	1,024	1,361	1,389	1,411	1,452	1,494	1,526	1,562	6.5	3.3	2.5
Tanzania	..	6,801	8,639	9,079	9,646	10,345	10,931	11,667	12,461	..	2.7	6.5
Togo	964	1,071	1,340	1,329	1,327	1,382	1,419	1,461	1,480	1.5	3.6	2.5
Uganda	..	3,077	5,610	5,926	6,219	6,613	6,926	7,306	7,786	2.3	7.2	5.6
Zambia	2,730	3,028	3,126	3,238	3,396	3,508	3,688	3,887	4,090	1	0.2	4.7
Zimbabwe	4,376	6,734	8,034	7,399	7,199	6,883	6,167	5,933	5,618	3.3	2.7	–5.7
NORTH AFRICA	126,904	176,633	234,042	241,901	251,458	260,036	269,560	282,196	294,925	3.4	3.2	4
Algeria	35,291	46,367	53,611	54,790	56,215	58,857	62,918	66,190	69,698	2.9	1.7	5.2
Egypt, Arab Rep.	38,553	65,574	94,738	99,839	103,357	106,649	109,964	114,559	119,714	5.5	4.3	3.6
Libya	14,354	..	34,104	34,495	36,053	37,228	36,204	38,014	40,409	–7	..	2.7
Morocco	18,308	26,717	33,018	33,334	35,433	36,563	38,582	40,220	40,910	4.2	2.4	4.3
Tunisia	8,622	12,237	18,571	19,443	20,401	20,738	21,891	23,213	24,194	3.2	4.6	4.5
ALL AFRICA	356,401	451,457	564,126	583,400	605,543	626,261	650,902	684,580	720,082	2.4	2.7	4.3

a. Provisional.

Table 2.8
Gross national income per capita

	Dollars[a]									Annual average		
	1980	1990	1999	2000	2001	2002	2003	2004	2005[a]	1980–89	1990–99	2000–05
SUB–SAHARAN AFRICA	664	584	503	488	480	471	514	608	751	587	540	552
Excluding South Africa	535	378	315	306	314	320	352	403	477	424	329	362
Excl. S. Africa & Nigeria	452	401	322	311	310	317	345	396	459	400	343	356
Angola	..	730	390	430	470	620	710	940	1,410	740	452	763
Benin	..	..	..	..	430	460	..	..	..	..	..	445
Botswana	960	2,450	3,110	3,270	3,470	3,120	3,670	4,380	5,590	1,202	2,923	3,917
Burkina Faso	310	350	260	250	240	250	290	350	400	284	287	297
Burundi	220	210	140	120	110	100	90	90	100	231	166	102
Cameroon	620	960	590	570	640	640	730	890	1,010	883	748	747
Cape Verde	..	..	..	..	..	..	..	..	..	..	..	..
Central African Republic	340	460	280	270	260	250	260	310	350	345	365	283
Chad	230	260	200	180	190	200	220	330	400	217	238	253
Comoros	..	540	410	400	400	400	470	550	650	383	501	478
Congo, Dem. Rep.	630	230	80	90	80	90	100	120	120	361	151	100
Congo, Rep.	820	880	450	520	570	620	640	750	950	990	658	675
Côte d'Ivoire	1,120	730	710	640	600	570	640	760	870	811	712	680
Djibouti	..	..	810	840	..	..	..	..	..	..	803	840
Equatorial Guinea	..	360	1,170	..	..	..	..	..	..	365	582	..
Eritrea	..	..	183	160	160	150	160	180	..	..	168	162
Ethiopia	..	170	130	130	130	120	110	130	160	154	140	130
Gabon	4,790	4,780	3,180	3,090	3,080	2,990	3,340	4,080	5,010	4,403	4,232	3,598
Gambia, The	380	310	340	340	320	270	300	460	..	309	337	338
Ghana	430	390	..	295	351	270	310	..	..	392	398	307
Guinea	..	..	..	..	370	360	380	410	380	..	..	380
Guinea-Bissau	..	..	..	160	140	130	140	160	180	..	..	152
Kenya	450	380	360	350	420	410	430	480	530	374	320	437
Lesotho	..	..	..	640	600	540	590	730	940	..	..	673
Liberia	620	..	..	130	130	140	100	120	130	510	..	125
Madagascar	440	..	..	..	..	230	290	320	..	388	260	280
Malawi	190	180	180	150	140	140	150	160	160	168	187	150
Mali	270	270	240	250	230	230	270	..	..	217	265	245
Mauritania	460	550	400	370	360	340	..	..	..	469	478	357
Mauritius	1,148	2,478	3,590	..	..	..	..	..	..	1,358	3,255	..
Mozambique	..	170	220	210	210	220	230	280	..	267	173	230
Namibia	..	..	..	1,870	1,750	1,650	1,930	2,370	..	1,474	..	1,914
Niger	390	280	170	160	160	160	180	210	240	289	213	185
Nigeria	810	280	280	280	330	340	380	430	560	496	270	387
Rwanda	250	370	240	240	220	210	190	200	..	293	248	212
São Tomé and Principe	..	430	270	290	300	310	340	380	420	490	348	340
Senegal	500	660	460	450	440	420	490	600	700	474	560	517
Seychelles	2,080	5,020	7,290	7,440	7,380	6,840	7,450	8,080	8,180	2,764	6,420	7,562
Sierra Leone	390	200	150	140	160	190	200	210	220	280	175	187
Somalia	110	120	..	..	..	..	..	..	..	126	120	..
South Africa	2,550	3,390	3,150	3,050	2,830	2,630	2,870	3,700	4,990	2,695	3,472	3,345
Sudan	..	610	330	330	340	380	430	520	650	757	355	442
Swaziland	..	..	..	1,380	1,330	1,240	1,340	1,650	..	..	..	1,388
Tanzania	..	190	250	260	270	290	300	320	340	..	188	297
Togo	410	380	290	270	250	240	270	310	350	306	326	282
Uganda	..	190	320	280	240	230	230	250	280	208	243	252
Zambia	630	450	320	310	330	340	380	..	..	460	368	340
Zimbabwe	930	850	500	460	540	780	790	580	350	858	659	583
NORTH AFRICA	1,276	1,376	1,581	1,644	1,673	1,645	1,699	1,817	2,024	1,305	1,378	1,751
Algeria	2,060	2,420	1,560	1,610	1,690	1,750	1,950	2,290	2,730	2,462	1,758	2,003
Egypt, Arab Rep.	530	810	1,370	1,490	1,530	1,470	1,390	..	..	671	999	1,470
Libya	10,460	..	..	..	..	..	..	..	..	7,432	..	..
Morocco	970	1,030	1,190	1,180	1,900	..	..	..	..	805	1,156	1,540
Tunisia	1,360	1,430	2,090	2,090	2,060	2,000	2,260	2,650	2,880	1,264	1,808	2,323
ALL AFRICA	780	738	694	690	687	674	718	818	971	725	697	760

a. Calculated by the *World Bank Atlas* method.
b. Provisional.

Table 2.9

Gross domestic product deflator (local currency series)

	1980	1990	1999	2000	2001	2002	2003	2004	2005[a]	1980–89	1990–99	2000–05
				Index (2000 = 100)						Annual average		
SUB-SAHARAN AFRICA	14	38	94	100	105	110	116	122	131	22.6	65.4	113.8
Excluding South Africa	15	39	94	100	105	109	115	121	130	23.6	65.2	113.6
Excl. S. Africa & Nigeria	17	39	95	100	105	109	114	121	130	24.8	65.9	113.3
Angola	..	..	19	100	208	460	931	1,329	1,907	0.0	2.6	822.5
Benin	38	50	97	100	103	111	113	113	116	47.1	72.5	109.5
Botswana	13	41	89	100	106	107	110	117	130	21.8	62.0	111.7
Burkina Faso	45	68	95	100	105	109	111	119	123	59.6	79.2	111.3
Burundi	21	31	88	100	105	107	120	130	151	23.9	50.5	118.9
Cameroon	34	58	97	100	102	106	106	107	112	50.4	78.5	105.6
Cape Verde	..	66	101	100	103	105	106	113	109	59.8	81.0	105.8
Central African Republic	32	70	98	100	103	107	110	108	111	54.5	83.9	106.4
Chad	46	60	95	100	114	116	115	127	156	55.3	77.6	121.5
Comoros	36	70	96	100	109	113	119	121	124	54.3	82.5	114.3
Congo, Dem. Rep.	..	..	..	..	..	..	..	..	..	..	..	..
Congo, Rep.	29	38	68	100	86	84	82	87	111	38.6	49.8	91.8
Côte d'Ivoire	39	50	101	100	104	109	111	112	116	49.7	75.5	108.8
Djibouti	..	69	98	100	102	102	105	109	112	..	84.7	105.0
Equatorial Guinea	..	24	68	100	88	88	90	102	147	25.6	40.8	102.5
Eritrea	..	..	80	100	114	131	147	180	206	..	65.6	146.4
Ethiopia	..	49	94	100	95	90	102	107	116	41.2	80.4	101.7
Gabon	35	53	78	100	94	94	93	99	116	44.3	63.4	99.4
Gambia, The	15	64	96	100	115	134	170	194	203	30.6	81.8	152.7
Ghana	0	11	79	100	135	166	213	244	280	3.0	37.3	189.8
Guinea	5	48	90	100	105	108	121	147	192	17.3	77.0	128.6
Guinea-Bissau	0	6	97	100	95	98	95	97	105	1.0	47.4	98.3
Kenya	10	24	94	100	102	101	107	117	126	15.8	57.2	108.6
Lesotho	12	38	96	100	107	117	124	129	136	21.4	64.7	118.7
Liberia	2	2	101	100	112	141	145	146	166	1.8	22.2	134.9
Madagascar	4	21	93	100	107	124	127	145	172	10.3	53.6	129.2
Malawi	2	7	77	100	126	146	160	180	207	3.3	28.9	153.1
Mali	35	57	95	100	100	116	117	116	119	49.8	79.1	111.4
Mauritania	20	42	99	100	108	116	119	133	157	29.5	75.1	122.2
Mauritius	21	54	96	100	104	111	118	124	130	32.8	74.2	114.5
Mozambique	0	7	91	100	116	136	148	161	179	1.4	48.1	139.9
Namibia	12	39	90	100	114	127	126	130	133	21.4	62.6	121.8
Niger	49	63	96	100	104	107	108	106	114	62.8	77.7	106.6
Nigeria	2	7	72	100	111	115	139	167	209	3.1	41.0	140.1
Rwanda	19	31	97	100	100	100	109	122	131	23.9	65.5	110.3
São Tomé and Principe	..	..	..	..	..	..	..	..	..	..	..	..
Senegal	39	63	98	100	103	106	106	106	109	55.1	80.7	105.0
Seychelles	57	88	99	100	105	110	116	121	123	70.8	92.7	112.7
Sierra Leone	0	5	94	100	102	98	106	123	140	0.6	40.9	111.5
Somalia	..	..	..	..	..	..	..	..	..	..	..	..
South Africa	9	38	92	100	108	119	125	132	138	18.5	64.9	120.2
Sudan	..	..	..	..	..	..	..	..	..	..	..	..
Swaziland	11	32	89	100	111	125	139	145	153	18.7	57.5	128.9
Tanzania	..	15	93	100	107	114	122	132	142	11.4	49.1	119.7
Togo	35	58	102	100	103	105	101	105	106	48.5	78.3	103.2
Uganda	..	30	96	100	107	102	112	119	129	4.4	71.6	111.6
Zambia	0	1	77	100	124	149	179	214	255	0.2	31.9	170.2
Zimbabwe	2	7	64	100	177	394	1,883	9,064	30,632	3.9	23.6	7,041.8
NORTH AFRICA	30	54	95	100	102	104	111	123	132	43.6	77.0	112.1
Algeria	6	16	80	100	101	103	111	123	142	8.6	50.2	113.3
Egypt, Arab Rep.	13	43	95	100	102	104	111	124	132	20.4	72.6	112.3
Libya	143	..	81	100	98	128	166	204	263	153.1	80.9	160.0
Morocco	38	75	99	100	102	102	102	104	105	54.8	89.7	102.6
Tunisia	30	64	97	100	103	105	107	110	112	46.2	81.7	106.3
ALL AFRICA	15	39	94	100	104	109	113	122	131	23.5	66.2	113.1

a. Provisional.

Table 2.10

Gross domestic product deflator
(U.S. dollar series)

	1980	1990	1999	2000	2001	2002	2003	2004	2005[a]	Annual average 1980–89	1990–99	2000–05
SUB–SAHARAN AFRICA	122	110	100	100	95	96	114	133	148	108	108	114
Excluding South Africa	149	117	97	100	100	107	114	127	147	123	104	116
Excl. S. Africa & Nigeria	130	126	102	100	99	109	115	127	142	121	112	115
Angola	..	121	69	100	95	106	125	160	220	95	91	134
Benin	130	131	112	100	100	113	138	153	157	103	116	127
Botswana	88	112	99	100	93	86	114	127	130	77	108	108
Burkina Faso	153	178	110	100	102	111	137	160	166	130	125	129
Burundi	164	131	113	100	92	83	80	85	101	153	123	90
Cameroon	106	127	108	100	91	99	120	134	140	102	125	114
Cape Verde	..	112	117	100	100	107	130	152	147	95	117	123
Central African Republic	109	184	113	100	100	109	135	146	149	118	144	123
Chad	156	157	110	100	111	119	142	172	211	121	129	143
Comoros	91	138	111	100	106	116	146	163	167	89	125	133
Congo, Dem. Rep.	205	122	102	100	111	127	123	134	136	133	126	122
Congo, Rep.	98	100	79	100	84	86	100	118	150	84	81	106
Côte d'Ivoire	132	130	116	100	101	112	136	151	157	108	123	126
Djibouti	..	69	98	100	102	102	105	109	112	..	85	105
Equatorial Guinea	..	64	79	100	85	90	110	138	198	54	65	120
Eritrea	..	..	94	100	97	91	79	84	128	..	99	97
Ethiopia	..	192	102	100	93	86	97	101	110	162	153	98
Gabon	119	138	90	100	91	96	114	134	157	96	104	115
Gambia, The	113	104	108	100	94	86	80	83	91	91	109	89
Ghana	169	180	161	100	103	114	134	148	169	177	166	128
Guinea	434	128	113	100	94	95	106	115	92	420	136	100
Guinea-Bissau	97	131	112	100	92	100	117	131	141	105	116	114
Kenya	103	81	102	100	98	97	107	113	127	86	86	107
Lesotho	110	102	109	100	87	77	113	138	148	92	115	111
Liberia	69	89	99	100	94	93	100	109	119	76	101	103
Madagascar	130	94	100	100	110	122	139	105	116	108	101	115
Malawi	124	151	103	100	104	114	98	98	104	118	132	103
Mali	116	149	110	100	97	118	144	157	161	108	132	129
Mauritania	102	125	113	100	101	102	108	124	139	108	140	112
Mauritius	76	89	99	100	96	94	105	116	115	71	104	104
Mozambique	157	108	108	100	87	89	96	110	120	173	101	100
Namibia	108	104	103	100	92	84	116	140	145	90	111	113
Niger	165	165	111	100	101	109	132	143	155	137	127	123
Nigeria	204	81	80	100	101	97	109	128	162	127	76	116
Rwanda	80	145	113	100	88	82	79	83	92	105	116	87
São Tomé and Principe	..	..	..	..	..	..	..	..	..	..	..	..
Senegal	131	165	113	100	99	108	129	143	147	120	136	121
Seychelles	51	94	106	100	103	115	123	126	128	65	103	116
Sierra Leone	118	64	109	100	108	98	95	96	99	98	98	99
Somalia	..	..	..	..	..	..	..	..	..	..	..	..
South Africa	85	101	104	100	87	78	114	141	151	88	115	112
Sudan	137	185	92	100	102	107	121	140	167	195	108	123
Swaziland	98	86	101	100	89	82	128	156	167	83	101	120
Tanzania	..	63	100	100	98	94	94	97	101	76	77	97
Togo	118	152	118	100	100	107	124	141	143	106	131	119
Uganda	..	140	107	100	91	88	90	93	112	164	114	96
Zambia	142	109	100	100	107	105	117	140	178	111	111	125
Zimbabwe	153	130	74	100	142	318	120	79	61	136	101	137
NORTH AFRICA	104	97	97	100	94	85	90	97	106	96	93	95
Algeria	120	134	91	100	98	97	108	128	146	128	101	113
Egypt, Arab Rep.	60	66	96	100	94	82	75	69	75	62	76	83
Libya	248	..	89	100	83	52	66	80	103	263	89	81
Morocco	103	97	107	100	96	99	114	124	126	80	106	110
Tunisia	101	100	112	100	98	101	114	121	119	89	111	109
ALL AFRICA	114	105	98	100	94	91	104	118	131	103	102	106

a. Provisional.

Table 2.11 Gross domestic savings

	Share of GDP (%)									Annual average		
	1980	1990	1999	2000	2001	2002	2003	2004	2005[a]	1980–89	1990–99	2000–05
SUB–SAHARAN AFRICA	29.9	19.8	16.0	21.2	19.3	17.9	19.5	20.4	21.3	23.2	16.5	19.9
Excluding South Africa	27.1	17.4	13.9	22.7	19.4	17.0	20.0	23.1	24.5	20.7	14.4	21.1
Excl. S. Africa & Nigeria	22.1	15.2	12.8	17.0	15.0	15.0	16.6	18.3	19.5	20.5	12.4	16.9
Angola	..	29.7	20.7	41.8	15.1	23.9	19.2	25.1	32.8	24.0	22.0	26.3
Benin	−6.3	2.2	4.8	6.0	6.5	3.7	6.0	5.5	6.9	−2.4	3.8	5.8
Botswana	26.7	42.6	42.2	54.5	56.6	51.4	49.7	50.2	51.8	35.3	39.6	52.3
Burkina Faso	−7.2	5.2	8.1	6.5	5.0	4.7	3.9	..	..	−2.7	7.6	5.0
Burundi	−0.6	−5.4	−2.5	−6.0	−7.8	−9.7	−8.7	−11.0	−23.1	3.1	−5.2	−11.1
Cameroon	21.7	20.7	19.2	20.3	19.0	19.0	17.8	18.5	16.2	24.2	18.5	18.5
Cape Verde	..	−8.1	−17.5	−14.2	−15.1	−15.7	−15.8	..	..	−2.2	−5.6	−15.2
Central African Republic	−8.9	−0.6	11.0	7.8	11.1	10.3	..	..	..	−1.1	3.7	9.7
Chad	..	−7.7	−0.2	5.5	5.3	..	18.1	24.5	35.6	−8.1	−0.5	17.8
Comoros	−10.1	−3.2	−5.7	−5.7	−5.2	−4.0	−5.8	−10.6	−12.9	−4.5	−4.5	−7.4
Congo, Dem. Rep.	10.1	9.3	9.1	4.5	3.2	4.0	5.0	4.0	5.9	10.9	8.8	4.4
Congo, Rep.	35.7	23.8	41.0	59.3	50.5	51.0	51.3	51.3	58.7	31.9	28.8	53.7
Côte d'Ivoire	20.4	11.3	21.3	17.9	19.0	26.3	20.6	20.5	20.4	19.6	17.8	20.8
Djibouti	..	−10.4	−2.4	−6.5	−0.6	4.9	5.2	4.8	7.3	..	−6.4	2.5
Equatorial Guinea	..	−20.1	..	72.0	80.8	78.1	78.7	83.0	86.9	..	13.7	79.9
Eritrea	..	..	−41.2	−34.7	−27.0	−33.7	−59.7	−61.4	−26.8	..	−30.9	−40.6
Ethiopia	..	9.6	1.8	6.8	7.4	7.8	6.6	3.7	−1.6	10.5	7.5	5.1
Gabon	60.6	36.9	47.7	58.3	51.7	43.7	48.2	53.9	67.2	44.3	43.6	53.8
Gambia, The	5.8	10.7	11.0	8.5	12.0	12.9	11.1	10.5	4.4	6.5	7.4	9.9
Ghana	4.9	5.5	3.3	5.3	7.1	7.7	11.4	7.3	3.4	4.8	7.5	7.0
Guinea	..	22.2	15.5	15.4	14.1	9.5	7.8	7.3	11.1	16.6	18.3	10.9
Guinea-Bissau	−1.0	2.8	−1.2	−8.5	−19.3	−12.1	1.2	−3.0	1.5	−0.9	1.5	−6.7
Kenya	18.1	18.5	10.7	9.4	11.3	13.1	13.3	12.4	9.0	17.9	15.6	11.4
Lesotho	−52.0	−52.9	−22.6	−20.6	−16.6	−19.8	−17.3	−14.7	−4.8	−65.5	−38.3	−15.6
Liberia	14.8	..	..	..	−3.4	−3.3	−3.2	−0.7	2.4	2.2	..	−1.6
Madagascar	−1.4	5.5	7.2	7.7	15.3	7.7	8.9	9.4	8.4	2.9	4.2	9.6
Malawi	10.8	13.4	−0.6	3.8	3.8	−10.1	−10.7	−9.1	−9.5	12.7	3.4	−5.3
Mali	1.1	6.4	9.5	12.0	14.0	11.3	13.3	8.6	9.8	−0.4	7.6	11.5
Mauritania	−3.5	4.9	−1.2	−8.6	3.1	−1.9	−5.0	−3.1	−15.0	3.1	2.4	−5.1
Mauritius	14.5	23.5	23.3	23.9	26.0	25.2	24.8	23.4	18.9	20.0	24.1	23.7
Mozambique	−8.9	−5.8	13.7	11.6	8.0	11.0	11.7	14.3	11.9	−6.2	1.0	11.4
Namibia	38.4	18.2	12.5	14.0	17.0	17.8	26.2	26.7	29.5	10.8	12.7	21.9
Niger	14.6	1.2	3.7	3.5	4.4	5.3	5.0	6.1	9.3	7.3	2.7	5.6
Nigeria[b]	31.4	29.4	19.1	42.3	34.9	25.5	32.1	39.4	39.5	17.5	24.0	35.6
Rwanda	4.2	6.2	0.0	1.3	2.6	0.0	−0.8	2.4	2.0	5.0	−5.5	1.2
São Tomé and Principe	..	..	..	..	..	..	..	..	..	..	..	..
Senegal	2.1	2.4	10.9	11.2	9.4	6.8	8.8	8.0	9.9	4.3	5.4	9.0
Seychelles	27.1	20.3	25.6	22.6	19.1	20.0	21.2	23.0	−14.7	24.1	21.7	15.2
Sierra Leone	0.9	8.7	−10.3	−13.3	−11.6	−9.4	−7.4	−1.9	−2.3	9.1	2.9	−7.6
Somalia	−12.9	−12.5	..	..	..	..	..	..	..	−6.3	−12.5	..
South Africa	37.9	23.2	19.0	18.9	19.2	19.7	18.8	16.8	16.6	28.5	19.4	18.3
Sudan	2.1	..	7.7	15.9	9.8	13.3	15.7	18.7	13.8	5.0	7.3	14.5
Swaziland	1.2	6.6	0.3	3.0	3.1	19.5	19.9	16.8	13.3	3.7	2.0	12.6
Tanzania	..	1.3	4.5	10.2	8.8	11.8	12.0	11.2	10.9	..	2.0	10.8
Togo	23.2	14.7	3.2	−2.2	1.0	0.6	5.3	4.5	4.9	12.3	6.7	2.4
Uganda	−0.4	0.6	7.6	8.1	6.5	4.7	6.3	8.4	7.1	2.3	4.3	6.9
Zambia	19.3	16.6	−1.1	8.3	17.3	17.7	18.7	18.2	17.0	14.0	7.1	16.2
Zimbabwe	13.8	17.5	16.0	13.3	11.6	7.1	6.2	4.1	0.6	16.5	16.9	7.2
NORTH AFRICA	41.3	22.8	19.7	24.5	23.0	23.6	26.8	30.3	34.9	29.4	20.0	27.2
Algeria	43.1	27.1	31.6	44.8	42.0	40.9	44.9	47.7	54.4	31.5	30.1	45.8
Egypt, Arab Rep.	15.2	16.1	13.4	12.9	13.4	13.9	14.3	15.6	15.7	15.5	14.2	14.3
Libya	56.9	..	..	..	..	..	..	..	..	46.9	..	..
Morocco	14.9	19.9	18.8	17.1	19.4	19.4	19.9	18.3	18.0	16.7	17.0	18.7
Tunisia	24.0	20.0	24.1	23.7	23.3	21.4	21.2	21.2	20.7	22.7	22.3	21.9
ALL AFRICA	32.8	20.9	17.5	22.5	20.9	20.1	21.9	23.4	25.4	25.0	17.8	22.4

a. Provisional.
b. For 1994–2000 Nigeria's values were distorted because the official exchange rate used by the government for oil exports and oil value added was significantly overvalued.

Table 2.12 Gross national savings

	1980	1990	1999	2000	2001	2002	2003	2004	2005[a]	1980–89	1990–99	2000–05
SUB–SAHARAN AFRICA	11.8	13.5	13.5	17.1	16.2	14.5	15.9	16.3	17.5	11.9	13.3	16.3
Excluding South Africa	2.6	10.0	11.4	17.4	16.3	13.2	15.7	17.4	19.4	5.4	10.7	16.5
Excl. S. Africa & Nigeria	4.0	8.3	9.7	12.9	12.6	12.5	13.9	14.4	15.7	6.1	9.1	13.6
Angola	..	..	−1.7	23.8	−1.4	9.8	7.6	12.6	20.5	..	4.8	12.1
Benin	..	..	9.9	10.9	12.5	7.3	9.4	8.9	10.6	..	10.8	9.9
Botswana	28.7	43.3	42.0	52.3	57.6	43.2	44.5	45.1	50.5	33.7	41.5	48.9
Burkina Faso	..	..	..	..	..	..	..	..	..	..	..	..
Burundi	..	..	−0.1	1.2	1.6	2.9	6.0	5.2	1.1	..	1.4	3.0
Cameroon	5.1	16.1	15.9	14.7	15.9	15.1	15.5	16.9	14.7	19.2	13.5	15.5
Cape Verde	..	17.6	8.1	9.1	8.0	9.4	9.2	..	..	24.2	21.2	8.9
Central African Republic	..	..	12.0	8.0	12.3	7.6	..	..	14.0	..	12.0	10.5
Chad	..	−2.7	2.4	7.9	6.6	..	4.9	13.7	21.3	−3.3	3.5	10.9
Comoros	..	10.1	2.5	9.9	12.5	9.6	7.2	6.5	5.9	..	6.8	8.6
Congo, Dem. Rep.	7.9	0.8	1.1	−1.3	0.1	5.3	9.9	6.1	6.1	5.9	1.1	4.4
Congo, Rep.	..	..	11.0	30.1	20.7	24.0	26.7	26.3	33.5	..	3.2	26.9
Côte d'Ivoire	..	−4.3	11.7	8.0	10.6	16.8	12.3	12.4	10.9	9.2	6.2	11.8
Djibouti	..	..	10.6	5.4	11.6	15.6	20.6	18.5	20.5	..	11.4	15.4
Equatorial Guinea	..	−22.0	..	43.1	24.0	38.6	21.5	20.2	33.3	..	6.0	30.1
Eritrea	..	..	4.9	20.4	28.7	26.3	9.4	0.0	10.6	..	11.7	15.9
Ethiopia	..	11.9	7.7	14.9	16.6	17.8	19.4	16.1	11.8	11.8	13.2	16.1
Gabon	..	25.4	35.1	40.2	35.4	31.0	33.3	39.9	52.3	23.5	30.0	38.7
Gambia, The	..	..	14.2	13.6	14.8	18.2	18.6	14.3	9.1	..	16.2	14.8
Ghana	..	..	9.2	15.5	21.3	20.2	24.9	25.7	21.4	..	14.6	21.5
Guinea	..	14.6	12.9	13.3	12.7	9.2	6.8	5.7	9.1	8.8	14.2	9.5
Guinea-Bissau	−6.3	15.3	−3.3	−2.7	−15.7	−8.0	5.1	16.2	11.2	−0.3	5.5	1.0
Kenya	15.4	18.6	13.7	15.2	15.7	16.6	16.4	13.3	11.8	15.8	16.1	14.8
Lesotho	34.5	39.0	22.5	22.8	26.5	24.6	25.3	29.2	37.5	33.8	29.5	27.7
Liberia	..	..	..	..	−21.4	−11.1	−6.4	33.1	39.9	..	..	6.8
Madagascar	..	9.2	9.5	9.4	17.2	8.3	13.0	15.2	11.7	5.0	4.9	12.5
Malawi	..	..	−2.5	2.2	2.4	−12.0	−5.1	−5.2	−4.3	..	−0.9	−3.7
Mali	..	..	..	16.0	12.9	8.5	15.0	9.8	9.9	..	..	12.0
Mauritania	..	..	..	..	..	..	..	..	..	..	..	..
Mauritius	..	26.3	24.9	25.3	27.6	26.6	26.3	23.8	20.1	25.5	26.5	25.0
Mozambique	−6.9	2.1	14.7	15.4	6.4	11.1	12.8	14.2	11.4	−3.8	4.0	11.9
Namibia	26.9	34.8	24.3	27.7	27.7	27.7	41.6	39.7	40.0	18.5	27.3	34.1
Niger	13.0	−1.2	2.8	2.8	4.4	4.7	5.5	..	..	5.5	1.0	4.4
Nigeria[b]	..	..	13.9	33.6	29.4	15.8	22.2	27.4	30.5	..	13.9	26.5
Rwanda	..	..	−1.3	−0.5	0.2	−2.2	−3.8	−0.6	..	..	−9.2	−1.4
São Tomé and Principe	..	..	..	..	..	..	..	..	..	..	..	..
Senegal	0.1	−0.5	12.2	14.6	13.9	11.8	16.0	13.3	16.2	0.5	5.3	14.3
Seychelles	..	..	23.2	17.9	16.8	12.0	16.4	20.1	−18.2	..	22.0	10.8
Sierra Leone	0.5	2.6	−5.6	−7.9	−3.2	5.2	6.3	8.7	7.6	7.2	0.1	2.8
Somalia	−5.8	..	..	..	..	..	..	..	..	3.2	..	..
South Africa	33.9	19.1	15.9	15.8	15.4	16.7	15.6	14.1	13.9	24.3	16.6	15.2
Sudan	4.0	..	0.0	3.5	1.8	9.5	12.3	16.3	13.2	6.5	0.9	9.4
Swaziland	16.7	24.8	16.2	13.2	13.9	24.6	22.1	22.9	18.9	20.2	19.6	19.3
Tanzania	..	..	2.5	10.1	9.1	11.1	11.8	10.7	10.4	..	2.0	10.5
Togo	..	..	3.8	0.4	3.1	4.1	7.3	6.5	..	..	4.5	4.3
Uganda	−0.9	0.6	7.7	9.1	7.6	5.9	7.1	9.7	10.0	2.6	6.5	8.2
Zambia	7.3	6.7	−6.6	2.9	12.1	13.7	15.2	10.0	10.2	2.2	−1.2	10.7
Zimbabwe	..	15.7	16.1	9.6	9.4	7.0	5.9	4.0	−0.4	17.3	16.0	5.9
NORTH AFRICA	4.3	11.5	19.9	21.9	22.8	24.3	25.8	27.6	29.3	5.8	18.4	25.3
Algeria	..	..	28.5	41.3	40.1	38.8	43.5	46.3	51.3	..	27.8	43.6
Egypt, Arab Rep.	..	..	..	..	..	..	..	..	..	..	..	..
Libya	53.5	..	..	..	..	..	..	..	..	40.5	..	..
Morocco	..	..	22.1	22.0	27.4	26.6	27.5	26.7	27.9	..	21.7	26.3
Tunisia	..	..	24.3	23.2	23.7	22.3	22.1	22.4	22.6	..	21.9	22.7
ALL AFRICA	9.4	12.8	16.1	19.1	18.9	18.3	19.4	20.1	21.5	9.7	15.2	19.6

a. Provisional.
b. For 1994–2000 Nigeria's values were distorted because the official exchange rate used by the government for oil exports and oil value added was significantly overvalued.

NATIONAL ACCOUNTS

Table 2.13

General government final consumption

	Share of GDP (%)									Annual average		
	1980	1990	1999	2000	2001	2002	2003	2004	2005[a]	1980–89	1990–99	2000–05
SUB-SAHARAN AFRICA	**13.3**	**16.6**	**15.0**	**15.8**	**16.7**	**16.1**	**17.1**	**17.0**	**17.0**	**14.8**	**16.1**	**16.6**
Excluding South Africa	12.5	14.6	12.7	14.3	15.8	15.0	15.7	15.2	15.0	13.0	13.5	15.2
Excl. S. Africa & Nigeria	13.1	14.4	12.5	12.3	12.5	12.7	13.4	13.0	12.7	13.0	13.6	12.7
Angola	..	34.5	..	..	..	..	..	..	..	31.5	40.7	..
Benin	8.6	11.0	10.0	11.6	11.6	12.5	13.3	13.6	15.0	12.7	10.5	12.9
Botswana	21.3	24.1	27.1	22.3	19.7	21.7	22.3	21.8	21.2	24.3	26.8	21.5
Burkina Faso	9.2	13.2	12.5	12.6	12.2	13.1	12.8	..	..	12.2	13.6	12.7
Burundi	9.2	10.8	18.2	17.5	19.9	19.1	22.7	26.1	26.5	9.3	17.0	22.0
Cameroon	9.7	12.8	9.5	9.5	10.2	10.2	10.0	10.2	10.4	10.0	10.6	10.1
Cape Verde	..	14.7	19.4	21.3	11.3	11.7	14.7	..	..	13.1	17.0	14.8
Central African Republic	15.1	14.9	11.5	11.3	11.4	11.8	..	..	..	15.6	13.9	11.5
Chad	..	10.0	6.9	7.7	7.5	7.7	7.6	4.9	4.5	11.3	8.1	6.7
Comoros	30.9	24.5	14.6	11.7	16.2	17.4	14.7	14.3	13.5	28.6	20.3	14.6
Congo, Dem. Rep.	8.4	11.5	6.0	7.5	6.0	5.5	6.3	8.2	8.3	9.0	9.9	7.0
Congo, Rep.	17.6	13.8	15.1	11.6	14.1	18.4	17.0	16.0	13.2	17.7	18.1	15.1
Côte d'Ivoire	16.9	16.8	6.5	7.2	7.5	7.8	8.2	8.3	8.2	16.5	11.9	7.9
Djibouti	..	31.5	29.5	29.7	26.9	28.3	29.3	29.7	27.6	..	31.8	28.6
Equatorial Guinea	..	39.7	..	4.6	3.3	5.1	3.8	3.1	3.0	27.4	25.1	3.8
Eritrea	..	..	69.5	63.8	51.5	44.0	51.5	52.6	44.6	..	39.7	51.3
Ethiopia	..	13.2	16.0	18.5	15.2	16.4	19.1	14.7	13.8	11.2	10.1	16.3
Gabon	13.2	13.4	14.2	9.4	10.0	11.5	10.7	9.3	7.7	18.3	12.6	9.8
Gambia, The	31.2	13.7	13.0	13.7	14.4	12.9	11.0	11.1	..	29.1	13.8	12.6
Ghana	11.2	9.3	8.0	7.8	7.9	11.5	17.5	16.5	15.3	9.0	11.4	12.8
Guinea	..	11.0	7.0	6.8	6.9	7.5	7.8	6.3	5.6	11.8	8.2	6.8
Guinea-Bissau	27.6	10.3	10.8	14.0	12.6	13.0	12.8	14.5	18.2	18.9	8.4	14.2
Kenya	19.8	18.6	15.8	15.1	16.0	17.4	18.5	17.7	16.7	18.3	15.8	16.9
Lesotho	21.8	14.1	19.5	19.2	18.0	17.7	17.9	17.2	17.0	19.2	16.8	17.9
Liberia	19.1	..	..	..	14.4	13.7	8.5	10.4	11.2	22.0	..	11.6
Madagascar	12.1	8.0	7.2	9.0	9.1	8.1	9.2	9.8	8.4	9.8	7.9	8.9
Malawi	19.3	15.1	13.4	14.6	15.8	14.7	16.3	16.9	16.7	17.5	16.6	15.8
Mali	11.6	13.8	15.9	8.6	9.2	8.7	8.4	10.0	9.9	12.3	12.7	9.2
Mauritania	45.3	25.9	20.5	25.8	23.7	22.3	30.1	21.9	22.7	30.6	14.5	24.4
Mauritius	14.4	12.8	12.7	13.1	12.9	12.8	14.1	14.2	14.4	13.5	13.0	13.6
Mozambique	12.2	13.5	9.5	10.1	10.0	9.7	10.3	10.4	10.0	13.8	11.0	10.1
Namibia	17.4	30.6	30.3	28.8	28.4	26.4	26.5	24.5	23.6	27.9	31.0	26.4
Niger	10.4	15.0	14.9	13.0	12.4	12.2	11.3	13.0	11.5	11.9	14.6	12.2
Nigeria	12.1	15.1	13.4	20.9	27.1	24.2	23.7	22.1	21.5	13.9	12.9	23.3
Rwanda	12.5	10.1	11.0	10.5	11.7	11.8	15.1	12.9	13.3	13.0	11.5	12.6
São Tomé and Principe	..	..	..	..	..	..	..	..	..	..	..	..
Senegal	24.8	18.4	13.3	12.8	12.6	13.3	13.4	13.9	12.7	19.3	15.0	13.1
Seychelles	28.7	27.7	26.9	24.2	24.8	22.7	25.5	25.4	24.2	33.1	29.0	24.5
Sierra Leone	8.4	7.8	11.5	14.3	17.6	16.4	15.3	13.1	12.3	7.7	10.4	14.8
Somalia	15.6	..	..	..	..	..	..	..	..	17.6	..	..
South Africa	14.3	19.7	18.4	18.1	18.3	18.4	19.3	19.6	20.0	17.4	19.4	18.9
Sudan	16.0	..	6.5	7.6	8.6	4.5	10.8	11.8	16.8	12.1	6.0	10.0
Swaziland	27.0	18.1	24.6	24.5	17.7	18.6	18.6	22.2	26.6	20.6	22.6	21.4
Tanzania	..	17.8	7.9	10.6	11.5	12.4	14.8	15.9	17.0	..	14.0	13.7
Togo	22.4	14.2	9.7	10.2	10.0	8.4	9.8	9.7	10.0	16.9	12.8	9.7
Uganda	..	7.5	12.9	13.7	13.8	15.3	14.8	14.7	14.4	9.9	11.1	14.4
Zambia	25.5	19.0	12.9	9.5	12.8	13.0	13.5	12.7	13.4	23.0	17.7	12.5
Zimbabwe	18.5	19.4	13.6	13.9	17.7	17.9	16.6	23.3	27.2	20.1	17.2	19.4
NORTH AFRICA	**14.0**	**16.2**	**15.7**	**14.5**	**15.0**	**15.2**	**15.3**	**14.9**	**14.0**	**17.4**	**16.6**	**14.8**
Algeria	15.2	16.1	16.8	13.6	14.7	15.4	14.8	13.8	12.2	17.2	16.6	14.1
Egypt, Arab Rep.	15.7	11.3	11.6	11.2	11.3	12.5	12.7	12.8	12.7	16.2	10.9	12.2
Libya	21.8	24.4	21.9	20.5	21.6	16.7	..	..	..	30.0	24.3	19.6
Morocco	18.3	15.5	19.1	19.1	19.8	20.1	21.0	21.0	22.1	16.6	17.2	20.5
Tunisia	14.5	16.4	15.5	15.6	15.6	15.9	15.7	15.4	15.5	16.5	16.0	15.6
ALL AFRICA	**13.3**	**16.4**	**15.3**	**15.3**	**16.0**	**15.7**	**16.5**	**16.3**	**16.1**	**15.5**	**16.1**	**16.0**

a. Provisional.

Table 2.14 Final consumption expenditure

	Share of GDP (%)									Annual average		
	1980	1990	1999	2000	2001	2002	2003	2004	2005a	1980–89	1990–99	2000–05
SUB-SAHARAN AFRICA	70.1	80.2	84.0	78.8	80.7	82.1	80.5	79.6	78.7	76.8	83.5	80.1
Excluding South Africa	72.9	82.6	86.1	77.3	80.6	83.0	80.0	76.9	75.5	79.3	85.6	78.9
Excl. S. Africa & Nigeria	77.9	84.8	87.2	83.0	85.0	85.0	83.4	81.7	80.5	79.5	87.6	83.1
Angola	..	70.3	79.3	58.2	84.9	76.1	80.8	74.9	67.2	76.0	78.0	73.7
Benin	106.3	97.8	95.2	94.0	93.5	96.3	94.0	94.5	93.1	102.4	96.2	94.2
Botswana	73.3	57.4	57.8	45.5	43.4	48.6	50.3	49.8	48.2	64.7	60.4	47.7
Burkina Faso	107.2	94.8	91.9	93.5	95.0	95.3	96.1	..	..	102.7	92.4	95.0
Burundi	100.6	105.4	102.5	106.0	107.8	109.7	108.7	111.0	123.1	96.9	105.2	111.1
Cameroon	78.3	79.3	80.8	79.7	81.0	81.0	82.2	81.5	83.8	75.8	81.5	81.5
Cape Verde	..	108.1	117.5	114.2	115.1	115.7	115.8	..	..	102.2	105.6	115.2
Central African Republic	108.9	100.6	89.0	92.2	88.9	89.7	..	..	..	101.1	96.3	90.3
Chad	..	107.7	100.2	94.5	94.7	..	81.9	75.5	64.4	108.1	100.5	82.2
Comoros	110.1	103.2	105.7	105.7	105.2	104.0	105.8	110.6	112.9	104.5	104.5	107.4
Congo, Dem. Rep.	89.9	90.7	90.9	95.5	96.8	96.0	95.0	96.0	94.1	89.1	91.2	95.6
Congo, Rep.	64.3	76.2	59.0	40.7	49.5	49.0	48.7	48.7	41.3	68.1	71.2	46.3
Côte d'Ivoire	79.6	88.7	78.7	82.1	81.0	73.7	79.4	79.5	79.6	80.4	82.2	79.2
Djibouti	..	110.4	102.4	106.5	100.6	95.1	94.8	95.2	92.7	..	106.4	97.5
Equatorial Guinea	..	120.1	..	28.0	19.2	21.9	21.3	17.0	13.1	..	86.3	20.1
Eritrea	..	..	141.2	134.7	127.0	133.7	159.7	161.4	126.8	..	130.9	140.6
Ethiopia	..	90.4	98.2	93.2	92.6	92.2	93.4	96.3	101.6	89.5	92.5	94.9
Gabon	39.4	63.1	52.3	41.7	48.3	56.3	51.8	46.1	32.8	55.7	56.4	46.2
Gambia, The	94.2	89.3	89.0	91.5	88.0	87.1	88.9	89.5	95.6	93.5	92.6	90.1
Ghana	95.1	94.5	96.7	94.7	92.9	92.3	88.6	92.7	96.6	95.2	92.5	93.0
Guinea	..	77.8	84.5	84.6	85.9	90.5	92.2	92.7	88.9	84.9	81.7	89.1
Guinea-Bissau	101.0	97.2	101.2	108.5	119.3	112.1	98.8	103.0	98.5	100.9	98.5	106.7
Kenya	81.9	81.5	89.3	90.6	88.7	86.9	86.7	87.6	91.0	82.1	84.4	88.6
Lesotho	152.0	152.9	122.6	120.6	116.6	119.8	117.3	114.7	104.8	165.5	138.3	115.6
Liberia	85.2	..	..	..	103.4	103.3	103.2	100.7	97.6	97.8	..	101.6
Madagascar	101.4	94.5	92.8	92.3	84.7	92.3	91.1	90.6	91.6	97.1	95.8	90.4
Malawi	89.2	86.6	100.6	96.2	96.2	110.1	110.7	109.1	109.5	87.3	96.6	105.3
Mali	98.9	93.6	90.5	88.0	86.0	88.7	86.7	91.4	90.2	100.4	92.4	88.5
Mauritania	103.5	95.1	101.2	108.6	96.9	101.9	105.0	103.1	115.0	96.9	97.6	105.1
Mauritius	85.5	76.5	76.7	76.1	74.0	74.8	75.2	76.6	81.1	80.0	75.9	76.3
Mozambique	108.9	105.8	86.3	88.4	92.0	89.0	88.3	85.7	88.1	106.2	99.0	88.6
Namibia	61.6	81.8	87.5	86.0	83.0	82.2	73.8	73.3	70.5	89.2	87.3	78.1
Niger	85.4	98.8	96.3	96.5	95.6	94.7	95.0	93.9	90.7	92.7	97.3	94.4
Nigeria	68.6	70.6	80.9	57.7	65.1	74.5	67.9	60.6	60.5	82.5	76.0	64.4
Rwanda	95.8	93.8	100.0	98.7	97.4	100.0	100.8	97.6	98.0	95.0	105.5	98.8
São Tomé and Principe	..	..	..	..	..	..	..	..	..	..	..	..
Senegal	97.9	97.6	89.1	88.8	90.6	93.2	91.2	92.0	90.1	95.7	94.6	91.0
Seychelles	72.9	79.7	74.4	77.4	80.9	80.0	78.8	77.0	114.7	75.9	78.3	84.8
Sierra Leone	99.1	91.3	110.3	113.3	111.6	109.4	107.4	101.9	102.3	90.9	97.1	107.6
Somalia	112.9	112.5	..	..	..	..	..	..	..	106.3	112.5	..
South Africa	62.1	76.8	81.0	81.1	80.8	80.3	81.2	83.2	83.4	71.5	80.6	81.7
Sudan	97.9	..	92.3	84.1	90.2	86.7	84.3	81.3	86.2	95.0	92.7	85.5
Swaziland	98.8	93.4	99.7	97.0	96.9	80.5	80.1	83.2	86.7	96.3	98.0	87.4
Tanzania	..	98.7	95.5	89.8	91.2	88.2	88.0	88.8	89.1	..	98.0	89.2
Togo	76.8	85.3	96.8	102.2	99.0	99.4	94.7	95.5	95.1	87.7	93.3	97.6
Uganda	100.4	99.4	92.4	91.9	93.5	95.3	93.7	91.6	92.9	97.7	95.7	93.1
Zambia	80.7	83.4	101.1	91.7	82.7	82.3	81.3	81.8	83.0	86.0	92.9	83.8
Zimbabwe	86.2	82.5	84.0	86.7	88.4	92.9	93.8	95.9	99.4	83.5	83.1	92.8
NORTH AFRICA	58.7	77.2	80.3	75.5	77.0	76.4	73.2	69.7	65.1	70.6	80.0	72.8
Algeria	56.9	72.9	68.4	55.2	58.0	59.1	55.1	52.3	45.6	68.5	69.9	54.2
Egypt, Arab Rep.	84.8	83.9	86.6	87.1	86.6	86.1	85.7	84.4	84.3	84.5	85.8	85.7
Libya	43.1	72.8	82.2	67.1	76.5	73.6	..	..	..	53.1	82.4	72.4
Morocco	85.1	80.1	81.2	82.9	80.6	80.6	80.1	81.7	82.0	83.3	83.0	81.3
Tunisia	76.0	80.0	75.9	76.3	76.7	78.6	78.8	78.8	79.3	77.3	77.7	78.1
ALL AFRICA	67.2	79.1	82.5	77.5	79.1	79.9	78.1	76.6	74.6	75.0	82.2	77.6

a. Provisional.

Table 2.15

Final consumption expenditure per capita

					Dollars					Annual average		
	1980	1990	1999	2000	2001	2002	2003	2004	2005[a]	1980–89	1990–99	2000–05
SUB-SAHARAN AFRICA	502	469	428	406	398	413	493	584	666	458	458	493
Excluding South Africa	401	326	280	260	275	306	323	358	420	335	291	324
Excl. S. Africa & Nigeria	348	351	288	269	279	311	325	362	414	324	308	327
Angola	..	685	361	384	534	595	749	956	1,383	586	478	767
Benin	403	349	325	295	299	353	422	468	473	313	317	385
Botswana	742	1,523	1,872	1,603	1,483	1,629	2,352	2,766	2,853	781	1,735	2,115
Burkina Faso	314	347	236	215	229	254	324	..	..	277	252	256
Burundi	224	210	130	116	108	101	92	101	130	215	171	108
Cameroon	603	759	582	540	513	570	711	802	867	692	667	667
Cape Verde	..	1,030	1,558	1,347	1,373	1,509	1,910	..	..	806	1,189	1,535
Central African Republic	373	499	252	233	224	241	..	..	..	352	344	233
Chad	..	309	194	159	191	..	245	353	389	221	235	267
Comoros	406	593	445	395	420	464	596	681	728	394	507	547
Congo, Dem. Rep.	462	224	88	82	89	101	99	113	116	288	154	100
Congo, Rep.	609	859	417	381	390	405	460	545	616	681	593	466
Côte d'Ivoire	971	757	603	512	501	488	620	688	704	681	637	586
Djibouti	..	895	792	822	786	750	778	814	828	..	849	796
Equatorial Guinea	..	450	..	782	727	1,007	1,315	1,695	1,963	..	463	1,248
Eritrea	..	..	284	240	230	218	230	242	279	..	251	240
Ethiopia	..	213	119	115	111	102	109	131	162	189	158	122
Gabon	2,420	3,926	1,961	1,663	1,755	2,102	2,338	2,427	2,051	2,501	2,637	2,056
Gambia, The	348	303	302	293	271	231	227	243	291	276	315	259
Ghana	374	359	384	237	243	274	319	380	468	340	348	320
Guinea	..	334	354	312	303	330	371	408	315	1,127	380	340
Guinea-Bissau	141	233	171	171	169	156	155	181	187	177	205	170
Kenya	365	299	384	375	367	350	388	423	510	301	312	402
Lesotho	508	591	625	575	488	457	677	841	850	472	687	648
Liberia	435	..	..	..	178	180	131	143	157	446	..	158
Madagascar	452	242	219	221	230	237	283	218	248	301	231	240
Malawi	179	172	159	146	140	176	158	165	176	150	180	160
Mali	254	255	206	183	188	240	297	339	354	206	230	267
Mauritania	456	478	471	444	399	417	466	535	688	433	551	492
Mauritius	1,020	1,725	2,778	2,865	2,800	2,813	3,226	3,766	4,103	1,078	2,412	3,262
Mozambique	319	194	196	186	186	195	222	261	304	277	173	226
Namibia	1,354	1,376	1,598	1,549	1,383	1,310	1,662	2,083	2,145	1,474	1,666	1,689
Niger	345	289	171	147	152	163	199	205	221	259	202	181
Nigeria	643	222	245	225	260	283	314	340	446	385	221	311
Rwanda	214	342	258	223	198	201	194	202	233	272	283	208
São Tomé and Principe	..	..	..	..	..	..	..	..	..	..	..	..
Senegal	575	700	455	403	417	458	559	642	665	521	550	524
Seychelles	1,667	4,196	5,762	5,864	6,166	6,672	6,718	6,442	9,806	2,170	5,142	6,944
Sierra Leone	337	145	167	159	192	209	208	205	221	250	181	199
Somalia	105	155	..	..	..	..	..	..	..	136	155	..
South Africa	1,818	2,444	2,514	2,450	2,137	1,964	2,951	3,885	4,306	2,094	2,782	2,949
Sudan	373	..	306	316	359	380	430	497	663	488	314	441
Swaziland	949	1,070	1,347	1,288	1,144	881	1,381	1,770	2,003	812	1,299	1,411
Tanzania	..	160	242	234	243	238	245	268	293	..	188	253
Togo	314	351	294	253	238	258	285	329	326	270	303	282
Uganda	99	241	235	224	212	214	218	224	281	231	220	229
Zambia	518	328	302	277	276	274	311	386	517	397	330	340
Zimbabwe	788	686	401	509	714	1,591	539	349	261	700	531	661
NORTH AFRICA	846	1,133	1,312	1,301	1,276	1,166	1,209	1,262	1,335	971	1,159	1,258
Algeria	1,281	1,789	1,107	992	1,036	1,075	1,177	1,374	1,413	1,697	1,217	1,178
Egypt, Arab Rep.	443	650	1,190	1,292	1,233	1,082	997	916	1,021	540	843	1,090
Libya	5,040	4,857	4,814	4,360	4,241	2,559	..	..	..	5,044	5,142	3,720
Morocco	832	865	1,040	992	971	1,021	1,217	1,370	1,403	659	1,001	1,162
Tunisia	1,041	1,205	1,670	1,551	1,584	1,691	2,001	2,231	2,267	961	1,467	1,888
ALL AFRICA	573	592	583	562	550	543	617	703	784	557	585	626

a. Provisional.

Table 2.16 Agriculture value added

	Constant prices (2000 $ millions)									Average annual growth (%)		
	1980	1990	1999	2000	2001	2002	2003	2004	2005a	1980–89	1990–99	2000–05
SUB-SAHARAN AFRICA	35,543	42,936	56,625	57,696	60,060	61,389	63,115	65,992	69,775	2.2	3.2	3.7
Excluding South Africa	32,459	39,215	52,846	53,736	56,236	57,310	59,150	62,144	65,723	2.1	3.5	3.9
Excl. S. Africa & Nigeria	25,114	30,774	41,452	42,006	44,064	44,612	45,552	47,614	49,916	2.0	3.5	3.2
Angola	..	686	473	517	610	684	767	875	1,024	..	-2.9	14.1
Benin	316	467	774	824	849	911	932	985	1,028	5.2	5.8	4.6
Botswana	132	155	139	139	144	143	147	141	130	1.8	-0.9	-1.1
Burkina Faso	410	531	850	881	848	919	919	..	..	3.6	4.3	2.1
Burundi	218	300	269	255	247	257	248	247	231	3.1	-1.9	-1.5
Cameroon	1,023	1,298	1,973	2,062	2,139	2,218	2,295	2,395	2,460	2.5	5.3	3.7
Cape Verde	..	50	59	64	64	60	63	..	..	..	4.2	-0.8
Central African Republic	298	332	450	478	498	517	536	533	547	1.7	3.6	2.6
Chad	306	321	578	563	620	617	648	612	694	3.1	5.5	3.1
Comoros	51	75	90	98	104	109	113	113	118	4.0	2.2	3.5
Congo, Dem. Rep.	1,565	2,011	2,407	2,126	2,043	2,053	2,078	2,090	2,150	2.5	2.2	0.4
Congo, Rep.	..	..	..	..	..	..	..	..	..	..	..	..
Côte d'Ivoire	1,628	1,756	2,216	2,400	2,407	2,351	2,379	2,474	2,438	-0.4	3.2	0.5
Djibouti	..	18	17	17	18	18	19	19	20	..	-1.1	3.6
Equatorial Guinea	..	..	..	121	112	106	102	103	105	..	..	-2.9
Eritrea	..	..	157	89	115	80	89	95	103	..	5.4	0.8
Ethiopia	..	2,891	3,385	3,494	3,858	3,776	3,345	3,925	4,449	0.1	2.3	3.3
Gabon	236	252	299	315	324	309	313	317	328	1.5	1.9	0.4
Gambia, The	87	89	120	133	145	104	124	138	145	1.2	2.2	1.4
Ghana	1,226	1,268	1,716	1,756	1,820	1,895	1,993	2,133	2,221	0.9	3.3	5.0
Guinea	..	395	594	593	636	668	687	709	731	..	4.4	4.1
Guinea-Bissau	45	79	108	112	114	113	121	128	136	5.0	4.3	4.0
Kenya	2,192	3,138	3,696	3,649	4,075	3,934	4,031	4,100	4,377	3.2	1.8	2.8
Lesotho	92	122	126	138	126	118	118	116	116	2.1	1.8	-3.2
Liberia	..	..	..	..	..	..	..	..	..	..	..	..
Madagascar	696	860	1,015	1,026	1,068	1,054	1,067	1,100	1,133	2.4	1.8	1.7
Malawi	263	302	590	622	585	600	636	653	594	2.1	8.5	0.5
Mali	656	792	1,046	938	1,043	1,005	1,183	1,128	1,214	2.6	3.1	4.9
Mauritania	239	283	303	277	266	241	252	233	251	2.0	0.6	-2.4
Mauritius	224	274	300	230	304	318	269	278	288	3.1	0.7	2.0
Mozambique	..	698	1,000	887	971	1,076	1,173	1,271	1,292	7.3	5.5	8.3
Namibia	179	223	312	338	304	334	347	336	354	1.3	3.5	1.6
Niger	479	537	743	680	770	785	832	..	..	1.8	3.6	6.4
Nigeria	7,011	8,447	11,399	11,730	12,176	12,692	13,513	14,392	15,572	2.9	3.3	5.8
Rwanda	535	558	687	750	812	930	901	901	951	0.8	1.5	4.3
São Tomé and Principe	..	..	..	..	..	..	..	..	..	..	..	..
Senegal	506	602	773	791	801	623	751	771	843	2.5	2.1	1.1
Seychelles	18	17	17	17	17	17	15	15	15	-1.7	-0.5	-2.9
Sierra Leone	..	..	..	..	..	..	..	..	..	..	..	..
Somalia	..	..	..	..	..	..	..	..	..	..	..	..
South Africa	3,073	3,692	3,777	3,956	3,827	4,077	3,991	3,923	4,133	2.9	0.7	0.8
Sudan	1,713	2,144	4,653	4,963	5,239	5,633	..	..	..	2.3	9.1	..
Swaziland	126	144	156	150	136	138	142	144	147	2.0	1.0	0.3
Tanzania	..	2,767	3,650	3,773	3,980	4,178	4,346	4,597	4,834	..	3.2	5.0
Togo	220	342	477	455	461	494	489	505	524	5.7	4.5	2.8
Uganda	..	1,401	1,908	2,014	2,111	2,193	2,243	2,361	2,481	1.5	3.6	4.1
Zambia	371	471	634	644	627	616	647	675	671	4.1	4.3	1.4
Zimbabwe	599	858	1,137	1,174	1,128	872	863	838	754	2.8	4.2	-8.5
NORTH AFRICA	17,435	23,679	29,283	28,631	31,174	31,791	35,372	36,251	35,444	4.0	2.4	4.8
Algeria	2,459	3,246	4,842	4,600	5,210	5,144	6,158	6,349	6,469	4.3	4.0	7.3
Egypt, Arab Rep.	8,751	11,474	15,003	15,513	16,088	16,667	17,478	17,723	18,301	2.7	3.1	3.4
Libya	..	..	..	..	..	..	..	..	..	..	..	..
Morocco	4,094	5,925	5,472	4,610	5,882	6,212	7,330	7,469	6,147	7.0	0.1	6.9
Tunisia	1,213	1,787	2,424	2,399	2,351	2,093	2,542	2,800	2,660	2.0	2.1	3.6
ALL AFRICA	52,868	66,572	85,886	86,326	91,207	93,153	98,585	102,295	105,077	2.8	2.9	4.0

a. Provisional.

Table 2.17 Industry value added

Table 2.17

	Constant prices (2000 $ millions)									Average annual growth (%)		
	1980	1990	1999	2000	2001	2002	2003	2004	2005[a]	1980–89	1990–99	2000–05
SUB–SAHARAN AFRICA	83,896	92,618	102,894	106,656	110,668	112,443	119,788	127,192	134,514	0.9	1.5	4.8
Excluding South Africa	51,217	57,141	66,533	68,388	71,695	72,407	79,658	85,331	91,048	1.1	1.9	6.0
Excl. S. Africa & Nigeria	..	36,718	44,239	44,663	47,380	50,180	52,056	56,555	60,919	4.0	2.5	6.2
Angola	..	4,861	6,359	6,584	6,853	7,850	8,146	9,014	11,126	..	3.9	10.5
Benin	115	203	287	313	341	362	372	370	387	3.3	4.1	3.8
Botswana	619	1,905	3,037	3,406	3,584	3,706	3,880	4,187	4,394	11.8	5.0	5.2
Burkina Faso	252	333	398	422	457	460	460	..	..	4.2	2.2	2.7
Burundi	98	159	127	119	111	104	98	92	86	4.6	–4.7	–6.2
Cameroon	1,977	3,710	3,196	3,355	3,389	3,416	3,434	3,427	3,365	7.5	–2.0	0.2
Cape Verde	..	59	97	95	95	108	114	..	..	..	5.1	7.1
Central African Republic	146	157	159	173	180	187	200	205	210	1.6	0.2	4.2
Chad	61	166	153	151	172	214	341	833	875	7.9	0.5	49.1
Comoros	19	15	23	23	24	25	28	27	25	–2.3	4.6	2.5
Congo, Dem. Rep.	2,497	2,288	1,061	863	840	909	1,025	1,162	1,265	2.3	–8.9	9.0
Congo, Rep.	..	..	..	..	..	..	..	..	..	..	..	..
Côte d'Ivoire	1,227	1,575	2,573	2,288	2,214	2,117	1,960	2,034	2,023	5.1	6.6	–2.7
Djibouti	..	127	71	74	78	81	83	90	95	..	–6.2	5.1
Equatorial Guinea	..	..	..	1,055	1,829	2,205	2,472	3,320	3,543	..	..	25.5
Eritrea	..	..	145	135	144	155	158	158	..	..	18.3	4.1
Ethiopia	..	837	894	942	990	1,072	1,105	1,215	1,313	4.5	3.5	6.8
Gabon	2,276	2,951	3,146	2,851	2,875	2,913	3,035	3,075	3,129	0.4	2.8	2.0
Gambia, The	28	42	46	48	51	56	60	62	64	4.3	0.7	5.9
Ghana	866	962	1,208	1,264	1,325	1,409	1,418	1,483	1,612	2.6	2.3	4.6
Guinea	..	623	918	951	1,002	1,049	1,053	1,086	1,127	..	4.8	3.2
Guinea-Bissau	24	34	25	26	28	31	30	30	32	1.3	–2.5	3.6
Kenya	1,189	1,752	1,943	1,908	2,013	2,060	2,187	2,276	2,380	3.7	1.5	4.5
Lesotho	117	186	303	320	335	353	360	381	413	4.1	5.4	4.9
Liberia	..	..	..	..	..	..	..	..	..	..	..	..
Madagascar	450	389	467	500	537	426	488	520	533	0.7	2.0	1.0
Malawi	175	236	285	282	252	248	261	288	333	2.4	2.0	3.8
Mali	166	248	443	464	561	661	599	597	646	4.7	6.4	5.1
Mauritania	155	218	295	298	284	288	300	337	330	5.4	3.3	3.1
Mauritius	319	704	1,158	1,208	1,294	1,328	1,335	1,356	1,335	9.0	5.5	1.9
Mozambique	..	307	817	906	1,095	1,203	1,324	1,392	1,499	–4.5	11.9	10.0
Namibia	689	670	861	873	905	975	1,021	1,170	1,173	–0.3	2.5	6.8
Niger	306	275	313	319	327	337	350	..	..	–2.0	1.8	3.1
Nigeria	22,498	20,202	22,169	23,522	24,141	22,207	27,172	28,433	29,849	–2.1	0.9	5.5
Rwanda	459	566	358	371	399	431	450	460	493	2.8	–5.5	5.6
São Tomé and Principe	..	..	..	..	..	..	..	..	..	..	..	..
Senegal	489	661	921	960	1,008	1,066	1,128	1,198	1,243	3.3	3.7	5.5
Seychelles	44	65	158	178	177	187	165	171	167	3.8	11.9	–1.5
Sierra Leone	..	..	..	..	..	..	..	..	..	..	..	..
Somalia	..	..	..	..	..	..	..	..	..	..	..	..
South Africa	32,864	35,440	36,511	38,387	39,132	40,177	40,507	42,338	44,053	0.5	0.9	2.7
Sudan	..	1,431	2,558	2,523	2,904	3,122	..	..	..	1.7	6.0	..
Swaziland	107	313	427	432	444	451	460	468	476	11.8	3.9	1.9
Tanzania	..	967	1,232	1,319	1,410	1,542	1,702	1,871	2,070	..	2.5	9.6
Togo	216	212	228	237	230	255	291	312	332	0.7	1.7	8.1
Uganda	..	381	1,040	1,095	1,168	1,260	1,351	1,426	1,571	4.4	12.6	7.3
Zambia	886	1,018	709	729	796	873	949	1,050	1,153	0.7	–4.4	9.6
Zimbabwe	1,235	1,714	1,770	1,586	1,456	1,296	1,108	1,069	944	2.9	1.1	–10.0
NORTH AFRICA	47,958	64,915	88,156	92,250	94,263	97,787	103,171	107,222	112,842	2.9	3.2	4.2
Algeria	19,854	25,580	29,102	30,360	30,260	31,578	33,802	35,165	37,114	2.9	1.4	4.4
Egypt, Arab Rep.	11,983	17,227	29,112	30,702	31,679	32,838	34,757	35,923	37,781	3.2	5.1	4.3
Libya	..	..	..	..	..	..	..	..	..	..	..	..
Morocco	5,868	8,041	10,347	10,644	11,172	11,472	11,765	12,346	13,087	2.7	3.1	4.0
Tunisia	2,462	3,521	5,275	5,558	5,839	6,013	6,086	6,370	6,529	2.9	4.5	3.1
ALL AFRICA	133,666	159,309	191,911	199,738	205,904	211,068	223,911	235,554	248,591	1.7	2.2	4.5

a. Provisional.

NATIONAL ACCOUNTS

Table 2.18 Services value added

Table 2.18 Services value added

	Constant prices (2000 $ millions)									Average annual growth (%)		
	1980	1990	1999	2000	2001	2002	2003	2004	2005[a]	1980–89	1990–99	2000–05
SUB-SAHARAN AFRICA	94,383	121,788	148,351	153,749	159,395	165,905	172,692	180,674	189,788	2.6	2.4	4.3
Excluding South Africa	46,124	60,542	72,954	75,284	78,082	81,180	84,311	88,103	92,102	2.7	2.2	4.1
Excl. S. Africa & Nigeria	41,542	53,976	64,338	65,954	68,442	70,918	73,293	76,285	79,394	2.7	2.1	3.7
Angola	..	2,556	2,035	2,028	1,935	2,233	2,194	2,442	2,792	..	−2.8	6.7
Benin	679	752	1,073	1,118	1,178	1,195	1,266	1,292	1,304	1.1	4.0	3.2
Botswana	295	1,086	2,121	2,233	2,379	2,557	2,718	2,822	2,924	14.8	8.0	5.6
Burkina Faso	598	877	1,311	1,298	1,439	1,490	1,671	..	..	3.9	4.6	8.2
Burundi	163	298	242	258	304	338	346	396	438	5.5	−3.4	10.4
Cameroon	3,345	4,022	3,767	3,899	4,186	4,494	4,827	5,130	5,340	3.5	0.0	6.7
Cape Verde	..	196	342	373	393	407	433	..	..	..	6.4	5.0
Central African Republic	236	254	233	215	204	173	112	121	121	1.3	−0.3	−12.9
Chad	313	537	612	617	690	758	815	878	963	7.4	0.6	9.0
Comoros	66	91	86	81	80	83	82	82	88	3.3	−0.5	1.4
Congo, Dem. Rep.	3,932	4,607	1,328	1,265	1,250	1,294	1,376	1,497	1,631	2.3	−13.0	5.5
Congo, Rep.	..	..	..	..	..	..	..	..	..	..	..	..
Côte d'Ivoire	4,857	4,958	6,043	5,738	5,811	5,796	5,741	5,729	5,749	−0.1	2.5	−0.1
Djibouti	..	431	392	390	401	406	414	429	438	..	−1.5	2.3
Equatorial Guinea	..	..	..	52	67	82	93	100	118	..	..	16.7
Eritrea	..	..	364	365	382	383	417	416	..	..	6.9	3.5
Ethiopia	..	2,221	2,682	2,934	3,048	3,128	3,263	3,494	3,777	3.6	4.0	5.0
Gabon	1,190	1,325	1,824	1,902	1,961	1,945	1,968	1,995	2,077	0.3	3.2	1.4
Gambia, The	100	136	185	190	203	221	227	232	..	2.5	3.9	5.4
Ghana	672	1,115	1,865	1,952	2,031	2,120	2,256	2,362	2,521	5.3	5.9	5.3
Guinea	..	1,006	1,356	1,382	1,410	1,438	1,460	1,495	1,518	..	3.7	1.9
Guinea-Bissau	38	59	54	61	60	67	63	63	63	3.1	−0.7	0.7
Kenya	2,625	4,235	5,613	5,718	5,710	5,866	6,019	6,322	6,618	4.9	3.4	3.1
Lesotho	149	218	317	314	325	332	348	363	375	3.9	4.8	3.7
Liberia	..	..	..	..	..	..	..	..	..	..	..	..
Madagascar	1,638	1,635	1,896	1,987	2,108	1,773	1,959	2,078	2,198	−0.2	2.0	1.6
Malawi	445	592	685	669	671	691	701	738	785	3.2	1.9	3.2
Mali	531	636	819	854	905	911	994	1,084	1,144	2.1	2.8	6.2
Mauritania	262	263	387	427	474	508	538	563	602	0.2	4.5	6.8
Mauritius	780	1,319	2,289	2,433	2,587	2,719	2,874	3,049	3,249	4.8	6.4	5.9
Mozambique	..	1,079	1,520	1,611	1,831	1,936	2,024	2,203	2,398	7.2	3.4	7.7
Namibia	775	1,185	1,797	1,869	1,942	2,064	2,135	2,223	2,366	3.7	4.6	4.7
Niger	738	695	768	798	828	862	889	..	..	−1.3	1.6	3.7
Nigeria	4,512	6,618	8,662	9,367	9,680	10,298	11,024	11,785	12,626	2.7	3.1	6.3
Rwanda	500	712	666	690	721	748	784	860	911	3.9	−2.5	5.8
São Tomé and Principe	..	..	..	..	..	..	..	..	..	..	..	..
Senegal	1,395	1,774	2,294	2,382	2,453	2,577	2,697	2,868	3,042	2.3	2.7	5.1
Seychelles	228	310	412	419	408	405	392	370	381	3.3	2.6	−2.3
Sierra Leone	..	..	..	..	..	..	..	..	..	..	..	..
Somalia	..	..	..	..	..	..	..	..	..	..	..	..
South Africa	48,244	61,244	75,379	78,441	81,288	84,698	88,338	92,515	97,573	2.4	2.6	4.4
Sudan	..	3,072	4,024	4,377	4,530	4,713	..	..	..	4.3	2.2	
Swaziland	165	264	367	383	396	414	432	439	444	4.7	3.5	3.1
Tanzania	..	2,444	3,100	3,286	3,467	3,682	3,887	4,131	4,416	..	2.4	6.1
Togo	539	516	633	637	635	627	631	634	608	−0.5	3.7	−0.7
Uganda	..	1,065	2,147	2,285	2,474	2,672	2,841	3,022	3,293	2.1	8.3	7.4
Zambia	1,250	1,159	1,449	1,512	1,585	1,647	1,726	1,763	1,850	0.0	2.0	4.0
Zimbabwe	1,993	2,893	3,856	3,588	3,563	3,692	3,294	2,836	2,019	2.8	3.4	−10.0
NORTH AFRICA	45,353	77,021	101,057	106,243	110,280	114,034	116,668	123,500	130,498	5.6	3.3	4.1
Algeria	10,412	14,452	16,640	16,843	17,492	18,455	19,118	20,464	21,640	3.3	1.8	5.2
Egypt, Arab Rep.	15,596	32,762	43,441	46,451	48,080	49,413	49,673	52,619	55,561	8.2	3.7	3.4
Libya	..	..	..	..	..	..	..	..	..	..	..	..
Morocco	8,702	13,209	17,386	18,080	18,588	19,122	19,887	20,790	21,789	4.2	2.7	3.8
Tunisia	4,930	6,896	10,860	11,486	12,229	12,680	13,293	14,070	15,070	3.7	5.3	5.4
ALL AFRICA	140,632	199,330	249,513	259,990	269,664	279,982	289,519	304,275	320,358	3.6	2.7	4.2

a. Provisional.

Table 2.19

Gross fixed capital formation

	Share of GDP (%)									Annual average		
	1980	1990	1999	2000	2001	2002	2003	2004	2005[a]	1980–89	1990–99	2000–05
SUB–SAHARAN AFRICA	22.2	17.1	18.3	18.0	18.7	18.4	19.5	19.5	19.4	18.9	17.7	18.9
Excluding South Africa	19.0	16.8	19.7	19.3	20.6	19.6	21.1	20.9	20.2	16.6	18.5	20.3
Excl. S. Africa & Nigeria	17.6	17.2	18.9	19.0	19.6	17.9	20.4	20.5	19.8	16.4	18.2	19.5
Angola	..	11.7	27.1	15.1	13.4	12.6	12.7	9.1	7.5	14.8	19.9	11.7
Benin	15.2	14.2	17.5	18.9	19.2	17.7	18.8	18.2	19.6	15.1	16.3	18.7
Botswana	40.1	37.4	32.6	35.5	40.4	39.9	40.5	38.9	30.7	30.0	29.9	37.6
Burkina Faso	15.1	18.2	23.8	22.7	18.9	17.8	18.7	..	..	17.4	21.7	19.5
Burundi	13.9	14.5	5.9	6.1	6.2	6.4	10.6	13.3	10.8	16.6	9.1	8.9
Cameroon	21.0	17.8	14.9	16.7	20.3	19.8	17.5	18.9	18.1	23.8	14.8	18.6
Cape Verde	..	22.9	20.9	19.7	18.3	20.9	18.7	..	..	26.9	29.6	19.4
Central African Republic	7.0	12.3	14.4	10.8	14.0	14.8	..	..	..	10.9	11.4	13.2
Chad	..	6.8	13.7	23.3	40.3	60.2	52.4	24.3	20.2	6.3	13.1	36.8
Comoros	33.2	19.7	14.9	10.1	10.1	11.0	10.3	9.4	9.3	28.8	18.1	10.0
Congo, Dem. Rep.	10.0	9.1	3.1	3.5	5.2	9.0	12.2	12.8	14.2	11.7	7.6	9.5
Congo, Rep.	35.8	15.9	27.8	22.6	26.4	23.4	25.7	24.2	22.4	32.5	25.9	24.1
Côte d'Ivoire	26.5	6.7	13.1	10.8	11.2	10.1	10.1	10.8	10.3	16.5	11.3	10.5
Djibouti	..	14.1	8.6	8.8	7.9	10.0	14.3	22.0	24.3	..	11.1	14.5
Equatorial Guinea	..	17.4	..	58.8	71.5	31.3	58.3	44.5	37.7	..	59.5	50.4
Eritrea	..	..	36.0	31.9	28.7	26.0	25.4	22.8	20.1	..	25.0	25.8
Ethiopia	..	12.9	14.4	19.2	19.5	22.4	21.6	21.4	20.5	15.7	14.4	20.8
Gabon	27.5	21.7	26.2	21.9	25.7	24.5	24.0	24.5	22.7	34.6	26.0	23.9
Gambia, The	26.7	22.3	17.8	17.4	17.4	21.2	20.3	28.1	25.0	19.7	20.1	21.6
Ghana	5.6	14.4	20.9	23.9	26.7	19.7	23.2	28.4	29.0	7.8	19.9	25.2
Guinea	..	24.5	19.8	19.7	15.4	13.5	10.2	11.3	13.8	16.4	21.3	14.0
Guinea-Bissau	28.2	29.9	16.8	11.3	15.0	9.6	12.6	13.2	14.6	32.0	25.9	12.7
Kenya	24.5	24.2	15.5	17.4	19.3	16.7	17.9	18.2	16.4	22.7	18.3	17.6
Lesotho	37.0	52.7	49.0	42.6	40.8	41.6	41.2	35.9	35.1	39.9	56.5	39.5
Liberia	..	..	..	..	4.9	4.7	9.4	13.2	16.5	..	..	9.7
Madagascar	15.0	17.0	14.9	15.0	18.5	14.3	17.9	24.3	22.5	10.6	12.4	18.8
Malawi	24.7	23.0	14.7	13.6	14.9	11.4	11.8	15.3	15.3	19.4	17.7	13.7
Mali	15.5	23.0	21.2	24.6	31.0	18.6	24.2	21.0	22.7	17.2	22.5	23.7
Mauritania	26.3	20.0	12.5	19.4	22.0	21.1	25.9	46.4	44.8	27.5	13.6	29.9
Mauritius	25.4	30.7	25.5	25.9	23.3	21.4	22.7	24.1	23.3	23.5	28.4	23.4
Mozambique	7.6	22.1	36.7	33.5	25.9	29.8	27.4	22.6	21.7	12.2	25.2	26.8
Namibia	30.6	33.7	23.3	19.5	23.4	19.7	29.8	25.5	27.3	18.4	22.6	24.2
Niger	28.1	8.1	10.2	11.4	12.1	14.2	14.2	16.4	18.5	15.3	8.9	14.5
Nigeria	21.3	14.7	23.4	20.3	24.1	26.2	23.9	22.3	21.3	16.5	19.8	23.0
Rwanda	16.1	14.6	17.2	17.5	18.4	16.9	18.4	20.5	22.4	15.3	14.5	19.0
São Tomé and Principe	..	..	..	..	..	..	..	..	..	..	..	..
Senegal	16.6	9.1	17.9	20.5	18.4	17.2	21.0	21.1	25.6	16.5	12.5	20.6
Seychelles	38.3	24.6	43.3	25.2	40.3	25.6	10.0	14.7	12.3	26.4	30.3	21.4
Sierra Leone	16.2	10.0	5.4	8.0	6.7	10.1	13.9	10.7	17.4	12.2	7.4	11.1
Somalia	42.4	15.5	..	..	..	..	..	..	..	28.8	15.5	..
South Africa	29.9	17.7	16.4	15.9	15.3	16.1	16.9	17.5	18.0	23.4	16.7	16.6
Sudan	14.7	..	16.8	18.3	17.6	19.5	20.0	22.5	23.6	14.4	15.7	20.2
Swaziland	40.7	19.1	18.7	18.6	18.4	19.8	18.0	18.4	18.0	27.2	21.1	18.5
Tanzania	..	26.1	15.5	17.6	17.0	19.2	18.7	18.3	18.2	..	21.3	18.2
Togo	28.4	26.6	13.3	17.8	20.4	18.5	18.9	18.0	18.4	19.5	16.3	18.7
Uganda	6.2	12.7	19.5	20.0	18.6	19.3	20.5	22.3	21.2	8.5	16.1	20.3
Zambia	23.3	17.3	17.6	18.7	20.0	23.0	26.1	26.0	25.8	16.1	14.1	23.3
Zimbabwe	16.9	17.4	14.4	13.6	10.3	8.0	11.4	14.2	16.8	17.3	19.5	12.4
NORTH AFRICA	26.6	26.4	22.4	21.1	21.1	22.7	22.5	23.7	22.6	27.4	22.5	22.3
Algeria	39.1	28.6	28.5	25.0	27.3	31.2	30.5	33.3	30.1	33.9	28.5	29.6
Egypt, Arab Rep.	27.5	28.8	21.6	19.6	18.3	18.3	16.9	16.9	18.0	28.6	20.9	18.0
Libya	22.1	18.6	11.2	13.1	12.2	15.0	..	..	..	26.5	14.0	13.5
Morocco	24.2	25.3	23.1	23.6	22.9	22.7	24.1	25.0	25.9	24.1	22.1	24.0
Tunisia	29.4	27.1	26.3	27.3	27.9	25.7	25.1	24.2	23.4	28.8	26.6	25.6
ALL AFRICA	23.5	20.6	20.0	19.2	19.7	20.1	20.6	21.0	20.5	21.9	19.5	20.2

a. Provisional.

Table 2.20

2.20 General government fixed capital formation

					Share of GDP (%)						Annual average	
	1980	1990	1999	2000	2001	2002	2003	2004	2005ᵃ	1980–89	1990–99	2000–05
SUB-SAHARAN AFRICA	..	..	4.6	4.5	5.7	5.1	5.0	5.1	5.2	..	4.3	5.1
Excluding South Africa	..	..	6.7	6.5	7.8	6.5	7.0	7.2	7.2	..	6.3	7.0
Excl. S. Africa & Nigeria	..	5.6	5.9	5.6	6.1	5.7	6.2	6.6	6.5	5.7	5.8	6.1
Angola	..	..	12.8	6.1	6.4	6.8	7.6	4.9	4.7	..	7.8	6.1
Benin	..	7.4	6.3	7.6	7.8	6.6	6.1	5.4	6.7	9.1	7.5	6.7
Botswana	0.0	12.7	11.8	10.7	9.3	10.4	11.1	10.4	9.2	0.0	12.4	10.2
Burkina Faso	..	3.9	14.9	12.1	8.2	7.2	7.5	..	..	6.7	9.5	8.7
Burundi	12.8	12.5	5.4	5.4	3.7	4.6	8.3	10.7	8.8	13.8	9.3	6.9
Cameroon	4.4	5.5	2.4	2.1	2.2	2.3	2.3	2.6	3.1	6.9	2.9	2.4
Cape Verde	..	10.3	6.5	12.5	10.8	13.0	9.8	..	..	19.3	20.3	11.5
Central African Republic	3.7	4.7	6.8	7.1	7.4	7.6	..	..	..	5.5	6.2	7.4
Chad	..	..	9.6	10.5	8.8	10.1	12.5	7.8	7.0	3.8	7.4	9.5
Comoros	23.2	5.2	5.4	3.9	4.4	5.8	5.4	4.4	4.5	18.7	7.0	4.7
Congo, Dem. Rep.	5.1	4.0	1.1	0.5	0.1	1.0	2.7	2.8	3.7	4.4	1.7	1.8
Congo, Rep.	..	5.6	6.1	7.0	10.0	8.7	6.5	7.0	5.4	11.1	6.4	7.4
Côte d'Ivoire	11.4	3.6	4.2	2.8	1.9	3.2	2.7	2.8	1.9	7.1	5.6	2.5
Djibouti	..	9.1	3.1	2.7	2.5	4.5	6.7	7.7	9.3	..	6.1	5.6
Equatorial Guinea	..	10.5	..	5.1	7.4	8.4	9.8	14.0	10.1	..	6.9	9.1
Eritrea	..	..	30.3	26.8	23.5	21.7	17.7	17.2	15.4	..	16.4	20.4
Ethiopia	..	4.0	6.9	7.3	8.6	10.7	9.4	9.0	9.1	4.9	4.8	9.0
Gabon	5.3	3.9	4.1	2.9	4.7	4.0	3.7	4.2	4.2	6.7	6.5	4.0
Gambia, The	..	7.4	4.7	4.6	11.2	7.9	5.7	10.9	9.0	10.4	7.8	8.2
Ghana	..	7.5	8.7	9.2	12.8	6.1	9.2	12.4	12.0	6.3	11.0	10.3
Guinea	..	9.7	4.9	4.9	4.9	4.0	4.4	3.9	3.3	7.5	6.1	4.2
Guinea-Bissau	..	27.4	10.8	10.3	14.8	9.0	13.1	19.9	10.4	33.3	20.2	12.9
Kenya	0.0	9.7	4.5	4.6	6.5	6.3	5.8	5.8	6.5	0.8	7.0	5.9
Lesotho	9.9	23.0	8.8	8.0	10.5	11.2	8.7	7.6	7.8	15.4	16.2	9.0
Liberia	..	..	..	..	0.0	0.0	0.0	0.0	0.0	..	..	0.0
Madagascar	..	7.9	6.9	6.7	7.3	4.8	7.8	12.5	10.3	6.9	6.9	8.2
Malawi	17.5	7.7	10.3	10.0	10.3	7.7	9.3	12.6	11.0	9.5	9.2	10.2
Mali	..	10.5	9.4	8.6	7.0	7.0	6.9	7.5	7.7	10.2	10.1	7.5
Mauritania	..	6.2	..	..	..	..	..	..	..	7.6	5.0	..
Mauritius	9.1	4.6	3.4	7.8	6.8	7.0	7.9	7.7	6.6	6.0	3.7	7.3
Mozambique	7.6	12.0	11.6	10.4	15.4	12.5	11.7	9.4	8.1	9.5	11.7	11.3
Namibia	15.7	8.2	11.0	6.1	8.7	6.2	7.0	7.2	7.5	10.7	8.2	7.1
Niger	20.4	7.4	6.4	6.6	7.1	8.8	8.3	9.3	9.8	11.2	5.6	8.3
Nigeria	..	..	10.4	9.6	13.8	10.0	9.7	9.1	9.3	..	8.7	10.2
Rwanda	12.2	5.9	6.3	6.0	6.6	4.9	5.6	8.5	10.1	12.1	7.2	7.0
São Tomé and Principe	..	..	..	..	..	..	..	..	..	..	..	..
Senegal	4.7	4.1	6.0	4.5	5.1	5.7	6.2	6.7	10.0	3.7	4.5	6.4
Seychelles	..	8.2	1.4	13.8	25.2	9.4	2.2	3.8	5.3	12.0	9.9	9.9
Sierra Leone	5.3	3.9	2.4	6.3	4.4	4.4	4.8	4.6	5.8	4.0	3.3	5.1
Somalia	..	..	..	..	..	..	..	..	..	..	..	..
South Africa	0.0	0.0	1.5	1.4	1.9	1.9	2.0	2.0	2.0	0.0	0.3	1.9
Sudan	6.9	..	1.2	2.3	2.3	3.0	2.9	5.0	5.4	4.3	0.7	3.5
Swaziland	11.9	5.7	6.7	6.3	8.0	7.4	5.7	8.2	8.5	8.0	6.6	7.3
Tanzania	..	10.5	3.1	6.0	5.6	7.6	7.4	7.3	7.2	..	5.8	6.9
Togo	20.2	7.3	3.1	3.0	2.3	1.4	3.7	5.3	4.2	11.2	3.7	3.3
Uganda	..	6.2	5.4	6.4	5.8	5.3	4.7	5.2	4.6	4.4	5.6	5.3
Zambia	..	6.2	10.6	10.0	11.9	11.8	11.5	9.2	8.9	..	6.8	10.5
Zimbabwe	1.8	3.4	1.7	0.7	2.1	2.1	2.1	5.1	1.5	2.9	2.9	2.3
NORTH AFRICA	..	9.2	8.6	8.6	8.4	9.3	8.8	8.7	8.4	11.8	8.6	8.7
Algeria	11.0	8.2	5.8	7.8	8.4	10.0	10.8	10.5	9.8	13.8	7.2	9.6
Egypt, Arab Rep.	..	14.7	10.9	9.9	8.7	9.4	8.5	8.7	8.8	16.9	12.0	9.0
Libya	19.4	..	..	..	..	..	..	..	..	19.4	..	..
Morocco	..	4.8	4.3	4.7	5.1	4.2	3.9	3.9	3.7	7.1	4.3	4.2
Tunisia	15.0	8.7	12.5	12.3	..	..	..	..	..	14.1	11.5	12.3
ALL AFRICA	..	6.4	6.1	6.1	6.8	6.6	6.4	6.3	6.3	7.7	5.8	6.4

a. Provisional.

Table 2.21

Private sector fixed capital formation

	1980	1990	1999	2000	2001	2002	2003	2004	2005[a]	Annual average		
										1980–89	1990–99	2000–05
SUB–SAHARAN AFRICA	12.3	12.6	13.1	12.5	12.3	12.7	13.4	13.2	13.3	13.3	13.2	12.9
Excluding South Africa	..	8.6	12.5	11.8	11.9	12.6	13.1	12.5	12.2	8.3	11.2	12.3
Excl. S. Africa & Nigeria	..	9.5	12.4	12.1	12.4	11.7	12.8	12.2	12.3	8.7	11.3	12.2
Angola	..	1.7	16.0	8.9	7.1	5.8	5.1	4.2	2.8	9.2	16.5	5.6
Benin	..	6.0	11.2	11.3	11.4	11.6	12.0	12.1	12.2	4.5	8.3	11.8
Botswana	34.5	19.7	13.2	11.0	11.5	11.6	10.3	9.8	9.7	29.0	14.8	10.6
Burkina Faso	..	13.6	8.9	10.6	10.8	10.6	11.2	..	..	11.5	12.2	10.8
Burundi	1.1	2.7	0.4	0.8	2.5	1.5	2.3	2.3	1.7	2.3	–0.3	1.9
Cameroon	15.6	11.9	12.3	13.9	18.1	17.5	15.8	15.7	14.7	14.2	11.7	15.9
Cape Verde	..	12.6	14.4	7.2	7.5	7.9	8.9	..	..	7.6	9.3	7.9
Central African Republic	3.2	6.7	7.7	3.7	6.6	7.2	..	..	..	4.7	5.0	5.9
Chad	..	..	7.4	10.5	27.8	49.6	36.3	14.9	12.0	0.6	4.3	25.2
Comoros	5.3	6.7	6.5	6.2	5.6	5.2	4.9	5.0	4.8	5.5	7.7	5.3
Congo, Dem. Rep.	3.7	8.9	2.0	3.0	5.1	8.0	9.5	10.0	10.5	7.1	6.3	7.7
Congo, Rep.	..	11.6	20.4	14.0	16.2	13.8	18.6	16.6	16.6	11.4	18.5	16.0
Côte d'Ivoire	13.0	4.9	10.2	7.5	10.6	6.0	7.8	7.1	8.4	8.7	6.2	7.9
Djibouti	..	5.1	5.6	6.1	5.4	5.6	7.6	14.3	15.0	..	5.8	9.0
Equatorial Guinea	..	6.9	..	53.7	64.1	22.9	48.5	30.5	27.6	..	52.6	41.2
Eritrea	..	..	5.6	5.1	5.2	4.3	7.7	5.6	4.7	..	8.6	5.4
Ethiopia	..	8.9	7.5	11.8	10.9	11.7	12.2	12.4	11.4	12.8	9.6	11.7
Gabon	21.4	17.6	22.0	19.0	21.0	20.5	20.2	20.3	18.5	27.2	18.9	19.9
Gambia, The	..	14.9	13.1	12.8	6.2	13.3	13.5	13.9	18.5	8.6	12.3	13.0
Ghana	..	6.9	12.0	14.8	13.8	13.6	14.0	16.0	17.0	3.8	8.7	14.9
Guinea	..	8.8	14.0	14.0	9.6	9.2	5.7	7.3	10.4	8.9	11.7	9.4
Guinea-Bissau	..	8.4	6.0	1.0	0.2	0.6	–0.5	–6.7	4.2	10.0	7.7	–0.2
Kenya	8.2	10.9	11.1	12.2	11.6	11.2	10.3	10.5	11.6	10.7	10.6	11.2
Lesotho	25.7	29.7	39.2	36.9	32.9	32.3	31.8	28.2	27.1	24.0	40.8	31.5
Liberia	..	..	..	..	2.0	2.2	4.8	4.2	4.3	..	..	3.5
Madagascar	..	6.9	8.0	8.3	11.2	9.5	10.1	11.8	12.3	3.6	5.5	10.5
Malawi	4.7	12.4	2.4	2.3	3.5	2.7	1.5	1.9	3.4	6.3	6.0	2.6
Mali	..	12.4	11.8	15.9	24.0	11.6	17.3	13.5	15.0	9.9	12.4	16.2
Mauritania	..	13.7	..	..	..	..	..	..	..	19.0	13.9	..
Mauritius	15.1	23.7	21.6	17.5	16.3	15.3	14.3	14.5	14.8	15.1	23.4	15.4
Mozambique	0.0	10.1	25.1	23.2	10.5	17.3	15.7	13.2	13.6	2.7	13.6	15.6
Namibia	11.4	13.0	12.0	12.7	13.2	14.9	22.1	17.9	18.8	7.8	12.8	16.6
Niger	5.1	4.0	3.6	4.6	4.8	5.2	5.7	7.1	8.8	3.0	3.4	6.0
Nigeria	..	3.8	13.0	10.7	10.3	16.2	14.2	13.2	12.0	5.9	10.9	12.8
Rwanda	..	8.7	10.9	11.6	11.8	12.0	12.8	12.0	12.2	7.8	7.2	12.1
São Tomé and Principe	..	..	..	..	..	..	..	..	..	..	..	..
Senegal	9.9	13.9	16.4	17.9	17.7	19.2	15.1	16.2	15.6	13.7	15.4	16.9
Seychelles	..	14.8	40.1	11.4	15.1	16.2	7.8	11.0	7.1	10.1	19.3	11.4
Sierra Leone	9.5	5.7	3.0	1.7	2.2	5.7	9.0	6.1	11.6	7.3	3.5	6.1
Somalia	..	..	..	..	..	..	..	..	..	..	..	..
South Africa	25.9	19.1	13.9	13.8	13.2	13.1	13.9	14.3	15.1	23.1	16.0	13.9
Sudan	3.8	..	9.2	9.7	8.8	10.1	11.2	12.2	13.5	8.9	7.5	10.9
Swaziland	23.1	12.7	12.1	12.3	10.4	12.3	12.3	10.2	9.5	17.3	13.8	11.2
Tanzania	..	15.3	12.3	11.4	11.2	11.4	11.1	10.9	10.8	..	15.2	11.1
Togo	8.0	18.0	10.3	14.8	19.0	17.4	17.2	15.9	18.1	7.8	11.8	17.1
Uganda	..	6.5	13.8	13.3	12.4	13.7	15.4	16.9	16.4	5.4	10.3	14.7
Zambia	..	7.2	5.4	7.2	6.8	9.8	13.3	15.4	15.8	4.9	5.8	11.4
Zimbabwe	12.3	14.8	11.6	11.1	10.1	8.1	11.7	12.0	19.5	13.1	17.2	12.1
NORTH AFRICA	..	16.0	14.1	12.0	12.2	13.1	12.8	13.2	13.9	13.4	13.6	12.9
Algeria	22.8	18.8	18.6	12.9	14.3	14.5	13.2	13.6	14.1	18.1	19.0	13.8
Egypt, Arab Rep.	..	12.3	9.9	9.1	9.0	8.4	7.9	7.7	9.1	9.3	8.3	8.5
Libya	1.8	..	..	..	..	..	..	..	..	1.8	..	..
Morocco	16.7	19.2	19.4	19.4	17.2	18.7	20.0	20.7	21.6	16.1	17.7	19.6
Tunisia	13.3	15.6	13.0	13.7	..	..	..	..	..	13.5	13.8	13.7
ALL AFRICA	..	13.9	13.5	12.4	12.3	12.9	13.4	13.5	13.8	13.4	13.5	13.0

a. Provisional.

Table 2.22

Resource balance (exports minus imports)

	1980	1990	1999	2000	2001	2002	2003	2004	2005[a]	Annual average 1980–89	1990–99	2000–05
SUB–SAHARAN AFRICA	**2.7**	**1.7**	**−2.4**	**3.1**	**0.6**	**−0.5**	**0.0**	**0.9**	**2.2**	**−0.2**	**−0.9**	**1.1**
Excluding South Africa	0.2	−0.8	−5.8	3.2	−1.3	−2.5	−1.2	2.1	4.5	−3.3	−3.7	0.8
Excl. S. Africa & Nigeria	−4.8	−3.2	−6.0	−2.1	−4.7	−2.8	−3.8	−2.4	−0.1	−4.2	−5.0	−2.6
Angola	..	18.0	−6.4	26.8	1.7	11.3	6.6	16.0	25.3	9.1	2.2	14.6
Benin	−21.5	−12.0	−12.7	−12.9	−12.7	−13.9	−12.8	−12.7	−12.6	−17.5	−12.5	−13.0
Botswana	−13.4	5.3	9.6	18.9	16.2	11.5	9.2	11.3	21.1	5.3	9.7	14.7
Burkina Faso	−22.3	−13.0	−15.7	−16.2	−13.9	−13.1	−14.8	..	..	−20.2	−14.1	−14.5
Burundi	−14.5	−19.9	−8.4	−12.2	−14.0	−16.2	−19.3	−24.3	−33.9	−13.5	−14.4	−20.0
Cameroon	0.8	2.9	4.3	3.6	−1.3	−0.8	0.3	−0.4	−1.9	0.4	3.7	−0.1
Cape Verde	..	−31.0	−38.4	−33.9	−33.4	−36.6	−34.5	..	..	−29.0	−35.2	−34.6
Central African Republic	−15.9	−12.9	−3.4	−3.1	−2.9	−4.5	..	..	..	−12.1	−7.7	−3.5
Chad	−11.9	−14.4	−13.9	−17.8	−35.0	..	−34.3	0.2	15.5	−13.5	−13.6	−14.3
Comoros	−43.2	−22.9	−20.7	−15.8	−15.3	−15.0	−16.1	−19.9	−22.2	−33.3	−22.6	−17.4
Congo, Dem. Rep.	0.1	0.3	6.0	1.0	−2.0	−4.9	−7.2	−8.8	−8.2	−0.8	1.2	−5.0
Congo, Rep.	−0.1	7.9	13.2	36.7	24.1	27.6	25.6	27.0	36.3	−0.5	2.9	29.5
Côte d'Ivoire	−6.2	4.6	8.2	7.1	7.8	16.2	10.4	9.7	10.2	3.2	6.5	10.2
Djibouti	..	−24.6	−11.0	−15.3	−8.5	−5.2	−9.1	−17.2	−17.0	..	−17.5	−12.0
Equatorial Guinea	..	−37.4	..	13.2	9.3	46.9	20.3	38.5	49.1	−28.6	−45.8	29.5
Eritrea	..	..	−77.2	−66.6	−55.7	−59.7	−85.1	−84.2	−46.9	..	−55.8	−66.4
Ethiopia	..	−3.3	−12.6	−12.4	−12.1	−14.7	−15.0	−17.7	−22.1	−5.3	−6.9	−15.7
Gabon	33.1	15.2	21.5	36.4	26.0	19.2	24.3	29.5	44.5	9.7	17.7	30.0
Gambia, The	−20.9	−11.7	−6.8	−8.9	−5.4	−8.3	−9.2	−17.6	−20.6	−13.2	−12.6	−11.7
Ghana	−0.7	−9.0	−17.6	−18.5	−19.5	−12.1	−11.9	−21.1	−25.6	−3.1	−12.4	−18.1
Guinea	3.1	−2.4	−4.4	−4.3	−1.3	−4.0	−2.4	−3.9	−2.7	0.8	−3.0	−3.1
Guinea-Bissau	−29.2	−27.1	−18.0	−19.8	−34.3	−21.7	−11.4	−16.2	−13.1	−32.9	−24.5	−19.4
Kenya	−6.4	−5.6	−4.9	−8.0	−8.0	−3.6	−4.6	−5.8	−7.4	−4.9	−2.7	−6.2
Lesotho	−89.1	−105.6	−71.6	−63.1	−57.3	−61.4	−58.4	−50.6	−39.9	−105.4	−94.8	−55.1
Liberia	−0.1	..	−27.1	−4.5	−8.4	−8.1	−12.6	−13.9	−14.1	2.9	−39.6	−10.2
Madagascar	−16.4	−11.4	−7.7	−7.3	−3.2	−6.6	−9.0	−14.9	−14.1	−7.7	−8.2	−9.2
Malawi	−14.0	−9.6	−15.3	−9.7	−11.1	−21.4	−22.5	−24.4	−24.8	−6.7	−14.3	−19.0
Mali	−14.4	−16.6	−11.7	−12.6	−17.0	−7.3	−10.9	−12.4	−12.9	−17.6	−14.9	−12.2
Mauritania	−29.8	−15.1	−13.7	−28.0	−18.9	−23.0	−30.9	−49.4	−59.8	−24.4	−11.2	−35.0
Mauritius	−10.9	−7.2	−2.2	−1.9	2.7	3.8	2.1	−0.6	−4.4	−3.5	−4.3	0.3
Mozambique	−16.5	−27.9	−22.9	−21.9	−17.9	−18.8	−15.8	−8.3	−9.8	−18.4	−24.2	−15.4
Namibia	7.8	−15.5	−10.8	−5.5	−6.4	−2.0	−3.6	1.2	2.3	−7.6	−10.0	−2.3
Niger	−13.5	−6.9	−6.5	−7.9	−7.7	−8.9	−9.2	−10.3	−9.2	−8.0	−6.2	−8.9
Nigeria[b]	10.2	14.6	−4.2	22.1	10.8	−0.8	8.2	17.1	18.3	1.1	4.1	12.6
Rwanda	−11.9	−8.5	−17.3	−16.2	−15.8	−16.9	−19.3	−18.1	−20.4	−10.3	−19.9	−17.8
São Tomé and Principe	..	..	..	..	..	..	..	..	..	..	..	..
Senegal	−14.5	−6.8	−7.0	−9.3	−9.0	−10.4	−12.2	−13.1	−15.7	−12.1	−7.1	−11.6
Seychelles	−11.2	−4.3	−17.6	−2.6	−21.2	−5.6	11.1	8.3	−26.9	−2.3	−8.6	−6.2
Sierra Leone	−15.4	−1.3	−15.7	−21.3	−18.2	−19.5	−21.3	−15.5	−18.3	−3.1	−4.5	−19.0
Somalia	−55.3	−28.0	..	..	..	..	..	..	..	−35.1	−28.0	..
South Africa	8.0	5.5	2.6	3.0	3.9	3.7	1.9	−0.7	−1.4	5.1	2.8	1.7
Sudan	−12.6	..	−9.1	−2.4	−7.8	−6.2	−4.2	−3.8	−9.8	−9.4	−8.5	−5.7
Swaziland	−39.4	−12.5	−18.4	−15.6	−15.4	−0.3	1.9	−1.6	−4.7	−23.5	−19.1	−5.9
Tanzania	..	−24.8	−11.1	−7.4	−8.2	−7.4	−6.6	−7.1	−7.3	..	−19.3	−7.3
Togo	−5.3	−11.9	−10.1	−20.0	−19.4	−18.0	−13.6	−13.5	−13.4	−7.2	−9.6	−16.3
Uganda	−6.6	−12.1	−12.0	−11.9	−12.1	−14.7	−14.2	−13.9	−14.0	−6.2	−11.7	−13.5
Zambia	−4.0	−0.7	−18.7	−10.4	−2.8	−5.3	−7.4	−7.7	−8.8	−2.1	−7.0	−7.1
Zimbabwe	−3.2	0.1	1.6	−0.3	1.3	−0.9	−5.2	−10.1	−16.2	−0.8	−2.6	−5.2
NORTH AFRICA	**5.0**	**−3.6**	**−2.6**	**3.4**	**1.9**	**0.8**	**3.3**	**4.1**	**7.7**	**−3.2**	**−2.4**	**3.5**
Algeria	4.0	−1.5	3.1	19.8	14.6	9.7	14.4	14.4	24.2	−2.5	1.6	16.2
Egypt, Arab Rep.	−12.4	−12.7	−8.3	−6.6	−4.9	−4.4	−2.6	−1.4	−2.3	−13.2	−6.7	−3.7
Libya	34.8	8.6	6.7	19.8	11.3	11.4	..	..	..	20.4	3.6	14.1
Morocco	−9.4	−5.4	−4.3	−6.5	−3.5	−3.3	−4.2	−6.7	−7.9	−7.4	−5.1	−5.4
Tunisia	−5.4	−7.0	−2.3	−3.6	−4.6	−4.3	−3.9	−2.9	−2.6	−6.1	−4.3	−3.7
ALL AFRICA	**3.2**	**−0.3**	**−2.5**	**3.2**	**1.1**	**0.0**	**1.2**	**2.0**	**4.0**	**−1.4**	**−1.5**	**1.9**

a. Provisional.
b. For 1994–2000 Nigeria's values were distorted because the official exchange rate used by the government for oil exports and oil value added was significantly overvalued.

Table 2.23 Exports of goods and services, nominal

	Current prices ($ millions)									Annual average		
	1980	1990	1999	2000	2001	2002	2003	2004	2005[a]	1980–89	1990–99	2000–05
SUB-SAHARAN AFRICA	**82,661**	**79,589**	**95,222**	**116,657**	**109,477**	**112,721**	**144,063**	**183,946**	**230,383**	**65,793**	**87,489**	**149,541**
Excluding South Africa	53,543	52,155	61,417	79,623	73,981	76,452	97,690	126,934	165,571	39,121	55,726	103,375
Excl. S. Africa & Nigeria	34,079	40,240	48,759	54,672	53,218	57,379	68,696	87,565	112,945	31,740	43,513	72,413
Angola	..	3,993	5,311	8,182	6,847	8,406	9,716	13,780	24,121	2,613	4,265	11,842
Benin	222	264	385	342	360	380	487	539	577	214	327	448
Botswana	563	2,087	2,743	3,248	2,933	2,811	3,739	4,491	5,519	999	2,350	3,790
Burkina Faso	173	352	287	237	260	272	357	..	..	184	287	281
Burundi	81	89	61	55	45	39	50	64	91	111	89	57
Cameroon	1,880	2,251	2,255	2,343	2,104	2,169	2,757	3,061	3,958	2,240	2,198	2,732
Cape Verde	..	43	113	146	167	194	253	..	..	41	79	190
Central African Republic	201	220	117	126	121	126	..	..	..	181	185	124
Chad	175	234	282	234	251	253	675	2,255	3,239	153	254	1,151
Comoros	11	36	29	34	34	40	51	46	48	22	40	42
Congo, Dem. Rep.	2,372	2,759	1,109	964	875	1,174	1,483	1,994	2,450	2,016	1,595	1,490
Congo, Rep.	1,024	1,502	1,702	2,585	2,163	2,462	2,825	3,662	5,160	1,092	1,393	3,143
Côte d'Ivoire	3,561	3,421	5,067	4,211	4,357	5,695	6,280	7,445	8,097	3,142	4,129	6,014
Djibouti	..	244	200	193	213	228	248	246	259	..	210	231
Equatorial Guinea	..	42	..	1,236	1,760	2,139	2,859	4,766	7,277	32	160	3,340
Eritrea	..	..	66	96	133	128	80	82	85	..	132	101
Ethiopia	..	672	918	984	980	983	1,140	1,494	1,858	608	715	1,240
Gabon	2,770	2,740	2,780	3,498	2,782	2,642	3,350	4,412	5,844	1,964	2,728	3,755
Gambia, The	103	190	199	202	150	157	158	185	207	108	195	176
Ghana	376	993	2,488	2,440	2,399	2,613	3,073	3,487	3,869	554	1,686	2,980
Guinea	2,084	829	749	735	809	785	806	845	924	2,021	798	817
Guinea-Bissau	14	24	56	68	57	61	77	84	114	15	32	77
Kenya	2,144	2,207	2,687	2,743	2,968	3,281	3,590	4,207	5,126	1,805	2,594	3,652
Lesotho	91	104	216	256	319	390	520	763	695	70	187	490
Liberia	613	..	64	120	126	111	133	171	201	519	43	144
Madagascar	539	512	909	1,190	1,317	704	1,264	1,425	1,355	414	673	1,209
Malawi	307	447	498	446	480	471	480	511	566	295	465	492
Mali	263	415	680	649	876	1,066	1,153	1,237	1,333	255	514	1,052
Mauritania	261	465	496	500	379	382	356	473	659	387	465	458
Mauritius	539	1,529	2,716	2,801	2,978	2,757	3,099	3,350	3,556	764	2,191	3,090
Mozambique	383	201	586	744	1,004	1,188	1,353	1,828	2,164	215	373	1,380
Namibia	1,712	1,220	1,563	1,558	1,446	1,548	2,300	2,644	2,961	1,139	1,543	2,076
Niger	617	372	321	320	329	330	438	491	512	420	325	403
Nigeria	18,859	12,366	12,832	24,954	20,774	19,093	28,993	39,344	52,575	7,725	12,563	30,955
Rwanda	168	145	114	151	157	133	139	189	228	173	107	166
São Tomé and Principe	..	..	..	..	..	..	..	..	..	..	..	..
Senegal	837	1,453	1,445	1,310	1,401	1,523	1,826	2,123	2,221	989	1,347	1,734
Seychelles	100	230	422	464	499	550	671	687	714	123	298	597
Sierra Leone	252	146	84	115	129	153	197	239	281	187	155	186
Somalia	200	90	..	..	..	..	..	..	..	119	90	..
South Africa	28,555	27,149	33,742	37,034	35,495	36,268	46,372	57,032	64,904	26,088	31,523	46,184
Sudan	806	..	828	1,891	1,711	1,996	2,613	3,822	4,973	875	658	2,834
Swaziland	405	658	1,006	1,133	1,156	1,131	1,580	1,986	2,095	394	886	1,513
Tanzania	..	538	1,285	1,527	1,505	1,631	2,022	2,538	2,964	..	962	2,031
Togo	580	545	455	409	421	498	595	691	743	464	441	559
Uganda	242	312	735	663	690	697	778	933	1,145	371	500	818
Zambia	1,608	1,180	701	682	980	875	891	1,059	1,192	1,060	1,083	946
Zimbabwe	1,561	2,009	2,767	2,660	2,369	2,019	1,854	2,002	1,941	1,530	2,469	2,141
NORTH AFRICA	**45,633**	**46,844**	**53,435**	**69,926**	**66,817**	**66,986**	**80,271**	**99,796**	**125,672**	**35,544**	**48,949**	**84,911**
Algeria	14,541	14,546	13,040	22,560	20,002	20,012	26,028	34,067	48,690	12,221	12,420	28,560
Egypt, Arab Rep.	6,992	8,647	13,654	16,175	17,066	16,091	18,074	22,258	27,214	6,654	12,435	19,480
Libya	23,523	11,468	7,275	12,078	9,054	9,164	..	..	..	17,320	8,527	10,099
Morocco	3,273	6,830	10,624	10,452	11,166	12,198	14,236	16,619	18,809	3,790	8,399	13,913
Tunisia	3,518	5,353	8,843	8,661	9,530	9,520	10,950	13,199	13,766	3,312	7,168	10,938
ALL AFRICA	**126,916**	**126,570**	**148,632**	**186,587**	**176,300**	**179,710**	**224,813**	**284,586**	**357,053**	**101,562**	**136,485**	**234,842**

a. Provisional.

Table 2.24 Imports of goods and services, nominal

	Current prices ($ millions)									Annual average		
	1980	1990	1999	2000	2001	2002	2003	2004	2005[a]	1980–89	1990–99	2000–05
SUB–SAHARAN AFRICA	75,159	74,458	103,059	105,964	107,564	114,480	144,042	179,001	216,632	66,401	90,312	144,614
Excluding South Africa	53,109	53,700	72,832	72,881	76,712	82,319	100,918	120,374	148,181	44,841	62,469	100,231
Excl. S. Africa & Nigeria	40,315	45,418	58,524	58,058	61,094	62,800	76,622	93,334	113,199	37,338	51,142	77,518
Angola	..	2,147	5,705	5,736	6,697	7,110	8,801	10,621	15,834	1,895	4,032	9,133
Benin	524	486	688	634	662	772	944	1,055	1,119	447	579	864
Botswana	705	1,888	2,204	2,079	1,958	2,130	2,979	3,380	3,313	842	1,896	2,640
Burkina Faso	603	758	729	658	650	693	977	..	..	579	659	744
Burundi	214	314	129	151	146	151	171	205	291	254	234	186
Cameroon	1,829	1,931	1,800	1,981	2,228	2,254	2,712	3,128	4,282	2,219	1,816	2,764
Cape Verde	..	148	337	326	351	419	529	..	..	118	237	406
Central African Republic	327	411	153	155	149	174	..	..	..	292	282	159
Chad	298	485	495	480	850	..	1,611	2,243	2,328	305	469	1,502
Comoros	64	93	75	66	68	77	103	118	134	67	93	94
Congo, Dem. Rep.	2,354	2,731	827	920	971	1,447	1,892	2,573	2,792	2,107	1,537	1,766
Congo, Rep.	1,026	1,282	1,391	1,404	1,490	1,629	1,913	2,488	2,994	1,093	1,309	1,986
Côte d'Ivoire	4,190	2,927	4,041	3,471	3,529	3,837	4,848	5,939	6,466	2,906	3,406	4,682
Djibouti	..	355	259	278	262	259	305	361	379	..	295	307
Equatorial Guinea	..	92	..	1,071	1,599	1,124	2,256	2,882	3,583	61	270	2,086
Eritrea	..	..	597	518	507	505	577	617	540	..	482	544
Ethiopia	..	1,069	1,882	1,961	1,938	2,073	2,347	3,171	4,367	1,093	1,330	2,643
Gabon	1,354	1,837	1,777	1,656	1,557	1,694	1,882	2,298	1,983	1,586	1,823	1,845
Gambia, The	153	227	228	239	173	188	192	255	302	137	242	225
Ghana	407	1,522	3,841	3,362	3,437	3,355	3,979	5,356	6,610	709	2,511	4,350
Guinea	1,878	892	901	867	849	912	892	1,005	1,012	1,953	905	923
Guinea-Bissau	46	90	96	111	125	105	104	127	153	67	91	121
Kenya	2,608	2,691	3,312	3,757	4,002	3,741	4,257	5,150	6,540	2,154	2,942	4,575
Lesotho	475	753	864	794	750	812	1,127	1,430	1,276	503	977	1,032
Liberia	614	..	184	146	171	156	184	235	275	491	180	195
Madagascar	1,202	864	1,197	1,474	1,463	993	1,756	2,073	2,067	668	942	1,637
Malawi	480	629	769	616	672	886	878	975	1,080	384	716	851
Mali	520	817	982	954	1,322	1,311	1,630	1,841	2,015	536	882	1,512
Mauritania	473	619	660	803	591	647	753	1,239	1,758	576	607	965
Mauritius	665	1,701	2,808	2,888	2,854	2,584	2,988	3,389	3,830	809	2,334	3,089
Mozambique	965	888	1,500	1,571	1,665	1,958	2,108	2,320	2,830	773	1,001	2,075
Namibia	1,542	1,584	1,927	1,746	1,652	1,610	2,461	2,573	2,819	1,284	1,844	2,144
Niger	957	545	452	462	479	523	688	795	825	583	448	629
Nigeria	12,324	8,203	14,304	14,807	15,601	19,447	24,200	26,965	34,855	7,362	11,214	22,646
Rwanda	307	364	448	445	427	425	464	521	667	354	405	491
São Tomé and Principe	..	..	..	..	..	..	..	..	..	..	..	..
Senegal	1,302	1,728	1,806	1,746	1,842	2,078	2,657	3,162	3,431	1,283	1,664	2,486
Seychelles	117	246	531	480	630	589	593	629	908	123	344	638
Sierra Leone	421	154	188	250	276	336	408	406	499	225	191	362
Somalia	534	346	..	..	..	..	..	..	..	403	346	..
South Africa	22,073	21,016	30,287	33,107	30,889	32,211	43,139	58,561	68,412	21,441	27,961	44,386
Sudan	1,763	..	1,802	2,189	2,756	2,924	3,367	4,650	7,701	1,853	1,551	3,931
Swaziland	619	768	1,260	1,349	1,350	1,134	1,543	2,023	2,217	515	1,116	1,603
Tanzania	..	1,595	2,241	2,200	2,283	2,353	2,703	3,344	3,881	..	2,000	2,794
Togo	640	738	615	674	678	763	833	969	1,026	542	586	824
Uganda	324	834	1,455	1,366	1,378	1,554	1,662	1,879	2,370	619	1,042	1,701
Zambia	1,764	1,203	1,287	1,018	1,080	1,072	1,212	1,478	1,835	1,148	1,313	1,282
Zimbabwe	1,771	2,002	2,670	2,680	2,232	2,218	2,238	2,477	2,495	1,598	2,661	2,390
NORTH AFRICA	39,100	53,024	59,364	61,717	62,205	65,195	72,156	88,641	101,546	40,426	53,495	75,243
Algeria	12,847	15,472	11,520	11,700	11,920	14,491	16,239	21,808	24,020	13,875	11,636	16,696
Egypt, Arab Rep.	9,822	14,109	21,144	22,780	21,802	19,917	20,219	23,330	29,246	10,787	16,572	22,882
Libya	11,167	8,996	5,246	5,252	5,674	6,979	..	..	..	10,722	7,464	5,968
Morocco	5,033	8,227	12,142	12,616	12,363	13,387	16,056	19,989	22,885	4,955	9,980	16,216
Tunisia	3,987	6,220	9,313	9,369	10,446	10,421	11,918	14,026	14,525	3,834	7,842	11,784
ALL AFRICA	114,047	127,869	162,420	167,684	169,771	179,671	216,817	268,476	319,552	107,081	143,927	220,329

a. Provisional.

Table **2.25** Exports of goods and services, real

						Constant prices (2000 $ millions)				Average annual growth (%)		
	1980	1990	1999	2000	2001	2002	2003	2004	2005[a]	1980–89	1990–99	2000–05
SUB–SAHARAN AFRICA	**72,127**	**77,415**	**109,996**	**119,417**	**121,895**	**120,096**	**130,399**	**138,648**	**144,627**	**1.3**	**4.8**	**4.2**
Excluding South Africa	53,614	55,278	75,981	82,595	84,450	82,282	93,167	100,845	104,079	1.1	4.4	5.3
Excl. S. Africa & Nigeria	29,742	40,345	55,811	58,367	61,769	62,898	65,889	73,311	77,637	3.1	4.0	5.8
Angola	..	..	..	..	..	..	..	..	..	..	..	..
Benin	391	247	344	342	359	359	376	378	397	–4.5	2.0	2.7
Botswana	691	1,994	2,682	3,248	3,168	3,059	2,961	3,137	3,818	13.8	4.0	2.2
Burkina Faso	226	253	262	237	244	273	300	..	..	–1.7	–0.1	8.5
Burundi	..	..	..	..	..	..	..	..	..	..	..	..
Cameroon	1,054	1,870	2,466	2,343	2,342	2,301	2,299	2,505	2,507	6.5	2.7	1.6
Cape Verde	..	42	96	146	167	182	208	..	..	..	13.9	12.1
Central African Republic	..	..	..	..	..	..	..	..	..	..	..	..
Chad	160	215	256	234	226	213	476	1,310	1,533	7.4	2.8	55.6
Comoros	9	26	29	34	32	34	35	28	29	11.0	–2.2	–3.3
Congo, Dem. Rep.	667	1,224	1,000	964	983	1,062	1,065	1,279	1,391	11.2	–2.5	7.8
Congo, Rep.	..	..	..	..	..	..	..	..	..	..	..	..
Côte d'Ivoire	3,048	4,084	4,337	4,211	4,147	4,384	4,142	4,855	4,782	1.2	1.5	3.1
Djibouti	..	355	205	193	210	223	238	229	234	..	–6.1	3.7
Equatorial Guinea	..	..	..	1,236	1,938	2,282	2,633	3,644	3,907	..	..	24.9
Eritrea	..	..	67	96	131	127	86	80	80	..	–1.4	–7.6
Ethiopia	..	579	761	984	1,033	1,172	1,350	1,836	1,904	3.7	5.9	15.9
Gabon	2,157	3,178	3,940	3,498	3,296	2,931	3,166	3,300	3,250	1.8	3.4	–0.8
Gambia, The	107	174	182	202	167	170	166	192	245	0.5	–0.9	4.0
Ghana	857	1,010	2,420	2,440	2,441	2,400	2,464	2,746	3,001	1.4	10.5	4.1
Guinea	..	688	743	735	791	780	750	760	803	..	0.1	0.8
Guinea-Bissau	22	17	55	68	71	71	76	79	83	–3.9	14.2	4.1
Kenya	1,479	2,374	2,712	2,743	2,943	3,044	3,268	3,700	3,873	3.3	1.2	7.4
Lesotho	58	83	204	256	339	428	396	441	377	4.7	10.7	7.9
Liberia	..	..	..	..	..	..	..	..	..	..	..	..
Madagascar	992	769	1,048	1,190	1,304	706	993	1,008	964	–1.8	3.3	–4.1
Malawi	315	354	479	446	491	499	480	465	554	2.1	4.8	2.5
Mali	175	266	657	649	811	1,067	907	905	984	4.7	10.1	6.7
Mauritania	437	532	493	500	491	458	405	442	470	3.5	–1.5	–2.1
Mauritius	732	1,739	2,859	2,801	3,101	3,394	3,123	3,060	3,235	10.1	5.8	1.7
Mozambique	436	237	564	744	1,127	1,364	1,776	1,807	1,897	–8.9	10.5	19.9
Namibia	1,096	954	1,571	1,558	1,525	1,739	2,139	1,994	2,040	1.4	4.3	7.0
Niger	..	..	..	..	..	..	..	..	..	..	..	..
Nigeria	21,372	15,781	21,442	24,954	23,975	21,360	28,111	28,976	28,466	–1.5	5.1	4.4
Rwanda	171	210	138	151	264	279	274	304	297	4.2	–6.4	11.4
São Tomé and Principe	..	..	..	..	..	..	..	..	..	..	..	..
Senegal	671	989	1,344	1,310	1,330	1,378	1,376	1,440	1,486	1.8	4.3	2.5
Seychelles	..	252	378	464	503	533	613	638	711	..	4.9	8.9
Sierra Leone	..	..	..	..	..	..	..	..	..	..	..	..
Somalia	..	..	..	..	..	..	..	..	..	..	..	..
South Africa	19,504	22,613	34,192	37,034	37,687	37,888	37,991	38,937	41,527	1.6	5.6	1.9
Sudan	764	334	845	1,891	1,736	1,790	2,135	2,434	2,751	–5.0	8.8	9.1
Swaziland	424	778	1,006	1,133	1,318	1,345	1,264	1,278	1,355	7.5	3.5	2.1
Tanzania	..	698	1,340	1,527	1,759	1,827	2,214	2,546	2,859	..	10.3	13.5
Togo	499	414	426	409	460	476	508	523	562	0.4	1.4	6.0
Uganda	..	229	715	663	757	844	911	968	1,011	1.4	16.0	8.7
Zambia	812	559	797	682	880	939	1,034	1,164	1,307	–3.0	3.5	12.7
Zimbabwe	638	1,011	2,502	2,660	2,606	2,195	1,918	1,952	1,887	4.3	10.8	–7.5
NORTH AFRICA	**31,796**	**52,076**	**72,867**	**76,210**	**78,842**	**79,225**	**83,953**	**92,313**	**102,606**	**4.8**	**3.8**	**5.9**
Algeria	11,053	16,673	21,303	22,560	21,951	23,158	24,988	25,762	27,257	4.2	2.9	4.4
Egypt, Arab Rep.	6,930	11,111	15,584	16,175	16,707	15,404	17,535	21,974	26,924	4.4	3.3	10.5
Libya	..	..	..	..	..	..	..	..	..	..	..	..
Morocco	2,848	6,337	10,196	10,452	11,529	12,276	11,899	12,309	13,353	7.6	5.5	4.1
Tunisia	3,303	5,408	8,228	8,661	9,660	9,299	9,304	10,027	10,352	5.1	5.1	2.9
ALL AFRICA	**104,296**	**128,692**	**181,840**	**194,762**	**199,759**	**198,214**	**213,340**	**229,613**	**245,262**	**2.5**	**4.4**	**4.8**

a. Provisional.

Table 2.26 Imports of goods and services, real

	Constant prices (2000 $ millions)									Average annual growth (%)		
	1980	1990	1999	2000	2001	2002	2003	2004	2005[a]	1980–89	1990–99	2000–05
SUB-SAHARAN AFRICA	86,589	67,505	104,183	104,247	108,582	115,008	124,060	134,976	150,387	–4.1	5.8	7.6
Excluding South Africa	68,510	49,436	73,473	71,637	76,072	80,894	86,876	92,184	103,385	–5.4	4.7	7.3
Excl. S. Africa & Nigeria	37,723	39,401	58,144	56,403	59,435	60,546	64,389	69,394	75,384	0.6	4.9	5.8
Angola	..	..	..	..	..	..	..	..	..	..	..	..
Benin	797	484	615	634	660	668	670	678	706	–7.4	1.8	1.8
Botswana	714	1,728	2,171	2,079	2,093	2,287	2,321	2,320	2,265	8.2	3.7	2.2
Burkina Faso	517	650	752	658	718	762	1,000	..	..	2.6	1.7	14.1
Burundi	..	..	..	..	..	..	..	..	..	..	..	..
Cameroon	795	1,261	1,706	1,981	2,259	2,087	2,162	2,427	2,993	4.9	4.1	6.8
Cape Verde	..	145	288	326	351	393	435	..	..	..	8.2	10.2
Central African Republic	..	..	..	..	..	..	..	..	..	..	..	..
Chad	320	537	449	480	767	..	1,135	1,304	1,101	11.5	–2.8	19.0
Comoros	66	67	60	66	64	67	71	72	80	0.3	–0.9	4.2
Congo, Dem. Rep.	566	1,063	785	920	1,012	1,387	1,767	2,233	2,626	13.1	–6.5	25.2
Congo, Rep.	..	..	..	..	..	..	..	..	..	..	..	..
Côte d'Ivoire	3,347	2,315	4,318	3,471	3,623	3,554	4,005	4,511	4,709	–2.2	8.9	6.8
Djibouti	..	518	265	278	257	253	292	335	342	..	–8.0	5.8
Equatorial Guinea	..	..	..	1,071	1,627	1,154	1,986	2,235	2,776	..	..	19.6
Eritrea	..	..	607	518	520	502	508	434	429	..	9.9	–4.1
Ethiopia	..	1,116	1,962	1,961	1,980	2,157	2,271	2,721	3,373	4.6	5.3	11.2
Gabon	1,890	1,967	1,982	1,656	1,662	1,765	1,731	1,817	1,478	–2.1	1.2	–0.9
Gambia, The	306	220	236	239	198	217	182	238	263	–7.5	0.0	2.4
Ghana	1,897	1,548	4,100	3,362	3,622	3,464	3,730	4,064	4,337	–0.5	11.8	5.0
Guinea	..	1,074	956	867	872	918	844	837	785	..	–1.0	–2.0
Guinea-Bissau	79	84	82	111	107	92	84	91	97	1.1	–2.5	–3.5
Kenya	1,913	1,854	3,687	3,757	4,080	3,971	3,972	4,450	5,085	0.9	10.3	5.2
Lesotho	520	761	846	794	850	989	966	1,008	856	3.4	2.1	2.5
Liberia	..	..	..	..	..	..	..	..	..	..	..	..
Madagascar	1,911	1,075	1,265	1,474	1,647	1,235	1,638	2,045	2,045	–7.7	3.3	7.6
Malawi	803	743	787	616	704	907	806	777	786	–1.5	–0.3	4.1
Mali	392	683	938	954	1,238	1,110	1,260	1,225	1,270	6.8	3.1	4.4
Mauritania	621	749	579	803	791	812	792	1,129	1,640	0.7	–0.8	14.1
Mauritius	829	1,793	2,853	2,888	2,955	3,108	3,009	3,003	3,147	9.5	5.2	1.3
Mozambique	1,232	851	1,610	1,571	1,246	1,512	1,710	1,767	1,989	–4.4	5.5	6.9
Namibia	1,107	1,151	1,842	1,746	1,918	1,983	2,096	1,868	1,897	0.5	6.0	1.1
Niger	..	..	..	..	..	..	..	..	..	..	..	..
Nigeria	26,740	9,817	14,933	14,807	16,126	19,442	21,428	21,859	26,518	–15.4	3.9	11.9
Rwanda	177	210	496	445	447	422	445	490	571	4.3	6.1	4.6
São Tomé and Principe	..	..	..	..	..	..	..	..	..	..	..	..
Senegal	987	1,376	1,699	1,746	1,777	1,838	2,025	2,001	2,228	2.0	1.5	4.9
Seychelles	..	208	487	480	629	546	546	590	784	..	11.1	6.7
Sierra Leone	..	..	..	..	..	..	..	..	..	..	..	..
Somalia	..	..	..	..	..	..	..	..	..	..	..	..
South Africa	19,907	18,795	31,429	33,107	33,179	34,859	37,943	43,278	47,642	–1.0	7.9	8.0
Sudan	1,742	1,083	2,064	2,189	2,182	2,346	2,470	..	..	–7.5	9.6	4.4
Swaziland	580	770	1,260	1,349	1,480	1,477	1,418	1,437	1,528	2.6	4.7	1.4
Tanzania	..	1,503	2,253	2,200	1,928	2,275	2,413	2,539	2,727	..	3.8	5.8
Togo	708	803	710	674	681	716	736	758	780	3.0	1.0	3.1
Uganda	..	687	1,397	1,366	1,408	1,667	1,711	1,832	2,229	4.7	10.7	9.8
Zambia	1,977	1,180	1,274	1,018	1,295	1,219	1,264	1,401	1,689	–1.7	2.6	8.4
Zimbabwe	618	984	2,470	2,680	2,435	2,419	2,255	2,293	2,234	2.7	9.8	–3.3
NORTH AFRICA	51,425	50,082	60,587	61,336	63,042	64,676	65,187	72,859	82,087	–1.8	2.4	5.6
Algeria	17,636	14,054	11,806	11,700	12,156	14,527	14,875	16,586	17,880	–4.0	–1.4	9.2
Egypt, Arab Rep.	20,494	17,932	23,581	22,780	22,524	21,172	21,443	25,140	31,130	–2.2	3.3	5.6
Libya	..	..	..	..	..	..	..	..	..	..	..	..
Morocco	4,673	7,642	11,786	12,616	12,714	13,604	13,501	14,795	15,888	4.0	4.7	4.7
Tunisia	4,539	6,476	8,602	9,369	10,641	10,237	10,191	10,552	10,670	0.6	3.5	1.8
ALL AFRICA	137,518	117,568	164,753	165,564	171,612	179,681	189,262	207,874	232,528	–3.2	4.4	6.9

a. Provisional.

Table 3.1

Millennium Development Goal 1: eradicate extreme poverty and hunger

	Share of population below national poverty line[a] (poverty headcount ratio)				International poverty line							
					Share of population below PPP $1 a day[a]				Poverty gap ratio at $1 a day[a] (incidence × depth of poverty)			
	Surveys 1990–99		Surveys 2000–05		Surveys 1990–99		Surveys 2000–05		Surveys 1990–99		Surveys 2000–05	
	Year[b]	Percent	Year[b]	Percent	Year[b]	Percent	Year[b]	Percent	Year[b]	Percent	Year[b]	Percent
SUB-SAHARAN AFRICA												
Angola	..	..	..	..	..	..	..	..	..	..	..	..
Benin	1999	29.0	..	..	..	..	2003	30.9	..	..	2003	8.2
Botswana	..	..	..	..	1993	28.0	..	..	1993	9.9	..	..
Burkina Faso	1998	54.6	2003	46.4	1998	44.9	2003	27.2	1998	14.4	2003	7.3
Burundi	1990	36.4	..	..	1998	54.6	..	..	1998	22.7	..	..
Cameroon	1996	53.3	2001	40.2	1996	32.5	2001	17.1	1996	9.1	2001	4.1
Cape Verde	..	..	..	..	..	..	..	..	..	..	..	..
Central African Republic	..	..	..	..	1993	66.6	..	..	1993	38.1	..	..
Chad	1996	64.0	..	..	..	..	..	..	..	..	..	..
Comoros	..	..	..	..	..	..	..	..	..	..	..	..
Congo, Dem. Rep.	..	..	..	..	..	..	..	..	..	..	..	..
Congo, Rep.	..	..	..	..	..	..	..	..	..	..	..	..
Côte d'Ivoire	..	..	..	..	1998	15.5	2002	14.8	1998	3.8	2002	4.1
Djibouti	..	..	..	..	..	..	..	..	..	..	..	..
Equatorial Guinea	..	..	..	..	..	..	..	..	..	..	..	..
Eritrea	1994	53.0	..	..	..	..	..	..	..	..	..	..
Ethiopia	1996	45.5	2000	44.2	1995	31.3	2000	23.0	1995	8.0	2000	4.8
Gabon	..	..	..	..	..	..	..	..	..	..	..	..
Gambia, The	1998	57.6	..	..	1998	59.3	..	..	1998	28.8	..	..
Ghana	1999	39.5	..	..	1998	44.8	..	..	1998	17.3	..	..
Guinea	1994	40.0	..	..	..	..	..	..	..	..	..	..
Guinea-Bissau	..	..	..	..	..	..	..	..	..	..	..	..
Kenya	1997	52.0	..	..	1997	22.8	..	..	1997	5.9	..	..
Lesotho	..	..	..	..	1995	36.4	..	..	1995	19.0	..	..
Liberia	..	..	..	..	..	..	..	..	..	..	..	..
Madagascar	1999	71.3	..	..	1999	66.0	2001	61.0	1999	29.4	2001	27.9
Malawi	1998	65.3	..	..	..	..	2004	20.8	..	..	2004	4.7
Mali	1998	63.8	..	..	1994	72.3	2001	36.1	1994	37.4	2001	12.2
Mauritania	1996	50.0	2000	46.3	1996	28.6	2000	25.9	1996	9.1	2000	7.6
Mauritius	..	..	..	..	..	..	..	..	..	..	..	..
Mozambique	1997	69.4	..	..	1997	37.9	2002	36.2	1997	12.0	2002	11.6
Namibia	..	..	..	..	1993	34.9	..	..	1993	14.0	..	..
Niger	1993	63.0	..	..	1995	60.6	..	..	1995	34.0	..	..
Nigeria	1993	34.1	..	..	1996	77.9	2003	70.8	1996	44.1	2003	34.5
Rwanda	1993	51.2	2000	60.3	..	..	2000	60.3	..	..	2000	25.6
São Tomé and Principe	..	..	..	..	..	..	..	..	..	..	..	..
Senegal	1992	33.4	..	..	1995	24.0	2001	17.0	1995	6.3	2001	3.6
Seychelles	..	..	..	..	..	..	..	..	..	..	..	..
Sierra Leone	..	..	2004	70.2	..	..	..	..	..	..	..	..
Somalia	..	..	..	..	..	..	..	..	..	..	..	..
South Africa	..	..	..	..	1995	6.3	2000	10.7	1995	0.6	2000	1.7
Sudan	..	..	..	..	..	..	..	..	..	..	..	..
Swaziland	..	..	..	..	1995	8.0	..	..	1995	2.5	..	..
Tanzania	1991	38.6	2001	35.7	1991	61.5	2000	57.8	1991	22.7	2000	20.7
Togo	..	..	..	..	..	..	..	..	..	..	..	..
Uganda	..	..	2003	37.7	..	..	..	..	..	..	..	..
Zambia	1998	72.9	2004	68.0	1998	65.7	2004	63.8	1998	34.0	2004	32.6
Zimbabwe	1996	34.9	..	..	1996	56.1	..	..	1996	24.2	..	..
NORTH AFRICA												
Algeria	1995	22.6	..	..	1995	2.0	..	..	1995	0.5	..	..
Egypt, Arab Rep.	1996	22.9	2000	16.7	1995	2.6	2000	3.1	1995	0.5	2000	0.5
Libya	..	..	..	..	..	..	..	..	..	..	..	..
Morocco	1999	19.0	..	..	1999	2.0	..	..	1999	0.5	..	..
Tunisia	1995	7.6	..	..	1995	2.0	2000	2.0	1995	0.5	2000	0.5

a. Data are based on expenditure shares, except for Namibia and Swaziland, for which data are based on income shares.
b. Data are for most recent year available during the period specified.

| Share of poorest quintile in national consumption or income[a] | | | | Prevalence of child malnutrition, underweight (% of children under age 5) | | | | Population below minimum dietary energy consumption | |
| Surveys 1990–99 | | Surveys 2000–05 | | Surveys 1990–99 | | Surveys 2000–05 | | Share (%) | Millions |
Year[b]	Percent	Year[b]	Percent	Year[b]	Percent	Year[b]	Percent	2004	2004
..	..	..	..	1996	40.6	2001	30.5	35	4.8
..	..	2003	7.4	1996	29.2	2005	30.0	12	0.8
1993	3.2	..	..	1996	17.2	2000	12.5	32	0.6
1998	5.9	2003	6.9	1999	34.3	2003	37.7	15	2.0
1998	5.1	..	..	..	..	2000	45.1	66	4.5
1996	5.7	2001	5.6	1998	22.2	2004	18.1	26	4.2
..	..	..	..	1994	13.5	..	..	..	..
1993	2.0	..	..	1995	23.2	2000	24.3	44	1.7
..	..	..	..	1997	38.8	2004	36.7	35	3.0
..	..	..	..	1996	25.8	2000	25.4	60	0.5
..	..	..	..	1995	34.4	2001	31.0	74	39.0
..	..	..	..	1999	13.0	..	..	33	1.2
1998	5.8	2002	5.2	1999	21.2	2004	17.2	13	2.2
..	..	..	..	1996	18.2	2002	26.8	24	0.2
..	..	..	..	..	..	2000	18.6	..	..
..	..	..	..	1995	43.7	2002	39.6	75	3.1
1995	7.2	2000	9.1	1992	47.7	2005	38.4	46	32.7
..	..	..	..	..	..	2001	11.9	5	0.1
1998	4.8	..	..	1996	26.2	2000	17.2	29	0.4
1998	5.6	..	..	1999	24.9	2003	22.1	11	2.3
..	..	2003	7.0	1999	23.2	2000	32.7	24	2.0
1993	5.2	..	..	..	..	2000	25.0	39	0.6
1997	6.0	..	..	1998	22.1	2003	19.9	31	9.9
1995	1.5	..	..	1996	16.0	2000	18.0	13	0.2
..	..	..	..	..	..	2000	26.5	50	1.7
1999	5.9	2001	4.9	1997	40.0	2004	41.9	38	6.6
..	..	2004	7.0	1995	29.9	2002	21.9	35	4.2
1994	4.6	2001	6.1	1996	26.9	2001	33.2	29	3.8
1996	6.3	2000	6.2	1996	23.0	2001	31.8	10	0.3
..	..	..	..	1995	14.9	..	..	5	0.1
1997	6.5	2002	5.4	1997	26.1	2003	23.7	44	8.3
1993	1.4	..	..	1992	26.2	2000	24.0	24	0.5
1995	2.6	..	..	1998	49.6	2000	40.1	32	3.9
1996	3.7	2003	5.0	1999	27.3	2003	28.7	9	11.4
..	..	2000	5.3	1996	27.3	2005	22.5	33	2.8
..	..	..	..	..	..	2000	12.9	10	0.0
1995	6.5	2001	6.6	1996	22.3	2000	22.7	20	2.1
..	..	..	..	..	..	..	..	9	0.0
..	..	..	..	1990	28.7	2000	27.2	51	2.5
..	..	..	..	1997	18.0	2000	25.8	..	..
1995	3.6	2000	3.5	1999	11.5	..	..	3	0.0
..	..	..	..	1993	33.9	2000	40.7	26	8.7
1995	2.5	2001	4.3	..	..	2000	10.3	22	0.2
1991	7.4	2000	7.3	1999	29.4	2005	21.8	44	16.4
..	..	..	..	1998	25.1	..	..	24	1.2
..	..	2002	5.7	1995	25.5	2001	22.9	19	4.8
1998	3.4	2004	3.6	1999	25.0	2003	23.0	46	5.0
1996	4.6	..	..	1999	13.0	..	..	47	6.0
1995	7.0	..	..	1995	12.8	2002	10.4	4	1.4
1995	8.8	2000	8.6	1998	10.7	2003	8.6	4	2.6
..	..	..	..	1995	4.7	..	..	3	0.0
1999	6.5	..	..	1997	9.0	2004	10.2	6	1.8
1995	5.6	2000	6.0	1997	3.8	2000	4.0	3	0.0

Table 3.2 Millennium Development Goal 2: achieve universal primary education

	Net primary enrollment ratio (% of relevant age group)			Primary completion rate (% of relevant age group)			Share of cohort reaching grade 5 (% of grade 1 students)			Youth literacy rate (% of ages 15–24)		
	1991	2000	2005	1991	2000	2005	1991	2000	2005a	1991	2000	2000–05b
SUB-SAHARAN AFRICA												
Angola	50.3	..	..	34.7	..	..	..	..	..	..	..	72.2
Benin	41.0	51.9	78.2	20.8	34.9	65.0	54.8	84.0	51.6	..	..	45.3
Botswana	83.4	79.6	83.4	82.9	87.5	92.0	84.0	89.5	..	89.3	..	94.0
Burkina Faso	29.2	35.8	45.2	21.3	25.2	30.9	69.7	69.1	75.5	20.2	..	33.0
Burundi	52.9	43.3	60.5	45.9	25.1	35.7	61.7	56.1	66.9	53.6	73.3	73.3
Cameroon	73.6	..	..	55.9	53.3	62.4	..	..	..	88.2	..	96.3
Cape Verde	91.1	97.7	90.1	..	101.8	81.4	..	..	92.5	..	..	..
Central African Republic	51.9	..	..	26.7	..	22.5	23.0	..	..	..	58.5	58.5
Chad	34.7	53.7	..	18.3	22.9	31.6	50.5	53.9	33.2	..	37.6	37.6
Comoros	56.7	55.1	..	..	..	50.5	..	..	80.3	..	..	..
Congo, Dem. Rep.	54.1	..	..	46.1	..	..	54.7	..	..	..	..	70.4
Congo, Rep.	79.4	..	43.5	54.1	..	57.5	60.1	..	..	..	..	97.4
Côte d'Ivoire	44.7	53.0	..	43.4	39.6	..	72.5	87.6	..	..	60.7	60.7
Djibouti	28.7	27.7	33.3	27.1	29.3	31.8	87.3	..	..	73.2	..	..
Equatorial Guinea	90.6	84.1	..	..	..	54.3	..	..	..	..	94.9	94.9
Eritrea	15.5	40.9	47.0	..	40.3	50.9	..	60.5	79.1	..	..	..
Ethiopia	22.0	36.1	61.4	..	36.7	55.0	18.3	..	..	..	..	49.9
Gabon	85.5	..	..	..	..	..	..	..	..	..	..	96.2
Gambia, The	48.0	66.7	..	..	..	..	..	..	..	..	..	..
Ghana	53.7	60.7	65.0	62.8	..	72.1	80.5	66.2	..	..	70.7	70.7
Guinea	27.2	47.0	65.5	16.8	33.3	54.5	58.6	..	76.0	..	..	46.6
Guinea-Bissau	38.1	45.2	..	..	27.0	..	..	..	..	..	..	..
Kenya	..	66.8	79.9	..	..	95.0	76.7	..	82.9	..	80.3	80.3
Lesotho	71.5	81.6	86.7	58.5	61.2	66.9	65.9	66.7	73.3	..	..	..
Liberia	..	65.7	..	..	..	..	..	..	..	..	..	67.4
Madagascar	64.2	65.0	92.5	33.3	35.6	57.7	21.1	..	42.7	..	70.2	70.2
Malawi	48.4	..	94.5	28.5	67.2	60.7	64.4	51.9	38.3	..	..	..
Mali	20.9	..	50.9	10.8	28.5	38.1	69.7	91.7	..	..	..	..
Mauritania	35.3	62.7	72.2	32.9	51.6	44.5	75.3	59.6	52.9	..	61.3	61.3
Mauritius	91.3	92.9	95.1	106.6	104.7	97.5	97.4	99.3	97.0	91.2	94.5	94.5
Mozambique	42.8	55.5	78.7	27.1	16.2	42.0	34.2	51.9	62.4	..	..	..
Namibia	..	74.1	72.2	..	85.4	75.3	62.3	94.2	..	88.1	..	92.3
Niger	22.3	25.3	39.9	16.5	16.8	28.1	62.4	74.0	64.8	..	..	36.5
Nigeria	57.8	..	90.9	..	..	81.8	89.1	..	..	71.2	..	84.2
Rwanda	66.0	..	73.7	32.9	22.4	39.0	59.9	39.1	..	74.9	77.6	77.6
São Tomé and Principe	..	..	96.7	..	..	77.2	..	..	76.3	93.8	..	95.4
Senegal	43.5	54.4	76.2	..	36.0	52.2	84.5	72.3	..	..	..	49.1
Seychelles	..	..	..	..	112.9	..	92.7	91.0	..	..	..	99.1
Sierra Leone	43.3	..	..	..	..	..	..	..	..	..	..	47.9
Somalia	9.0	..	..	..	..	..	..	..	..	..	..	..
South Africa	89.5	90.4	..	75.5	89.0	..	..	..	..	..	77.2	77.2
Sudan	40.0	43.2	..	41.4	38.9	49.7	93.8	..	78.6	..	88.4	88.4
Swaziland	77.1	76.1	..	59.9	64.3	..	77.0	73.9	..	..	..	78.4
Tanzania	49.4	51.4	91.4	61.2	..	54.2	81.3	81.4	75.8	..	..	..
Togo	64.0	76.6	78.1	34.9	61.0	65.3	48.0	73.8	74.6	..	74.4	74.4
Uganda	..	..	..	..	..	..	36.0	56.7	..	69.8	..	76.6
Zambia	..	62.6	88.9	..	56.3	77.5	..	..	..	66.4	..	..
Zimbabwe	..	82.2	..	98.6	..	..	76.1	..	..	..	..	97.7
NORTH AFRICA												
Algeria	88.8	91.5	96.6	79.5	82.5	95.8	94.5	97.2	95.6	77.3	..	..
Egypt, Arab Rep.	84.1	92.9	..	..	97.3	..	..	99.0	..	61.3	..	..
Libya	95.9	..	..	..	..	..	..	..	..	91.0	..	..
Morocco	55.9	76.7	86.1	46.6	58.2	80.3	75.1	80.1	79.2	55.3	..	..
Tunisia	94.1	94.4	..	74.4	87.5	..	86.4	93.1	..	84.1	..	..

a. Provisional.
b. Data are for most recent year available during the period specified.

Table 3.3 Millennium Development Goal 3: promote gender equity and empower women

	Ratio of girls to boys in primary and secondary school (%)			Ratio of young literate women to men (% of ages 15–24)		Women in national parliament (% of total seats)			Share of women employed in the nonagricultural sector (%)		
	1991	2000	2005a	1990	2006a	1990	2000	2006	1990	2000	2004
SUB–SAHARAN AFRICA											
Angola	..	..	..	..	75.4	15.0	16.0	15.0	..	..	..
Benin	48.6	63.2	72.5	43.6	56.1	3.0	6.0	7.2	46.0	..	..
Botswana	108.0	100.9	102.0	110.0	103.8	5.0	..	11.1	33.5	40.2	43.0
Burkina Faso	61.1	69.6	76.8	..	64.6	..	8.0	11.7	12.5	13.9	14.6
Burundi	81.2	78.1	82.8	76.7	91.6	..	6.0	30.5	13.3	..	..
Cameroon	..	82.0	83.0	87.9	..	14.0	6.0	8.9	20.7	21.1	21.6
Cape Verde	..	..	99.7	87.5	..	12.0	11.0	15.3	39.1	..	..
Central African Republic	58.9	..	..	60.1	66.6	4.0	7.0	10.5	30.4	..	..
Chad	..	55.0	59.8	64.5	41.7	..	2.0	6.5	3.8	10.2	12.8
Comoros	..	83.9	83.9	77.8	..	0.0	..	3.0	17.0	..	..
Congo, Dem. Rep.	..	..	..	71.8	80.9	5.0	..	8.4	21.8	20.6	20.1
Congo, Rep.	83.4	82.9	89.1	95.2	..	14.0	12.0	8.5	26.1	..	..
Côte d'Ivoire	..	67.8	..	62.0	73.6	6.0	..	8.5	25.9	..	..
Djibouti	70.4	71.0	75.3	78.1	..	0.0	0.0	10.8	..	..	..
Equatorial Guinea	..	85.4	..	91.9	100.2	13.0	5.0	18.0	10.5	..	..
Eritrea	..	76.3	..	68.0	..	..	15.0	22.0	..	..	..
Ethiopia	67.6	64.6	76.1	66.1	..	..	2.0	21.9	40.6	40.7	40.6
Gabon	..	94.0	..	..	..	13.0	8.0	9.2	37.7	..	..
Gambia, The	..	79.8	..	67.6	..	8.0	2.0	13.2	20.9	..	..
Ghana	78.0	87.9	90.8	85.5	86.2	..	9.0	10.9	56.5	..	..
Guinea	45.2	62.6	73.9	42.5	57.4	..	9.0	19.3	30.3	..	..
Guinea-Bissau	..	64.7	..	..	..	20.0	..	14.0	10.8	..	..
Kenya	..	96.6	..	93.4	101.1	1.0	4.0	7.3	21.4	33.2	38.7
Lesotho	120.9	105.8	102.8	125.8	..	..	4.0	11.7	..	..	..
Liberia	..	73.1	..	51.2	..	..	..	12.5	23.6	..	..
Madagascar	97.2	95.7	95.9	85.6	93.9	7.0	8.0	6.9	24.2	..	..
Malawi	79.7	91.8	..	67.6	86.1	10.0	8.0	13.6	10.5	11.8	12.4
Mali	58.1	70.2	74.6	..	52.3	..	12.0	10.2	..	..	..
Mauritania	65.4	87.2	95.8	65.0	81.9	..	4.0	..	37.0	..	..
Mauritius	101.3	96.3	98.3	99.9	101.7	7.0	8.0	17.1	36.7	38.6	37.5
Mozambique	..	73.6	..	47.9	..	16.0	..	34.8	11.4	..	..
Namibia	108.3	104.5	..	103.7	102.6	7.0	22.0	26.9	..	48.8	..
Niger	..	68.2	72.2	37.4	44.2	5.0	1.0	12.4	11.0	8.5	7.8
Nigeria	..	..	..	82.3	..	..	..	6.4	34.0	..	..
Rwanda	..	94.7	99.1	86.4	97.9	17.0	17.0	48.8	14.6	..	..
São Tomé and Principe	..	..	99.1	..	..	12.0	9.0	7.3	..	..	..
Senegal	..	80.8	89.6	60.4	70.0	13.0	12.0	19.2	25.7	..	..
Seychelles	..	104.1	..	..	100.6	16.0	24.0	29.4	..	..	..
Sierra Leone	..	..	..	..	63.0	..	9.0	14.5	21.2	..	..
Somalia	..	..	..	..	..	4.0	..	7.8	21.9	..	..
South Africa	102.6	101.3	..	99.7	100.8	3.0	30.0	32.8	42.6	45.4	45.9
Sudan	77.6	..	89.0	71.5	84.4a	..	..	14.7	22.2	18.2	16.8
Swaziland	94.3	94.1	..	100.9	103.2	4.0	3.0	10.8	36.1	31.8	29.9
Tanzania	96.2	96.9	94.9	86.5	94.2	..	16.0	30.4	..	..	..
Togo	58.2	68.0	72.3	60.1	76.0	5.0	..	8.6	41.0	..	..
Uganda	81.2	92.2	..	75.8	86.1	12.0	18.0	29.8	35.6	..	..
Zambia	..	90.4	..	88.1	91.2	7.0	10.0	14.6	29.4	..	..
Zimbabwe	90.8	93.6	..	94.6	..	11.0	14.0	16.0	15.4	20.4	21.8
NORTH AFRICA											
Algeria	..	94.4	102.1	79.1	91.6	2.0	3.0	6.2	14.7	15.8	17.0
Egypt, Arab Rep.	79.0	..	..	72.0	87.6	4.0	2.0	2.0	20.5	19.0	20.6
Libya	..	..	..	83.5	..	..	..	7.7	15.0	..	..
Morocco	69.2	82.5	87.6	61.8	74.9	0.0	1.0	10.8	24.8	21.7	21.8
Tunisia	84.4	99.4	..	81.0	95.7	4.0	12.0	22.8	22.9	24.6	25.0

a. Provisional.

Table 3.4
Millennium Development Goal 4: reduce child mortality

	Under-five mortality rate (per 1,000)			Infant mortality rate (per 1,000 live births)			Child immunization rate, measles (% of children ages 12–23 months)		
	1990	2000	2005	1990	2000	2005	1990	2000	2005
SUB-SAHARAN AFRICA									
Angola	260	260	260	154	154	154	38	41	45
Benin	185	160	150	111	95	89	79	68	85
Botswana	58	101	120	45	74	87	87	90	90
Burkina Faso	210	196	191	113	100	96	79	59	84
Burundi	190	190	190	114	114	114	74	75	75
Cameroon	139	151	149	85	88	87	56	49	68
Cape Verde	60	42	35	45	31	26	79	80	65
Central African Republic	168	193	193	102	115	115	83	36	35
Chad	201	205	208	120	122	124	32	28	23
Comoros	120	84	71	88	62	53	87	70	80
Congo, Dem. Rep.	205	205	205	129	129	129	38	46	70
Congo, Rep.	110	108	108	83	81	81	75	34	56
Côte d'Ivoire	157	188	195	103	115	118	56	73	51
Djibouti	175	147	133	116	97	88	85	50	65
Equatorial Guinea	170	200	205	103	120	123	88	51	51
Eritrea	147	97	78	88	61	50	..	86	84
Ethiopia	204	151	127	122	92	80	38	52	59
Gabon	92	91	91	60	60	60	76	55	55
Gambia, The	151	142	137	103	99	97	86	85	84
Ghana	122	112	112	75	68	68	61	84	83
Guinea	234	183	160	139	110	97	35	42	59
Guinea-Bissau	253	215	200	153	132	124	53	59	80
Kenya	97	117	120	64	77	79	78	75	69
Lesotho	101	108	132	81	86	102	80	74	85
Liberia	235	235	235	157	157	157	..	52	94
Madagascar	168	137	119	103	84	74	47	56	59
Malawi	221	155	125	131	95	79	81	73	82
Mali	250	224	218	140	124	120	43	49	86
Mauritania	133	125	125	85	79	78	38	62	61
Mauritius	23	18	15	20	16	13	76	84	98
Mozambique	235	178	145	158	122	100	59	71	77
Namibia	86	69	62	60	50	46	57	69	73
Niger	320	270	256	191	159	150	25	34	83
Nigeria	230	207	194	120	107	100	54	35	35
Rwanda	173	203	203	103	118	118	83	74	89
São Tomé and Principe	118	118	118	75	75	75	71	69	88
Senegal	149	133	119	72	66	61	51	48	74
Seychelles	19	15	13	17	13	12	86	97	99
Sierra Leone	302	286	282	175	167	165	..	37	67
Somalia	225	225	225	133	133	133	30	38	35
South Africa	60	63	68	45	50	55	79	77	82
Sudan	120	97	90	74	65	62	57	47	60
Swaziland	110	142	160	78	98	110	85	72	60
Tanzania	161	141	122	102	88	76	73	78	91
Togo	152	142	139	88	80	78	73	58	70
Uganda	160	145	136	93	85	79	52	61	86
Zambia	180	182	182	101	102	102	90	85	84
Zimbabwe	80	117	132	53	73	81	87	70	85
NORTH AFRICA									
Algeria	69	44	39	54	37	34	83	80	83
Egypt, Arab Rep.	104	49	33	76	40	28	86	98	98
Libya	41	22	19	35	20	18	89	92	97
Morocco	89	54	40	69	45	36	80	93	97
Tunisia	52	31	24	41	25	20	93	95	96

Table 3.5

Millennium Development Goal 5: improve maternal health

	Maternal mortality ratio, modeled estimate (per 100,000 live births)	Births attended by skilled health staff (% of total)			
		Surveys 1990–99		Surveys 2000–05	
	2000	Year[a]	Percent	Year[a]	Percent
SUB–SAHARAN AFRICA					
Angola	1,700	1996	23	2001	45
Benin	850	1996	60	2005	75
Botswana	100	1996	87	2000	94
Burkina Faso	1,000	1999	31	2003	38
Burundi	1,000	..	..	2000	25
Cameroon	730	1998	55	2004	62
Cape Verde	150	1998	89	..	..
Central African Republic	1,100	1995	46	2000	44
Chad	1,100	1997	15	2004	14
Comoros	480	1996	52	2000	62
Congo, Dem. Rep.	990	..	..	2001	61
Congo, Rep.	510	..	..	2005	86
Côte d'Ivoire	690	1999	47	2004	68
Djibouti	730	..	..	2003	61
Equatorial Guinea	880	1994	5	2000	65
Eritrea	630	1995	21	2002	28
Ethiopia	850	..	..	2005	6
Gabon	420	..	..	2000	86
Gambia, The	540	1990	44	2000	55
Ghana	540	1998	44	2003	47
Guinea	740	1999	35	2003	56
Guinea-Bissau	1,100	1995	25	2000	35
Kenya	1,000	1998	44	2003	42
Lesotho	550	1993	50	2004	55
Liberia	760	..	..	2000	51
Madagascar	550	1997	47	2004	51
Malawi	1,800	1992	55	2004	56
Mali	1,200	1996	24	2001	41
Mauritania	1,000	1991	40	2001	57
Mauritius	24	1999	99	2004	99
Mozambique	1,000	1997	44	2003	48
Namibia	300	1992	68	2000	76
Niger	1,600	1998	18	2000	16
Nigeria	800	1999	42	2003	35
Rwanda	1,400	1992	26	2005	39
São Tomé and Principe	..	..	..	2003	76
Senegal	690	1997	47	2002	58
Seychelles	..	..	..	..	..
Sierra Leone	2,000	..	..	2000	42
Somalia	1,100	1999	34	2002	25
South Africa	230	1998	84	2003	92
Sudan	590	1993	86	2000	87
Swaziland	370	1994	56	2002	74
Tanzania	1,500	1999	36	2005	43
Togo	570	1998	51	2003	61
Uganda	880	1995	38	2001	39
Zambia	750	1999	47	2002	43
Zimbabwe	1,100	1999	73	..	..
NORTH AFRICA					
Algeria	140	1992	77	2002	96
Egypt, Arab Rep.	84	1998	55	2005	74
Libya	97	1995	94	..	..
Morocco	220	1995	40	2004	63
Tunisia	120	1995	81	2000	90

a. Data are for most recent year available during the period specified.

Table 3.6

Millennium Development Goal 6: combat HIV/AIDS, malaria, and other diseases

	Prevalence of HIV (% of ages 15–49)	Contraceptive prevalence (% of women ages 15–49)				Deaths due to malaria (per 100,000 people)	
		Surveys 1990–99		Surveys 2000–05		Surveys 2000–05	
	2005	Year[a]	Percent	Year[a]	Percent	Year[a]	Number
SUB-SAHARAN AFRICA							
Angola	3.7	..	..	2001	6.0	2000	354
Benin	1.8	1996	16.4	2001	18.6	2000	177
Botswana	24.1	..	..	2000	48.0	2000	15
Burkina Faso	2.0	1999	11.9	2003	13.8	2000	292
Burundi	3.3	..	..	2000	16.0	2000	143
Cameroon	5.4	1998	19.3	2004	26.0	2000	108
Cape Verde	..	1998	52.9	..	..	2000	22
Central African Republic	10.7	1995	14.8	2000	28.0	2000	137
Chad	3.5	1997	4.1	2004	2.8	2000	207
Comoros	0.1	1996	21.0	2000	26.0	2000	80
Congo, Dem. Rep.	3.2	..	..	2001	31.0	2000	224
Congo, Rep.	5.3	..	..	2005	44.3	2000	78
Côte d'Ivoire	7.1	1999	15.0	..	..	2000	76
Djibouti	3.1	..	..	2002	9.0	..	..
Equatorial Guinea	3.2	..	..	..	..	2000	152
Eritrea	2.4	1995	8.0	2002	8.0	2000	74
Ethiopia	..	1990	4.3	2005	14.7	2000	198
Gabon	7.9	..	..	2000	32.7	2000	80
Gambia, The	2.4	..	..	2001	18.0	2000	52
Ghana	2.3	1998	22.0	2003	25.2	2000	70
Guinea	1.5	1999	6.2	2003	7.0	2000	200
Guinea-Bissau	3.8	..	..	2000	8.0	2000	150
Kenya	6.1	1998	39.0	2003	39.3	2000	63
Lesotho	23.2	1991	23.2	2000	30.0	2000	84
Liberia	..	..	..	2000	10.0	2000	201
Madagascar	0.5	1997	19.4	2004	27.1	2000	184
Malawi	14.1	1996	22.0	2000	30.6	2000	275
Mali	1.7	1996	6.7	2001	8.1	2000	454
Mauritania	0.7	..	..	2001	8.0	2000	108
Mauritius	0.6	1991	75.0	2002	76.0	..	..
Mozambique	16.1	1997	5.6	2003	25.5	2000	232
Namibia	19.6	1992	28.9	2000	43.7	2000	52
Niger	1.1	1998	8.2	2000	14.0	2000	469
Nigeria	3.9	1999	15.3	2003	12.6	2000	141
Rwanda	3.1	1992	21.2	2005	17.4	2000	200
São Tomé and Principe	..	..	..	2000	29.0	2000	80
Senegal	0.9	1997	12.9	2000	10.5	2000	72
Seychelles	..	..	..	..	..	..	..
Sierra Leone	1.6	..	..	2000	4.0	2000	312
Somalia	0.9	..	..	..	..	2000	81
South Africa	18.8	1998	56.3	2003	60.3	2000	0
Sudan	1.6	1993	10.0	2000	7.0	2000	70
Swaziland	33.4	..	..	2002	48.0	2000	0
Tanzania	6.5	1999	25.4	2005	26.4	2000	130
Togo	3.2	1998	23.5	2000	26.0	2000	47
Uganda	6.7	1995	14.8	2001	22.8	2000	152
Zambia	17.0	1999	53.5	2002	34.2	2000	141
Zimbabwe	20.1	1999	53.5	..	..	2000	1
NORTH AFRICA							
Algeria	0.1	1992	50.8	2002	57.0	..	..
Egypt, Arab Rep.	0.1	1998	51.7	2005	59.2	..	..
Libya	..	1995	45.0	..	..	..	..
Morocco	0.1	1997	59.0	2004	63.0	..	..
Tunisia	0.1	1995	60.0	2000	66.0	..	..

a. Data are for most recent year available during the period specified.

Children sleeping under insecticide-treated bednets (% of children under age 5)		Incidence of tuberculosis (per 100,000 people)				Tuberculosis cases detected under DOTS (% of estimated cases)			
Surveys 2000–05		Surveys 1990–99		Surveys 2000–05		Surveys 1990–99		Surveys 2000–05	
Year[a]	Percent	Year[a]	Number	Year[a]	Number	Year[a]	Percent	Year[a]	Percent
2001	2.0	1999	243.5	2005	268.8	1999	51.3	2005	85.4
2001	7.0	1999	84.0	2005	87.9	1999	84.7	2005	83.3
..	..	1999	577.2	2005	654.5	1999	68.5	2005	68.5
2003	2.0	1999	178.1	2005	223.3	1999	16.4	2005	17.6
2000	1.0	1999	282.8	2005	333.7	1999	37.1	2005	29.6
2004	1.0	1999	147.7	2005	174.3	1999	21.6	2005	105.8
..	..	1999	167.1	2005	174.4	..	..	2005	33.9
2000	2.0	1999	265.9	2005	313.8	1996	61.4	2005	40.4
2000	0.6	1999	230.2	2005	271.6	1999	36.2	2005	21.7
2000	9.0	1999	58.5	2005	45.0	1998	54.5	2005	48.9
2001	1.0	1999	301.9	2005	356.2	1999	53.9	2005	72.4
..	..	1999	310.7	2005	366.6	1998	50.0	2005	57.4
2004	4.0	1999	324.1	2005	382.4	1999	43.8	2005	37.6
..	..	1999	690.4	2005	762.3	1999	74.2	2005	42.1
2000	1.0	1999	197.2	2005	232.7	1998	81.0	2004	80.8
2002	4.0	1999	255.3	2005	281.9	1999	13.7	2005	12.5
2005	1.5	1999	291.5	2005	343.9	1999	25.1	2005	32.7
..	..	1999	209.0	2005	307.5	..	..	2005	57.5
2000	15.0	1999	219.6	2005	242.4	1998	75.7	2005	69.4
2003	4.0	1999	212.0	2005	205.0	1999	30.8	2005	37.5
2003	4.0	1999	185.6	2005	235.9	1999	52.3	2005	55.6
2000	7.0	1999	186.8	2005	206.3	..	..	2005	79.1
2003	5.0	1999	390.9	2005	641.0	1999	54.6	2005	42.8
..	..	1999	527.0	2005	695.8	1998	74.8	2005	84.8
..	..	1999	255.4	2005	301.4	1998	41.5	2005	50.0
2000	0.2	1999	211.5	2005	233.9	1998	67.6	2005	67.0
2004	15.0	1999	419.4	2005	409.4	1999	41.8	2005	38.6
2003	8.0	1999	288.6	2005	277.8	1999	16.4	2005	21.1
2004	2.0	1999	269.9	2005	298.0	..	..	2005	28.2
..	..	1999	64.9	2005	62.3	1999	35.6	2005	31.7
..	..	1999	379.1	2005	447.3	1999	46.0	2005	48.7
2000	3.0	1999	591.0	2005	697.3	1999	83.2	2005	89.9
2000	6.0	1999	148.1	2005	163.6	1999	35.0	2005	49.6
2003	1.0	1999	239.5	2005	282.6	1999	13.2	2005	21.6
2005	13.0	1999	306.0	2005	361.0	1999	43.5	2005	29.1
2000	22.8	1999	116.2	2005	105.4	..	..	..	..
2005	14.0	1999	230.7	2005	254.7	1999	48.2	2005	50.7
..	..	1999	37.2	2005	33.7	1998	69.2	2005	65.3
2000	2.0	1999	349.0	2005	475.4	1998	36.0	2005	37.4
..	..	1999	262.0	2005	224.1	1999	43.3	2005	85.8
..	..	1999	508.4	2005	599.9	1999	57.5	2005	103.1
2000	0.0	1999	206.7	2005	228.2	1999	27.6	2005	34.6
2000	0.0	1999	699.3	2005	1261.9	..	..	2005	42.3
2005	16.0	1999	327.7	2005	342.0	1999	50.6	2005	44.9
2005	54.0	1999	357.7	2005	372.8	1999	11.1	2005	17.9
2001	0.0	1999	323.8	2005	368.8	1999	57.0	2005	45.1
2002	7.0	1999	605.4	2005	600.1	..	..	2005	51.6
..	..	1999	614.8	2005	601.0	1999	46.9	2005	41.3
..	..	1999	46.9	2005	55.3	1997	132.5	2005	105.9
..	..	1999	31.8	2005	25.0	1999	31.3	2005	62.7
..	..	1999	23.5	2005	18.4	1999	146.2	2005	177.7
..	..	1999	113.8	2005	89.2	1999	91.1	2005	101.0
..	..	1999	26.8	2005	24.4	1999	93.5	2005	82.5

Table 3.7

3.7 Millennium Development Goal 7: ensure environmental sustainability

	Forest area (% of total land area)			Nationally protected areas (% of total land area)	GDP per unit of energy use (constant 2000 PPP $ per kg of oil equivalent)		
	1990	2000	2005	2004	1990	2000	2004
SUB-SAHARAN AFRICA							
Angola	48.9	47.9	47.4	10.1	3.7	3.1	3.3
Benin	30.0	24.2	21.3	23.9	2.6	3.4	3.3
Botswana	24.2	22.1	21.1	30.9	6.2	7.3	8.6
Burkina Faso	26.1	25.3	24.8	15.4	..	..	..
Burundi	11.3	7.7	5.9	5.7	..	..	..
Cameroon	52.7	48.0	45.6	8.0	4.7	4.4	4.5
Cape Verde	14.4	20.3	20.8	0.2	..	..	..
Central African Republic	37.2	36.8	36.5	16.6	..	..	..
Chad	10.4	9.8	9.5	9.5	..	..	..
Comoros	5.4	3.6	2.2	..	..	..	..
Congo, Dem. Rep.	62.0	59.6	58.9	8.6	5.0	2.3	2.2
Congo, Rep.	66.5	66.0	65.8	18.0	2.3	3.9	3.3
Côte d'Ivoire	32.1	32.5	32.7	17.1	5.2	3.8	3.7
Djibouti	0.3	0.3	0.3	0.4	..	..	..
Equatorial Guinea	66.3	60.9	58.2	16.2	..	..	..
Eritrea	..	15.6	15.4	5.0	..	..	..
Ethiopia	13.7	13.7	13.0	18.6	2.6	2.7	2.8
Gabon	85.1	84.7	84.5	3.4	4.8	5.0	4.9
Gambia, The	44.2	46.1	47.1	3.5	..	..	..
Ghana	32.7	26.8	24.2	16.2	4.6	4.8	5.4
Guinea	30.1	28.1	27.4	6.4	..	..	..
Guinea-Bissau	78.8	75.4	73.7	0.0	..	..	..
Kenya	6.5	6.3	6.2	12.6	2.2	2.1	2.1
Lesotho	0.2	0.2	0.3	0.2	..	..	..
Liberia	42.1	35.9	32.7	15.8	..	..	..
Madagascar	23.5	22.4	22.1	3.1	..	..	..
Malawi	41.4	37.9	36.2	20.6	..	..	..
Mali	11.5	10.7	10.3	3.8	..	..	..
Mauritania	0.4	0.3	0.3	0.2	..	..	..
Mauritius	19.2	18.7	18.2	3.3	..	..	..
Mozambique	25.5	24.9	24.6	5.8	1.3	2.2	2.6
Namibia	10.6	9.8	9.3	5.6	..	11.1	10.2
Niger	1.5	1.0	1.0	7.7	..	..	..
Nigeria	18.9	14.4	12.2	6.0	1.1	1.2	1.4
Rwanda	12.9	13.9	19.5	7.9	..	..	..
São Tomé and Principe	28.1	28.1	28.1	..	..	..	..
Senegal	48.6	46.2	45.0	11.2	5.0	6.0	6.5
Seychelles	87.0	87.0	87.0	8.3	..	..	..
Sierra Leone	42.5	39.8	38.5	4.5	..	..	..
Somalia	13.2	12.0	11.4	0.3	..	..	..
South Africa	7.6	7.6	7.6	6.1	3.9	3.7	3.7
Sudan	32.1	29.7	28.4	5.2	2.7	4.1	3.7
Swaziland	27.4	30.1	31.5	3.5	..	..	..
Tanzania	46.9	42.2	39.9	42.4	1.4	1.3	1.3
Togo	12.6	8.9	7.1	11.9	4.3	3.7	3.1
Uganda	25.0	20.6	18.4	32.6	..	..	..
Zambia	66.1	60.1	57.1	42.0	1.5	1.3	1.5
Zimbabwe	57.5	49.4	45.3	14.9	3.0	3.1	2.6
NORTH AFRICA							
Algeria	0.8	0.9	1.0	5.0	5.7	5.6	6.0
Egypt, Arab Rep.	0.0	0.1	0.1	5.6	5.1	5.3	4.9
Libya	0.1	0.1	0.1	0.1	..	..	..
Morocco	9.6	9.7	9.8	1.1	11.9	9.9	10.3
Tunisia	4.1	6.2	6.8	1.5	6.7	7.9	8.2

a. Data are for most recent year available during the period specified.

Carbon dioxide emissions (metric tons per capita)			Solid fuels use (% of population)	Population with sustainable access to an improved water source (%)			Population with sustainable access to improved sanitation (%)		
1990	2000	2003	2000–05[a]	1990	2000	2004	1990	2000	2004
0.4	0.5	0.6	..	36	46	53	29	30	31
0.1	0.2	0.3	95.6	63	65	67	12	26	33
1.5	2.3	2.3	..	93	95	95	38	41	42
0.1	0.1	0.1	97.5	38	54	61	7	11	13
0.0	0.0	0.0	..	69	77	79	44	38	36
0.1	0.2	0.2	82.6	50	61	66	48	50	51
0.2	0.3	0.3	..	..	80	80	..	41	43
0.1	0.1	0.1	..	52	70	75	23	26	27
0.0	0.0	0.0	..	19	35	42	7	8	9
0.2	0.2	0.2	..	93	88	86	32	34	33
0.1	0.0	0.0	..	43	45	46	16	25	30
0.5	0.3	0.4	83.2	..	57	58	..	27	27
0.4	0.4	0.3	..	69	83	84	21	33	37
0.6	0.5	0.5	..	72	73	73	79	81	82
0.3	0.4	0.3	..	..	43	43	..	52	53
..	0.2	0.2	..	43	54	60	7	8	9
0.1	0.1	0.1	89.0	23	22	22	3	8	13
6.3	1.2	0.9	34.1	..	86	88	..	36	36
0.2	0.2	0.2	..	..	82	82	..	53	53
0.2	0.3	0.4	91.8	55	70	75	15	18	18
0.2	0.2	0.1	79.8	44	49	50	14	17	18
0.2	0.2	0.2	..	..	58	59	..	34	35
0.2	0.3	0.3	87.1	45	57	61	40	43	43
..	..	..	62.1	..	79	79	37	37	37
0.2	0.1	0.1	..	55	61	61	39	28	27
0.1	0.1	0.1	98.3	40	45	46	14	27	32
0.1	0.1	0.1	97.8	40	64	73	47	58	61
0.0	0.0	0.0	95.9	34	45	50	36	43	46
1.3	0.9	0.9	70.5	38	47	53	31	33	34
1.4	2.3	2.6	..	100	100	100	..	94	94
0.1	0.1	0.1	96.9	36	42	43	20	27	32
0.0	0.9	1.2	65.9	57	80	87	24	25	25
0.1	0.1	0.1	..	39	44	46	7	11	13
0.5	0.4	0.4	76.6	49	49	48	39	42	44
0.1	0.1	0.1	99.4	59	70	74	37	40	42
0.6	0.6	0.6	..	..	79	79	..	24	25
0.4	0.4	0.4	58.7	65	73	76	33	50	57
1.6	7.0	6.6	..	88	87	88	..	..	..
0.1	0.1	0.1	..	..	57	57	..	38	39
0.0	..	..	..	..	29	29	..	25	26
8.1	7.4	7.9	..	83	87	88	69	66	65
0.2	0.2	0.3	..	64	69	70	33	34	34
0.6	1.0	0.9	..	..	62	62	..	48	48
0.1	0.1	0.1	98.1	46	58	62	47	47	47
0.2	0.3	0.4	..	50	51	52	37	34	35
0.0	0.1	0.1	97.4	44	55	60	42	43	43
0.3	0.2	0.2	83.6	50	55	58	44	51	55
1.6	1.2	0.9	..	78	80	81	50	52	53
3.0	5.4	5.1	..	94	89	85	88	91	92
1.4	2.1	2.0	..	94	97	98	54	65	70
8.7	8.8	8.9	..	71	71	71	97	97	97
1.0	1.2	1.3	..	75	79	81	56	69	73
1.6	2.1	2.1	..	81	90	93	75	83	85

JOLIET JUNIOR COLLEGE
JOLIET, IL 60431

3.8 Millennium Development Goal 8: develop a global partnership for development

	Debt sustainability					
	Heavily Indebted Poor Countries (HIPC) Debt Initiative		Debt service relief committed ($ millions)	Public and publicly guaranteed debt service (% of exports)		
	Decision point 2006	Completion point 2006	2006	1990	2000	2004–05[a]
SUB-SAHARAN AFRICA						
Angola	..	..	..	7.1	20.4	9.0
Benin	Jul. 2000	Mar. 2003	460	8.6	10.7	..
Botswana			..	4.3	2.0	0.9
Burkina Faso	Jul. 2000	Apr. 2002	930	7.7	15.1	..
Burundi	Oct. 2000	Floating	1,472	40.7	25.1	41.2
Cameroon	Oct. 2000	Apr. 2006	4,917	12.5	14.0	
Cape Verde	..	..	..	8.9	10.5	8.3
Central African Republic	..	..	..	7.5	..	..
Chad	May 2001	Floating	260	2.4	..	..
Comoros	..	..	..	2.5	..	..
Congo, Dem. Rep.	Jul. 2003	Floating	10,389	..	..	..
Congo, Rep.	..	..	2,881	31.6	0.5	2.0
Côte d'Ivoire	Mar. 1998	..	..	14.7	14.9	1.9
Djibouti	..	..	..	..	..	..
Equatorial Guinea	..	..	..	2.5	..	..
Eritrea	..	..	..	..	2.8	..
Ethiopia	Nov. 2001	Apr. 2004	3,275	33.1	12.2	4.1
Gabon	..	..	..	3.8	8.8	..
Gambia, The	Dec. 2000	Floating	90	17.9	..	14.1
Ghana	Feb. 2002	Jul. 2004	3,500	19.9	12.0	5.9
Guinea	Dec. 2000	Floating	800	17.7	17.3	..
Guinea-Bissau	Dec. 2000	Floating	790	22.0	..	..
Kenya	..	..	..	22.7	15.7	3.8
Lesotho	..	..	..	4.1	10.3	5.0
Liberia	..	..	..	..	..	..
Madagascar	Dec. 2000	Oct. 2004	1,900	31.9	8.4	14.5
Malawi	Dec. 2000	Floating	1,000	22.4	10.8	..
Mali	Aug. 2000	Mar. 2003	895	9.7	10.2	..
Mauritania	Feb. 2000	Jun. 2002	1,100	24.8	..	..
Mauritius	..	..	..	4.5	16.4	5.4
Mozambique	Apr. 2000	Sep. 2001	4,300	17.2	7.0	2.5
Namibia	..	..	..	..	..	..
Niger	Dec. 2000	Jun. 2004	1,190	3.2	6.0	..
Nigeria	..	..	..	22.3	8.2	16.7
Rwanda	Dec. 2000	Jun. 2005	1,316	10.2	14.8	6.8
São Tomé and Principe	Dec. 2000	Floating	200	28.6	21.0	..
Senegal	Jun. 2000	Apr. 2004	850	13.7	13.2	..
Seychelles	..	..	..	7.6	3.3	6.6
Sierra Leone	Mar. 2002	Floating	950	7.8	29.6	7.6
Somalia	..	..	..	..	..	..
South Africa	..	..	..	..	5.5	1.5
Sudan	..	..	..	4.5	10.1	7.2
Swaziland	..	..	..	5.6	2.4	1.8
Tanzania	Apr. 2000	Nov. 2001	3,000	25.1	10.8	2.2
Togo	..	..	..	8.6	3.2	..
Uganda	Feb. 2000	May 2000	1,950	47.1	6.5	9.5
Zambia	Dec. 2000	Apr. 2005	3,900	12.6	16.9	..
Zimbabwe	..	..	..	18.2	..	..
NORTH AFRICA						
Algeria	..	..	..	63.3	..	..
Egypt, Arab Rep.	..	..	..	23.2	8.5	6.2
Libya	..	..	..	..	..	..
Morocco	..	..	..	23.1	23.0	12.2
Tunisia	..	..	..	23.0	20.0	12.0

Note: 0 indicates less than 1.

a. Data are for most recent year available during the period specified.

Youth unemployment rate (ages 15–24)						Information and communications								
Total (share of total labor force)		Male (share of male labor force)		Female (share of female labor force)		Fixed-line and mobile telephone subscribers (per 1,000 people)			Personal computers (per 1,000 people)			Internet users (per 1,000 people)		
Year	Percent	Year	Percent	Year	Percent	1990	2000	2005	1990	2000	2005	1995	1999	2005
..	..	..	..	..	..	7	7	75	..	1	..	..	1	11
..	..	..	..	..	..	3	15	98	..	1	4	..	2	50
2001	39.7	2001	33.9	2001	46.1	19	192	541	..	34	..	1	14	34
..	..	..	..	..	..	2	7	51	0	1	2	..	1	5
..	..	..	..	..	..	1	6	..	..	1	..	0	1	5
..	..	..	..	..	..	4	13	..	..	3	..	..	3	15
..	..	..	..	..	..	23	165	302	..	56	..	..	18	49
..	..	..	..	..	..	2	4	27	..	2	3	..	1	3
..	..	..	..	..	..	1	2	..	..	1	..	..	0	4
..	..	..	..	..	..	8	13	55	0	6	..	..	3	33
..	..	..	..	..	..	1	1	48	..	..	..	..	0	2
..	..	..	..	..	..	6	27	..	..	3	..	..	0	13
..	..	..	..	..	..	6	44	..	..	5	..	0	2	11
..	..	..	..	..	..	10	14	69	2	9	24	0	2	13
..	..	..	..	..	..	4	25	212	..	5	..	..	2	14
..	..	..	..	..	..	..	9	18	..	2	8	0	1	16
2005	7.7	2005	4.1	2005	11.2	3	4	14	..	1	..	0	0	2
..	..	..	..	..	..	22	125	498	..	9	33	..	12	48
..	..	..	..	..	..	7	30	192	..	11	..	0	9	..
2000	15.9	2000	12.7	2000	19.4	3	17	143	0	3	..	0	2	18
..	..	..	..	..	..	2	8	..	..	3	..	0	1	5
..	..	..	..	..	..	6	8	..	..	..	..	..	2	20
..	..	..	..	..	..	8	14	143	0	5	..	0	3	32
..	..	..	..	..	..	8	25	163	..	..	..	..	2	..
..	..	..	..	..	..	4	3	..	..	..	..	..	0	..
..	..	..	..	..	..	3	7	31	..	2	..	..	2	5
..	..	..	..	..	..	3	8	41	..	1	2	..	1	4
..	..	..	..	..	..	1	4	70	..	1	3	..	1	4
..	..	..	..	..	..	3	13	256	..	10	..	..	2	7
2005	25.9	2005	20.5	2005	34.3	55	388	863	4	101	..	..	73	..
..	..	..	..	..	..	4	8	..	..	3	..	..	1	..
2001	44.8	2001	40.4	2001	49.3	38	101	..	..	40	..	0	16	..
..	..	..	..	..	..	1	2	23	..	0	1	..	0	2
..	..	..	..	..	..	3	5	151	..	6	..	..	1	38
..	..	..	..	..	..	2	7	..	..	..	..	..	1	6
..	..	..	..	..	..	19	33	..	..	..	..	..	47	..
..	..	..	..	..	..	6	44	171	2	16	21	0	4	46
..	..	..	..	..	..	124	574	928	..	136	189	..	74	249
..	..	..	..	..	..	3	7	..	..	..	..	0	1	..
..	..	..	..	..	..	2	15	73	..	..	..	0	2	11
2003	60.1	2003	55.8	2003	64.8	94	302	825	7	66	85	7	55	109
..	..	..	..	..	..	2	13	69	..	3	90	0	1	77
..	..	..	..	..	..	18	62	208	..	12	..	0	10	..
..	..	..	..	..	..	3	8	..	..	3	..	..	1	..
..	..	..	..	..	..	3	17	82	..	19	30	0	19	49
..	..	..	..	..	..	2	8	56	..	3	9	0	2	17
..	..	..	..	..	..	8	17	89	..	7	..	0	2	..
2002	24.9	2002	28.2	2002	21.4	12	41	79	0	16	92	0	4	77
2004	43.4	2004	42.8	2004	46.3	32	61	494	1	7	11	0	5	58
2002	27.1	2002	21.4	2002	40	29	102	325	..	12	38	0	7	68
..	..	..	..	..	..	51	122	..	..	..	..	..	2	..
2003	17	2003	17.4	2003	15.9	17	135	455	..	13	25	0	7	153
2005	30.7	2005	31.4	2005	29.3	37	112	692	3	22	57	0	27	95

Table 4.1 Status of Paris Declaration indicators

	PDI-1. Operational development strategies Comprehensive Development Framework composite rating of national development strategy[a] 2005	PDI-2a. Reliable public financial management Benchmark rating of public expenditure management systems (0–15)[b] 2005	PDI-6. Avoidance of parallel project implementation units Number of existing parallel project implementation units 2005	PDI-11. Monitorable performance assessment frameworks Overall rating[a] 2005	PDI-12. Mutual accountability Independent assessment framework in place? 2005
SUB–SAHARAN AFRICA					
Angola	..	..	..	..	..
Benin	C	4	29	C	No
Botswana	..	..	..	..	..
Burkina Faso	C	4	131	C	No
Burundi	D	2.5	37	D	No
Cameroon	..	..	..	D	Yes
Cape Verde	C	3.5	10	..	..
Central African Republic	..	..	..	..	..
Chad	..	..	..	..	..
Comoros	..	..	..	..	No
Congo, Dem. Rep.	..	..	34	..	No
Congo, Rep.	D	2.5	..	D	..
Côte d'Ivoire	..	..	..	..	..
Djibouti	..	..	..	..	..
Equatorial Guinea	..	..	..	..	..
Eritrea	..	..	..	..	..
Ethiopia	C	3.5	103	C	Yes
Gabon	..	..	..	..	..
Gambia, The	..	..	..	..	..
Ghana	C	3.5	45	C	Yes
Guinea	..	..	..	..	..
Guinea-Bissau	..	..	..	..	..
Kenya	D	3.5	17	C	No
Lesotho	..	..	..	..	..
Liberia	..	..	..	..	..
Madagascar	..	..	..	..	..
Malawi	C	3	69	C	Yes
Mali	C	4	65	D	No
Mauritania	B	2	23	C	No
Mauritius	..	..	..	..	..
Mozambique	C	3.5	40	C	Yes
Namibia	..	..	..	..	..
Niger	C	3.5	52	D	No
Nigeria	..	..	..	..	..
Rwanda	B	3.5	48	C	No
São Tomé and Principe	..	..	..	..	..
Senegal	C	3.5	23	C	No
Seychelles	..	..	..	..	..
Sierra Leone	..	..	..	..	..
Somalia	..	..	..	..	..
South Africa	..	..	15	..	Yes
Sudan	..	..	..	..	..
Swaziland	..	..	..	..	..
Tanzania	B	4.5	56	B	Yes
Togo	..	..	..	..	..
Uganda	B	4	54	B	No
Zambia	C	3	24	D	Yes
Zimbabwe	..	..	..	..	..

Note: See technical notes for further details. PDI is Paris Declaration Indicator.

a. Ratings range from A to E, where A means the development strategy substantially achieves good practices; B means it is largely developed toward achieving good practices; C means it reflects action taken toward achieving good practices; D means it incorporates some elements of good practice; and E means it reflects little action toward achieving good practices.

b. Ratings range from 0 to 15 and indicate the total number of the 15 required standard benchmarks that a country has met. The higher the number the less system upgrading is required.

Table 5.1 Business environment

	Number of startup procedures to register a business 2006	Time to start a business (days) 2006	Cost to start a business (% of GNI per capita) 2006	Number of procedures to register property 2006	Time to register property (days) 2006	Number of procedures to enforce a contract 2006	Time to enforce a contract (days) 2006	Protecting investors disclosure index (0 low to 10 high) 2006	Time to resolve insolvency (years) 2006	Rigidity of employment index (0 least rigid to 100 most rigid) 2006
SUB–SAHARAN AFRICA	**11**	**61**	**164**	**7**	**109**	**39**	**595**	**4**	**4**	**47**
Angola	13	124	487	7	334	47	1,011	5	6	64
Benin	7	31	173	3	50	49	720	5	4	46
Botswana	11	108	11	4	30	26	501	8	1	20
Burkina Faso	8	34	121	8	107	41	446	6	4	64
Burundi	11	43	222	5	94	47	403	..	4	59
Cameroon	12	37	152	5	93	58	800	8	3	56
Cape Verde	12	52	46	6	83	40	465	1	..	44
Central African Republic	10	14	209	3	69	45	660	4	5	73
Chad	19	75	226	6	44	52	743	3	10	60
Comoros	11	23	192	5	24	60	721	6	..	46
Congo, Dem. Rep.	13	155	481	8	57	51	685	3	5	78
Congo, Rep.	8	71	215	7	137	47	560	4	3	69
Côte d'Ivoire	11	45	134	6	32	25	525	6	2	45
Djibouti	11	37	222	7	49	59	1,225	5	5	46
Equatorial Guinea	20	136	101	6	23	38	553	6	..	66
Eritrea	13	76	116	12	101	35	305	4	2	20
Ethiopia	7	16	46	13	43	30	690	4	2	34
Gabon	10	60	163	8	60	32	880	5	5	59
Gambia, The	8	27	292	5	371	26	247	2	3	27
Ghana	12	81	50	7	382	29	552	7	2	34
Guinea	13	49	187	6	104	44	276	5	4	41
Guinea-Bissau	17	233	261	9	211	40	1,140	0	..	77
Kenya	13	54	46	8	73	25	360	4	5	28
Lesotho	8	73	40	6	101	58	695	2	3	35
Liberia	..	..	..	..	..	..	..	..	..	..
Madagascar	10	21	35	8	134	29	591	5	..	57
Malawi	10	37	135	6	118	40	337	4	3	21
Mali	13	42	202	5	33	28	860	6	4	51
Mauritania	11	82	122	4	49	40	400	0	8	59
Mauritius	6	46	8	6	210	37	630	6	2	30
Mozambique	13	113	86	8	42	38	1,010	7	5	54
Namibia	10	95	18	9	23	31	270	5	2	27
Niger	11	24	417	5	49	33	360	4	5	77
Nigeria	9	43	54	16	80	23	457	6	2	21
Rwanda	9	16	188	5	371	27	310	2	..	49
São Tomé and Principe	10	144	147	7	62	67	405	6	..	67
Senegal	10	58	113	6	114	33	780	4	3	61
Seychelles	9	38	9	4	33	29	720	4	..	34
Sierra Leone	9	26	1,195	8	235	58	515	3	3	63
Somalia	..	..	..	..	..	..	..	..	..	..
South Africa	9	35	7	6	23	26	600	8	2	41
Sudan	10	39	59	6	9	67	770	0	..	55
Swaziland	13	61	41	11	46	31	972	1	2	17
Tanzania	13	30	92	10	123	21	393	3	3	67
Togo	13	53	253	7	242	37	535	4	3	58
Uganda	17	30	114	13	227	19	484	7	2	7
Zambia	6	35	30	6	70	21	404	3	3	23
Zimbabwe	10	96	36	4	30	33	410	8	3	34
NORTH AFRICA	**10**	**17**	**28**	**8**	**87**	**42**	**626**	**4**	**2**	**52**
Algeria	14	24	22	15	51	49	397	6	3	45
Egypt, Arab Rep.	10	19	69	7	193	55	1,010	5	4	53
Libya	..	..	..	..	..	..	..	..	..	..
Morocco	6	12	13	4	46	42	615	6	2	63
Tunisia	10	11	9	5	57	21	481	0	1	46

Table 5.2 Investment climate

	Private investment (% of GDP) 2005[a]	Net foreign direct investment ($ millions) 2005	Domestic credit to private sector (% of GDP) 2005	Viewed by firms as a major constraint (% of firms)									
				Policy uncertainty 2006	Corruption 2006	Courts 2006	Lack of confidence in courts to uphold property rights 2006	Crime 2006	Tax rates 2006	Finance 2006	Electricity 2006	Labor regulations 2006	Labor skills 2006
SUB–SAHARAN AFRICA	**13.3**	**20,037.6**	..	..	..	..	..	..	..	..	..	..	..
Angola	2.8	1,639.0	4.8	1.6	12.5	..	51.0	6.2	3.0	11.6	34.5	..	1.1
Benin	12.2	13.6	16.6	..	..	..	..	..	..	..	..	..	..
Botswana	9.7	59.8	19.0	0.7	7.9	1.4	31.4	10.9	7.3	24.3	1.7	1.5	9.4
Burkina Faso	..	22.8	17.3	..	5.1	0.7	29.9	1.4	18.8	37.0	19.6	..	..
Burundi	1.7	1.5	20.8	14.3	2.2	0.2	36.9	2.9	3.7	16.0	40.7	..	0.1
Cameroon	14.7	302.9	9.4	..	5.2	1.2	37.3	2.9	32.6	13.4	15.1	1.2	..
Cape Verde	..	41.3	39.0	..	..	2.0	35.2	1.0	13.3	16.3	35.7	1.0	4.1
Central African Republic	..	..	6.7	..	..	..	..	..	..	..	..	..	..
Chad	12.0	123.8	3.1	..	..	..	..	..	..	..	..	..	..
Comoros	4.8	2.0	8.1	..	..	..	..	..	..	..	..	..	..
Congo, Dem. Rep.	10.5	551.0	1.9	5.3	0.5	..	56.5	1.8	9.6	14.5	45.5	..	1.0
Congo, Rep.	16.6	732.3	2.9	..	..	..	..	..	..	..	..	..	..
Côte d'Ivoire	8.4	283.1	13.8	..	..	..	..	..	..	..	..	..	..
Djibouti	15.0	60.0	20.1	..	..	..	..	..	..	..	..	..	..
Equatorial Guinea	27.6	1,869.5	5.4	..	..	..	..	..	..	..	..	..	..
Eritrea	4.7	..	31.0	..	..	..	..	..	..	..	..	..	..
Ethiopia	11.4	149.7	25.3	..	..	..	..	..	..	..	..	..	..
Gabon	18.5	−276.4	8.9	..	..	..	..	..	..	..	..	..	..
Gambia, The	18.5	46.4	13.0	2.1	0.6	2.3	28.4	2.3	6.5	11.6	53.7	..	1.7
Ghana	17.0	145.0	15.5	..	..	..	..	..	..	..	..	..	..
Guinea	10.4	63.9	5.1	1.4	2.7	0.4	59.0	1.7	3.1	8.3	61.0	..	..
Guinea-Bissau	4.2	..	2.1	5.0	6.1	1.4	70.3	0.7	5.3	19.6	41.4	..	..
Kenya	11.6	134.0	25.9	..	..	..	..	..	..	..	..	..	..
Lesotho	27.1	68.7	8.4	..	..	..	..	..	..	..	..	..	..
Liberia	4.3	0.0	6.6	..	..	..	..	..	..	..	..	..	..
Madagascar	12.3	85.7	9.9	..	..	..	..	..	..	..	..	..	..
Malawi	3.4	26.5	10.5	..	..	..	..	..	..	..	..	..	..
Mali	15.0	61.2	18.4	..	..	..	..	..	..	..	..	..	..
Mauritania	..	863.6	..	0.7	1.5	0.8	35.6	1.2	12.8	21.6	13.0	0.4	3.8
Mauritius	14.8	−32.0	76.7	..	..	..	..	..	..	..	..	..	..
Mozambique	13.6	105.4	11.2	..	..	..	..	..	..	..	..	..	..
Namibia	18.8	252.3	61.4	0.8	9.3	0.6	24.9	20.6	17.2	11.8	3.1	4.4	9.4
Niger	8.8	40.7	6.8	..	..	..	..	..	..	..	..	..	..
Nigeria	12.0	6,409.4	14.9	..	..	..	..	..	..	..	..	..	..
Rwanda	12.2	10.6	13.5	0.9	0.8	..	34.6	..	26.9	13.6	31.8	..	2.8
São Tomé and Principe	..	31.4	44.7	..	..	..	..	..	..	..	..	..	..
Senegal	15.6	100.5	23.8	..	..	..	..	..	..	..	..	..	..
Seychelles	7.1	78.1	40.6	..	..	..	..	..	..	..	..	..	..
Sierra Leone	11.6	27.2	4.5	..	..	..	..	..	..	..	..	..	..
Somalia	..	..	..	..	..	..	..	..	..	..	..	..	..
South Africa	15.1	2,305.3	143.5	..	..	..	..	..	..	..	..	..	..
Sudan	13.5	2,355.0	10.0	..	..	..	..	..	..	..	..	..	..
Swaziland	9.5	34.1	20.0	0.6	5.2	1.0	56.7	18.5	15.4	10.3	6.8	0.4	2.3
Tanzania	10.8	495.0	10.4	0.5	0.5	..	35.4	1.9	3.9	9.3	72.9	..	1.4
Togo	18.1	115.5	16.8	..	..	..	..	..	..	..	..	..	..
Uganda	16.4	245.4	6.7	0.3	2.4	0.1	35.6	0.2	11.0	6.7	63.3	..	0.4
Zambia	15.8	380.0	7.6	..	..	..	..	..	..	..	..	..	..
Zimbabwe	19.5	13.0	26.9	..	..	..	..	..	..	..	..	..	..
NORTH AFRICA	**13.9**	**7,393.3**	..	..	..	..	..	..	..	..	..	..	..
Algeria	14.1	1,020.0	11.8	..	..	..	..	..	..	..	..	..	..
Egypt, Arab Rep.	9.1	3,862.8	52.4	..	..	..	..	..	..	..	..	..	..
Libya	..	..	9.0	..	..	..	..	..	..	..	..	..	..
Morocco	21.6	1,698.1	62.2	..	..	..	..	..	..	..	..	..	..
Tunisia	..	812.4	65.6	..	..	..	..	..	..	..	..	..	..

a. Provisional.

	Regulation and tax administration							Interest rate spread (lending rate minus deposit rate) 2005			
Number of tax payments 2006	Time to prepare, file, and pay taxes (hours) 2006	Total tax payable (% of profit) 2006	Highest marginal tax rate, corporate rate (%) 2006	Time dealing with officials (% of management time) 2006	Average time to clear customs (days) 2006	Bank branches (per 100,000 people) 2004		Listed domestic companies 2006[a]	Market capitalization of listed companies (% of GDP) 2005[a]	Turnover ratio for traded stocks (%) 2006[a]
40.8	331	70.6	..	..	5.0	..	..	..	..	..
42	272	64.4	..	7.1	16.5	..	54.3	..	..	..
72	270	68.5	38.0	..	..	..	..	..	..	..
24	140	53.3	15.0	5.0	1.2	3.8	6.5	18.0	23.6	2.4
45	270	51.1	..	9.5	3.1	..	..	..	..	..
40	140	286.7	..	5.7	4.4	..	..	..	..	..
39	1,300	46.2	..	12.8	4.3	..	12.8	..	..	..
49	100	54.4	..	12.2	10.0	..	8.9	..	..	..
54	504	209.5	..	..	..	..	12.8	..	..	..
65	122	68.2	..	..	..	..	12.8	..	..	..
20	100	47.5	..	..	..	..	8.0	..	..	..
34	312	235.4	40.0	6.3	3.6	..	..	..	..	..
94	576	57.3	..	..	..	..	12.8	..	..	..
71	270	45.7	35.0	..	..	..	..	40.0	14.2	3.7
36	114	41.7	..	..	..	..	10.3	..	..	..
48	212	62.4	..	..	..	..	12.8	..	..	..
18	216	86.3	..	..	..	..	..	..	..	..
20	212	32.8	..	..	..	0.4	3.5	..	..	..
27	272	48.3	..	..	..	..	12.8	..	..	..
47	376	291.4	..	7.3	5.0	..	17.6	..	..	..
35	304	32.3	25.0	..	..	1.6	..	32.0	12.8	3.4
55	416	49.4	..	2.6	4.1	..	..	..	..	..
47	208	47.5	..	2.9	5.6	..	..	..	..	..
17	432	74.2	..	..	..	1.4	7.8	51.0	34.1	15.8
21	352	25.6	..	..	..	..	7.8	..	..	..
..	..	..	..	..	..	..	13.6	..	..	..
25	304	43.2	..	..	..	0.7	8.3	..	..	..
29	878	32.6	..	..	..	..	22.2	..	..	..
60	270	50.0	..	..	..	..	..	..	..	..
61	696	104.3	..	5.8	3.9	..	15.1	..	..	..
7	158	24.8	25.0	..	..	11.9	13.8	41.0	41.6	6.0
36	230	39.2	32.0	..	..	..	11.7	..	..	..
34	..	25.6	35.0	2.9	1.3	4.5	4.4	9.0	6.8	4.6
44	270	46.0	..	..	..	..	..	..	..	..
35	1,120	31.4	..	..	..	1.6	7.4	202.0	19.6	13.8
43	168	41.1	..	5.9	6.7	..	..	..	..	..
42	424	55.2	..	..	..	..	..	..	..	..
59	696	47.7	..	..	..	..	..	..	..	..
15	76	48.8	..	..	..	..	6.3	..	..	..
20	399	277.0	..	..	..	..	13.5	..	..	..
..	..	..	..	..	..	..	..	..	..	..
23	350	38.3	29.0	..	..	6.0	4.6	401.0	236.0	49.5
66	180	37.1	..	..	..	..	..	..	..	..
34	104	39.5	30.0	4.4	1.9	..	6.6	..	7.2	..
48	248	45.0	30.0	4.0	4.8	0.6	10.4	..	4.9	..
51	270	48.3	..	..	..	..	..	..	..	..
31	237	32.2	30.0	5.2	2.9	0.5	10.9	..	1.2	..
37	131	22.2	..	..	..	1.5	17.0	..	13.6	..
59	216	37.0	..	..	..	3.3	144.6	80.0	71.2	7.9
43.8	444	59.6	..	..	..	..	..	..	..	..
61	504	76.4	..	..	..	..	6.3	..	..	..
41	536	50.4	..	..	..	3.6	5.9	603.0	89.1	55.2
..	..	..	..	..	..	..	4.0	..	..	..
28	468	52.7	..	..	..	6.6	..	65.0	52.7	32.9
45	268	58.8	..	..	..	..	..	48.0	10.0	15.2

Table 6.1 International trade and tariff barriers

	Merchandise trade (% of GDP) 2005[a]	Exports ($ millions) 2005[a]	Imports ($ millions) 2005[a]	Exports (% of GDP) 2005[a]	Imports (% of GDP) 2005[a]	Annual growth (%) Exports 2005[a]	Annual growth (%) Imports 2005[a]	Terms of trade index (2000=100) 2005[a]
SUB–SAHARAN AFRICA	**71**	**230,383**	**216,632**	**36.6**	**34.4**	**..**	**11.4**	**..**
Angola	121.8	24,121	15,834	73.5	48.3	..	..	..
Benin	39.6	577	1,119	13.5	26.1	5.0	1.0	91.8
Botswana	84.6	5,519	3,313	52.8	34.6	21.7	1.0	98.8
Burkina Faso	..	..	..	..	21.9	..	..	..
Burundi	47.7	91	291	11.4	36.3	..	..	..
Cameroon	48.8	3,958	4,282	23.5	25.4	0.1	1.2	110.3
Cape Verde	..	..	..	..	..	..	..	..
Central African Republic	..	..	..	..	..	..	..	..
Chad	94.4	3,239	2,328	54.9	39.3	17.0	0.8	100.0
Comoros	47.2	48	134	12.5	34.7	2.8	1.1	100.0
Congo, Dem. Rep.	73.8	2,450	2,792	34.5	39.3	8.8	1.2	165.6
Congo, Rep.	136.6	5,160	2,994	86.4	54.8	..	..	..
Côte d'Ivoire	90.7	8,097	6,466	50.4	42.4	-1.5	1.0	123.3
Djibouti	90	259	379	36.5	53.5	2.1	1.0	100.0
Equatorial Guinea	144.4	7,277	3,583	96.8	..	7.2	1.2	144.3
Eritrea	64.5	85	540	8.8	55.7	-0.1	1.0	84.6
Ethiopia	54.7	1,858	4,367	16.3	39.1	3.7	1.2	75.4
Gabon	90.3	5,844	1,983	67.4	38.5	-1.5	0.8	134.0
Gambia, The	110.2	207	302	44.8	65.4	27.3	1.1	73.5
Ghana	97.7	3,869	6,610	36.1	61.7	9.3	1.1	84.6
Guinea	58.2	924	1,012	27.8	29.6	5.6	0.9	89.1
Guinea-Bissau	88.5	114	153	37.7	55.2	5.0	1.1	86.6
Kenya	60.8	5,126	6,540	26.7	34.9	4.7	1.1	102.9
Lesotho	135.3	695	1,276	47.7	88	-14.4	0.8	123.6
Liberia	90	201	275	38	50.2	..	..	..
Madagascar	67.9	1,355	2,067	26.9	40.3	-4.4	1.0	139.1
Malawi	79.3	566	1,080	27.3	53	19.0	1.0	74.3
Mali	63.1	1,333	2,015	25.1	37.2	8.7	1.0	85.3
Mauritania	131.6	659	1,758	35.9	95	6.2	1.5	131.0
Mauritius	117.4	3,556	3,830	56.5	60.9	5.7	1.0	90.3
Mozambique	73.2	2,164	2,830	31.7	42.3	5.0	1.1	80.2
Namibia	93.5	2,961	2,819	47.9	45	2.3	1.0	97.6
Niger	39.3	512	825	15.1	24.2	..	..	..
Nigeria	90.1	52,575	34,855	54.2	35.2	-1.8	1.2	140.5
Rwanda	41.5	228	667	10.6	31	-2.2	1.2	65.8
São Tomé and Principe	..	..	..	..	99.4	..	..	..
Senegal	65.7	2,221	3,431	25.8	41.6	3.2	1.1	97.1
Seychelles	224.4	714	908	98.7	120.5	11.3	1.3	86.7
Sierra Leone	65.4	281	499	23.5	42.7	..	..	..
Somalia	..	..	..	..	..	..	..	..
South Africa	55.1	64,904	68,412	26.8	28.6	6.7	1.1	108.8
Sudan	45.4	4,973	7,701	17.8	28	13.0	..	..
Swaziland	165	2,095	2,217	80.2	95.4	6.0	1.1	106.5
Tanzania	54.4	2,964	3,881	23.5	26.3	12.3	1.1	72.8
Togo	83.9	743	1,026	35.2	46.6	7.5	1.0	100.4
Uganda	40.3	1,145	2,370	13.1	27.2	4.4	1.2	106.6
Zambia	41.6	1,192	1,835	16.4	25.2	12.3	1.2	83.9
Zimbabwe	129.8	1,941	2,495	56.8	52.9	-3.4	1.0	92.2
NORTH AFRICA	**72.5**	**125,672**	**101,546**	**40.1**	**32.4**	**..**	**12.7**	**..**
Algeria	71.4	48,690	24,020	47.8	23.5	5.8	1.1	133.0
Egypt, Arab Rep.	63	27,214	29,246	30.3	32.7	22.5	1.2	107.6
Libya	..	..	..	..	..	..	..	..
Morocco	80.8	18,809	22,885	36.4	42.9	8.5	1.1	97.8
Tunisia	98.6	13,766	14,525	48	50.6	3.2	1.0	97.7

a. Provisional.
b. Data are for the most recent year available during the period specified.

Structure of merchandise exports (% of total)					Structure of merchandise imports (% of total)					Export diversification index (0 low to 100 high) 2000–05ᵇ
Food 2000–05ᵇ	Agricultural raw materials 2000–05ᵇ	Fuel 2000–05ᵇ	Ores and metals 2000–05ᵇ	Manufactures 2000–05ᵇ	Food 2000–05ᵇ	Agricultural raw materials 2000–05ᵇ	Fuel 2000–05ᵇ	Ores and metals 2000–05ᵇ	Manufactures 2000–05ᵇ	
..	..	..	..	..	..	..	..	..	..	
..	..	..	..	..	..	..	..	..	..	1.1
24.8	61.0	0.7	0.5	12.8	29.8	4.2	20.4	0.9	43.9	2.9
2.4	0.1	0.0	10.7	86.4	13.9	0.8	4.4	1.1	75.1	1.3
16.4	72.3	2.8	0.6	8.0	12.0	0.6	24.4	0.6	62.5	1.4
86.8	4.2	0.1	2.5	6.2	6.5	1.4	8.5	0.8	82.3	1.3
17.1	13.0	49.6	5.5	3.3	18.0	1.8	26.4	1.1	52.8	3.6
10.4	5.9	48.5	0.1	89.5	30.2	1.9	7.6	0.3	60.0	2.6
0.8	41.2	0.4	16.9	36.1	17.1	27.2	16.9	1.5	36.7	3.5
..	..	..	..	..	..	..	..	..	..	1.1
88.7	0.0	..	0.0	8.2	21.9	0.4	4.1	0.2	72.5	2.6
..	..	..	..	..	..	..	..	..	..	4.1
55.8	9.2	12.8	0.2	20.0	21.7	0.6	17.1	1.2	48.5	1.3
..	..	..	..	..	..	..	..	..	..	5.6
..	..	..	..	..	..	..	..	..	..	14.8
..	..	..	..	..	..	..	..	..	..	1.2
..	..	..	..	..	..	..	..	..	..	15.4
62.0	25.9	0.0	0.7	11.4	21.5	0.7	12.0	1.5	64.0	3.6
1.2	9.8	76.2	5.5	7.0	24.2	0.6	3.2	1.2	69.7	1.7
78.4	4.3	0.8	0.3	16.9	37.7	1.4	16.1	1.0	43.5	4.6
77.1	5.0	3.3	2.2	12.1	20.8	1.3	1.6	2.1	74.2	4.3
2.0	0.8	0.1	71.6	25.3	23.1	1.2	21.7	0.8	53.0	3.3
..	..	..	..	..	..	..	..	..	..	1.1
39.7	12.0	23.0	4.2	21.1	10.4	2.1	24.3	1.6	61.3	15.2
..	..	..	..	..	..	..	..	..	..	5.6
..	..	..	..	..	..	..	..	..	..	1.8
60.7	6.2	4.4	5.1	22.5	13.5	0.4	23.3	0.4	61.8	12.2
79.5	3.8	0.0	0.2	16.3	18.2	1.0	10.5	0.8	68.3	2.8
9.6	22.3	11.3	0.3	54.6	16.2	0.7	21.9	0.7	60.3	1.5
..	..	..	..	..	..	..	..	..	..	2.9
27.6	0.5	0.1	0.5	69.9	16.7	1.9	16.5	1.0	63.9	9.9
11.7	3.8	15.0	58.1	7.0	14.4	1.0	1.6	0.4	49.4	1.8
48.3	1.3	1.0	7.3	40.9	14.9	0.7	10.4	3.6	69.4	5.2
30.4	3.6	1.6	54.9	7.9	33.5	4.3	16.9	1.2	44.0	1.6
0.0	0.0	97.9	0.0	2.1	15.5	0.6	16.0	1.6	66.3	1.2
52.3	7.3	6.8	23.3	10.3	11.7	4.0	15.6	2.0	66.7	3.1
..	..	..	..	..	..	..	..	..	..	3.0
28.8	2.1	21.1	2.8	43.4	28.1	1.6	22.9	2.2	45.1	5.7
57.0	0.0	36.4	0.0	6.5	21.5	1.0	23.5	0.3	48.3	3.5
91.6	0.8	..	0.1	7.5	22.5	7.6	39.7	0.8	29.3	2.5
..	..	..	..	..	..	..	..	..	..	5.6
8.5	2.0	10.3	22.4	56.7	4.4	1.1	14.3	1.8	69.6	23.1
6.8	4.8	87.3	0.4	0.1	13.0	0.7	1.2	1.0	83.2	1.3
14.6	7.8	0.7	0.2	76.4	18.2	2.2	12.6	1.0	64.4	18.9
56.7	16.7	0.2	11.7	14.4	11.9	1.3	9.9	1.1	75.7	18.7
21.5	8.9	1.2	10.3	58.1	15.5	0.8	29.0	2.1	52.6	7.6
64.0	11.6	5.1	2.3	17.0	15.0	1.5	16.9	1.2	64.5	5.8
13.1	5.4	0.7	71.9	8.8	6.3	1.3	11.6	2.7	77.9	3.1
30.9	15.7	1.6	23.2	28.5	18.7	1.8	13.7	9.8	54.2	13.9
..	..	..	..	..	..	..	..	..	..	..
0.2	0.0	97.4	0.4	2.0	21.9	1.9	0.9	1.3	73.9	2.1
9.8	7.0	43.1	3.7	30.6	22.2	5.1	8.3	3.5	49.8	22.6
..	..	..	..	..	16.8	0.6	0.7	0.9	81.1	1.1
21.5	1.9	2.5	9.0	65.2	10.7	2.8	21.9	2.8	61.7	34.7
11.1	0.7	9.6	1.1	77.6	8.6	2.8	10.3	2.7	75.6	30.6

Table 6.1 International trade and tariff barriers (continued)

	Competitiveness indicator (%)		Tariff barriers, all products (%)					
	Sectoral effect 1999–2003	Global effect 1999–2003	Binding coverage 2005	Simple mean bound rate 2005	Simple mean tariff 2005	Weighted mean tariff 2005	Share of lines with international peaks 2005	Share of lines with specific rates 2005
SUB–SAHARAN AFRICA	..	..	..	..	..	..	..	..
Angola	13.5	23.4	100.0	59.2	7.6	6.0	10.3	0.0
Benin	–8.3	–11.0	39.1	28.6	14.4	12.4	57.6	0.0
Botswana	9.7	488.1	96.3	19.0	9.9	11.2	23.6	0.2
Burkina Faso	–7.4	2.2	39.3	41.9	13.1	11.7	48.6	0.0
Burundi	6.9	14.2	20.9	67.5	19.6	19.9	46.5	0.0
Cameroon	4.0	–7.4	12.6	79.9	18.4	16.5	52.6	0.0
Cape Verde	–4.9	–1.1	..	..	..	..	..	..
Central African Republic	–1.0	–20.8	..	..	17.9	16.8	58.0	0.0
Chad	–10.4	473.8	..	..	17.2	12.5	48.7	0.0
Comoros	–14.5	–8.4	..	..	..	..	..	..
Congo, Dem. Rep.	5.8	–16.4	..	..	..	..	..	..
Congo, Rep.	11.5	10.1	..	..	19.1	17.7	56.4	0.0
Côte d'Ivoire	1.1	–6.6	33.2	11.2	12.6	10.3	44.3	0.0
Djibouti	–3.1	–30.4	..	..	..	..	..	..
Equatorial Guinea	10.4	36.9	..	..	..	..	..	..
Eritrea	–4.9	1.8	..	..	..	..	..	..
Ethiopia	–5.6	19.2	..	..	..	..	..	..
Gabon	11.7	–12.0	100.0	21.4	19.9	16.8	60.6	0.0
Gambia, The	–7.5	–6.5	..	..	..	..	..	..
Ghana	0.0	–4.2	..	..	..	..	..	..
Guinea	–0.7	–6.7	39.0	20.1	14.2	12.7	58.6	0.0
Guinea-Bissau	10.6	–18.7	..	..	14.1	14.0	55.8	0.0
Kenya	–6.7	2.2	14.0	95.1	12.1	7.5	36.4	0.0
Lesotho	–10.2	26.1	..	..	9.9	16.8	24.1	0.8
Liberia	3.5	–15.1	..	..	..	..	..	..
Madagascar	–8.7	–5.4	29.7	27.4	11.6	5.2	37.1	0.0
Malawi	–11.9	3.5	..	..	..	..	..	..
Mali	–4.7	–7.7	40.7	28.8	12.4	10.7	43.7	0.0
Mauritania	13.3	–13.6	..	..	..	..	..	..
Mauritius	–5.6	–7.2	18.0	94.0	8.5	4.7	19.7	0.0
Mozambique	–4.1	18.9	..	..	13.1	8.6	38.2	0.0
Namibia	–0.8	60.2	96.3	19.4	5.6	1.3	15.2	0.0
Niger	4.6	–23.4	96.8	44.3	12.7	12.8	47.6	0.0
Nigeria	14.8	–1.7	18.2	117.8	11.6	10.8	41.0	0.0
Rwanda	41.3	–50.6	100.0	89.5	17.2	9.7	47.0	0.0
São Tomé and Principe	–1.8	–16.0	..	..	..	..	..	..
Senegal	–2.8	–9.9	100.0	30.0	14.0	9.2	53.8	0.0
Seychelles	–5.3	8.5	..	..	18.3	46.0	23.9	0.0
Sierra Leone	1.3	19.8	..	..	..	..	..	..
Somalia	–4.0	–7.0	..	..	..	..	..	..
South Africa	2.1	–5.0	96.3	19.4	8.5	5.4	21.3	1.0
Sudan	11.5	19.5	..	..	..	..	..	..
Swaziland	–5.9	20.2	96.3	19.4	10.8	10.5	26.6	0.0
Tanzania	–2.5	9.5	13.4	120.0	12.9	8.4	38.0	0.0
Togo	–6.0	–6.4	13.2	80.0	14.6	10.4	55.3	0.0
Uganda	–3.0	1.9	14.9	73.5	12.4	9.0	38.3	0.0
Zambia	7.3	11.2	15.9	105.7	14.6	9.4	34.5	0.0
Zimbabwe	–2.5	–11.6	..	..	..	..	..	..
NORTH AFRICA	..	..	..	..	..	..	..	..
Algeria	–1.4	14.9	..	..	15.8	10.6	38.6	0.0
Egypt, Arab Rep.	–2.6	13.1	99.1	36.6	18.9	12.0	21.8	0.0
Libya	11.2	4.4	..	..	..	..	..	..
Morocco	–4.3	2.5	100.0	41.3	19.4	13.7	57.0	0.0
Tunisia	–4.0	1.5	57.9	57.7	13.4	9.1	31.0	0.0

a. Provisional.
b. Data are for most recent year available during the period specified.

TRADE

Tariff barriers, primary products (%)		Tariff barriers, manufactured products (%)		Average cost to ship 20 ft container from port to final destination ($)		Average time to clear customs (days)
Simple mean tariff 2005	Weighted mean tariff 2005	Simple mean tariff 2005	Weighted mean tariff 2005	Export 2006	Import 2006	
..	..	..	..	1,750	2,181	5.0
12.0	13.1	6.8	4.4	1,850	2,325	16.5
15.4	12.0	14.2	12.8	1,167	1,202	..
5.1	1.0	10.1	12.9	2,328	2,595	1.2
13.6	10.1	13.0	12.6	2,096	3,522	3.1
26.1	25.5	18.5	18.7	2,147	3,705	4.4
20.9	19.5	18.0	15.5	524	1,360	4.3
..	..	..	..	..	..	10.0
21.8	24.8	17.4	13.2	4,581	4,534	..
22.1	25.0	16.5	10.3	4,867	5,520	..
..	..	..	..	..	..	..
..	..	..	..	3,120	3,308	3.6
22.9	22.1	18.5	16.2	2,201	2,201	..
14.9	11.2	12.2	9.9	1,653	2,457	..
..	..	..	..	..	..	..
..	..	..	..	..	..	..
..	..	..	..	935	1,185	..
..	..	..	..	1,617	2,793	..
22.9	19.4	19.3	15.8	..	..	..
..	..	..	..	..	..	5.0
..	..	..	..	822	842	..
16.3	14.3	13.9	11.2	570	995	4.1
16.3	13.3	13.6	14.7	..	..	5.6
15.9	8.6	11.6	6.7	1,980	2,325	..
7.4	3.3	10.0	17.6	1,188	1,210	..
..	..	..	..	..	..	..
16.9	4.1	11.0	5.9	982	1,282	..
..	..	..	..	1,623	2,500	..
14.4	11.7	12.2	10.4	1,752	2,680	..
..	..	..	..	3,733	3,733	3.9
9.0	5.3	8.3	4.2	683	683	..
16.4	9.1	12.6	8.5	1,155	1,185	..
3.7	0.5	5.9	1.6	1,539	1,550	1.3
14.9	14.7	12.4	12.1	2,945	2,946	..
14.9	14.9	11.3	9.3	798	1,460	..
12.7	5.5	17.7	12.2	3,840	4,080	6.7
..	..	..	..	690	577	..
14.9	8.2	13.8	10.4	828	1,720	..
30.5	110.1	15.7	15.5	..	..	..
..	..	..	..	1,282	1,242	..
..	..	..	..	..	..	..
5.4	1.7	8.8	6.5	1,087	1,195	..
..	..	..	..	1,870	1,970	..
10.3	4.3	10.8	10.8	..	..	1.9
18.7	10.6	12.2	7.7	822	917	4.8
15.4	9.7	14.4	11.0	463	695	..
16.7	10.1	11.9	8.4	1,050	2,945	2.9
14.9	9.3	14.5	9.4	2,098	2,840	..
..	..	..	..	1,879	2,420	..
..	..	..	..	1,023	1,259	..
15.3	9.0	15.7	11.0	1,606	1,886	..
85.8	16.4	11.6	10.5	1,014	1,049	..
..	..	..	..	..	..	..
23.3	12.1	18.8	14.3	700	1,500	..
27.4	13.8	12.0	7.5	770	600	..

Table 6.2 Top three exports and share in total exports, 2005

	First		Second	
	Product	Share of total exports (%)	Product	Share of total exports (%)
SUB-SAHARAN AFRICA				
Angola	Crude petroleum	95.8		
Benin	Cotton, not carded, combed	55.3	Edible nuts fresh, dried	16.5
Botswana	Diamonds excluding industrial	88.2	Nickel mattes, sinters, and the like	8.1
Burkina Faso	Cotton, not carded, combed	84.5		
Burundi	Coffee, not roasted	88.0		
Cameroon	Crude petroleum	48.8	Wood, nonconiferous, sawn	14.1
Cape Verde	Fish, frozen, excluding fillets	61.4	Trousers, breeches, and the like	6.3
Central African Republic	Diamonds excluding industrial	40.0	Wood, nonconiferous, rough, untreated	33.8
Chad	Crude petroleum	94.9		
Comoros	Spices, excluding pepper, pimento	57.9	Essential oils	14.2
Congo, Dem. Rep.	Diamonds excluding industrial	42.6	Other nonferrous ore, concentrated	17.2
Congo, Rep.	Crude petroleum	88.7		
Côte d'Ivoire	Cocoa beans	38.2	Crude petroleum	12.0
Djibouti	Bovine animals, live	20.0	Trousers, breeches, and the like	7.2
Equatorial Guinea	Crude petroleum	92.6		
Eritrea	Natural gums, resins, and the like	17.3	Sesame (sesamum) seeds	8.7
Ethiopia	Coffee, not roasted	47.8	Sesame (sesamum) seeds	20.2
Gabon	Crude petroleum	76.7	Wood, nonconiferous, rough, untreated	10.6
Gambia, The	Edible nuts fresh, dried	43.5	Mechanical shovel and the like, self-propelled	9.9
Ghana	Cocoa beans	46.1	Manganese ores, concentrates	7.2
Guinea	Aluminium ore, concentrate	50.9	Alumina (aluminium oxide)	17.2
Guinea-Bissau	Edible nuts fresh, dried	93.5		
Kenya	Tea	16.8	Cut flowers and foliage	14.2
Lesotho	Jerseys, pullovers, and the like, knit	29.2	Trousers, breeches, and the like	22.0
Liberia	Ships, boats, other vessels	73.9	Special purpose vessels and the like	8.9
Madagascar	Jerseys, pullovers, and the like, knit	19.4	Crustaceans, frozen	13.2
Malawi	Tobacco, stemmed, stripped	59.2	Tea	7.6
Mali	Cotton, not carded, combed	81.8		
Mauritania	Iron ore, concentrates not agglomerated	51.3	Molluscs	24.0
Mauritius	Sugars, beet or cane, raw	21.4	T-shirts, other vests knit	18.7
Mozambique	Aluminium, aluminium alloy, unwrought	73.4	Crustaceans, frozen	4.7
Namibia	Diamonds excluding industrial	39.1	Radioactive chemicals	11.4
Niger	Radioactive chemicals	79.5		
Nigeria	Crude petroleum	92.2		
Rwanda	Coffee, not roasted	51.9	Ores and concentrates of molybdenum, niobium, and the like	19.0
São Tomé and Principe	Cocoa beans	55.2	Vessels, other floating structures	10.9
Senegal	Inorganic acid, oxide, and the like	38.8	Molluscs	9.8
Seychelles	Fish, prepared, preserved, not elsewhere specified	44.1	Fish, frozen excluding fillets	27.5
Sierra Leone	Diamonds excluding industrial	62.7	Cocoa beans	7.2
Somalia	Sheep and goats, live	34.6	Bovine animals, live	19.7
South Africa	Platinum	12.5	Other coal, not agglomerated	8.0
Sudan	Crude petroleum	89.2		
Swaziland	Sugars, beet or cane, raw	14.1	Food preparations, not elsewhere specified	9.3
Tanzania	Gold, nonmonetary excluding ores	10.9	Fish fillets, fresh, chilled	9.7
Togo	Cocoa beans	22.4	Natural calcium phosphates	19.8
Uganda	Coffee, not roasted	31.1	Fish fillets, fresh, chilled	24.3
Zambia	Copper, anodes, alloys	55.8	Cobalt, cadmium, and the like, unwrought	7.0
Zimbabwe	Tobacco, stemmed, stripped	13.9	Nickel, nickel alloy, unwrought	12.6
NORTH AFRICA				
Algeria	Crude petroleum	67.2	Natural gas, liquefied	13.2
Egypt, Arab Rep.	Natural gas, liquefied	15.8	Crude petroleum	10.3
Libya	Crude petroleum	95.3		
Morocco	Inorganic acid, oxide, and the like	7.2	Insulated wire, and the like, conductor	6.8
Tunisia	Crude petroleum	9.0	Trousers, breeches, and the like	8.7
AFRICAᵃ	**Crude petroleum**	49.2 (18.0)	**Diamonds excluding industrial**	3.7 (12.6)

Note: Products are reported when accounting for more than 4 percent of total exports.
a. Values in parentheses are Africa's share of total world exports.

Product	Third Share of total exports (%)	Number of exports accounting for 75 percent of total exports
		1
Other nonferrous metal waste	6.4	3
		1
		1
		1
Bananas, fresh or dried	8.7	4
Gas turbines, not elsewhere specified	4.0	4
Cotton, not carded, combed	8.9	3
		1
Fish, frozen excluding fillets	12.7	3
Crude petroleum	16.7	3
		1
Cocoa paste	7.7	7
Other ferrous waste, scrap	7.0	17
		1
Molluscs	7.6	14
		5
Manganese ores, concentrates	6.9	1
Groundnuts (peanuts)	7.7	6
Wood, nonconiferous, sawn	6.7	8
Copper ores, concentrates	7.8	3
		1
Other fresh, chilled vegetables	8.1	27
Diamonds excluding industrial	15.0	4
Natural rubber latex	8.0	2
Spices, excluding pepper, pimento	9.0	14
Sugars, beet or cane, raw	5.3	4
		1
Fish, frozen excluding fillets	13.5	2
Shirts	7.6	10
		2
Zinc, zinc alloy, unwrought	9.7	5
		1
		1
Tin ores, concentrates	9.8	3
Drawing, measuring instrument	7.6	4
Fish, fresh, chilled, whole	6.4	8
Ships, boats, other vessels	11.0	3
Cultivating machinery and the like	4.1	4
Fish, frozen excluding fillets	7.8	5
Gold, nonmonetary excluding ores	7.9	39
		1
Flavors, industrial use	9.0	20
Copper ores, concentrates	8.6	15
Cotton, not carded, combed	18.6	8
Tobacco, stemmed, stripped	7.5	5
Cotton, not carded, combed	5.7	5
Nickel ores, concentrates	12.3	16
Natural gas, gaseous	5.6	2
Portland cement, and the like	4.7	46
		1
Natural calcium phosphates	5.6	32
Insulated wire, and the like, conductor	6.7	36
Nickel ores, concentrates	**2.8 (17.5)**	**26**

Table 6.3 Regional integration, trade blocs

	Year established	Merchandise exports within bloc ($ millions)								
		1990	1995	1999	2000	2001	2002	2003	2004	2005
Economic and Monetary Community of Central African States (CEMAC)	1994	139	120	127	97	118	136	148	176	201
Economic Community of the Countries of the Great Lakes (CEPGL)	1976	7	8	9	10	11	13	15	19	22
Common Market for Eastern and Southern Africa (COMESA)	1994	963	1,386	1,348	1,653	1,819	2,031	2,436	2,849	3,330
Cross-Border Initiative (CBI)	1992	613	1,002	964	1,166	1,070	1,373	1,536	1,705	1,913
East African Community (EAC)	1996	230	530	438	595	664	685	706	750	857
Economic Community of Central African States (ECCAS)	1983	163	163	179	191	203	199	198	238	272
Economic Community of West African States (ECOWAS)	1975	1,557	1,936	2,364	2,835	2,371	3,229	3,140	4,499	5,673
Indian Ocean Commission (IOC)	1984	73	127	91	106	134	105	179	155	159
Mano River Union (MRU)	1973	0	1	4	5	4	5	5	6	6
Southern African Development Community (SADC)	1992	1,630	3,373	4,224	4,282	3,771	4,316	5,377	6,384	6,384
Central African Customs and Economic Union (UDEAC)	1964	139	120	126	96	117	134	146	174	198
West African Economic and Monetary Union (WAEMU/UEMOA)	1994	621	560	805	741	775	857	1,076	1,233	1,390

	Year established	Merchandise exports within bloc (% of total bloc exports)								
		1990	1995	1999	2000	2001	2002	2003	2004	2005
Economic and Monetary Community of Central African States (CEMAC)	1994	2.3	2.1	1.7	1.1	1.4	1.5	1.4	1.3	0.9
Economic Community of the Countries of the Great Lakes (CEPGL)	1976	0.5	0.5	0.8	0.8	0.8	0.9	1.2	1.2	1.3
Common Market for Eastern and Southern Africa (COMESA)	1994	6.6	7.7	7.4	6.1	7.9	7.4	7.4	6.8	5.9
Cross-Border Initiative (CBI)	1992	10.3	11.9	12.1	11.8	11.5	14.5	13.0	13.8	14.0
East African Community (EAC)	1996	13.4	17.4	14.4	20.5	21.4	19.3	18.2	16.6	15.0
Economic Community of Central African States (ECCAS)	1983	1.4	1.5	1.3	1.1	1.3	1.1	1.0	0.9	0.6
Economic Community of West African States (ECOWAS)	1975	7.9	9.0	10.4	7.9	8.5	10.9	8.6	9.4	9.5
Indian Ocean Commission (IOC)	1984	4.1	6.0	4.8	4.4	5.6	4.3	6.2	4.3	4.6
Mano River Union (MRU)	1973	0.0	0.1	0.4	0.4	0.3	0.2	0.3	0.3	0.3
Southern African Development Community (SADC)	1992	17.0	31.6	11.9	9.3	8.6	9.5	9.8	9.5	7.7
Central African Customs and Economic Union (UDEAC)	1964	2.3	2.1	1.7	1.0	1.4	1.4	1.4	1.2	0.9
West African Economic and Monetary Union (WAEMU/UEMOA)	1994	13.0	10.3	13.1	13.1	12.7	12.2	13.3	12.9	13.4

Note: **Economic and Monetary Community of Central Africa (CEMAC),** Cameroon, the Central African Republic, Chad, the Republic of Congo, Equatorial Guinea, Gabon, and São Tomé and Principe; **Economic Community of the Countries of the Great Lakes (CEPGL),** Burundi, the Democratic Republic of Congo, and Rwanda; **Common Market for Eastern and Southern Africa (COMESA),** Angola, Burundi, Comoros, the Democratic Republic of Congo, Djibouti, the Arab Republic of Egypt, Eritrea, Ethiopia, Kenya, Madagascar, Malawi, Mauritius, Namibia, Rwanda, Seychelles, Sudan, Swaziland, Uganda, Tanzania, Zambia, and Zimbabwe; **Cross Border Initiative,** Burundi, Comoros, Kenya, Madagascar, Malawi, Mauritius, Namibia, Rwanda, Seychelles, Swaziland, Tanzania, Uganda, Zambia, and Zimbabwe; **East African Community (EAC),** Kenya, Tanzania, and Uganda; **Economic Community of Central African States (ECCAS),** Angola, Burundi, Cameroon, the Central African Republic, Chad, the Democratic Republic of Congo, the Republic of Congo, Equatorial Guinea, Gabon, Rwanda, and São Tomé and Principe; **Economic Community of West African States (ECOWAS),** Benin, Burkina Faso, Cape Verde, Côte d'Ivoire, the Gambia, Ghana, Guinea, Guinea-Bissau, Liberia, Mali, Mauritania, Niger, Nigeria, Senegal, Sierra Leone, and Togo; **Indian Ocean Commission,** Comoros, Madagascar, Mauritius, Réunion, and Seychelles; **Mano River Union (MRU),** Guinea, Liberia, and Sierra Leone; **Southern African Development Community (SADC; formerly Southern African Development Coordination Conference),** Angola, Botswana, the Democratic Republic of Congo, Lesotho, Malawi, Mauritius, Mozambique, Namibia, Seychelles, South Africa, Swaziland, Tanzania, Zambia, and Zimbabwe; **Central African Customs and Economic Union (UDEAC; formerly Union Douanière et Economique de l'Afrique Centrale),** Cameroon, the Central African Republic, Chad, the Republic of Congo, Equatorial Guinea, and Gabon; **West African Economic and Monetary Union (UEMOA),** Benin, Burkina Faso, Côte d'Ivoire, Guinea-Bissau, Mali, Niger, Senegal, and Togo.

Table 7.1 Water and sanitation

| | Access, supply side | Access, demand side | | | | | | Quality of supply | Financing | |
| | Internal fresh water resources per capita (cubic meters) | Population with sustainable access to improved water source (%) | | | Population with sustainable access to improved sanitation (%) | | | Water supply failure for firms receiving water (average days per year) | Committed nominal investment in water projects with private participation ($ millions) | Average annual ODA disburse-ments for water supply and sanitation sector ($ millions) |
	2005	Total 2000–05[a]	Urban 2000–05[a]	Rural 2000–05[a]	Total 2000–05[a]	Urban 2000–05[a]	Rural 2000–05[a]	2000–05[a]	2000–05[a]	2000–05
SUB-SAHARAN AFRICA		**56**	**80**	**43**	**37**	**53**	**28**			**93.5**
Angola	9,284	53	75	40	31	56	16	..	..	4.2
Benin	1,221	67	78	57	33	59	11	19.2	..	5.5
Botswana	1,360	95	100	90	42	57	25			2.4
Burkina Faso	945	61	94	54	13	42	6	..	..	61.3
Burundi	1,338	79	92	77	36	47	35	..		0.4
Cameroon	16,726	66	86	44	51	58	43			2.7
Cape Verde	592	80	86	73	43	61	19			9.6
Central African Republic	34,921	75	93	61	27	47	12	..		0.0
Chad	1,539	42	41	43	9	24	4			14.4
Comoros	1,998	86	92	82	33	41	29			5.2
Congo, Dem. Rep.	15,639	46	82	29	30	42	25			3.4
Congo, Rep.	55,515	58	84	27	27	28	25			0.0
Côte d'Ivoire	4,231	84	97	74	37	46	29	..	..	0.1
Djibouti	378	73	76	59	82	88	50	..	..	..
Equatorial Guinea	51,637	43	45	42	53	60	46	..	..	3.5
Eritrea	636	60	74	57	9	32	3	79.2	..	0.6
Ethiopia	1,712	22	81	11	13	44	7	0.0	..	9.2
Gabon	118,511	88	95	47	36	37	30	..	..	17.7
Gambia, The	1,978	82	95	77	53	72	46	..		2.3
Ghana	1,370	75	88	64	18	27	11	..		321.5
Guinea	24,037	50	78	35	18	31	11			12.6
Guinea-Bissau	10,086	59	79	49	35	57	23			0.5
Kenya	604	61	83	46	43	46	41	85.2		118.7
Lesotho	2,897	79	92	76	37	61	32	19.2		17.2
Liberia	60,915	61	72	52	27	49	7	..		0.3
Madagascar	18,113	46	77	35	32	48	26	5.2	..	18.7
Malawi	1,250	73	98	68	61	62	61	21.3		2.8
Mali	4,438	50	78	36	46	59	39	2.1		50.2
Mauritania	130	53	59	44	34	49	8	..		3.0
Mauritius	2,252	100	100	100	94	95	94	16.7	..	0.1
Mozambique	5,068	43	72	26	32	53	19	..	..	4.0
Namibia	3,052	87	98	81	25	50	13	..	..	9.2
Niger	251	46	80	36	13	43	4	0.1	3.4	14.4
Nigeria	1,680	48	67	31	44	53	36	..	..	3.2
Rwanda	1,051	74	92	69	42	56	38	..	..	22.5
São Tomé and Principe	14,055	79	89	73	25	32	20	..	..	0.0
Senegal	2,213	76	92	60	57	79	34	5.6	..	3.2
Seychelles	..	88	100	75	..	..	100	..	..	0.1
Sierra Leone	28,957	57	75	46	39	53	30	..	..	18.2
Somalia	729	29	32	27	26	48	14	..	..	3.1
South Africa	956	88	99	73	65	79	46	4.8	31.3	67.3
Sudan	828	70	78	64	34	50	24	..	..	0.3
Swaziland	2,299	62	87	54	48	59	44	..		0.2
Tanzania	2,192	62	85	49	47	53	43	105.0	8.5	4.9
Togo	1,871	52	80	36	35	71	15	..		9.0
Uganda	1,353	60	87	56	43	54	41	2.7		32.2
Zambia	6,873	58	90	40	55	59	52	13.6		38.6
Zimbabwe	946	81	98	72	53	63	47	..		0.2
NORTH AFRICA		**91**	**96**	**86**	**77**	**91**	**62**			**..**
Algeria	341	85	88	80	92	99	82	31.0	510.0	
Egypt, Arab Rep.	24	98	99	97	70	86	58	5.2	..	
Libya	103	71	72	68	97	97	96	..	..	..
Morocco	961	81	99	56	73	88	52	1.3	..	..
Tunisia	419	93	99	82	85	96	65	..	..	

a. Data are for most recent year available during the period specified.

Table 7.2 Transportation

| | Access, supply side | | | | Access, demand side | | |
| | | | Road density | | Rural access (% of rural population within 2 km of an all-season road) 2000–05[a] | Vehicle fleet (per 1,000 people) | |
	Road network (km) 2000–05[a]	Rail lines (km) 2000–05[a]	Ratio to arable land (road km/1,000 sq km arable land) 2000–05[a]	Ratio to total land (road km/1,000 sq km of land area) 2000–05[a]		Commercial vehicles 2000–05[a]	Passenger vehicles 2000–05[a]
SUB-SAHARAN AFRICA							
Angola	51,429	2,761	17.1	41.3	..	..	..
Benin	19,000	578	..	171.8	32.0	..	..
Botswana	24,455	888	66.9	43.2	..	105.0	42.0
Burkina Faso	15,272	622	..	55.8	25.0	..	..
Burundi	12,322	..	..	479.8	..	..	..
Cameroon	50,000	974	..	107.4	20.0	..	..
Cape Verde	1,350	..	30.7	335.0	..	..	..
Central African Republic	..	..	..	..	..	..	..
Chad	..	..	..	..	5.0	..	..
Comoros	..	..	..	..	..	..	..
Congo, Dem. Rep.	153,497	3,641	..	67.7	26.0	..	..
Congo, Rep.	17,289	795	..	50.6	..	..	..
Côte d'Ivoire	80,000	639	..	251.6	..	..	..
Djibouti	..	781	..	..	..	..	..
Equatorial Guinea	..	..	..	..	..	..	..
Eritrea	..	306	..	..	..	..	..
Ethiopia	36,469	..	3.1	36.5	17.0	2.0	1.0
Gabon	9,170	810	26.0	35.6	..	..	..
Gambia, The	3,742	..	11.9	374.2	..	7.0	5.0
Ghana	47,787	977	11.4	210.0	..	..	..
Guinea	44,348	1,115	40.3	180.5	..	..	..
Guinea-Bissau	3,455	..	11.5	122.9	..	..	..
Kenya	63,265	1,917	14.2	111.2	..	18.0	9.0
Lesotho	..	..	..	..	..	..	..
Liberia	..	490	..	..	..	..	..
Madagascar	..	732	..	..	..	..	..
Malawi	15,451	710	6.3	164.2	..	..	..
Mali	18,709	733	3.9	15.3	..	..	..
Mauritania	..	717	..	..	..	..	..
Mauritius	2,015	..	20.2	992.6	..	130.0	96.0
Mozambique	..	3,070	..	..	..	82.4	41.6
Namibia	42,237	..	51.8	51.3	..	82.4	41.6
Niger	14,565	..	..	11.5	37.0	..	..
Nigeria	193,200	3,528	..	212.1	47.0	..	17.0
Rwanda	14,008	..	..	567.8	..	..	..
São Tomé and Principe	..	..	..	..	..	..	..
Senegal	13,576	906	5.5	70.5	..	..	..
Seychelles	458	..	458.0	995.7	..	..	..
Sierra Leone	11,300	..	21.1	157.8	..	3.6	2.2
Somalia	..	..	..	..	..	..	..
South Africa	364,131	20,047	24.7	299.8	..	144.4	91.8
Sudan	..	5,478	..	..	..	..	..
Swaziland	3,594	301	20.2	209.0	..	83.1	39.9
Tanzania	78,891	2,600	19.7	89.3	38.0	..	..
Togo	..	568	..	..	..	..	..
Uganda	70,746	259	13.6	358.9	..	..	..
Zambia	91,440	1,273	17.4	123.0	..	..	..
Zimbabwe	97,267	..	30.2	251.4	..	50.4	43.9
NORTH AFRICA							
Algeria	108,302	3,572	..	45.5	..	..	..
Egypt, Arab Rep.	92,370	5,150	31.2	92.8	..	..	..
Libya	..	2,757	..	..	..	..	..
Morocco	57,493	1,907	6.8	128.8	..	..	..
Tunisia	19,232	1,909	6.8	123.8	..	..	..

a. Data are for most recent year available during the period specified.

INFRASTRUCTURE

| Quality | | | | Pricing | | | | Financing | |
| Roads | | Average time to ship 20 ft container from port to final destination (days) | | Average cost to ship 20 ft container from port to final destination ($) | | Price of diesel fuel (U.S. cents/ liter) | Price of gasoline (U.S. cents/ liter) | Committed nominal investment in transport projects with private participation ($ millions) | Average annual ODA disbursements for trans- portation and storage ($ millions) |
Road network in good or fair condition (%) 2000–05[a]	Ratio of paved to total roads (%) 2000–05[a]	Import 2006	Export 2006	Import 2006	Export 2006	2004	2004	2003–05[a]	2003–05
		53	**43**	**2,181**	**1,750**				**248.3**
..	10.4	58	64	2,325	1,850	29	39	55.0	0.4
..	9.5	41	34	1,202	1,167	72	77	..	60.6
..	36.5	43	33	2,595	2,328	61	66	..	0.0
69.3	31.2	54	45	3,522	2,096	94	118	..	27.3
87.6	10.4	71	47	3,705	2,147	108	104	..	100.5
23.4	10.0	53	39	1,360	524	83	95	..	13.5
..	69.0	..	..	..	..	81	140	..	2.8
..	..	66	57	4,534	4,581	114	129	..	0.5
71.3	..	102	78	5,520	4,867	101	117	..	11.7
..	..	..	..	..	..	..	..	0.5	5.6
23.2	1.8	62	50	3,308	3,120	81	92	..	9.6
..	5.0	62	50	2,201	2,201	59	87	..	0.8
64.6	8.1	43	23	2,457	1,653	95	114	140.0	0.0
..	..	..	..	..	..	..	..	130.0	..
..	..	..	..	..	..	..	..	23.0	0.0
..	..	69	69	1,185	935	40	80	..	3.6
63.6	19.1	42	46	2,793	1,617	42	60	..	43.9
78.0	10.2	..	..	..	..	69	90	91.8	23.3
94.6	19.3	..	..	..	..	73	75	..	1.4
71.9	17.9	55	47	842	822	43	49	10.0	79.2
44.2	9.8	32	33	995	570	69	75	..	60.9
..	27.9	..	..	..	..	..	..	..	6.2
67.2	14.1	62	45	2,325	1,980	76	92	..	209.1
71.5	..	49	44	1,210	1,188	68	73	..	17.7
..	..	..	..	..	..	77	75	..	0.0
..	..	48	48	1,282	982	79	105	12.5	126.1
..	45.0	54	45	2,500	1,623	88	95	..	6.3
62.0	18.0	65	44	2,680	1,752	90	116	55.4	195.9
..	..	40	42	3,733	3,733	59	80	..	21.3
..	100.0	16	16	683	683	56	74	..	0.0
63.5	..	38	27	1,185	1,155	79	88	186.9	34.5
..	12.8	24	29	1,550	1,539	65	68	..	20.7
63.1	25.0	68	59	2,946	2,945	91	102	..	17.3
..	15.0	53	41	1,460	798	45	39	2,355.4	0.2
..	19.0	92	63	4,080	3,840	99	98	..	5.6
..	..	29	27	577	690	..	..	..	11.7
27.4	29.3	26	20	1,720	828	90	110	55.4	18.0
..	96.0	..	..	..	..	..	..	..	0.0
..	8.0	34	31	1,242	1,282	89	76	..	60.8
..	..	..	..	..	..	49	63	..	0.3
..	17.3	35	30	1,195	1,087	80	81	17.0	0.9
..	..	83	56	1,970	1,870	29	47	..	9.3
..	..	..	..	..	..	73	76	..	0.0
55.0	8.6	51	30	917	822	87	93	27.7	83.4
..	..	43	34	695	463	83	85	..	0.0
58.6	23.0	67	42	2,945	1,050	88	102	..	4.2
..	22.0	64	53	2,840	2,098	98	110	15.6	6.2
..	19.0	67	52	2,420	1,879	65	61	..	0.0
		28	**20**	**1,259**	**1,023**				**..**
..	70.2	22	15	1,886	1,606	15	32	104.0	..
..	81.0	29	27	1,049	1,014	10	28	86.0	..
..	..	..	..	..	..	8	9	..	..
..	56.9	30	18	1,500	700	70	110	200.0	..
..	65.8	29	18	600	770	39	68	..	..

Table 7.3 Information and communication technology

	Access, supply side Telephone subscribers (per 1,000 people)			Access, demand side Households with own telephone					Quality	
	Total 2000–05a	Mainline telephone 2000–05a	Mobile telephone 2000–05a	Total (% of households) 2000–05a	Urban (% of urban households) 2000–05a	Rural (% of rural households) 2000–05a	Average delay for firm in obtaining a mainline phone connection (days) 2000–05a	Internet users (per 1,000 people) 2005	Duration of phone outages (hours) 2000–05a	Telephone faults (per 100 mainlines) 2000–05a
SUB-SAHARAN AFRICA	**149.7**	**17.0**	**124.5**					**29.0**		
Angola	74.5	5.9	68.6	..	..	..	..	11.0	..	..
Benin	97.9	9.0	88.9	4.4	10.3	1.0	159.7	50.4	6.1	5.8
Botswana	541.2	74.8	466.3	..	..	..	..	34.0	..	..
Burkina Faso	50.6	7.4	43.3	3.7	19.8	0.3	..	4.9	..	18.4
Burundi	17.6	3.8	20.3	..	..	..	..	5.3	..	6.0
Cameroon	102.0	6.2	138.4	2.3	4.8	0.0	..	15.3	..	..
Cape Verde	302.2	140.9	161.2	..	..	..	..	49.3	..	33.0
Central African Republic	27.2	2.5	24.8	..	..	..	..	2.7	..	56.0
Chad	14.4	1.4	21.5	0.9	4.3	0.0	..	4.1	..	60.8
Comoros	55.0	28.2	26.8	..	..	..	..	33.3	..	55.8
Congo, Dem. Rep.	47.9	0.2	47.7	..	..	..	..	2.4	..	..
Congo, Rep.	102.4	3.6	122.5	1.3	2.2	0.2	..	12.5	..	..
Côte d'Ivoire	108.1	14.4	120.6	..	..	..	..	11.0	..	81.0
Djibouti	69.1	13.6	55.5	..	..	..	..	12.6	..	136.0
Equatorial Guinea	212.3	19.9	192.4	..	..	..	..	13.9	..	..
Eritrea	17.8	8.6	9.2	..	..	..	256.3	15.9	..	54.3
Ethiopia	14.3	8.6	5.8	4.4	35.3	0.2	154.9	2.3	..	100.0
Gabon	497.8	28.3	469.6	15.3	20.0	1.8	..	48.4	..	45.0
Gambia, The	192.1	29.0	163.1	..	..	..	..	..	..	..
Ghana	143.1	14.5	128.5	7.5	17.0	0.7	..	18.1	..	5.6
Guinea	19.7	2.8	20.1	7.2	23.7	0.3	..	5.3	..	1.6
Guinea-Bissau	7.9	7.1	42.2	..	..	..	..	19.5	..	70.5
Kenya	142.9	8.2	134.6	12.3	37.4	6.0	99.4	32.4	27.2	130.4
Lesotho	163.3	26.7	136.5	16.9	45.8	10.6	73.8	..	26.4	75.0
Liberia	2.8	2.2	48.7	..	..	..	..	..	..	..
Madagascar	30.7	3.6	27.1	4.9	11.9	3.0	63.8	5.4	21.3	59.6
Malawi	41.3	8.0	33.3	6.0	26.7	2.1	107.7	4.1	28.0	..
Mali	69.9	5.5	64.3	3.5	12.8	0.1	70.6	4.4	10.3	177.6
Mauritania	256.3	13.4	243.0	3.6	8.0	0.2	..	6.5	..	..
Mauritius	862.5	288.8	573.7	..	..	..	22.6	..	5.3	41.5
Mozambique	40.0	3.6	61.6	2.1	6.1	0.1	..	..	..	66.0
Namibia	206.1	63.7	243.7	17.4	43.5	4.5	..	..	..	40.4
Niger	23.2	1.7	21.5	..	..	..	60.1	2.1	..	104.6
Nigeria	150.6	9.3	141.3	5.1	11.7	1.8	..	38.0	..	20.6
Rwanda	18.2	2.6	32.1	1.1	6.1	0.2	..	5.5	..	..
São Tomé and Principe	96.7	46.1	76.7	..	..	..	..	..	..	..
Senegal	171.3	22.9	148.4	19.8	35.9	7.5	12.0	46.3	11.4	17.3
Seychelles	928.0	253.3	674.6	..	..	..	..	248.5	..	6.0
Sierra Leone	18.6	4.9	22.1	..	..	..	..	..	..	..
Somalia	72.9	12.2	60.8	..	..	..	..	10.9	..	..
South Africa	825.1	100.9	724.3	..	..	..	8.2	108.8	3.9	48.2
Sudan	68.9	18.5	50.4	..	..	..	..	77.3	..	..
Swaziland	207.8	31.0	176.8	..	..	..	..	..	..	70.0
Tanzania	55.6	3.9	51.6	9.7	31.4	3.0	23.1	..	10.8	24.0
Togo	81.7	9.5	72.2	..	..	..	..	48.8	..	6.2
Uganda	56.4	3.5	52.9	3.1	18.5	0.9	33.4	17.4	16.9	..
Zambia	89.2	8.1	81.1	4.3	11.2	0.6	88.6	..	11.7	108.0
Zimbabwe	78.9	25.2	53.7	..	..	..	..	76.9	..	7.7
NORTH AFRICA	**414.3**	**105.8**	**308.4**					**84.8**		
Algeria	494.1	78.3	415.8	..	..	..	174.3	58.4	..	0.8
Egypt, Arab Rep.	324.5	140.4	184.1	..	..	..	136.9	67.5	..	0.1
Libya	155.8	133.2	40.9	..	..	..	..	..	..	..
Morocco	455.2	44.5	410.8	..	..	..	4.4	152.5	15.0	25.0
Tunisia	691.8	125.4	566.4	..	..	..	..	95.1	..	30.0

a. Data are for the most recent year available during the period specified.

INFRASTRUCTURE

	Pricing			Financing				
Price basket for Internet ($ per month) 2005	Cost of a 3 minute local call during peak hours ($) 2000–05ᵃ	Cost of 3 minute cellular local call during off-peak hours ($) 2000–05ᵃ	Cost of 3 minute call to US during peak hours ($) 2000–05ᵃ	Annual investment ($ millions)			Committed nominal investment in telecommunication projects with private participation ($ millions) 2000–05ᵃ	Average annual ODA disbursements for communication ($ millions) 2000–05
				Telephone service 2000–05ᵃ	Mobile communication 2000–05ᵃ	Telecommunications 2000–05ᵃ		
				85.4	20.3	21.7	..	17.2
34.3	0.1	0.1	3.2	..	..	..	119.8	0.6
20.7	0.1	0.7	4.8	..	3.6	26.4	5.8	0.3
21.3	0.1	0.1	2.9	..	..	19.0	19.0	0.3
90.6	0.2	0.7	1.1	..	23.2	61.2	5.3	0.3
52.0	0.1	0.5	2.5	..	..	..	6.0	0.1
44.6	0.1	0.9	..	..	..	111.2	29.0	0.2
40.3	0.1	0.8	6.1	12.4	1.6	8.9	..	1.0
147.8	0.6	0.6	2.0	..	..	0.1	..	0.2
86.3	0.1	..	9.1	..	..	..	1.4	0.2
37.9	0.2	0.7	..	..	..	4.2	..	0.1
93.2	..	..	..	..	..	..	42.0	0.5
84.5	..	..	5.4	..	..	..	7.0	0.0
67.1	0.3	0.6	2.2	32.2	83.2	95.2	20.0	0.1
41.1	..	..	4.7	..	..	..	..	..
32.7	..	..		..	..	..	..	..
28.6	0.0	0.3	3.6	..	17.2	17.4	40.0	0.1
23.3	0.0	0.1	4.0	14.5	5.2	35.3	..	0.4
40.1	0.3	0.5	2.8	..	..	53.0	9.0	0.2
17.8	0.0	0.5	1.8	..	..	3.7	6.6	0.0
23.6	0.2	0.1	0.4	..	..	59.4	51.6	0.4
24.7	0.1	0.4	4.6	..	..	0.8	32.6	0.1
75.0	..	0.0	..	..	..	..	0.6	0.7
75.9	0.1	0.4	3.0	..	..	80.5	421.0	1.0
38.6	0.2	0.1	3.3	..	..	7.1	3.0	0.0
..	..	0.0	..	..	..	..	15.8	0.0
45.9	0.2	0.7	0.6	..	..	14.8	12.6	0.2
41.9	0.1	0.4	3.6	..	..	..	0.9	0.4
28.4	0.1	0.8	12.3	..	..	17.7	82.6	2.7
54.3	0.1	0.4	..	..	..	84.7	1.6	0.0
17.5	0.1	0.1	1.6	..	..	29.7	25.7	0.1
32.9	0.1	0.2	1.2	..	..	19.7	14.0	9.7
48.7	0.0	0.4	4.3	..	..	20.5	8.8	0.2
101.8	0.1	0.7	8.8	..	..	..	47.2	0.5
50.4	0.1	0.1	1.5	..	..	386.9	2,312.0	0.5
30.1	0.1	0.4	2.4	..	..	..	33.0	0.0
53.2	0.2	0.0	5.1	..	..	2.2	..	0.4
25.6	0.2	0.6	1.0	..	19.8	106.0	157.0	6.6
31.5	0.2	1.2	3.8	..	..	4.1	14.9	0.0
10.6	0.0	0.4	..	..	..	..	0.3	0.6
..	0.1	0.0	..	..	..	..	1.4	0.2
63.2	0.2	1.2	0.8	..	360.3	871.2	1,183.5	7.4
65.5	0.1	0.3	39.2	..	..	128.5	152.0	0.2
51.7	0.1	0.9	3.0	..	..	27.6	3.0	0.0
93.6	0.2	0.2	3.2	..	..	9.4	88.5	0.9
44.7	0.1	0.6	4.0	26.4	..	30.0	..	0.2
99.6	0.2	0.5	3.2	..	..	68.0	77.0	1.3
68.4	0.1	0.4	1.4	..	36.9	42.5	74.0	0.7
24.6	0.1	1.2	4.4	..	20.3	21.7	13.0	0.7
				..	..	..	..	..
9.4	..	..	2.1	..	..	..	1,272.0	..
5.0	..	..	1.5	..	..	..	1,827.0	..
22.0	..	..	..	..	..	..	..	..
26.8	..	..	1.7	..	..	..	626.0	..
12.4	..	..	2.3	..	..	..	106.0	..

Table 7.4 Energy

| | Electric power consumption (kWh per capita) 2000–05[a] | GDP per unit of energy use (2000 PPP $ per kg of oil equivalent) 2000–05[a] | Access, demand side | | | | | |
| | | | Access to electricity | | | Solid fuels use | | |
			Total (% of total population) 2000–05[a]	Urban (% of urban population) 2000–05[a]	Rural (% of rural population) 2000–05[a]	Total (% of total population) 2000–05[a]	Urban (% of urban population) 2000–05[a]	Rural (% of rural population) 2000–05[a]
SUB-SAHARAN AFRICA								
Angola	123.8	3.3	..	..	..	..	..	..
Benin	66.6	3.3	22.0	50.9	5.6	95.6	89.5	99.1
Botswana	1,325.0	8.6	..	..	..	..	..	..
Burkina Faso	..	..	10.2	53.5	0.8	97.5	88.5	99.4
Burundi	..	..	..	..	..	..	..	..
Cameroon	207.0	4.5	45.8	76.7	16.3	82.6	67.1	97.3
Cape Verde	..	..	..	..	..	..	..	..
Central African Republic	..	..	..	..	..	..	..	..
Chad	..	..	4.3	19.9	0.3	..	..	..
Comoros	..	..	..	..	..	..	..	..
Congo, Dem. Rep.	92.9	2.2	..	..	..	..	..	..
Congo, Rep.	131.1	3.3	34.9	51.3	16.4	83.2	71.3	96.5
Côte d'Ivoire	176.1	3.7	..	..	..	..	..	..
Djibouti	..	..	..	..	..	..	..	..
Equatorial Guinea	..	..	..	..	..	..	..	..
Eritrea	..	..	..	..	..	..	..	..
Ethiopia	32.7	2.8	12.0	85.9	2.0	89.0	69.7	91.6
Gabon	927.8	4.9	75.2	90.6	31.4	34.1	16.4	84.4
Gambia, The	..	..	..	..	..	..	..	..
Ghana	247.0	5.4	44.3	77.0	20.9	91.8	82.7	98.3
Guinea	..	..	20.9	63.5	3.2	79.8	39.3	96.8
Guinea-Bissau	..	..	..	..	..	..	..	..
Kenya	140.0	2.1	13.1	51.4	3.6	87.1	46.0	97.3
Lesotho	..	..	5.7	28.1	0.8	62.1	9.5	73.5
Liberia	..	..	..	..	..	..	..	..
Madagascar	..	..	18.8	52.0	9.7	98.3	96.3	98.9
Malawi	..	..	7.5	34.0	2.5	97.8	88.7	99.5
Mali	..	..	12.8	41.3	2.7	95.9	97.6	95.3
Mauritania	..	..	23.4	50.7	2.7	70.5	51.9	84.4
Mauritius	..	..	..	..	..	..	..	..
Mozambique	366.9	2.6	11.0	29.8	1.5	96.9	91.9	99.5
Namibia	1,388.6	10.2	31.7	74.6	10.4	65.9	18.7	89.3
Niger	..	..	..	..	..	..	..	..
Nigeria	104.2	1.4	51.3	84.0	34.6	76.6	52.0	89.0
Rwanda	..	..	5.4	27.2	1.5	99.4	98.3	99.6
São Tomé and Principe	..	..	..	..	..	..	..	..
Senegal	176.1	6.5	46.4	82.1	19.0	58.7	24.3	85.2
Seychelles	..	..	..	..	..	..	..	..
Sierra Leone	..	..	..	..	..	..	..	..
Somalia	..	..	..	..	..	..	..	..
South Africa	4,884.8	3.7	..	..	..	..	..	..
Sudan	92.2	3.7	..	..	..	..	..	..
Swaziland	..	..	..	..	..	..	..	..
Tanzania	53.5	1.3	10.6	38.9	1.8	98.1	93.4	99.5
Togo	87.0	3.1	..	..	..	..	..	..
Uganda	..	..	8.4	47.5	2.6	97.4	87.8	98.8
Zambia	692.0	1.5	20.1	50.0	3.5	83.6	58.5	97.6
Zimbabwe	795.1	2.6	..	..	..	..	5.1	..
NORTH AFRICA								
Algeria	812.4	6.0	..	..	..	..	..	..
Egypt, Arab Rep.	1,215.3	4.9	..	..	..	..	..	..
Libya	2,519.4	..	..	..	..	..	..	..
Morocco	594.6	10.3	..	..	..	..	..	..
Tunisia	1,157.4	8.2	..	..	..	..	..	..

a. Data are for most recent year available during the period specified.

		Quality			Financing	
Average delay for firm in obtaining electrical connection (days) 2000–05[a]	Electric power transmission and distribution losses (% of output) 2000–05[a]	Electrical outages of firms (average number of days per year) 2000–05[a]	Firms that share or own their own generator (%) 2000–05[a]	Firms identifying electricity as major or very severe obstacle to business operation and growth (%) 2000–05[a]	Committed nominal investment in energy projects with private participation ($ millions) 2000–05[a]	Average annual ODA disbursements for energy ($ millions) 2000–05
..	14.5	..	..	..	45.0	0.7
55.6	..	77.3	29.9	68.5	..	63.3
..	10.4	..	..	..	..	0.0
..	..	..	..	..	..	7.0
..	..	..	..	..	..	..
..	19.2	..	..	..	21.5	0.2
..	..	..	..	..	..	0.1
..	..	..	..	..	..	1.3
..	..	..	..	..	..	0.0
..	..	..	..	..	..	..
..	3.1	..	..	..	..	0.0
..	73.6	..	..	..	..	12.8
..	15.7	..	..	..	20.0	0.5
..	..	..	..	..	..	..
..	..	..	..	..	..	0.2
65.4	..	93.9	43.0	36.7	..	50.4
105.5	10.0	0.0	17.1	42.5	300.0	0.9
..	17.8	..	..	..	..	..
..	..	..	..	..	..	0.1
..	14.7	..	..	..	184.0	1.6
..	..	..	..	..	..	6.7
..	..	..	..	..	..	0.2
43.7	17.4	83.6	70.9	47.1	..	188.9
43.3	..	19.1	26.1	35.1	..	0.0
..	..	..	..	..	..	..
49.5	..	78.0	21.5	41.3	..	2.6
84.4	..	63.2	49.1	19.2	..	1.0
32.0	..	10.5	45.3	24.0	365.9	0.2
..	..	..	..	..	..	8.8
20.0	..	6.0	39.5	12.7	..	131.2
..	10.1	..	..	..	5.8	24.5
..	18.4	..	..	..	1.0	0.1
16.5	..	11.1	24.8	1.6	..	0.2
..	33.7	..	..	..	539.0	0.6
..	..	..	..	..	..	5.4
..	..	..	..	..	50.0	0.1
10.3	14.7	26.1	62.5	30.5	87.0	6.0
..	..	..	..	..	..	..
..	..	..	..	..	..	41.2
..	..	..	..	..	..	0.1
5.3	6.1	5.5	9.5	9.0	7.0	0.1
..	15.6	..	..	..	..	0.0
..	..	..	..	..	..	9.9
44.0	23.3	60.6	55.4	..	32.0	58.3
..	34.0	..	..	..	67.7	..
25.6	..	70.8	36.0	..	124.0	4.9
142.4	4.0	30.0	38.2	39.6	12.4	2.1
..	15.1	..	..	..	..	0.0
94.3	15.9	12.4	29.5	11.4	400.0	..
80.1	12.2	13.9	19.3	26.5	678.0	..
..	28.4	..	..	..	..	..
7.7	16.1	5.8	13.8	8.9	360.0	..
..	11.8	..	..	..	30.0	..

Table 7.5 Financial sector infrastructure

	Macroeconomy				
	Foreign currency sovereign ratings		Gross national savings (% of GDP)	Money and quasi money (M2) (% of GDP)	Real interest rate (%)
	Long-term 2007	Short-term 2007	2005	2005	2005
SUB-SAHARAN AFRICA			**17.5**		
Angola			20.5	11.1	16.9
Benin	B	B	10.6	25.1	..
Botswana			50.5	26.5	6.4
Burkina Faso			..	20.9	..
Burundi			1.1	25.9	2.1
Cameroon	B	B	14.7	16.7	12.4
Cape Verde	B+	B	..	75.7	11.9
Central African Republic			14.0	16.5	15.0
Chad			21.3	7.6	-2.0
Comoros			5.9	21.4	8.5
Congo, Dem. Rep.			6.1	7.2	..
Congo, Rep.			33.5	14.8	9.8
Côte d'Ivoire			10.9	23.3	..
Djibouti			20.5	73.6	..
Equatorial Guinea			33.3	14.3	..
Eritrea			10.6	138.1	..
Ethiopia			11.8	44.8	1.0
Gabon			52.3	17.6	8.1
Gambia, The	CCC	C	9.1	43.9	29.4
Ghana	B+	B	21.4	27.6	..
Guinea			9.1	14.6	..
Guinea-Bissau			11.2	30.3	..
Kenya			11.8	36.9	8.2
Lesotho	BB-	B	37.5	26.9	8.3
Liberia			39.9	17.8	7.4
Madagascar			11.7	19.9	7.3
Malawi	B-	B	-4.3	20.5	15.3
Mali	B-	B	9.9	28.7	..
Mauritania			..	..	3.6
Mauritius			20.1	136.2	15.5
Mozambique	B	B	11.4	25.9	12.2
Namibia	BBB-	F3	40.0	42.6	2.8
Niger			..	13.4	..
Nigeria	BB-	B	30.5	18.8	-7.0
Rwanda	B-	B	..	19.5	..
São Tomé and Principe			..	60.4	..
Senegal			16.2	34.3	..
Seychelles			-18.2	114.6	8.9
Sierra Leone			7.6	18.1	10.2
Somalia			..	..	..
South Africa	BBB+	F2	13.9	56.4	5.6
Sudan			13.2	17.4	..
Swaziland			18.9	19.1	5.5
Tanzania			10.4	24.8	11.0
Togo			..	26.7	..
Uganda	B	B	10.0	19.3	11.0
Zambia			10.2	17.4	7.7
Zimbabwe			-0.4	44.9	-0.6
NORTH AFRICA			**29.3**		
Algeria			51.3	51.4	..
Egypt, Arab Rep.	BB+	B	..	92.4	7.6
Libya			..	28.8	..
Morocco	BBB-	F3	27.9	97.4	..
Tunisia	BBB	F2	22.6	57.3	..

a. Data are consolidated for regional security markets where they exist.

	Intermediation				Capital markets[a]		
Domestic credit to private sector (% of GDP) 2005	Interest rate spread (lending rate minus deposit rate) 2005	Ratio of bank non-performing loans to total gross loans (%) 2005	Bank branches (per 100,000 people) 2004	Listed domestic companies, total 2005	Market capitalization of listed companies (% of GDP) 2005	Turnover ratio for traded stocks (%) 2005
4.8	54.3	..	..	..	..	..
16.6	..	..	..	..	..	..
19.0	6.5	..	3.8	18.0	23.6	1.8
17.3	..	..	..	..	..	..
20.8	..	..	..	..	..	..
9.4	12.8	..	..	..	..	..
39.0	8.9	..	..	..	..	..
6.7	12.8	..	..	..	..	..
3.1	12.8	..	..	..	..	..
8.1	8.0	..	..	..	..	..
1.9	..	..	..	..	..	..
2.9	12.8	..	..	..	..	..
13.8	..	..	..	39.0	14.2	1.4
20.1	10.3	..	..	..	..	..
5.4	12.8	..	..	..	..	..
31.0	..	..	..	..	..	..
25.3	3.5	..	0.4	..	..	..
8.9	12.8	..	..	..	..	..
13.0	17.6	..	..	..	..	..
15.5	..	13.9	1.6	30.0	12.8	2.2
5.1	..	..	..	..	..	..
2.1	..	..	..	..	..	..
25.9	7.8	5.2	1.4	47.0	34.1	9.8
8.4	7.8	..	..	..	..	..
6.6	13.6	..	..	..	..	..
9.9	8.3	10.1	0.7	..	..	..
10.5	22.2	..	..	..	..	..
18.4	..	..	..	..	..	..
..	15.1	..	..	..	..	..
76.7	13.8	..	11.9	42.0	41.6	6.0
11.2	11.7	4.6	..	..	..	..
61.4	4.4	2.0	4.5	13.0	6.8	1.5
6.8	..	..	..	..	..	..
14.9	7.4	21.9	1.6	214.0	19.6	11.5
13.5	..	34.1	..	..	..	..
44.7	..	..	..	..	..	..
23.8	..	..	..	..	..	..
40.6	6.3	..	..	..	..	..
4.5	13.5	..	..	..	..	..
..	..	..	..	..	..	..
143.5	4.6	1.5	6.0	388.0	236.0	39.3
10.0	..	..	..	..	..	..
20.0	6.6	..	..	6.0	7.2	0.0
10.4	10.4	..	0.6	6.0	4.9	2.3
16.8	..	..	..	..	..	..
6.7	10.9	..	0.5	5.0	1.2	3.1
7.6	17.0	10.8	1.5	12.0	13.6	2.0
26.9	144.6	..	3.3	79.0	71.2	15.3
11.8	6.3	..	..	..	..	..
52.4	5.9	25.0	3.6	744.0	89.1	43.0
9.0	4.0	..	..	..	..	..
62.2	..	15.7	6.6	56.0	52.7	15.9
65.6	..	20.9	..	46.0	10.0	16.5

Table 8.1 Education

	Literacy rate (%)						Primary education						
	Youth (ages 15–24)			Adult (ages 15 and older)			Gross enrollment ratio (% of relevant age group)			Net enrollment ratio (% of relevant age group)			Student-teacher ratio
	Total 2000–05[a]	Male 2000–05[a]	Female 2000–05[a]	Total 2000–05[a]	Male 2000–05[a]	Female 2000–05[a]	Total 2005	Male 2005	Female 2005	Total 2005	Male 2005	Female 2005	2005
SUB-SAHARAN AFRICA							98	103	92				
Angola	72	84	63	67	83	54	..	..	..	..	..	..	..
Benin	45	59	33	35	48	23	96	107	85	78	86	70	47
Botswana	94	92	96	81	80	82	105	105	104	83	83	83	26
Burkina Faso	33	40	26	24	31	17	58	64	51	45	50	40	47
Burundi	73	77	70	59	67	52	85	91	78	60	63	58	49
Cameroon	..	..	..	68	77	60	117	126	107	..	..	..	48
Cape Verde	96	96	97	81	88	76	108	111	105	90	91	89	26
Central African Republic	59	70	47	49	65	33	56	67	44	..	..	..	..
Chad	38	56	23	26	41	13	77	92	62	..	..	..	63
Comoros	..	..	..	..	..	..	85	91	80	..	..	..	35
Congo, Dem. Rep.	70	78	63	67	81	54	..	..	..	..	..	..	..
Congo, Rep.	97	98	97	85	91	79	88	91	84	44	39	48	83
Côte d'Ivoire	61	71	52	49	61	39	..	..	..	..	..	..	..
Djibouti	..	..	..	..	..	..	40	44	36	33	37	30	35
Equatorial Guinea	95	95	95	87	93	80	114	117	111	..	..	..	48
Eritrea	..	..	..	..	..	..	64	71	57	47	51	43	48
Ethiopia	50	62	39	36	50	23	93	101	86	61	64	59	72
Gabon	96	97	95	84	88	80	..	..	..	..	..	..	..
Gambia, The	..	..	..	..	..	..	..	..	..	..	..	..	..
Ghana	71	76	65	58	66	50	88	90	87	65	65	65	33
Guinea	47	59	34	29	43	18	81	88	74	66	70	61	45
Guinea-Bissau	..	..	..	..	..	..	..	..	..	..	..	..	..
Kenya	80	80	81	74	78	70	114	116	112	80	80	80	40
Lesotho	..	..	..	82	74	90	132	132	131	87	84	89	42
Liberia	67	65	69	52	58	46	..	..	..	..	..	..	..
Madagascar	70	73	68	71	77	65	138	141	136	92	93	92	54
Malawi	..	..	..	..	..	..	122	121	124	95	92	97	64
Mali	..	..	..	24	33	16	66	74	59	51	56	45	54
Mauritania	61	68	55	51	60	43	93	93	94	72	72	72	40
Mauritius	95	94	95	84	88	81	102	102	102	95	94	96	22
Mozambique	..	..	..	..	..	..	105	114	96	79	82	75	66
Namibia	92	91	93	85	87	83	99	98	100	72	70	75	33
Niger	37	52	23	29	43	15	47	54	39	40	46	33	44
Nigeria	84	87	81	69	78	60	103	111	95	91	..	..	37
Rwanda	78	79	77	65	71	60	120	119	121	74	72	75	62
São Tomé and Principe	95	96	95	85	92	78	134	135	132	97	97	96	31
Senegal	49	58	41	39	51	29	88	89	86	76	77	75	47
Seychelles	99	99	99	92	91	92	..	..	..	..	..	..	..
Sierra Leone	48	60	37	35	47	24	155	171	139	..	..	..	67
Somalia	..	..	..	..	..	..	..	..	..	..	..	..	..
South Africa	..	..	..	..	..	..	..	..	..	..	..	..	..
Sudan	77	85	71	61	71	52	60	65	56	..	..	..	28
Swaziland	88	87	90	80	81	78	..	..	..	..	..	..	..
Tanzania	78	81	76	69	78	62	106	108	104	91	92	91	56
Togo	74	84	64	53	69	38	100	108	92	78	84	72	34
Uganda	77	83	71	67	77	58	118	118	117	..	..	..	50
Zambia	..	..	..	..	..	..	111	114	108	89	89	89	51
Zimbabwe	98	97	98	89	93	86	..	..	..	..	..	..	..
NORTH AFRICA							..	..	..				
Algeria	..	..	..	..	..	..	112	116	107	97	98	95	25
Egypt, Arab Rep.	..	..	..	..	..	..	..	..	..	..	..	..	..
Libya	..	..	..	..	..	..	107	108	106	..	..	..	..
Morocco	..	..	..	..	..	..	105	111	99	86	89	83	27
Tunisia	..	..	..	..	..	..	..	..	..	..	..	..	..

a. Data are for most recent year available during the period specified.

| Secondary education | | | | | | | Tertiary education | | | Public spending on education (%) | |
| Gross enrollment ratio (% of relevant age group) | | | Net enrollment ratio (% of relevant age group) | | | Student-teacher ratio | Gross enrollment ratio (% of relevant age group) | | | Share of government expenditure | Share of GDP |
Total 2005	Male 2005	Female 2005	Total 2005	Male 2005	Female 2005	2005	Total 2004	Male 2004	Female 2004	2000–05[a]	2000–05[a]
31	**35**	**28**									
..	..	..	..	..	..	..	..	..	..	..	3.0
33	41	23	..	..	..	..	..	..	..	21.0	3.0
75	73	77	55	51	58	14	5	5	4	28.0	11.0
14	16	12	11	13	9	31	2	3	1	..	5.0
13	15	11	..	..	..	19	2	3	1	18.0	5.0
44	49	39	..	..	..	33	6	7	5	11.0	2.0
68	65	70	58	55	60	23	7	7	7	34.0	7.0
..	..	..	..	..	..	..	2	..	..	..	..
16	23	8	..	..	..	34	1	2	0	..	2.0
35	40	30	..	..	..	14	..	..	..	..	4.0
..	..	..	..	..	..	..	..	..	..	..	..
..	..	..	..	..	..	34	..	..	..	9.0	2.0
..	..	..	..	..	..	..	..	..	..	22.0	5.0
24	29	19	23	27	18	..	2	3	2	34.0	8.0
..	..	..	..	..	..	..	..	..	..	..	1.0
31	40	23	25	30	20	51	..	..	..	..	5.0
31	38	24	28	34	22	54	3	4	1	14.0	4.0
..	..	..	..	..	..	..	..	..	..	..	4.0
..	..	..	..	..	..	42	..	..	..	14.0	2.0
44	47	40	37	39	35	19	5	7	4	..	5.0
30	39	21	24	31	17	33	3	5	1	..	2.0
..	..	..	..	..	..	..	..	..	..	..	..
49	50	48	42	42	42	32	..	..	..	35.0	7.0
39	34	43	25	19	30	26	3	3	4	31.0	13.0
..	..	..	..	..	..	..	3	3	2	29.0	3.0
28	31	25	24	25	22	..	..	..	..	..	6.0
24	..	..	..	..	..	..	3	3	2	..	4.0
21	22	19	15	17	14	28	3	5	2	13.0	2.0
89	89	88	82	81	82	17	17	15	19	14.0	4.0
14	16	11	7	8	6	..	..	..	..	26.0	4.0
61	60	61	38	32	44	..	..	..	..	22.0	7.0
9	10	7	8	9	6	31	1	1	1	..	2.0
34	37	31	27	29	25	..	..	..	..	..	..
14	15	13	..	..	..	26	3	3	2	16.0	4.0
44	43	46	32	30	34	..	..	..	..	..	..
26	30	23	21	23	18	26	5	..	..	..	5.0
..	..	..	..	..	..	14	..	..	..	..	5.0
30	34	26	..	..	..	..	..	..	..	..	5.0
..	..	..	..	..	..	..	..	..	..	..	..
..	..	..	..	..	..	..	..	..	..	19.0	5.0
34	35	33	..	..	..	25	..	..	..	..	..
..	..	..	..	..	..	..	4	4	5	18.0	6.0
..	..	..	..	..	..	..	1	2	1	..	..
40	54	27	..	..	..	34	..	..	..	25.0	3.0
16	18	14	13	14	12	19	..	..	..	24.0	5.0
28	31	25	26	29	23	34	..	..	..	17.0	2.0
..	..	..	..	..	..	..	..	..	..	..	5.0
83	80	86	..	..	..	21	20	17	24	..	..
..	..	..	..	..	..	17	..	..	..	..	..
..	..	..	..	..	..	..	..	..	..	..	..
50	54	46	..	..	..	19	11	12	10	32.0	7.0
..	..	..	..	..	..	18	..	..	..	..	7.0

Table 8.2 Health

	Life expectancy at birth (years)			Mortality Under-five mortality rate (per 1,000)			Infant mortality rate (per 1,000 live births)	Maternal mortality ratio, modeled estimate (per 100,000 live births)	Diseases Prevalence of HIV (% of ages 15–49)	Incidence of tuberculosis (per 100,000 people)	Deaths due to malaria (per 100,000 people)
	Total 2005	Male 2005	Female 2005	Total 2000–05[b]	Male 2000–05[b]	Female 2000–05[b]	2005	2000–05[b]	2005	2005	2000–05[b]
SUB-SAHARAN AFRICA											
Angola	41.4	40.0	42.9	260	276	243	154	1,700	3.7	269	354
Benin	55.0	54.2	55.8	150	152	153	89	850	1.8	88	177
Botswana	35.0	35.4	34.5	120	123	109	87	100	24.1	655	15
Burkina Faso	48.5	47.7	49.3	191	193	191	96	1,000	2.0	223	292
Burundi	44.6	43.7	45.7	190	196	184	114	1,000	3.3	334	143
Cameroon	46.1	45.5	46.6	149	156	143	87	730	5.4	174	108
Cape Verde	70.7	67.7	73.9	35	38	35	26	150	..	174	22
Central African Republic	39.4	38.8	40.1	193	201	185	115	1,100	10.7	314	137
Chad	44.0	43.0	45.1	208	212	188	124	1,100	3.5	272	207
Comoros	62.6	61.3	64.0	71	76	64	53	480	0.1	45	80
Congo, Dem. Rep.	44.0	43.0	45.1	205	217	192	129	990	3.2	356	224
Congo, Rep.	52.8	51.5	54.1	108	113	103	81	510	5.3	367	78
Côte d'Ivoire	46.2	45.4	46.9	195	225	162	118	690	7.1	382	76
Djibouti	53.4	52.3	54.5	133	131	120	88	730	3.1	762	..
Equatorial Guinea	42.3	42.0	42.6	205	213	195	123	880	3.2	233	152
Eritrea	54.9	53.1	56.8	78	89	75	50	630	2.4	282	74
Ethiopia	42.7	41.9	43.4	127	175	158	80	850	..	344	198
Gabon	53.8	53.4	54.3	91	102	80	60	420	7.9	308	80
Gambia, The	56.8	55.5	58.2	137	129	115	97	540	2.4	242	52
Ghana	57.5	57.0	58.0	112	113	111	68	540	2.3	205	70
Guinea	54.1	53.8	54.3	160	160	150	97	740	1.5	236	200
Guinea-Bissau	45.1	43.8	46.5	200	212	194	124	1,100	3.8	206	150
Kenya	49.0	49.8	48.1	120	129	110	79	1,000	6.1	641	63
Lesotho	35.2	34.5	35.9	132	87	76	102	550	23.2	696	84
Liberia	42.5	41.7	43.3	235	249	220	157	760	..	301	201
Madagascar	55.8	54.6	57.1	119	128	117	74	550	0.5	234	184
Malawi	40.5	40.8	40.2	125	179	172	79	1,800	14.1	409	275
Mali	48.6	48.0	49.3	218	230	208	120	1,200	1.7	278	454
Mauritania	53.7	52.1	55.3	125	134	115	78	1,000	0.7	298	108
Mauritius	73.0	69.7	76.5	15	17	14	13	24	0.6	62	..
Mozambique	41.8	41.4	42.3	145	154	150	100	1,000	16.1	447	232
Namibia	46.9	47.0	46.8	62	70	57	46	300	19.6	697	52
Niger	44.9	44.9	45.0	256	256	262	150	1,600	1.1	164	469
Nigeria	43.8	43.7	44.0	194	198	195	100	800	3.9	283	141
Rwanda	44.1	42.6	45.7	203	211	195	118	1,400	3.1	361	200
São Tomé and Principe	63.5	62.4	64.6	118	122	114	75	..	..	105	80
Senegal	56.5	55.2	57.7	119	141	132	61	690	0.9	255	72
Seychelles	..	..	..	13	14	13	12	..	..	34	..
Sierra Leone	41.4	40.0	42.8	282	296	269	165	2,000	1.6	475	312
Somalia	47.7	46.5	49.0	225	222	228	133	1,100	0.9	224	81
South Africa	47.7	46.7	48.7	68	72	62	55	230	18.8	600	0
Sudan	56.7	55.3	58.1	90	98	84	62	590	1.6	228	70
Swaziland	41.5	42.2	40.7	160	163	150	110	370	33.4	1,262	0
Tanzania	46.3	46.0	46.6	122	134	117	76	1,500	6.5	342	130
Togo	55.1	53.3	57.0	139	151	128	78	570	3.2	373	47
Uganda	50.0	49.3	50.6	136	144	132	79	880	6.7	369	152
Zambia	38.4	38.9	37.9	182	190	173	102	750	17.0	600	141
Zimbabwe	37.3	37.9	36.6	132	136	121	81	1,100	20.1	601	1
NORTH AFRICA											
Algeria	71.7	70.4	73.1	39	41	39	34	140	0.1	55	..
Egypt, Arab Rep.	70.5	68.4	72.8	33	36	36	28	84	0.1	25	..
Libya	74.4	72.1	76.8	19	20	19	18	97	..	18	..
Morocco	70.4	68.2	72.7	40	47	38	36	220	0.1	89	..
Tunisia	73.5	71.5	75.5	24	29	22	20	120	0.1	24	..

a. Diphtheria, pertussis, and tetanus toxoid.
b. Data are for most recent year available during the period specified.

		Prevention and treatment							
Child immunization rate (% of children ages 12–23 months)		Malnutrition (% of children under age 5)		Births attended by skilled health staff (% of total)	Contraceptive prevalence rate (% of women ages 15–49)	Children sleeping under insecticide-treated bednets (% of children under age 5)	Tuberculosis cases detected under DOTS (% of estimated cases)	Tuberculosis treatment success rate (% of registered cases)	Children under age 5 with fever receiving antimalarial drugs (%)
Measles 2005	DPT[a] 2005	Stunting 2000–05[b]	Underweight 2000–05[b]	2000–05[b]	2000–05[b]	2000–05[b]	2005	2000–05[b]	2000–05[b]
45	47	45.2	30.5	44.7	6.0	2.0	85.4	67.6	63.0
85	93	30.7	30.0	75.0	18.6	7.0	83.3	82.7	60.0
90	97	23.1	12.5	94.2	48.0	..	68.5	64.6	..
84	96	38.7	37.7	37.8	13.8	2.0	17.6	67.1	50.0
75	74	56.8	45.1	25.2	16.0	1.0	29.6	78.2	31.0
68	80	31.7	18.1	61.8	26.0	1.0	105.8	70.7	53.0
65	73	..	..	..	..	..	33.9	71.0	..
35	40	38.9	24.3	44.1	28.0	2.0	40.4	91.4	69.0
23	20	40.9	36.7	14.4	2.8	0.6	21.7	69.0	44.0
80	80	42.3	25.4	61.8	26.0	9.0	48.9	94.1	63.0
70	73	38.1	31.0	60.7	31.0	1.0	72.4	84.8	45.0
56	65	..	..	86.2	44.3	..	57.4	63.0	..
51	56	..	17.2	68.0	..	4.0	37.6	70.6	58.0
65	71	23.0	26.8	60.6	9.0	..	42.1	79.6	..
51	33	..	18.6	64.6	..	1.0	..	51.3	49.0
84	83	37.6	39.6	28.3	8.0	4.0	12.5	85.1	4.0
59	69	46.5	38.4	5.7	14.7	1.5	32.7	79.3	3.0
55	38	20.7	11.9	85.5	32.7	..	57.5	40.3	..
84	88	19.2	17.2	54.7	18.0	15.0	69.4	85.9	55.0
83	84	29.9	22.1	47.1	25.2	4.0	37.5	71.7	63.0
59	69	..	32.7	55.5	7.0	4.0	55.6	71.7	56.0
80	80	30.5	25.0	34.7	8.0	7.0	79.1	75.4	58.0
69	76	30.3	19.9	41.6	39.3	5.0	42.8	80.3	27.0
85	83	46.1	18.0	55.4	30.0	..	84.8	69.2	..
94	87	39.5	26.5	50.9	10.0	..	50.0	70.4	..
59	61	47.7	41.9	51.3	27.1	0.2	67.0	70.8	34.0
82	93	49.0	21.9	56.1	30.6	15.0	38.6	71.0	28.0
86	85	38.2	33.2	40.6	8.1	8.0	21.1	70.6	38.0
61	71	34.5	31.8	56.9	8.0	2.0	28.2	21.9	33.0
98	97	..	..	99.2	76.0	..	31.7	88.9	..
77	72	41.0	23.7	47.7	25.5	..	48.7	76.7	15.0
73	86	23.6	24.0	75.5	43.7	3.0	89.9	68.4	14.0
83	89	39.7	40.1	15.7	14.0	6.0	49.6	60.7	48.0
35	25	38.3	28.7	35.2	12.6	1.0	21.6	73.4	34.0
89	95	45.3	22.5	38.6	17.4	13.0	29.1	76.5	12.3
88	97	28.9	12.9	76.4	29.0	22.8	..	..	61.0
74	84	25.4	22.7	58.0	10.5	14.0	50.7	74.4	29.0
99	99	..	..	..	..	..	65.3	92.3	..
67	64	33.8	27.2	41.7	4.0	2.0	37.4	81.7	61.0
35	35	23.3	25.8	24.8	..	..	85.8	90.5	..
82	94	..	..	92.0	60.3	..	103.1	69.7	..
60	59	43.3	40.7	87.0	7.0	0.0	34.6	77.2	50.0
60	71	30.2	10.3	74.0	48.0	0.0	42.3	50.3	26.0
91	90	37.7	21.8	43.4	26.4	16.0	44.9	81.3	58.2
70	82	..	..	60.8	26.0	54.0	17.9	66.6	60.0
86	84	39.1	22.9	39.0	22.8	0.0	45.1	70.5	..
84	80	46.8	23.0	43.4	34.2	7.0	51.6	82.7	52.0
85	90	..	..	..	..	..	41.3	54.3	..
		..	..						..
83	88	19.1	10.4	95.9	57.0	..	105.9	90.9	..
98	98	15.6	8.6	74.2	59.2	..	62.7	70.1	..
97	98	..	..	..	..	..	177.7	63.9	..
97	98	18.1	10.2	62.6	63.0	..	101.0	87.0	..
96	98	12.3	4.0	89.9	66.0	..	82.5	89.9	..

Table 8.2 Health (continued)

	Water and sanitation						Human resources		
	Population with sustainable access to an improved water source (%)			Population with sustainable access to improved sanitation (%)			Health workers (per 1,000 people)		
	Total 2004	Urban 2004	Rural 2004	Total 2004	Urban 2004	Rural 2004	Physicians 2004	Nurses 2004	Midwives 2004
SUB-SAHARAN AFRICA									
Angola	53	75	40	31	56	16	0.1	..	..
Benin	67	78	57	33	59	11	0.0	0.8	..
Botswana	95	100	90	42	57	25	0.4	2.7	..
Burkina Faso	61	94	54	13	42	6	0.1	0.4	0.1
Burundi	79	92	77	36	47	35	0.0	0.2	..
Cameroon	66	86	44	51	58	43	0.2	1.6	..
Cape Verde	80	86	73	43	61	19	0.5	0.9	..
Central African Republic	75	93	61	27	47	12	0.1	0.3	0.1
Chad	42	41	43	9	24	4	0.0	0.3	0.0
Comoros	86	92	82	33	41	29	0.1	0.7	..
Congo, Dem. Rep.	46	82	29	30	42	25	0.1	0.5	..
Congo, Rep.	58	84	27	27	28	25	0.2	1.0	..
Côte d'Ivoire	84	97	74	37	46	29	0.1	0.6	..
Djibouti	73	76	59	82	88	50	0.2	0.4	0.1
Equatorial Guinea	43	45	42	53	60	46	0.3	0.5	0.1
Eritrea	60	74	57	9	32	3	0.1	0.6	..
Ethiopia	22	81	11	13	44	7	..	0.2	..
Gabon	88	95	47	36	37	30	0.3	5.2	..
Gambia, The	82	95	77	53	72	46	..	..	..
Ghana	75	88	64	18	27	11	0.2	0.9	..
Guinea	50	78	35	18	31	11	0.1	0.6	0.0
Guinea-Bissau	59	79	49	35	57	23	0.1	0.7	0.0
Kenya	61	83	46	43	46	41	0.1	1.1	..
Lesotho	79	92	76	37	61	32	..	..	..
Liberia	61	72	52	27	49	7	0.0	0.2	0.1
Madagascar	46	77	35	32	48	26	0.3	0.3	..
Malawi	73	98	68	61	62	61	0.0	0.6	..
Mali	50	78	36	46	59	39	0.1	0.5	0.0
Mauritania	53	59	44	34	49	8	0.1	0.6	..
Mauritius	100	100	100	94	95	94	1.1	3.7	0.0
Mozambique	43	72	26	32	53	19	0.0	0.2	0.1
Namibia	87	98	81	25	50	13	0.3	3.1	..
Niger	46	80	36	13	43	4	0.0	0.2	..
Nigeria	48	67	31	44	53	36	..	1.7	..
Rwanda	74	92	69	42	56	38	0.0	0.4	0.0
São Tomé and Principe	79	89	73	25	32	20	0.5	1.6	0.3
Senegal	76	92	60	57	79	34	0.1	0.3	..
Seychelles	88	100	75	..	..	100	1.5	7.9	..
Sierra Leone	57	75	46	39	53	30	0.0	0.4	..
Somalia	29	32	27	26	48	14	..	..	..
South Africa	88	99	73	65	79	46	0.8	4.1	..
Sudan	70	78	64	34	50	24	0.2	0.8	0.1
Swaziland	62	87	54	48	59	44	0.2	6.3	..
Tanzania	62	85	49	47	53	43	..	..	..
Togo	52	80	36	35	71	15	0.0	0.4	..
Uganda	60	87	56	43	54	41	0.1	0.6	0.1
Zambia	58	90	40	55	59	52	0.1	1.7	0.3
Zimbabwe	81	98	72	53	63	47	0.2	0.7	..
NORTH AFRICA									
Algeria	85	88	80	92	99	82	..	..	..
Egypt, Arab Rep.	98	99	97	70	86	58	..	..	..
Libya	..	..	..	97	97	96	..	..	..
Morocco	81	99	56	73	88	52	0.5	0.8	..
Tunisia	93	99	82	85	96	65	1.3	2.9	..

	Expenditure on health						
	Share of GDP (%)			Share of total health expenditure (%)		Out-of-pocket (% of private expenditure on health)	Health expenditure per capita ($)
	Total 2004	Public 2004	Private 2004	Public 2004	Private 2004	2004	2004
	1.9	1.5	0.4	79.4	20.6	100.0	25.5
	4.9	2.5	2.4	51.2	48.8	99.9	24.2
	6.4	4.0	2.4	62.9	37.1	27.9	328.6
	6.1	3.3	2.8	54.8	45.2	97.9	24.2
	3.2	0.8	2.4	26.2	73.8	100.0	3.0
	5.2	1.5	3.7	28.0	72.0	94.5	50.7
	5.2	3.9	1.3	75.8	24.2	99.8	97.8
	4.1	1.5	2.6	36.8	63.2	95.4	13.2
	4.2	1.5	2.7	36.9	63.1	95.8	19.6
	2.8	1.6	1.2	56.9	43.1	100.0	13.2
	4.0	1.1	2.9	28.1	71.9	100.0	4.7
	2.5	1.2	1.3	49.2	50.8	100.0	27.6
	3.8	0.9	2.9	23.8	76.2	88.7	33.0
	6.3	4.4	1.9	69.2	30.8	98.6	53.1
	1.6	1.2	0.4	77.1	22.9	75.1	168.2
	4.5	1.8	2.7	39.2	60.8	100.0	9.9
	5.3	2.7	2.6	51.5	48.5	78.3	5.6
	4.5	3.1	1.4	68.8	31.2	100.0	231.3
	6.8	1.8	5.0	27.1	72.9	68.2	18.5
	6.7	2.8	3.9	42.2	57.8	78.2	27.2
	5.3	0.7	4.6	13.2	86.8	99.5	21.8
	4.8	1.3	3.5	27.3	72.7	90.0	8.7
	4.1	1.8	2.3	42.7	57.3	81.9	20.1
	6.5	5.5	1.0	84.2	15.8	18.2	49.4
	5.6	3.6	2.0	63.9	36.1	98.5	8.6
	3.0	1.8	1.2	59.1	40.9	52.5	7.3
	12.9	9.6	3.3	74.7	25.3	35.2	19.3
	6.6	3.2	3.4	49.2	50.8	99.5	23.8
	2.9	2.0	0.9	69.4	30.6	100.0	14.5
	4.3	2.4	1.9	54.7	45.3	80.8	222.3
	4.0	2.7	1.3	68.4	31.6	38.5	12.3
	6.8	4.7	2.1	69.0	31.0	18.1	189.8
	4.2	2.2	2.0	52.5	47.5	85.1	8.6
	4.6	1.4	3.2	30.4	69.6	90.4	23.0
	7.5	4.3	3.2	56.8	43.2	36.9	15.5
	11.5	9.9	1.6	86.2	13.8	100.0	47.8
	5.9	2.4	3.5	40.3	59.7	94.5	39.4
	6.1	4.6	1.5	75.3	24.7	62.5	534.4
	3.3	1.9	1.4	59.0	41.0	100.0	6.6
	..	..	..	..	..	..	..
	8.6	3.5	5.1	40.4	59.6	17.2	390.2
	4.1	1.5	2.6	35.4	64.6	98.1	24.7
	6.3	4.0	2.3	63.8	36.2	40.2	145.8
	4.0	1.7	2.3	43.6	56.4	83.2	12.0
	5.5	1.1	4.4	20.7	79.3	84.9	17.9
	7.6	2.5	5.1	32.7	67.3	51.3	19.0
	6.3	3.4	2.9	54.7	45.3	71.4	29.6
	7.5	3.5	4.0	46.1	53.9	48.7	27.2
	3.6	2.6	1.0	72.5	27.5	94.6	93.9
	5.9	2.2	3.7	37.0	63.0	..	64.0
	3.8	2.8	1.0	74.9	25.1	100.0	195.4
	5.1	1.7	3.4	34.3	65.7	76.0	82.2
	..	..	..	..	..	..	..

Table 9.1 Rural development

	Rural population (%)		Rural population density (rural population per sq. km of arable land)	Share of rural population below the national poverty line			
	Share of total population 2005	Annual growth 2005	2000–05[a]	Surveys 1990–99		Surveys 2000–05	
				Year[a]	Percent	Year[a]	Percent
SUB-SAHARAN AFRICA	**64.7**	**1.4**					
Angola	46.7	1.5	219.0	..	..	..	..
Benin	59.9	2.6	181.0	1999	33.0	..	..
Botswana	42.6	−2.2	208.1	..	..	..	..
Burkina Faso	81.7	2.7	211.5	1998	61.1	2003	52.4
Burundi	90.0	3.3	643.7	1990	36.0	..	..
Cameroon	45.4	−0.3	124.8	1996	59.6	2001	49.9
Cape Verde	42.7	0.5	465.4	..	..	..	..
Central African Republic	62.0	1.2	126.8	..	..	..	..
Chad	74.7	2.6	191.4	1996	67.0	..	..
Comoros	63.0	1.1	462.5	..	..	..	..
Congo, Dem. Rep.	67.9	2.3	557.0	..	..	..	..
Congo, Rep.	39.8	2.0	308.9	..	..	..	..
Côte d'Ivoire	55.0	0.8	297.7	..	..	..	..
Djibouti	13.9	−2.2	11,487.9	..	..	..	..
Equatorial Guinea	61.1	2.2	226.3	..	..	..	..
Eritrea	80.6	3.5	586.0	..	..	..	..
Ethiopia	84.0	1.6	524.0	1996	47.0	2000	45.0
Gabon	16.4	−2.6	73.5	..	..	..	..
Gambia, The	46.1	0.6	219.2	1998	61.0	..	..
Ghana	52.2	0.6	272.3	1999	49.9	..	..
Guinea	67.0	1.3	534.4	..	..	..	..
Guinea-Bissau	70.4	3.0	350.3	..	..	..	..
Kenya	79.3	2.1	561.0	1997	53.0	..	..
Lesotho	81.3	−0.4	445.4	..	..	..	..
Liberia	41.9	−0.5	366.3	..	..	..	..
Madagascar	73.2	2.5	439.3	1999	76.7	..	..
Malawi	82.8	1.7	421.2	1998	66.5	..	..
Mali	69.5	2.2	195.7	1998	75.9	..	..
Mauritania	59.6	2.8	354.3	1996	65.5	2000	61.2
Mauritius	57.6	0.9	716.1	..	..	..	..
Mozambique	65.5	0.7	293.5	1997	71.3	..	..
Namibia	64.9	0.3	160.8	..	..	..	..
Niger	83.2	3.2	75.2	1993	66.0	..	..
Nigeria	51.8	0.8	236.3	1993	36.4	..	..
Rwanda	80.7	0.4	605.0	..	..	2000	65.7
São Tomé and Principe	42.0	0.1	818.9	..	..	..	..
Senegal	58.4	2.0	265.8	1992	40.4	..	..
Seychelles	47.1	0.2	3,962.8	..	..	..	..
Sierra Leone	59.3	2.2	545.9	..	..	2004	79.0
Somalia	64.8	2.7	483.6	..	..	..	..
South Africa	40.7	0.0	129.4	..	..	..	..
Sudan	59.2	0.4	125.2	..	..	..	..
Swaziland	75.9	0.8	473.4	..	..	..	..
Tanzania	75.8	2.1	699.6	1991	40.8	2001	38.7
Togo	59.9	1.4	142.5	..	..	..	..
Uganda	87.4	3.4	452.6	..	..	2003	41.7
Zambia	65.0	1.6	139.7	1998	83.1	2004	78.0
Zimbabwe	64.1	−0.1	259.4	1996	48.0	..	..
NORTH AFRICA	**46.6**	**0.9**					
Algeria	36.7	−0.4	160.9	1995	30.3	..	..
Egypt, Arab Rep.	57.2	1.8	1,411.6	1996	23.3	..	..
Libya	15.2	−0.3	49.2	..	..	..	..
Morocco	41.3	−0.7	148.7	1999	27.2	..	..
Tunisia	34.7	−0.1	125.1	1995	13.9	..	..

a. Data are for most recent year available during the period specified.

Share of rural population with sustainable access (%)				
To an improved water source 2000–05[a]	To improved sanitation facilities 2000–05[a]	To electricity 2000–05[a]	To transportation (within 2 km of an all-season road) 2000–05[a]	To landline telephone 2000–05[a]
42.7	**28.1**			
40.0	16.0	..	..	..
57.0	11.0	5.6	32.0	1.0
90.0	25.0	..	..	..
54.0	6.0	0.8	25.0	0.3
77.0	35.0	..	..	..
44.0	43.0	16.3	20.0	0.0
73.0	19.0	..	..	..
61.0	12.0	..	..	..
43.0	4.0	0.3	5.0	0.0
82.0	29.0	..	..	..
29.0	25.0	..	26.0	..
27.0	25.0	16.4	..	0.2
74.0	29.0	..	..	..
59.0	50.0	..	..	..
42.0	46.0	..	..	..
57.0	3.0	..	..	..
11.0	7.0	2.0	17.0	0.2
47.0	30.0	31.4	..	1.8
77.0	46.0	..	..	..
64.0	11.0	20.9	..	0.7
35.0	11.0	3.2	..	0.3
49.0	23.0	..	..	..
46.0	41.0	3.6	..	6.0
76.0	32.0	0.8	..	10.6
52.0	7.0	..	..	..
35.0	26.0	9.7	..	3.0
68.0	61.0	2.5	..	2.1
36.0	39.0	2.7	..	0.1
44.0	8.0	2.7	..	0.2
100.0	94.0	..	..	..
26.0	19.0	1.5	..	0.1
81.0	13.0	10.4	..	4.5
36.0	4.0	..	37.0	..
31.0	36.0	34.6	47.0	1.8
69.0	38.0	1.5	..	0.2
73.0	20.0	..	..	..
60.0	34.0	19.0	..	7.5
75.0	100.0	..	..	..
46.0	30.0	..	..	..
27.0	14.0	..	..	..
73.0	46.0	..	..	..
64.0	24.0	..	..	..
54.0	44.0	..	..	..
49.0	43.0	1.8	38.0	3.0
36.0	15.0	..	..	..
56.0	41.0	2.6	..	0.9
40.0	52.0	3.5	..	0.6
72.0	47.0	..	..	..
85.9	**61.9**			
80.0	82.0	..	..	..
97.0	58.0	..	..	..
68.0	96.0	..	..	..
56.0	52.0	..	..	..
82.0	65.0	..	..	..

Table 9.2 Agriculture

	Agriculture value added (% of GDP) 2005	Production index (1999–2001=100)			Cereal production (thousands of metric tons) 2004–05[a]	Trade			
						Agricultural		Food	
		Crop 2004–05[a]	Food 2004–05[a]	Livestock 2004–05[a]		Exports ($ millions) 2004–05[a]	Imports ($ millions) 2004–05[a]	Exports ($ millions) 2004–05[a]	Imports ($ millions) 2004–05[a]
SUB-SAHARAN AFRICA									
Angola	7.2	119.2	112.9	100.0	725	6	985	1	741
Benin	32.2	133.9	137.4	116.2	1,109	240	267	44	244
Botswana	1.8	113.1	104.3	102.4	45	52	126	49	92
Burkina Faso	..	130.0	115.2	110.3	2,902	338	169	63	108
Burundi	31.6	104.2	104.4	100.2	280	54	19	1	16
Cameroon	18.7	104.9	104.7	103.2	1,684	608	458	347	428
Cape Verde	..	85.4	91.8	102.1	4	0	113	0	88
Central African Republic	54.7	97.7	108.2	114.7	192	16	33	15	26
Chad	20.9	115.7	112.2	107.6	1,213	123	80	55	65
Comoros	51	105.9	104.6	95.9	21	29	34	26	30
Congo, Dem. Rep.	44.7	96.7	97.5	100.4	1,570	39	336	8	227
Congo, Rep.	4.7	105.5	108.8	121.1	9	40	261	30	301
Côte d'Ivoire	21.7	97.4	101.2	111.0	2,205	3,180	683	2,614	535
Djibouti	3.2	114.6	109.6	108.5	..	12	163	11	119
Equatorial Guinea	2.8	93.8	93.4	101.9	-	7	57	6	24
Eritrea	20.7	71.5	86.3	99.5	83	3	127	2	126
Ethiopia	42.9	110.5	112.1	115.8	9,280	382	425	125	385
Gabon	4.9	102.3	101.7	101.5	32	17	227	2	185
Gambia, The	29.6	65.6	69.0	103.1	213	17	155	15	127
Ghana	37.5	121.2	121.0	111.8	1,943	1,344	1,074	1,302	729
Guinea	18.6	110.4	113.8	115.3	1,142	70	220	42	154
Guinea-Bissau	59.3	109.8	109.7	109.1	171	62	44	62	35
Kenya	24.1	101.6	104.3	108.7	2,730	1,423	519	393	413
Lesotho	14.6	111.2	106.0	100.0	248	6	60	1	47
Liberia	66	99.3	97.3	110.0	110	96	121	3	105
Madagascar	25.8	108.8	107.6	104.4	3,391	122	90	104	80
Malawi	29.8	91.8	95.6	101.9	1,843	397	100	76	59
Mali	33.7	111.2	109.6	117.9	2,845	334	160	121	123
Mauritania	21.4	100.5	108.8	110.0	125	34	345	16	239
Mauritius	5.3	103.5	105.9	113.6	0	429	426	371	335
Mozambique	19.7	107.4	104.0	101.1	2,007	124	343	..	301
Namibia	10.7	110.8	114.0	113.9	107	249	278	145	197
Niger	..	122.1	118.4	104.6	2,672	71	262	65	226
Nigeria	23.4	105.9	106.2	108.8	22,783	623	2,285	548	2,024
Rwanda	42.3	113.1	113.2	109.9	319	34	58	1	50
São Tomé and Principe	17	109.3	109.2	107.7	3	4	20	4	14
Senegal	14.4	76.8	81.6	101.1	1,085	156	890	102	798
Seychelles	2.6	93.8	91.6	91.1	-	12	78	6	67
Sierra Leone	43.4	115.0	113.5	105.2	309	14	156	11	98
Somalia	..	..	..	..	..	88	152	85	148
South Africa	2.2	102.6	105.9	108.6	12,352	4,184	2,753	2,680	1,731
Sudan	32.3	109.7	107.8	107.2	3,643	626	642	307	572
Swaziland	6.5	100.8	105.9	111.1	71	272	74	262	54
Tanzania	42.4	106.8	105.6	109.6	5,020	534	342	146	278
Togo	43.6	110.9	104.2	109.2	787	96	85	50	64
Uganda	30	108.7	109.2	110.3	2,625	417	316	78	269
Zambia	16.8	108.2	108.0	98.9	1,364	322	173	159	139
Zimbabwe	13.4	66.1	86.4	99.0	837	847	468	115	371
NORTH AFRICA									
Algeria	8	128.4	116.8	104.8	3,998	61	3,971	50	3,456
Egypt, Arab Rep.	14	105.5	110.9	122.3	21,315	1,187	3,989	900	3,356
Libya	..	99.8	104.3	100.9	213	12	1,150	1	1,049
Morocco	14.1	148.6	132.1	99.8	8,604	1,430	2,367	1,168	1,776
Tunisia	11.6	101.7	101.6	98.8	2,155	974	1,206	783	874

a. Data are for most recent year available during the period specified.

AGRICULTURE, RURAL DEVELOPMENT, AND ENVIRONMENT

Share of land area (%)		Irrigated land (% of cropland) 2001–03[a]	Fertilizer consumption (100 grams per hectare of arable land) 2000–02[a]	Agricultural machinery Tractors per 100 sq km of arable land 2000–03[a]	Agricultural employment (% of total employment) 2000–05[a]	Incidence of drought 2000–05[a]	Agriculture value added per worker (2000 $) 2003–04[a]	Cereal yield (kilograms per hectare) 2005
Permanent cropland 2005	Cereal cropland 2005							
0.2	1.2	2.2	4.7	31.2	..	No	194	597
2.4	9.2	0.4	187.6	0.7	..	No	622	1,147
0.0	0.1	0.3	122.0	159.2	22.6	No	430	241
0.2	11.3	0.5	3.6	4.1	..	Yes	189	941
14.2	8.1	1.5	25.8	1.7	..	Yes	74	1,329
2.6	2.5	0.4	58.6	0.8	..	No	1,180	1,727
0.7	3.7	6.1	47.8	3.5	..	Yes	1,582	156
0.2	0.3	0.1	3.1	0.2	..	No	422	1,042
0.0	1.9	0.8	48.6	0.5	..	Yes	214	671
23.3	7.0	..	37.5	0.6	..	No	419	1,338
0.5	0.9	0.1	15.7	3.6	..	No	151	767
0.2	0.0	0.4	4.8	14.1	..	No	368	806
11.3	2.9	1.1	330.3	11.5	..	No	836	1,262
..	0.0	..	..	60.0	..	Yes	72	1,500
3.6	..	..	..	13.1	..	No	654	..
0.0	3.7	3.7	65.4	8.2	..	Yes	59	405
0.7	9.8	2.5	151.0	2.7	..	Yes	154	1,244
0.7	0.1	1.4	9.2	46.2	..	No	1,929	1,641
0.5	19.8	0.6	25.4	1.4	..	No	240	1,123
9.7	5.9	0.5	74.2	8.6	55.0	Yes	354	1,458
2.6	3.2	5.4	30.5	5.1	..	No	237	1,468
8.9	5.5	4.5	80.0	0.6	..	No	237	1,220
1.0	3.8	2.0	310.3	27.6	..	Yes	326	1,322
0.1	5.1	0.9	342.4	60.6	..	Yes	494	936
2.3	1.2	0.5	..	8.5	..	No	..	917
1.0	2.6	30.6	30.9	12.0	78.0	Yes	175	2,380
1.5	13.2	2.2	839.2	5.8	..	Yes	137	1,097
0.0	2.6	4.9	89.4	5.4	..	No	229	839
0.0	0.2	9.8	59.4	7.8	..	Yes	338	1,448
3.0	0.0	20.8	2,500.0	37.0	10.0	No	4,967	3,455
0.3	2.5	2.6	59.3	13.2	..	Yes	158	959
0.0	0.3	1.0	3.7	38.7	31.1	No	1,099	447
0.0	6.6	0.5	3.4	0.1	..	Yes	174	394
3.2	20.1	0.8	55.0	9.8	..	No	949	1,057
10.9	14.2	0.6	137.1	0.5	..	Yes	222	1,016
49.0	1.1	18.2	..	156.3	..	No	221	2,455
0.2	6.2	4.8	136.1	2.8	..	No	259	975
13.0	..	..	170.0	400.0	..	No	512	..
1.0	3.5	4.7	5.6	1.4	..	No	..	1,223
0.0	1.2	18.7	4.8	16.3	..	Yes	..	..
0.8	3.5	9.5	654.2	44.4	10.3	No	2,499	3,330
0.2	4.7	10.7	42.8	7.0	..	Yes	728	398
0.8	3.4	26.0	393.3	221.9	..	Yes	1,212	1,160
1.2	4.0	3.6	17.9	19.0	82.1	Yes	303	1,472
2.2	13.7	0.3	67.9	0.3	..	Yes	412	1,058
10.9	8.1	0.1	18.2	9.0	69.1	Yes	237	1,695
0.0	0.8	2.9	123.9	11.4	..	Yes	219	1,595
0.3	4.3	5.2	341.6	74.5	..	Yes	236	717
0.3	1.0	6.9	129.9	128.8	20.7	Yes	2,267	1,466
0.5	3.1	99.9	4,321.5	308.7	29.9	No	2,062	7,516
0.2	0.2	21.9	341.0	219.0	..	No	..	627
2.0	12.2	15.4	475.2	57.8	47.0	Yes	1,739	814
13.8	9.0	8.0	368.1	125.8	..	No	2,874	1,450

Table 9.3 Environment

	Forest area (% of land area)		Average annual deforestation (% change)	Renewable internal freshwater resources		Annual fresh water withdrawals	
				Total (billions of cubic meters)	Per capita (cubic meters)	Total (billions of cubic meters)	Share of internal resources (%)
	1990	2005	1990–2005	2005	2005	2002	2002
SUB-SAHARAN AFRICA							
Angola	48.9	47.4	0.2	148	9,284	9,284	0.2
Benin	30.0	21.3	1.9	10	1,221	1,221	1.3
Botswana	24.2	21.1	0.9	2	1,360	1,360	8.1
Burkina Faso	26.1	24.8	0.3	13	945	945	6.4
Burundi	11.3	5.9	3.2	10	1,338	1,338	2.9
Cameroon	52.7	45.6	0.9	273	16,726	16,726	0.4
Cape Verde	14.4	20.8	−3.0	0	592	592	7.3
Central African Republic	37.2	36.5	0.1	141	34,921	34,921	0.0
Chad	10.4	9.5	0.6	15	1,539	1,539	1.5
Comoros	5.4	2.2	3.9	1	1,998	1,998	0.8
Congo, Dem. Rep.	62.0	58.9	0.3	900	15,639	15,639	0.0
Congo, Rep.	66.5	65.8	0.1	222	55,515	55,515	0.0
Côte d'Ivoire	32.1	32.7	−0.1	77	4,231	4,231	1.2
Djibouti	0.3	0.3	0.0	0	378	378	6.3
Equatorial Guinea	66.3	58.2	0.8	26	51,637	51,637	0.4
Eritrea	..	15.4	0.3	3	636	636	10.7
Ethiopia	13.7	13.0	0.9	122	1,712	1,712	4.6
Gabon	85.1	84.5	0.0	164	118,511	118,511	0.1
Gambia, The	44.2	47.1	−0.4	3	1,978	1,978	1.0
Ghana	32.7	24.2	1.7	30	1,370	1,370	3.2
Guinea	30.1	27.4	0.6	226	24,037	24,037	0.7
Guinea-Bissau	78.8	73.7	0.4	16	10,086	10,086	1.1
Kenya	6.5	6.2	0.3	21	604	604	7.6
Lesotho	0.2	0.3	−4.0	5	2,897	2,897	1.0
Liberia	42.1	32.7	1.5	200	60,915	60,915	0.1
Madagascar	23.5	22.1	0.4	337	18,113	18,113	4.4
Malawi	41.4	36.2	0.8	16	1,250	1,250	6.3
Mali	11.5	10.3	0.7	60	4,438	4,438	10.9
Mauritania	0.4	0.3	2.4	0	130	130	425.0
Mauritius	19.2	18.2	0.3	3	2,252	2,252	21.8
Mozambique	25.5	24.6	0.2	100	5,068	5,068	0.6
Namibia	10.6	9.3	0.8	6	3,052	3,052	4.8
Niger	1.5	1.0	2.3	4	251	251	62.3
Nigeria	18.9	12.2	2.4	221	1,680	1,680	3.6
Rwanda	12.9	19.5	−3.4	10	1,051	1,051	1.6
São Tomé and Principe	28.1	28.1	0.0	2	14,055	14,055	..
Senegal	48.6	45.0	0.5	26	2,213	2,213	8.6
Seychelles	87.0	87.0	0.0	..	..	..	..
Sierra Leone	42.5	38.5	0.6	160	28,957	28,957	0.2
Somalia	13.2	11.4	0.9	6	729	729	54.8
South Africa	7.6	7.6	0.0	45	956	956	27.9
Sudan	32.1	28.4	0.8	30	828	828	124.4
Swaziland	27.4	31.5	−1.0	3	2,299	2,299	40.1
Tanzania	46.9	39.9	1.0	84	2,192	2,192	6.2
Togo	12.6	7.1	2.9	12	1,871	1,871	1.5
Uganda	25.0	18.4	1.8	39	1,353	1,353	0.8
Zambia	66.1	57.1	0.9	80	6,873	6,873	2.2
Zimbabwe	57.5	45.3	1.4	12	946	946	34.2
NORTH AFRICA							
Algeria	0.8	1.0	−1.8	11	341	341	54.2
Egypt, Arab Rep.	0.0	0.1	−3.5	2	24	24	3,794.4
Libya	0.1	0.1	0.0	1	103	103	711.3
Morocco	9.6	9.8	−0.1	29	961	961	43.4
Tunisia	4.1	6.8	−4.3	4	419	419	62.9

a. Data are for most recent year available during the period specified.

Water productivity (2000 $ per cubic meter of fresh water withdrawal)			Emissions of organic water pollutants (kilograms per day)		Energy production (kilotons of oil equivalent)		Energy use (kilotons of oil equivalent)		Combustible renewables and waste (% of total energy use)		Carbon dioxide emissions, industrial (thousands of metric tons)	
Total 2001–03[a]	Agriculture 2001–03[a]	Industry 2001–03[a]	1990	2001–03[a]	1990	2004	1990	2004	1990	2004	1990	2003
30.8	3.3	130.8	..	..	28,652	57,358	6,285	9,488	68.8	64.7	4,645	8,615
19.0	15.4	12.1	..	..	1,774	1,623	1,678	2,475	93.2	65.6	714	2,040
35.4	1.8	105.9	4,509	5,499	910	1,008	1,272	1,866	33.1	24.4	2,169	4,114
3.6	1.3	76.7	..	..	..	..	..	..	..	..	993	1,040
2.6	1.2	6.1	1,570	..	..	..	..	..	..	..	194	234
11.1	3.0	42.7	13,989	10,032	12,090	12,476	5,032	6,949	75.9	77.8	1,604	3,535
26.2	3.0	269.6	103	..	..	..	..	..	..	..	84	143
38.4	517.4	46.8	998	..	..	..	..	..	..	..	198	253
7.2	3.2	..	..	..	..	..	..	..	..	..	143	117
21.7	23.2	50.4	..	..	..	..	..	..	..	..	66	88
12.1	18.7	15.2	..	..	12,019	17,002	11,903	16,559	84.0	92.5	3,971	1,788
76.0	..	..	..	..	9,005	12,586	1,056	1,063	69.4	61.7	1,172	1,377
11.0	3.9	19.2	..	..	3,382	7,220	4,408	6,927	72.1	64.9	5,385	5,714
30.4	6.0	..	..	..	..	..	..	..	..	..	352	366
14.8	105.5	129.7	61	..	..	..	..	..	..	..	117	165
2.3	0.3	..	..	..	..	..	..	..	..	..	..	700
1.5	0.7	51.1	18,593	22,085	14,158	19,370	15,151	21,179	92.8	90.4	2,963	7,333
42.1	6.2	291.3	..	..	14,630	12,107	1,243	1,693	59.8	58.8	5,989	1,223
14.1	5.2	15.7	..	..	..	..	..	..	..	..	191	282
5.5	2.9	14.8	..	..	4,392	6,230	5,337	8,354	73.1	69.1	3,766	7,729
2.2	0.5	35.0	..	..	..	..	..	..	..	..	1,011	1,337
1.1	0.8	3.9	..	..	..	..	..	..	..	..	209	271
8.4	3.9	20.6	42,588	56,102	10,272	13,675	12,479	16,920	78.4	74.1	5,821	8,773
18.4	11.8	17.6	2,958	..	..	..	..	..	..	..	..	..
5.4	..	..	..	..	..	..	..	..	..	..	465	462
0.2	0.1	1.9	..	..	..	..	..	..	..	..	941	2,341
1.7	0.7	5.0	10,024	..	..	..	..	..	..	..	601	883
0.4	0.2	11.8	..	..	..	..	..	..	..	..	421	553
0.7	0.2	5.8	..	..	..	..	..	..	..	..	2,634	2,498
7.9	..	..	17,813	..	..	..	..	..	..	..	1,462	3,143
7.3	2.0	120.3	20,414	10,231	6,846	8,236	7,203	8,571	94.4	84.1	996	1,568
12.4	1.6	69.7	..	..	..	321	..	1,337	..	13.8	7	2,326
0.9	0.4	33.7	..	386	..	..	..	..	..	..	1,048	1,205
6.0	2.3	27.4	..	..	150,453	229,440	70,905	98,989	79.8	80.2	45,326	52,176
14.1	9.1	35.9	..	..	..	..	..	..	..	..	528	601
..	..	..	..	..	..	..	..	..	..	..	66	92
2.1	0.3	18.4	10,309	6,603	1,362	1,106	2,238	2,751	60.6	38.9	3,132	4,835
..	..	..	..	..	..	..	..	..	..	..	114	546
2.5	..	..	..	..	..	..	..	..	..	..	333	652
..	..	..	..	..	..	..	..	..	..	..	18	..
11.3	0.5	53.1	261,618	221,256	114,534	155,998	91,229	131,137	11.4	10.0	285,403	364,157
0.4	0.2	12.0	..	38,583	8,775	29,330	10,642	17,638	81.7	79.2	5,381	8,989
1.4	0.1	37.6	6,586	..	..	..	..	..	..	..	425	956
2.0	0.9	61.7	31,125	..	9,063	17,530	9,808	18,749	91.0	91.6	2,333	3,802
8.2	6.5	63.8	..	..	1,203	1,910	1,447	2,688	82.6	70.6	751	2,194
22.0	18.3	25.2	..	..	..	..	..	..	..	..	813	1,711
2.0	0.5	6.7	15,880	..	4,923	6,360	5,470	6,943	73.4	79.1	2,443	2,194
1.6	0.3	4.3	37,149	..	8,550	8,600	9,384	9,301	50.4	63.8	16,641	11,465
9.7	1.3	39.5	106,978	..	104,439	165,728	23,858	32,895	0.1	0.2	76,971	163,634
1.6	0.3	8.2	211,531	186,059	54,869	64,662	31,895	56,881	3.3	2.5	75,414	139,626
8.7	..	..	..	..	73,173	85,378	11,541	18,193	1.1	0.8	37,762	50,179
2.9	0.6	31.9	41,710	72,126	773	659	6,725	11,452	4.7	3.9	23,480	37,897
7.9	1.0	54.7	..	55,775	6,127	6,805	5,536	8,703	18.7	12.4	13,256	20,868

Table 10.1 Labor force participation

	Labor force ages 15 and older (thousands)			Participation rate (%)					
					Total				
	Total 2005	Male 2005	Female 2005	Ages 15 and older 2005	Ages 15–24 2005	Ages 25–54 2005	Ages 55–64 2005	Ages 65 and older 2005	
SUB-SAHARAN AFRICA	**296,962**	**170,084**	**126,878**	**73.9**	**65.6**	**83.5**	**73.6**	**48.6**	
Angola	6,939	3,742	3,197	81.3	79.2	87.7	78.8	54.5	
Benin	3,277	2,026	1,251	69.6	60.3	78.3	70.3	53.9	
Botswana	612	347	266	55.6	36.4	74.3	55.1	33.1	
Burkina Faso	5,796	3,109	2,687	83.0	77.3	90.9	84.1	58.9	
Burundi	3,775	1,813	1,962	91.0	87.4	97.6	94.4	79.7	
Cameroon	6,317	3,839	2,478	65.8	52.3	78.8	65.6	39.0	
Cape Verde	164	112	53	53.6	46.0	65.4	39.4	20.7	
Central African Republic	1,831	988	842	79.5	70.1	86.2	86.0	73.0	
Chad	3,465	1,779	1,686	67.4	56.0	81.3	82.3	69.9	
Comoros	333	200	133	71.9	60.2	82.2	75.2	50.8	
Congo, Dem. Rep.	23,003	13,554	9,449	75.8	71.8	81.7	71.0	50.0	
Congo, Rep.	1,627	962	665	77.0	58.4	79.9	76.8	72.4	
Côte d'Ivoire	6,763	4,820	1,943	64.1	55.7	72.5	66.1	48.8	
Djibouti	..	..	..	..	54.7	79.2	66.6	39.4	
Equatorial Guinea	196	124	72	69.8	68.6	75.2	73.8	40.6	
Eritrea	1,792	1,056	736	73.7	68.8	80.0	67.4	45.1	
Ethiopia	34,137	18,880	15,257	79.5	76.9	87.0	71.6	42.7	
Gabon	591	339	252	71.3	60.5	83.4	71.1	44.8	
Gambia, The	652	382	270	71.8	62.4	79.2	76.1	58.6	
Ghana	9,739	5,062	4,676	72.2	50.6	88.6	80.3	56.1	
Guinea	4,441	2,387	2,054	84.0	75.7	92.8	82.7	50.6	
Guinea-Bissau	643	378	265	77.2	74.3	81.0	71.6	53.8	
Kenya	15,413	8,725	6,688	78.7	70.4	88.5	81.5	52.7	
Lesotho	634	353	281	57.5	45.9	73.8	59.6	32.9	
Liberia	1,202	724	478	69.1	58.1	78.3	69.7	49.2	
Madagascar	8,540	4,413	4,127	82.0	68.2	92.2	88.1	71.8	
Malawi	5,934	2,987	2,947	87.5	80.3	93.5	90.6	77.6	
Mali	5,541	2,956	2,585	79.2	71.3	87.1	76.5	44.9	
Mauritania	1,202	717	485	68.7	57.4	79.3	66.9	41.3	
Mauritius	554	364	190	59.0	46.8	75.4	44.4	9.8	
Mozambique	9,265	4,288	4,977	83.6	67.3	94.4	92.5	82.6	
Namibia	641	365	276	53.9	33.0	73.9	48.4	25.8	
Niger	5,928	3,443	2,485	83.3	80.3	88.0	80.2	56.9	
Nigeria	46,958	30,562	16,395	64.1	53.5	74.9	73.0	46.5	
Rwanda	4,161	2,029	2,132	81.5	71.1	94.3	83.0	48.4	
São Tomé and Principe	..	..	..	..	37.5	68.4	47.0	21.1	
Senegal	4,592	2,678	1,914	68.6	58.9	80.1	63.8	35.7	
Seychelles	..	..	..	..	..	..	..	..	
Sierra Leone	2,342	1,436	906	74.1	73.7	79.1	67.3	50.7	
Somalia	3,513	2,133	1,380	76.4	76.9	79.5	68.1	52.7	
South Africa	19,780	12,177	7,603	61.9	49.7	76.4	48.9	11.5	
Sudan	10,041	7,559	2,482	45.6	32.7	57.5	52.4	37.7	
Swaziland	301	204	96	49.3	41.6	64.9	46.4	19.5	
Tanzania	19,235	9,718	9,516	87.4	80.6	96.0	90.2	61.8	
Togo	2,419	1,530	889	69.7	63.8	76.4	65.7	50.8	
Uganda	11,884	6,173	5,711	83.2	75.7	91.4	86.3	59.9	
Zambia	4,897	2,831	2,065	77.5	76.8	84.4	67.5	50.8	
Zimbabwe	5,659	3,216	2,443	72.5	59.8	87.3	83.8	58.8	
NORTH AFRICA	**64,379**	**47,798**	**16,580**	**50.5**	**36.7**	**63.7**	**45.4**	**17.8**	
Algeria	13,394	9,320	4,074	57.9	48.0	70.4	45.2	15.6	
Egypt, Arab Rep.	23,089	17,728	5,361	46.9	29.5	62.2	42.4	10.1	
Libya	2,291	1,706	585	56.0	40.1	71.7	50.9	24.2	
Morocco	11,686	8,663	3,023	53.9	43.0	64.1	47.6	19.3	
Tunisia	3,879	2,822	1,057	51.8	40.4	64.4	37.4	18.1	
AFRICA	**361,341**	**217,883**	**143,458**	**68.2**	**59.5**	**78.5**	**66.4**	**39.8**	

Male					Female				
Ages 15 and older 2005	Ages 15–24 2005	Ages 25–54 2005	Ages 55–64 2005	Ages 65 and older 2005	Ages 15 and older 2005	Ages 15–24 2005	Ages 25–54 2005	Ages 55–64 2005	Ages 65 and older 2005
85.7	73.8	96.5	89.5	67.4	62.4	57.4	70.7	59.4	33.6
89.8	86.1	97.1	88.6	76.1	73.2	72.5	78.6	70.3	37.6
86.0	73.0	95.9	88.4	79.6	53.2	47.3	60.2	55.2	35.5
65.1	40.0	90.5	78.8	48.9	46.8	32.8	59.1	36.3	23.1
89.3	81.3	97.0	92.2	74.2	76.7	73.2	84.9	75.4	46.5
91.4	86.3	99.0	96.9	84.9	90.5	88.5	96.3	92.7	76.5
81.1	61.1	95.3	85.5	61.3	51.0	43.3	62.6	47.7	20.6
78.1	61.1	92.4	66.5	46.5	32.2	30.9	41.9	23.9	6.7
89.4	77.3	98.0	94.2	85.0	70.4	63.1	75.1	79.4	64.4
70.6	54.4	91.7	94.1	83.0	64.2	57.6	71.3	71.8	59.5
86.8	69.7	98.4	95.1	83.7	57.2	50.5	65.9	57.1	24.8
90.9	81.8	97.9	93.4	76.2	61.2	61.7	65.8	51.8	30.3
92.7	69.2	98.6	94.8	88.5	61.8	47.7	61.6	61.2	60.1
88.8	75.8	98.6	91.1	78.2	37.9	35.6	44.2	36.6	17.8
..	65.4	95.6	86.5	61.9	..	43.8	62.8	48.2	21.4
90.5	88.6	96.8	95.3	51.3	50.0	48.8	54.1	55.2	32.0
90.4	80.0	98.3	93.0	76.2	58.3	57.7	63.1	47.9	25.4
89.1	81.7	97.2	90.2	62.3	70.1	72.1	77.2	54.5	26.2
82.9	66.5	96.0	82.7	61.9	60.0	54.5	71.1	59.4	31.1
85.6	72.0	94.7	91.2	76.8	58.4	52.9	64.3	62.1	43.0
74.7	50.6	91.7	84.7	65.1	69.8	50.6	85.4	76.1	48.0
88.5	77.6	95.6	90.8	68.9	79.3	73.7	89.9	74.8	34.7
93.0	84.7	98.8	93.8	82.4	62.1	64.1	64.0	51.6	30.6
89.3	79.5	97.5	92.3	78.5	68.1	61.2	79.5	71.8	30.4
72.5	56.3	93.8	81.1	56.2	45.6	35.9	60.4	44.6	15.8
83.9	64.7	97.3	90.4	74.4	54.6	51.4	59.6	50.9	29.1
85.6	68.5	97.3	93.5	81.2	78.4	67.9	87.2	83.2	63.8
89.8	80.2	97.0	93.5	83.3	85.2	80.4	90.2	88.0	72.7
86.5	74.3	93.9	86.5	58.7	72.2	68.1	80.8	68.7	34.6
83.9	68.0	95.8	87.4	63.5	54.3	46.7	63.6	49.1	23
78.8	58.7	96.2	62.8	17.2	39.9	34.7	54.3	28.0	4.7
82.3	61.9	97.0	95.9	87.1	84.7	72.7	92.2	89.8	79.3
62.7	35.5	85.7	64.3	31.6	45.5	30.5	62.7	34.7	21.2
95.1	91.6	98.4	95.1	85.1	71.2	68.4	77.0	67.1	34
83.2	71.3	95.9	91.4	69.5	44.8	35.1	53.6	56.1	27.3
83.6	72.5	96.3	86.7	61.5	79.6	69.8	92.5	79.9	38.5
..	55.2	95.8	82.6	40.5	..	19.5	42.6	19.1	4.3
83.0	67.6	96.3	78.8	53.4	55.2	50.2	65.1	52.3	21.5
..	..	..	..	..	..	..	..	..	..
93.0	86.6	99.5	95.2	87.1	56.1	60.8	59.5	42.7	21.9
94.4	87.8	99.5	96.2	87.3	59.0	66.0	60.2	42.7	23.9
78.6	57.3	96.4	77.1	22.9	46.1	41.9	57.2	25.1	4.2
68.8	46.3	87.4	83.0	62.7	22.5	18.8	27.5	23.9	16.3
71.6	55.6	96.1	77.6	37.6	29.7	27.8	39.9	20.6	5.4
89.5	80.5	97.6	96.0	77.3	85.4	80.7	94.4	85.2	50.0
90.1	80.3	98.1	87.3	78.9	50.1	47.3	55.6	46.4	28.9
87.1	78.8	94.3	90.5	67.5	79.5	72.6	88.4	82.5	53.5
89.7	83.4	98.3	91.3	74.6	65.2	70.2	69.9	46.6	31.7
83.6	71.7	97.2	89.5	62.1	61.7	47.9	77.6	78.9	56.1
75.2	51.3	95.1	77.9	32.6	25.9	21.6	32.1	15.0	5.7
80.4	66.0	95.2	70.9	27.0	35.4	29.3	44.9	21.9	6.2
72.5	41.0	98.4	77.4	19.5	21.7	17.8	25.9	9.0	2.6
80.5	59.5	97.0	79.6	42.4	29.6	19.9	44.9	13.7	4.2
81.2	63.3	95.0	84.3	38.8	27.4	22.2	33.7	15.9	4.7
75.5	49.4	94.8	65.5	35.6	28.2	31.1	33.8	10.8	3.0
83.1	69.0	96.2	86.5	57.4	53.6	49.8	61.0	48.3	25.8

Table 10.2 Labor force composition

| | Sector[a] | | | | | |
| | Agriculture | | Industry | | Services | |
	Male (% of male employment) 2000–05[b]	Female (% of female employment) 2000–05[b]	Male (% of male employment) 2000–05[b]	Female (% of female employment) 2000–05[b]	Male (% of male employment) 2000–05[b]	Female (% of female employment) 2000–05[b]
SUB-SAHARAN AFRICA						
Angola	..	..	..	..	..	..
Benin	..	..	..	..	..	..
Botswana	25.9	18.6	29.2	13.3	42.8	58.0
Burkina Faso	..	..	..	..	..	..
Burundi	..	..	..	..	..	..
Cameroon	..	..	..	..	..	..
Cape Verde	..	..	..	..	..	..
Central African Republic	..	..	..	..	..	..
Chad	..	..	..	..	..	..
Comoros	..	..	..	..	..	..
Congo, Dem. Rep.	..	..	..	..	..	..
Congo, Rep.	..	..	..	..	..	..
Côte d'Ivoire	..	..	..	..	..	..
Djibouti	..	..	..	..	..	..
Equatorial Guinea	..	..	..	..	..	..
Eritrea	..	..	..	..	..	..
Ethiopia	..	..	..	..	..	..
Gabon	..	..	..	..	..	..
Gambia, The	..	..	..	..	..	..
Ghana	59.8	50.3	13.5	14.5	26.5	35.6
Guinea	..	..	..	..	..	..
Guinea-Bissau	..	..	..	..	..	..
Kenya	..	..	..	..	..	..
Lesotho	..	..	..	..	..	..
Liberia	..	..	..	..	..	..
Madagascar	76.7	79.3	7.4	6.0	16.0	14.6
Malawi	..	..	..	..	..	..
Mali	..	..	..	..	..	..
Mauritania	..	..	..	..	..	..
Mauritius	10.5	8.9	34.2	28.8	55.1	62.2
Mozambique	..	..	..	..	..	..
Namibia	32.8	29.1	17.2	6.7	49.4	63.3
Niger	..	..	..	..	..	..
Nigeria	..	..	..	..	..	..
Rwanda	..	..	..	..	..	..
São Tomé and Principe	..	..	..	..	..	..
Senegal	..	..	..	..	..	..
Seychelles	..	..	..	..	..	..
Sierra Leone	..	..	..	..	..	..
Somalia	..	..	..	..	..	..
South Africa	12.6	7.4	33.3	13.6	53.9	78.9
Sudan	..	..	..	..	..	..
Swaziland	..	..	..	..	..	..
Tanzania	80.2	84.0	4.0	1.2	15.7	14.8
Togo	..	..	..	..	..	..
Uganda	60.1	77.3	10.7	4.8	28.2	16.7
Zambia	..	..	..	..	..	..
Zimbabwe	..	..	..	..	..	..
NORTH AFRICA						
Algeria	20.4	22.3	25.6	28.2	53.8	49.4
Egypt, Arab Rep.	27.7	39.0	22.9	6.2	49.3	54.7
Libya	..	..	..	..	..	..
Morocco	41.0	63.0	23.0	15.0	36.0	22.0
Tunisia	..	..	..	..	..	..

a. Components may not sum up to 100 percent because of unclassified data.
b. Data are for most recent year available during the period specified.

LABOR, MIGRATION, AND POPULATION

Status[a]								
Wage and salaried workers			Self-employed workers			Contributing family workers		
Total (% of total employed) 2000–05[b]	Male (% of males employed) 2000–05[b]	Female (% of females employed) 2000–05[b]	Total (% of total employed) 2000–05[b]	Male (% of males employed) 2000–05[b]	Female (% of females employed) 2000–05[b]	Total (% of total employed) 2000–05[b]	Male (% of males employed) 2000–05[b]	Female (% of females employed) 2000–05[b]
..	..	..	..	..	..	..	..	..
..	..	..	..	..	..	..	..	..
82.7	83.2	81.9	15.9	15.3	16.8	1.3	1.4	1.2
..	..	..	..	..	..	..	..	..
..	..	..	..	..	..	..	..	..
19.2	29.3	8.7	59.3	57.0	61.7	18.2	9.5	27.2
..	..	..	..	..	..	..	..	..
..	..	..	..	..	..	..	..	..
..	..	..	..	..	..	..	..	..
..	..	..	..	..	..	..	..	..
..	..	..	..	..	..	..	..	..
..	..	..	..	..	..	..	..	..
..	..	..	..	..	..	..	..	..
49.5	52.1	45.9	42.2	40.9	43.7	7.2	5.2	9.9
..	..	..	..	..	..	..	..	..
..	..	..	..	..	..	..	..	..
..	..	..	..	..	..	..	..	..
..	..	..	..	..	..	..	..	..
15.0	17.8	12.0	43.7	51.6	35.4	40.6	29.7	51.9
..	..	..	..	..	..	..	..	..
..	..	..	..	..	..	..	..	..
80.0	77.7	84.9	17.7	21.2	10.4	2.1	0.8	4.7
..	..	..	..	..	..	..	..	..
61.5	66.7	54.9	16.0	15.0	17.2	16.9	12.8	22.0
..	..	..	..	..	..	..	..	..
..	..	..	..	..	..	..	..	..
..	..	..	..	..	..	..	..	..
..	..	..	..	..	..	..	..	..
..	..	..	..	..	..	..	..	..
81.8	82.4	81.1	17.4	17.1	17.7	0.8	0.5	1.1
..	..	..	..	..	..	..	..	..
..	..	..	..	..	..	..	..	..
6.9	9.8	4.0	89.3	87.2	91.4	3.8	3.0	4.6
..	..	..	..	..	..	..	..	..
14.5	22.2	7.5	59.4	67.5	52.1	26.1	10.3	40.5
18.7	..	..	59.7	..	..	19.6	..	..
37.7	51	23.1	50.4	38.6	63.2	11.9	10.4	13.6
59.8	61.9	49.8	31.7	30.7	36.6	8.2	7.1	13.6
57.9	58.2	56.5	30.0	32.8	17.7	12.2	9.0	25.8
..	..	..	..	..	..	..	..	..
38.1	39.7	33.6	31.1	37.5	13.4	29.7	21.6	52.5
64.3	..	..	26.8	..	..	8.7	..	..

Table 10.3 Migration and population

	International migration				Population				
	Stock		Net migration	Workers remittances, received ($ millions)	Population dynamics				
	Share of population (%)	Total			Total (millions)	Male (% of total)	Female (% of total)	Annual growth rate (%)	Fertility rate (births per woman)
	2005	2005	2005	2005	2005	2005	2005	2005	2005
SUB-SAHARAN AFRICA	..	..	..	..	743.7	..	..	..	..
Angola	0.4	56,351	145,000	..	15.9	49.3	50.7	2.9	6.6
Benin	2.1	174,726	98,831	100.8	8.4	50.4	49.6	3.1	5.6
Botswana	4.5	80,064	−6,000	..	1.8	49.1	50.9	−0.2	3.0
Burkina Faso	5.8	772,817	100,000	49.4	13.2	50.3	49.7	3.1	5.9
Burundi	1.3	100,189	191,600	..	7.5	48.8	51.2	3.6	6.8
Cameroon	0.8	136,909	13,000	..	16.3	49.7	50.3	1.8	..
Cape Verde	2.2	11,183	−5,000	121.0	0.5	47.9	52.1	2.3	3.5
Central African Republic	1.9	76,484	−45,000	..	4.0	48.8	51.2	1.3	4.7
Chad	4.5	437,049	270,941	..	9.7	49.5	50.5	3.1	6.3
Comoros	11.2	67,185	−10,000	68.2	0.6	50.2	49.8	2.1	3.8
Congo, Dem. Rep.	0.9	538,838	−321,565	..	57.5	49.6	50.4	3.0	6.7
Congo, Rep.	7.2	287,603	−14,000	..	4.0	49.6	50.4	2.9	5.6
Côte d'Ivoire	13.1	2,371,277	−371,159	..	18.2	50.8	49.2	1.6	4.7
Djibouti	2.6	20,272	−9,794	..	0.8	49.9	50.1	1.8	4.7
Equatorial Guinea	1.2	5,800	0	..	0.5	49.6	50.4	2.3	5.9
Eritrea	0.3	14,612	279,932	223.1	4.4	49.1	50.9	3.9	5.2
Ethiopia	0.8	555,054	−150,335	173.5	71.3	49.7	50.3	1.8	5.3
Gabon	17.7	244,550	−15,000	4.5	1.4	49.8	50.2	1.6	3.7
Gambia, The	15.3	231,739	31,127	..	1.5	49.6	50.4	2.6	4.4
Ghana	7.5	1,669,267	11,690	25.6	22.1	50.6	49.4	2.0	4.1
Guinea	4.3	405,772	−299,219	1.1	9.4	51.2	48.8	1.9	5.6
Guinea-Bissau	1.2	19,171	1,181	16.8	1.6	49.4	50.6	3.0	7.1
Kenya	1	344,857	−211,519	..	34.3	50.1	49.9	2.3	5.0
Lesotho	0.3	5,886	−36,000	8.9	1.8	46.5	53.5	−0.2	3.4
Liberia	1.5	50,172	−244,548	..	3.3	49.9	50.1	1.3	6.8
Madagascar	0.3	62,787	0	..	18.6	49.7	50.3	2.7	5.0
Malawi	2.2	278,793	−20,000	161.6	12.9	49.7	50.3	2.2	5.8
Mali	0.3	46,318	−134,204	..	13.5	49.8	50.2	3.0	6.7
Mauritania	2.1	65,889	30,000	50.5	3.1	49.5	50.5	2.9	5.6
Mauritius	1.7	20,725	0	154.0	1.2	49.6	50.4	1.1	2.0
Mozambique	2.1	405,904	−20,000	..	19.8	48.4	51.6	1.9	5.3
Namibia	7.1	143,275	−5,500	31.6	2.0	49.6	50.4	1.1	3.7
Niger	0.9	123,687	−10,000	42.8	14.0	51.1	48.9	3.3	7.7
Nigeria	0.7	971,450	−170,000	..	131.5	50.6	49.4	2.4	5.5
Rwanda	1.3	121,183	45,000	..	9.0	48.5	51.5	1.7	5.8
São Tomé and Principe	4.8	7,499	−2,000	..	0.2	49.5	50.5	2.3	3.8
Senegal	2.8	325,940	−100,000	617.0	11.7	49.2	50.8	2.4	4.9
Seychelles	5.8	4,932	..	..	0.1	50.3	49.7	1.0	..
Sierra Leone	2.2	119,162	438,215	..	5.5	49.3	50.7	3.5	6.5
Somalia	3.4	281,702	170,000	..	8.2	49.6	50.4	3.3	6.2
South Africa	2.4	1,106,214	50,000	..	46.9	49.1	50.9	1.1	2.8
Sudan	1.8	638,596	−519,123	..	36.2	50.3	49.7	2.0	4.1
Swaziland	4	45,459	−6,000	..	1.1	48.2	51.8	1.0	3.9
Tanzania	2.1	792,328	−345,000	10.3	38.3	49.8	50.2	2.6	5.2
Togo	3	183,304	−3,570	151.3	6.1	49.4	50.6	2.6	5.0
Uganda	1.8	518,158	−15,000	413.6	28.8	50.0	50.0	3.5	7.1
Zambia	2.4	274,842	−65,000	..	11.7	50.1	49.9	1.6	5.4
Zimbabwe	3.9	510,637	−50,000	..	13.0	49.6	50.4	0.6	3.3
NORTH AFRICA	..	..	..	..	152.9	..	..	..	..
Algeria	0.7	242,446	−100,000	..	32.9	50.5	49.5	1.5	2.4
Egypt, Arab Rep.	0.2	166,047	−450,000	4,329.5	74.0	50.1	49.9	1.9	3.1
Libya	10.5	617,536	10,000	..	5.9	51.6	48.4	2.0	2.8
Morocco	0.4	131,654	−400,000	4,567.4	30.2	49.7	50.3	1.0	2.4
Tunisia	0.4	37,858	−20,000	1,392.7	10.0	50.4	49.6	1.0	2.0

	Population										Geographic distribution (%)			
	Age composition (% of total)										Share of total population		Annual growth	
	Ages 0–14			Ages 15–64			Ages 65 and older			Dependency ratio	Rural population	Urban population	Rural population	Urban population
	Total 2005	Male 2005	Female 2005	Total 2005	Male 2005	Female 2005	Total 2005	Male 2005	Female 2005	2005	2005	2005	2005	2005
	43.5	22.0	21.5	53.4	26.5	26.8	3.1	1.4	1.7	0.90	64.7	35.3	1.4	..
	46.5	23.2	23.3	51.1	25.1	26.0	2.5	1.1	1.4	1.00	46.7	53.3	1.5	4.1
	44.2	22.5	21.7	53.1	26.8	26.3	2.7	1.1	1.6	0.90	59.9	40.1	2.6	4.0
	37.6	19.0	18.7	59.0	28.9	30.2	3.3	1.3	2.0	0.70	42.6	57.4	−2.2	1.2
	47.2	23.9	23.2	50.1	25.1	25.0	2.7	1.2	1.5	1.00	81.7	18.3	2.7	5.1
	45.0	22.5	22.5	52.3	25.2	27.0	2.7	1.0	1.7	0.90	90.0	10.0	3.3	6.4
	41.2	20.7	20.5	55.1	27.3	27.8	3.7	1.7	2.0	0.80	45.4	54.6	−0.3	3.5
	39.5	19.8	19.7	56.2	26.6	29.6	4.3	1.5	2.8	0.80	42.7	57.3	0.5	3.7
	43.0	21.4	21.6	53.0	25.7	27.3	4.1	1.7	2.4	0.90	62.0	38.0	1.2	1.5
	47.3	23.6	23.6	49.7	24.5	25.2	3.0	1.3	1.7	1.00	74.7	25.3	2.6	4.6
	41.9	21.3	20.7	55.3	27.7	27.6	2.7	1.2	1.5	0.80	63.0	37.0	1.1	3.9
	47.3	23.7	23.6	50.1	24.8	25.3	2.7	1.1	1.5	1.00	67.9	32.1	2.3	4.4
	47.1	23.6	23.5	49.9	24.7	25.2	2.9	1.3	1.7	1.00	39.8	60.2	2.0	3.6
	41.9	20.9	20.9	54.9	28.2	26.6	3.3	1.7	1.6	0.80	55.0	45.0	0.8	2.5
	41.5	20.9	20.6	55.7	27.8	27.9	2.8	1.3	1.6	0.80	13.9	86.1	−2.2	2.4
	44.3	22.3	22.1	51.6	25.4	26.2	3.9	1.8	2.2	0.90	61.1	38.9	2.2	2.3
	44.8	22.5	22.2	52.9	25.7	27.3	2.3	0.9	1.4	0.90	80.6	19.4	3.5	5.6
	44.5	22.4	22.2	52.5	26.0	26.5	2.9	1.3	1.6	0.90	84.0	16.0	1.6	3.2
	40.1	20.2	19.8	55.6	27.6	28.0	4.4	1.9	2.4	0.80	16.4	83.6	−2.6	2.4
	40.1	20.2	19.9	56.1	27.7	28.5	3.7	1.7	2.0	0.80	46.1	53.9	0.6	4.4
	39.0	19.9	19.1	57.3	28.9	28.4	3.7	1.7	1.9	0.70	52.2	47.8	0.6	3.7
	43.7	22.5	21.2	52.7	27.1	25.7	3.5	1.6	1.9	0.90	67.0	33.0	1.3	3.1
	47.5	23.8	23.8	49.4	24.3	25.2	3.1	1.4	1.7	1.00	70.4	29.6	3.0	2.9
	42.8	21.5	21.3	54.4	27.2	27.1	2.8	1.3	1.5	0.80	79.3	20.7	2.1	3.3
	38.6	19.4	19.2	56.2	24.9	31.3	5.3	2.2	3.0	0.80	81.3	18.7	−0.4	0.8
	47.1	23.6	23.4	50.7	25.3	25.4	2.2	1.0	1.2	1.00	41.9	58.1	−0.5	2.6
	44.0	22.1	21.9	52.9	26.3	26.6	3.1	1.4	1.7	0.90	73.2	26.8	2.5	3.3
	47.3	23.8	23.5	49.6	24.4	25.2	3.0	1.4	1.6	1.00	82.8	17.2	1.7	4.6
	48.2	24.6	23.7	49.1	24.1	25.0	2.7	1.2	1.5	1.00	69.5	30.5	2.2	4.7
	43.0	21.6	21.4	53.6	26.3	27.3	3.4	1.5	1.9	0.90	59.6	40.4	2.8	3.1
	24.6	12.5	12.1	68.8	34.4	34.4	6.6	2.7	3.9	0.50	57.6	42.4	0.9	0.7
	44.0	22.1	21.9	52.7	24.9	27.8	3.3	1.4	1.9	0.90	65.5	34.5	0.7	4.1
	41.5	20.9	20.6	55.0	27.1	27.9	3.5	1.5	1.9	0.80	64.9	35.1	0.3	2.6
	49.0	25.2	23.9	49.0	25.1	23.9	2.0	0.9	1.1	1.00	83.2	16.8	3.2	4.1
	44.3	22.7	21.6	52.7	26.5	26.2	3.0	1.4	1.7	0.90	51.8	48.2	0.8	4.2
	43.5	21.6	21.9	54.0	25.8	28.2	2.5	1.1	1.4	0.90	80.7	19.3	0.4	7.6
	39.6	20.1	19.5	56.4	27.7	28.7	4.3	2.0	2.3	0.80	42.0	58.0	0.1	3.9
	42.6	21.5	21.1	54.3	26.3	28.0	3.1	1.4	1.7	0.80	58.4	41.6	2.0	2.8
	..	..	..	..	..	..	..	..	..	..	47.1	52.9	0.2	1.7
	42.8	21.4	21.4	53.8	26.5	27.4	3.3	1.5	1.9	0.90	59.3	40.7	2.2	5.3
	44.1	22.1	22.0	53.3	26.3	27.0	2.6	1.2	1.4	0.90	64.8	35.2	2.7	4.3
	32.6	16.4	16.2	63.1	31.0	32.1	4.2	1.7	2.6	0.60	40.7	59.3	0.0	1.9
	39.2	20.0	19.3	57.2	28.7	28.5	3.6	1.7	1.9	0.70	59.2	40.8	0.4	4.3
	41.0	20.6	20.4	55.5	26.1	29.4	3.5	1.6	2.0	0.80	75.9	24.1	0.8	1.7
	42.6	21.4	21.2	54.2	26.9	27.2	3.2	1.4	1.8	0.80	75.8	24.2	2.1	4.1
	43.5	21.7	21.7	53.4	26.3	27.1	3.1	1.4	1.8	0.90	59.9	40.1	1.4	4.3
	50.5	25.4	25.0	47.1	23.5	23.6	2.5	1.1	1.3	1.10	87.4	12.6	3.4	4.3
	45.8	23.0	22.8	51.2	25.7	25.5	3.0	1.3	1.7	1.00	65.0	35.0	1.6	1.8
	40.0	20.0	19.9	56.4	27.9	28.5	3.6	1.7	2.0	0.80	64.1	35.9	−0.1	1.7
	31.6	16.1	15.5	63.6	31.9	31.7	4.8	2.2	2.7	0.60	46.6	53.4	0.9	..
	29.6	15.2	14.5	65.8	33.3	32.6	4.5	2.1	2.5	0.50	36.7	63.3	−0.4	2.6
	33.6	17.1	16.4	61.7	30.9	30.8	4.8	2.1	2.7	0.60	57.2	42.8	1.8	2.0
	30.1	15.4	14.7	65.9	34.1	31.8	4.1	2.1	1.9	0.50	15.2	84.8	−0.3	2.4
	31.1	15.8	15.3	64.1	31.8	32.3	4.8	2.1	2.7	0.60	41.3	58.7	−0.7	2.2
	25.9	13.4	12.6	67.8	34.1	33.7	6.3	2.9	3.4	0.50	34.7	65.3	−0.1	1.6

Table 11.1 HIV/AIDS

| | Estimated number of people living with HIV/AIDS (thousands) | | | | Estimated prevalence rate (%) | | | | | | | | | Deaths of adults and children due to HIV/AIDS (thousands) | AIDS orphans (ages 0–17, thousands) |
| | | | | | Adults (ages 15–49) | | | Young men (ages 15–24) | | | Young women (ages 15–24) | | | | |
	Total 2005	Adults (ages 15 and older) 2005	Women (ages 15 and older) 2005	Children (ages 0–14) 2005	Point estimate 2005	Low estimate 2005	High estimate 2005	Point estimate 2005	Low estimate 2005	High estimate 2005	Point estimate 2005	Low estimate 2005	High estimate 2005	2000	2005
SUB-SAHARAN AFRICA	24,500	22,400	13,200	2,000	6.1	5.4	6.8	1.5	1.3	1.7	4.3	3.7	5.1	2,000	12,000
Angola	320	280	170	35	3.7	2.3	5.3	0.9	0.4	1.4	2.5	1.2	4.2	30	160
Benin	87	77	45	10	1.8	1.2	2.5	0.4	0.2	0.6	1.1	0.6	1.8	10	62
Botswana	270	260	140	14	24.1	23.0	32.0	5.7	5.6	7.5	15.3	15.2	20.3	18	120
Burkina Faso	150	140	80	17	2.0	1.5	2.5	0.5	0.3	0.6	1.4	0.8	2.0	12	120
Burundi	150	130	79	20	3.3	2.7	3.8	0.8	0.7	0.9	2.3	2.0	2.7	13	120
Cameroon	510	470	290	43	5.4	4.9	5.9	1.4	1.3	1.6	4.9	4.4	5.3	46	240
Cape Verde	..	..	..	..	..	..	..	..	..	..	..	..	..	..	..
Central African Republic	250	230	130	24	10.7	4.5	17.2	2.5	0.9	4.5	7.3	2.7	13.1	24	140
Chad	180	160	90	16	3.5	1.7	6.0	0.9	0.4	1.6	2.2	0.9	3.9	11	57
Comoros	<0.5	<0.5	<0.1	<0.1	<0.1	<0.2	<0.2	<0.1	<0.2	<0.2	<0.1	<0.2	<0.2	<0.1	..
Congo, Dem. Rep.	1,000	890	520	120	3.2	1.8	4.9	0.8	0.3	1.3	2.2	1.0	3.8	90	680
Congo, Rep.	120	100	61	15	5.3	3.3	7.5	1.2	0.6	1.9	3.7	1.9	5.7	11	110
Côte d'Ivoire	750	680	400	74	7.1	4.3	9.7	1.7	0.9	2.7	5.1	2.6	7.9	65	450
Djibouti	15	14	8	1	3.1	0.8	6.9	0.7	0.2	1.6	2.1	0.5	4.6	1	6
Equatorial Guinea	9	8	5	<1	3.2	2.6	3.8	0.7	0.6	0.9	2.3	1.8	2.7	<1	5
Eritrea	59	53	31	7	2.4	1.3	3.9	0.6	0.3	1.0	1.6	0.7	2.7	6	36
Ethiopia	..	..	..	..	..	0.9	3.5	..	0.2	0.8	..	0.5	2.3	..	..
Gabon	60	56	33	4	7.9	5.1	11.5	1.8	0.9	3.0	5.4	2.7	8.7	5	20
Gambia, The	20	19	11	1	2.4	1.2	4.1	0.6	0.2	1.0	1.7	0.7	2.9	1	4
Ghana	320	300	180	25	2.3	1.9	2.6	0.2	0.2	0.3	1.3	1.1	1.5	29	170
Guinea	85	78	53	7	1.5	1.2	1.8	0.5	0.4	0.5	1.4	1.1	1.6	7	28
Guinea-Bissau	32	29	17	3	3.8	2.1	6.0	0.9	0.4	1.5	2.5	1.1	4.3	3	11
Kenya	1,300	1,200	740	150	6.1	5.2	7.0	1.0	0.9	1.2	5.2	4.5	6.0	140	1,100
Lesotho	270	250	150	18	23.2	21.9	24.7	5.9	5.5	6.2	14.1	13.3	15.0	23	97
Liberia	..	..	..	..	2.0	5.0	..	..	..	..	..	..	..	..	..
Madagascar	49	47	13	2	0.5	0.2	1.2	0.6	0.2	1.3	0.3	0.1	0.6	3	13
Malawi	940	850	500	91	14.1	6.9	21.4	3.4	1.4	5.9	9.6	3.9	16.8	78	550
Mali	130	110	66	16	1.7	1.3	2.1	0.4	0.3	0.5	1.2	0.9	1.5	11	94
Mauritania	12	11	6	1	0.7	0.4	2.8	0.2	0.1	0.3	0.5	0.2	1.0	<1	7
Mauritius	4	4	<1	..	0.6	0.3	1.8	..	..	..	..	..	..	<0.1	..
Mozambique	1,800	1,600	960	140	16.1	12.5	20.0	3.6	2.0	5.3	10.7	6.0	15.8	140	510
Namibia	230	210	130	17	19.6	8.6	31.7	4.4	1.7	8.1	13.4	5.2	24.7	17	85
Niger	79	71	42	9	1.1	0.5	1.9	0.2	0.1	0.4	0.8	0.3	1.4	8	46
Nigeria	2,900	2,600	1,600	240	3.9	2.3	5.6	0.9	0.4	1.5	2.7	1.3	4.4	220	930
Rwanda	190	160	91	27	3.1	2.9	3.2	0.8	0.7	0.8	1.9	1.9	2.0	21	210
São Tomé and Principe	..	..	..	..	..	..	..	..	..	..	..	..	..	..	..
Senegal	61	56	33	5	0.9	0.4	1.5	0.2	0.1	0.4	0.6	0.2	1.1	5	25
Seychelles	..	..	..	..	..	..	..	..	..	..	..	..	..	..	..
Sierra Leone	48	43	26	5	1.6	0.9	2.4	0.4	0.2	0.6	1.1	0.6	1.7	5	31
Somalia	44	40	23	5	0.9	0.5	1.6	0.2	0.1	0.4	0.6	0.3	1.1	4	23
South Africa	5,500	5,300	3,100	240	18.8	16.8	20.7	4.5	4.0	4.9	14.8	13.2	16.3	320	1,200
Sudan	350	320	180	30	1.6	0.8	2.7	..	..	..	..	..	..	34	..
Swaziland	220	210	120	15	33.4	21.2	45.3	7.7	3.9	12.1	22.7	11.5	35.9	16	63
Tanzania	1,400	1,300	710	110	6.5	5.8	7.2	2.8	2.5	3.1	3.8	3.4	4.2	140	1,100
Togo	110	100	61	10	3.2	1.9	4.7	0.8	0.4	1.2	2.2	1.0	3.6	9	88
Uganda	1,000	900	520	110	6.7	5.7	7.6	2.3	1.9	2.6	5.0	4.2	5.7	91	1,000
Zambia	1,100	1,000	570	130	17.0	15.9	18.1	3.8	3.6	4.0	12.7	11.9	13.6	98	710
Zimbabwe	1,700	1,500	890	160	20.1	13.3	27.6	4.4	2.3	6.9	14.7	7.7	23.2	180	1,100
NORTH AFRICA	440	400	190	31	0.2	0.1	0.4	0.1	0.1	0.2	0.2	0.1	0.3	37	..
Algeria	19	19	4	..	0.1	0.2	0.2	..	..	..	..	..	..	<0.5	..
Egypt, Arab Rep.	5	5	<1	..	<0.1	0.2	0.2	..	..	..	..	..	..	<0.5	..
Libya	..	..	..	..	..	0.2	0.2	..	..	..	..	..	..	..	..
Morocco	19	19	4	..	0.1	0.1	0.4	..	..	..	..	..	..	1	..
Tunisia	9	9	2	..	0.1	0.1	0.3	..	..	..	..	..	..	<0.1	..

HIV/AIDS

Table 12.1 Malaria

	Population (millions) 2005	Risk of malaria (% of population)			Deaths due to malaria (per 100,000 population) 2000–05[a]	Under-five mortality rate (per 1,000) 2000–05[a]	Children sleeping under insecticide-treated bednets (% of children under age 5) 2000–05[a]	Children with fever receiving antimalarial treatment within 24 hours (% of children under age 5 with fever)		Pregnant women receiving two doses of intermittent preventive treatment (%) 2000–05[a]
		Endemic 2000–05[a]	Epidemic 2000–05[a]	Negligible 2000–05[a]				Effective antimalarial treatment 2000–05[a]	Any antimalarial treatment 2000–05[a]	
SUB–SAHARAN AFRICA	**743.7**					**163**				
Angola	15.9	90.5	8.4	1.2	354	260	2.0	20	63	..
Benin	8.4	100.0	0.0	0.0	177	150	7.0	19	60	..
Botswana	1.8	0.0	31.5	68.5	15	120	..	..	..	..
Burkina Faso	13.2	100.0	0.0	0.0	292	191	2.0	45	50	..
Burundi	7.5	67.6	17.3	15.2	143	190	1.0	..	31	..
Cameroon	16.3	93.6	4.4	2.0	108	149	1.0	27	53	..
Cape Verde	0.5	..	..	..	22	35	..	..	..	..
Central African Republic	4.0	100.0	0.0	0.0	137	193	2.0	..	66	..
Chad	9.7	96.5	3.5	0.0	207	208	0.6	..	56	..
Comoros	0.6	0.0	100.0	0.0	80	71	9.0	..	63	..
Congo, Dem. Rep.	57.5	91.6	2.6	5.8	224	205	1.0	..	45	..
Congo, Rep.	4.0	100.0	0.0	0.0	78	108	..	9	48	..
Côte d'Ivoire	18.2	100.0	0.0	0.0	76	195	4.0	..	58	..
Djibouti	0.8	..	..	..	..	133	..	..	..	..
Equatorial Guinea	0.5	98.0	1.5	0.5	152	205	1.0	..	49	..
Eritrea	4.4	92.2	6.9	1.0	74	78	4.0	8	4	..
Ethiopia	71.3	39.7	23.9	36.4	198	127	1.5	1	3	..
Gabon	1.4	96.5	0.0	3.5	80	91	..	..	..	..
Gambia, The	1.5	100.0	0.0	0.0	52	137	15.0	..	56	..
Ghana	22.1	100.0	0.0	0.0	70	112	4.0	44	63	0.8
Guinea	9.4	100.0	0.0	0.0	200	160	4.0	14	44	5.6
Guinea-Bissau	1.6	99.5	0.0	0.5	150	200	7.0	..	58	..
Kenya	34.3	53.4	24.4	22.2	63	120	5.0	11	27	3.9
Lesotho	1.8	..	..	..	84	132	..	..	..	..
Liberia	3.3	100.0	0.0	0.0	201	235	..	..	..	..
Madagascar	18.6	89.1	7.1	3.8	184	119	0.2	..	34	..
Malawi	12.9	96.7	2.5	0.7	275	125	15.0	23	27	46.5
Mali	13.5	99.1	0.9	0.0	454	218	8.0	..	38	..
Mauritania	3.1	65.3	34.5	0.2	108	125	2.0	12	33	..
Mauritius	1.2	..	..	..	..	15	..	..	..	..
Mozambique	19.8	99.5	0.3	0.2	232	145	..	8	15	..
Namibia	2.0	0.0	40.8	59.2	52	62	3.0	..	..	..
Niger	14.0	97.1	2.8	0.1	469	256	6.0	..	48	..
Nigeria	131.5	100.0	0.0	0.0	141	194	1.0	25	34	1.1
Rwanda	9.0	53.0	13.6	33.4	200	203	13.0	..	3	1
São Tomé and Principe	0.2	0.0	100.0	0.0	80	118	22.8	..	73	..
Senegal	11.7	100.0	0.0	0.0	72	119	14.0	12	36	10.1
Seychelles	0.1	..	..	..	..	13	..	..	..	..
Sierra Leone	5.5	100.0	0.0	0.0	312	282	2.0	..	61	..
Somalia	8.2	19.9	79.1	1.1	81	225	..	..	..	..
South Africa	46.9	0.0	19.8	80.2	0	68	..	..	..	..
Sudan	36.2	74.1	24.7	1.3	70	90	0.0	..	50	..
Swaziland	1.1	0.0	76.6	23.4	0	160	0.0	..	26	..
Tanzania	38.3	93.1	3.0	3.9	130	122	16.0	49	..	21.7
Togo	6.1	100.0	0.0	0.0	47	139	54.0	..	60	..
Uganda	28.8	90.2	2.9	6.9	152	136	0.0	..	..	..
Zambia	11.7	96.1	3.0	0.9	141	182	7.0	..	52	..
Zimbabwe	13.0	0.0	84.2	15.8	1	132	..	3	5	6.8
NORTH AFRICA	**152.9**					**35**				
Algeria	32.9	..	..	..	..	39	..	..	..	..
Egypt, Arab Rep.	74.0	..	..	..	..	33	..	..	..	..
Libya	5.9	..	..	..	..	19	..	..	..	..
Morocco	30.2	..	..	..	..	40	..	..	..	..
Tunisia	10.0	..	..	..	..	24	..	..	..	..

a. Data are for the most recent year available during the period specified.

Table 13.1 Aid and debt relief

	Net aid (2004 $ millions)		
	From all donors 2005	From DAC donors 2005	From multilateral donors 2005
SUB-SAHARAN AFRICA	**30,686**	**21,377**	**9,183**
Angola	442	258	183
Benin	349	207	142
Botswana	71	52	19
Burkina Faso	660	339	319
Burundi	365	181	184
Cameroon	414	336	77
Cape Verde	161	104	56
Central African Republic	95	62	33
Chad	380	167	213
Comoros	25	17	8
Congo, Dem. Rep.	1,828	1,034	793
Congo, Rep.	1,449	1,360	89
Côte d'Ivoire	119	151	-32
Djibouti	79	54	23
Equatorial Guinea	39	30	9
Eritrea	355	226	132
Ethiopia	1,937	1,202	706
Gabon	54	30	24
Gambia, The	58	15	43
Ghana	1,120	603	503
Guinea	182	128	54
Guinea-Bissau	79	39	40
Kenya	768	495	260
Lesotho	69	39	30
Liberia	236	149	87
Madagascar	929	500	429
Malawi	575	322	251
Mali	691	378	313
Mauritania	190	125	66
Mauritius	32	22	10
Mozambique	1,286	771	513
Namibia	123	99	23
Niger	515	256	259
Nigeria	6,437	5,966	471
Rwanda	576	292	284
São Tomé and Principe	32	18	13
Senegal	689	440	249
Seychelles	19	8	11
Sierra Leone	343	130	213
Somalia	236	146	90
South Africa	700	486	213
Sudan	1,829	1,472	315
Swaziland	46	20	26
Tanzania	1,505	871	622
Togo	87	59	27
Uganda	1,198	704	492
Zambia	945	836	109
Zimbabwe	368	179	189
NORTH AFRICA	**2,349**	**1,524**	**727**
Algeria	371	290	71
Egypt, Arab Rep.	926	659	238
Libya	24	17	4
Morocco	652	289	309
Tunisia	376	269	105

| Net aid | | | | | Heavily Indebted Poor Countries (HIPC) Debt Initiative | | Debt service relief committed ($ millions) |
Share of GDP (%) 2005	Per capita ($) 2005	Share of gross capital formation (%) 2005	Share of imports of goods and services (%) 2005	Share of central government expenditures (%) 2005	Decision point 2006	Completion point 2006	2006
4.9	41.3	25.1	6.7	28.1			52,315
1.3	27.7	17.9	1.1	..			..
8.1	41.4	41.6	20.6	54.3	Jul. 2000	Mar.2003	460
0.7	40.2	2.2	0.8	3.2			..
11.6	49.9	..	..	..	Jul. 2000	Apr. 2002	930
45.6	48.4	423.5	95.6	172.2	Oct. 2000	Floating	1,472
2.5	25.4	13.6	5.0	23.6	Oct.2000	Apr. 2006	4,917
16.1	316.9	..	..	..			..
7	23.6	..	..	..			..
6.4	39	31.9	6.8	143.1	May. 2001	Floating	260
6.5	42	70.0	13.8	48.4			..
25.7	31.8	181.2	34.9	310.3	Jul. 2003	Floating	10,389
24.3	362.3	108.1	17.8	183.2			2,881
0.7	6.6	7.2	0.8	9.0	Mar. 1998		
11.1	99.1	45.6	12.3	40.2			
0.5	77.5	1.4	0.4	17.3			
36.6	80.7	182.2	56.8	82.1			..
17	27.2	83.1	31.1	123.7	Nov. 2001	Apr. 2004	3,275
0.6	38.9	2.7	0.7	8.1			..
12.6	38.3	50.4	11.4	..	Dec. 2000	Floating	90
10.4	50.6	36.0	10.7	68.2	Feb. 2002	Jul. 2004	3,500
5.5	19.4	39.8	9.4	97.4	Dec. 2000	Floating	800
26.3	49.9	180.0	29.7	144.4	Dec. 2000	Floating	790
4	22.4	24.4	6.6	23.9			..
4.7	38.3	13.4	3.5	27.8			..
44.6	71.9	270.9	49.6	399.7			..
18.4	49.9	81.8	27.2	219.2	Dec. 2000	Oct. 2004	1,900
27.7	44.7	181.3	35.0	166.2	Dec. 2000	Floating	1,000
13	51.1	57.5	20.7	131.1	Aug. 2000	Mar.2003	895
10.4	62	23.1	7.9	45.8	Feb. 2000	Jun. 2002	1,100
0.5	25.7	2.2	0.4	3.5			..
18.8	65	86.8	25.7	188.8	Apr. 2000	Sep. 2001	4,300
2	60.7	7.3	2.1	8.5			..
15.2	36.9	81.8	38.6	131.9	Dec. 2000	Jun. 2004	1,190
6.6	48.9	31.2	7.4	30.8			..
26.7	63.7	119.5	64.4	200.6	Dec. 2000	Jun. 2005	1,316
28.3	203.8	..	..	..	Dec. 2000	Floating	200
8	59.1	31.3	12.2	63.3	Jun. 2000	Apr. 2004	850
2.6	222.6	21.2	1.2	10.8			..
28.8	62.1	165.9	44.0	233.2	Mar. 2002	Floating	950
..	28.7	..	..	..			..
0.3	14.9	1.6	0.5	1.4			..
6.6	50.5	27.7	14.4	39.1			..
1.8	40.7	9.8	1.1	6.6			..
12	39.3	65.8	22.0	70.2	Apr. 2000	Nov. 2001	3,000
4.1	14.1	22.4	4.9	40.9			..
13.7	41.6	64.8	34.1	95.4	Feb. 2000	May. 2000	1,950
13	81	50.3	31.2	96.8	Dec. 2000	Apr. 2005	3,900
10.8	28.3	64.0	8.3	39.6			..
0.7	15.4	3.3	1.2	5.9			..
0.4	11.3	1.2	0.5	3.0			..
1	12.5	5.7	1.6	8.1			..
0.1	4.2	..	..	..			..
1.3	21.6	4.9	1.6	5.7			..
1.3	37.5	5.6	1.3	8.5			..

Table 13.2 Capable states

	Investment climate (viewed by firms as major or very severe constraints, %)		Enforcing contracts		
	Courts 2006	Crime 2006	Number of procedures 2006	Time required (days) 2006	Cost (% of debt) 2006
SUB-SAHARAN AFRICA					
Angola	..	6.2	47	1,011	11.2
Benin	..	..	49	720	29.7
Botswana	1.4	10.9	26	501	24.8
Burkina Faso	0.7	1.4	41	446	95.4
Burundi	0.2	2.9	47	403	32.5
Cameroon	1.2	2.9	58	800	36.4
Cape Verde	2.0	1.0	40	465	15.0
Central African Republic	..	..	45	660	43.7
Chad	..	..	52	743	54.9
Comoros	..	..	60	721	29.4
Congo, Dem. Rep.	..	1.8	51	685	156.8
Congo, Rep.	..	..	47	560	45.6
Côte d'Ivoire	..	..	25	525	29.5
Djibouti	..	..	59	1,225	..
Equatorial Guinea	..	..	38	553	14.5
Eritrea	..	..	35	305	18.6
Ethiopia	..	..	30	690	14.8
Gabon	..	..	32	880	9.8
Gambia, The	2.3	2.3	26	247	35.9
Ghana	..	..	29	552	13.0
Guinea	0.4	1.7	44	276	43.8
Guinea-Bissau	1.4	0.7	40	1,140	27.0
Kenya	..	..	25	360	41.3
Lesotho	..	..	58	695	10.6
Liberia	..	..	..	..	..
Madagascar	..	..	29	591	22.8
Malawi	..	..	40	337	136.5
Mali	..	..	28	860	45.0
Mauritania	0.8	1.2	40	400	17.9
Mauritius	..	..	37	630	15.7
Mozambique	..	..	38	1,010	132.1
Namibia	0.6	20.6	31	270	28.3
Niger	..	..	33	360	42.0
Nigeria	..	..	23	457	27.0
Rwanda	..	..	27	310	43.2
São Tomé and Principe	..	..	67	405	69.5
Senegal	..	..	33	780	23.8
Seychelles	..	..	29	720	13.0
Sierra Leone	..	..	58	515	227.3
Somalia	..	..	..	..	..
South Africa	..	..	26	600	11.5
Sudan	..	..	67	770	20.6
Swaziland	1.0	18.5	31	972	20.1
Tanzania	..	1.9	21	393	51.5
Togo	..	..	37	535	24.3
Uganda	0.1	0.2	19	484	35.2
Zambia	..	..	21	404	28.7
Zimbabwe	..	..	33	410	..
NORTH AFRICA					
Algeria	..	..	49	397	..
Egypt, Arab Rep.	..	..	55	1,010	..
Libya	..	..	..	..	..
Morocco	..	..	42	615	..
Tunisia	..	..	21	481	..

a. Indexes range from 0 (least desirable) to 10 (most desirable).
b. Average of the disclosure, director liability and shareholder suits indexes.

Protecting investors[a]				Regulation and tax administration			Extractive Industries Transparency Initiative		Corruption Perceptions Index transparency index (mean score, 0 low to 10 high) 2006
Disclosure index 2006	Director liability index 2006	Shareholder suits index 2006	Investor protection index[b] 2006	Number of tax payments 2006	Time to prepare, file, and pay taxes (hours) 2006	Total tax payable (% of profit) 2006	Endorsed 2006	Report produced 2006	
5	6	6	5.7	42	272	64.4	No	No	2.2
5	8	4	5.7	72	270	68.5	No	No	2.5
8	2	3	4.3	24	140	53.3	No	No	5.6
6	5	3	4.7	45	270	51.1	No	No	3.2
..	..	..	..	40	140	286.7	No	No	2.4
8	2	6	5.3	39	1,300	46.2	Yes	Yes	2.3
1	5	6	4.0	49	100	54.4	No	No	..
4	6	7	5.7	54	504	209.5	No	No	2.4
3	4	7	4.7	65	122	68.2	Yes	No	2.0
6	4	5	5.0	20	100	47.5	No	No	..
3	3	5	3.7	34	312	235.4	Yes	No	2.0
4	5	6	5.0	94	576	57.3	Yes	No	2.2
6	5	3	4.7	71	270	45.7	Yes	No	2.1
5	2	0	2.3	36	114	41.7	..	..	..
6	4	5	5.0	48	212	62.4	Yes	No	2.1
4	5	5	4.7	18	216	86.3	No	No	2.9
4	4	5	4.3	20	212	32.8	No	No	2.4
5	4	5	4.7	27	272	48.3	Yes	Yes	3.0
2	1	5	2.7	47	376	291.4	No	No	2.5
7	5	6	6.0	35	304	32.3	Yes	Yes	3.3
5	7	2	4.7	55	416	49.4	Yes	Yes	1.9
0	5	6	3.7	47	208	47.5	No	No	..
4	2	10	5.3	17	432	74.2	No	No	2.2
2	1	8	3.7	21	352	25.6	No	No	3.2
..	..	..	..	..	..	..	Yes	No	..
5	6	6	5.7	25	304	43.2	Yes	No	3.1
4	7	5	5.3	29	878	32.6	No	No	2.7
6	5	3	4.7	60	270	50.0	Yes	No	2.8
0	0	0	0.0	61	696	104.3	Yes	No	3.1
6	8	9	7.7	7	158	24.8	No	No	5.1
7	2	6	5.0	36	230	39.2	No	No	2.8
5	5	6	5.3	34	..	25.6	No	No	4.1
4	5	5	4.7	44	270	46.0	Yes	No	2.3
6	7	4	5.7	35	1,120	31.4	Yes	Yes	2.2
2	5	1	2.7	43	168	41.1	No	No	2.5
6	1	6	4.3	42	424	55.2	Yes	No	..
4	4	4	4.0	59	696	47.7	No	No	3.3
4	8	5	5.7	15	76	48.8	No	No	3.6
3	6	5	4.7	20	399	277.0	Yes	No	2.2
..	..	..	..	..	..	..	No	No	..
8	8	8	8.0	23	350	38.3	No	No	4.6
0	6	5	3.7	66	180	37.1	No	No	2.0
1	1	5	2.3	34	104	39.5	No	No	2.5
3	4	7	4.7	48	248	45.0	No	No	2.9
4	3	5	4.0	51	270	48.3	No	No	2.4
7	5	4	5.3	31	237	32.2	No	No	2.7
3	6	7	5.3	37	131	22.2	No	No	2.6
8	..	..	..	59	216	37.0	No	No	2.4
									..
6	6	4	5.3	61	504	76.4	..	..	3.1
5	3	5	4.3	41	536	50.4	..	..	3.3
..	..	..	..	..	..	..	..	..	2.7
6	6	1	4.3	28	468	52.7	..	..	3.2
0	4	6	3.3	45	268	58.8	..	..	4.6

Table 13.3 Governance and anticorruption indicators

	Income category	Voice and accountability		Political stability and absence of violence	
		1996	2006	1996	2006
SUB–SAHARAN AFRICA					
Angola	Low income	−1.5	−1.3	−2.4	−0.5
Benin	Low income	0.7	0.3	1.0	0.4
Botswana	Upper middle income	0.7	0.6	0.7	1.2
Burkina Faso	Low income	−0.5	−0.3	−0.4	−0.2
Burundi	Low income	−1.3	−1.0	−2.0	−1.4
Cameroon	Low income	−1.1	−1.0	−1.2	−0.2
Cape Verde	Lower middle income	0.9	0.9	1.0	0.9
Central African Republic	Low income	−0.2	−1.1	−0.2	−1.7
Chad	Low income	−0.8	−1.4	−0.9	−1.8
Comoros	Low income	−0.2	−0.3	1.0	−0.2
Congo, Dem. Rep.	Low income	−1.3	−1.6	−2.0	−2.3
Congo, Rep.	Low income	−1.3	−1.1	−0.9	−1.0
Côte d'Ivoire	Low income	−0.3	−1.4	0.0	−2.1
Djibouti	Lower middle income	−0.9	−1.0	0.2	−0.2
Equatorial Guinea	Low income	−1.6	−1.8	−0.6	−0.2
Eritrea	Low income	−1.2	−1.8	0.2	−0.9
Ethiopia	Low income	−0.7	−1.1	−0.9	−1.8
Gabon	Upper middle income	−0.6	−1.0	−0.4	0.1
Gambia, The	Low income	−1.4	−0.9	0.0	0.2
Ghana	Low income	−0.4	0.4	−0.1	0.2
Guinea	Low income	−1.2	−1.2	−1.5	−1.7
Guinea-Bissau	Low income	−0.6	−0.4	−0.8	−0.6
Kenya	Low income	−0.6	−0.2	−0.7	−1.1
Lesotho	Low income	0.0	0.3	0.8	0.2
Liberia	Low income	−1.5	−0.6	−2.7	−1.2
Madagascar	Low income	0.2	−0.1	−0.1	0.1
Malawi	Low income	−0.5	−0.3	−0.2	0.0
Mali	Low income	0.3	0.3	0.5	0.0
Mauritania	Low income	−0.9	−1.0	0.5	−0.3
Mauritius	Upper middle income	0.8	0.9	0.9	0.9
Mozambique	Low income	−0.3	−0.1	−0.6	0.5
Namibia	Lower middle income	0.5	0.4	0.6	0.8
Niger	Low income	−0.5	−0.2	−0.3	−0.4
Nigeria	Low income	−1.6	−0.8	−1.8	−2.0
Rwanda	Low income	−1.5	−1.1	−1.5	−0.5
São Tomé and Principe	Low income	0.8	0.3	1.0	0.5
Senegal	Low income	−0.2	−0.1	−0.8	−0.3
Seychelles	Upper middle income	0.1	0.1	1.0	1.1
Sierra Leone	Low income	−1.5	−0.4	−2.5	−0.5
Somalia	Low income	−2.0	−2.1	−2.4	−2.8
South Africa	Lower middle income	0.6	0.6	−1.2	−0.1
Sudan	Low income	−1.7	−1.8	−2.8	−2.2
Swaziland	Lower middle income	−1.4	−1.1	0.0	−0.1
Tanzania	Low income	−0.9	−0.3	−0.2	−0.2
Togo	Low income	−1.1	−1.2	−0.7	−0.9
Uganda	Low income	−0.7	−0.5	−1.4	−1.2
Zambia	Low income	−0.2	−0.3	−0.7	0.3
Zimbabwe	Low income	−0.4	−1.6	−0.4	−1.2
NORTH AFRICA					
Algeria	Lower middle income	−1.2	−0.8	−2.9	−0.9
Egypt, Arab Rep.	Lower middle income	−0.8	−1.1	−0.6	−0.9
Libya	Upper middle income	−1.5	−1.9	−1.8	0.2
Morocco	Lower middle income	−0.7	−0.6	−0.6	−0.3
Tunisia	Lower middle income	−0.6	−1.2	0.0	0.2

Note: The rating scale for each criterion ranges from −2.5 (weak performance) to 2.5 (very high performance).

Government effectiveness		Regulatory quality		Rule of law		Control of corruption	
1996	2006	1996	2006	1996	2006	1996	2006
−1.3	−1.2	−1.5	−1.2	−1.5	−1.3	−1.1	−1.1
0.0	−0.5	0.1	−0.4	−0.1	−0.5	..	−0.8
0.5	0.7	0.6	0.5	0.8	0.6	0.5	0.8
−0.7	−0.8	−0.4	−0.4	−0.8	−0.5	−0.3	−0.4
−1.0	−1.3	−1.3	−1.2	−0.2	−1.0	..	−1.1
−1.1	−0.9	−0.8	−0.7	−1.2	−1.0	−1.2	−0.9
−0.1	0.2	−0.6	−0.2	0.0	0.6	..	0.7
−0.9	−1.4	−0.3	−1.2	−0.2	−1.6	..	−1.1
−0.7	−1.4	0.0	−1.2	−0.2	−1.4	..	−1.2
−0.7	−1.7	−0.7	−1.5	..	−0.9	..	−0.6
−1.7	−1.6	−2.2	−1.5	−1.9	−1.7	−2.1	−1.4
−1.2	−1.3	−0.8	−1.2	−1.3	−1.3	−0.9	−1.1
0.1	−1.4	−0.1	−1.1	−0.7	−1.5	0.5	−1.2
−1.1	−1.0	0.0	−0.9	..	−0.8	..	−0.7
−1.5	−1.3	−1.0	−1.4	..	−1.2	..	−1.5
−0.3	−1.2	−0.2	−1.9	−0.2	−1.0	..	−0.2
−0.6	−0.6	−1.3	−0.8	−0.3	−0.6	−1.1	−0.6
−1.0	−0.6	−0.5	−0.5	−0.4	−0.6	−1.3	−0.8
−0.3	−0.7	−1.6	−0.4	0.2	−0.3	0.4	−0.6
0.1	0.1	0.0	−0.1	−0.2	−0.1	−0.5	−0.1
−1.1	−1.4	0.0	−1.1	−1.1	−1.4	0.4	−1.0
−0.6	−1.2	0.1	−1.1	−1.7	−1.2	−1.1	−1.0
−0.6	−0.7	−0.4	−0.2	−0.8	−1.0	−1.1	−1.0
0.1	−0.3	−0.7	−0.6	−0.4	−0.3	..	−0.1
−1.8	−1.4	−3.0	−1.6	−2.2	−1.2	−1.8	−0.9
−1.0	−0.2	−0.1	−0.3	−0.9	−0.3	0.4	−0.3
−0.7	−0.9	−0.4	−0.6	−0.3	−0.5	−1.1	−0.7
−0.7	−0.4	0.1	−0.4	−0.8	−0.3	−0.3	−0.6
0.1	−0.6	−0.7	−0.2	−0.7	−0.4	..	−0.6
0.6	0.6	0.1	0.6	0.7	0.8	0.5	0.4
−0.5	−0.3	−1.1	−0.5	−1.3	−0.6	−0.5	−0.6
0.3	0.1	0.0	0.2	0.3	0.2	0.9	0.2
−1.1	−0.8	−1.0	−0.6	−1.3	−0.9	−0.3	−1.0
−1.3	−1.0	−1.0	−0.9	−1.3	−1.3	−1.3	−1.3
−1.2	−0.4	−1.1	−0.6	−0.2	−0.6	..	−0.1
−0.7	−0.9	−0.4	−0.8	..	−0.5	..	−0.5
−0.3	−0.2	−0.5	−0.3	−0.2	−0.3	−0.4	−0.4
−0.7	−0.1	−1.2	−0.6	..	0.0	..	0.1
−0.6	−1.1	−0.5	−1.1	−1.1	−1.2	−1.8	−1.2
−1.8	−2.2	−3.0	−2.7	−1.8	−2.5	−1.8	−1.8
0.5	0.8	0.2	0.7	0.3	0.2	0.7	0.6
−1.3	−1.1	−1.7	−1.2	−1.5	−1.3	−1.2	−1.1
−0.4	−0.7	0.0	−0.5	0.4	−0.7	..	−0.5
−1.2	−0.3	−0.4	−0.4	−0.8	−0.5	−1.1	−0.4
−0.8	−1.6	0.4	−0.9	−1.3	−1.0	−1.1	−1.0
−0.4	−0.5	0.1	−0.2	−0.9	−0.5	−0.5	−0.7
−0.8	−0.7	0.3	−0.6	−0.4	−0.6	−1.0	−0.8
0.0	−1.5	−0.8	−2.2	−0.3	−1.7	−0.1	−1.4
−0.6	−0.4	−0.8	−0.6	−0.7	−0.6	−0.4	−0.4
−0.3	−0.4	−0.1	−0.4	0.2	0.0	0.1	−0.4
−0.8	−0.9	−1.8	−1.4	−1.1	−0.7	−1.0	−0.9
−0.1	0.0	0.1	−0.2	0.1	0.0	0.3	−0.1
0.5	0.6	0.3	0.2	0.0	0.4	0.0	0.2

Table 13.4 Country Policy and Institutional Assessment ratings

	CPIA overall rating (IDA resource allocation index)[a] 2006	Economic management				Structural policies			
		Average[b] 2006	Macro-economic management 2006	Fiscal policy 2006	Debt policy 2006	Average[b] 2006	Trade 2006	Financial sector 2006	Business regulatory environment 2006
SUB-SAHARAN AFRICA									
Angola	2.7	2.7	3.0	3.0	2.0	2.8	4.0	2.5	2.0
Benin	3.6	4.0	4.5	4.0	3.5	3.8	4.5	3.5	3.5
Botswana[c]	..	..	..	..	..	..	..	..	..
Burkina Faso	3.7	4.3	4.5	4.5	4.0	3.3	4.0	3.0	3.0
Burundi	3.0	3.2	3.5	3.5	2.5	3.0	3.5	3.0	2.5
Cameroon	3.2	3.5	4.0	4.0	2.5	3.2	3.5	3.0	3.0
Cape Verde	4.1	4.3	4.5	4.5	4.0	3.8	4.0	4.0	3.5
Central African Republic	2.4	2.5	3.0	3.0	1.5	2.7	3.5	2.5	2.0
Chad	2.8	3.0	3.5	3.0	2.5	3.0	3.0	3.0	3.0
Comoros	2.4	2.0	2.5	2.0	1.5	2.5	2.5	2.5	2.5
Congo, Dem. Rep.	2.8	3.2	3.5	3.5	2.5	3.0	4.0	2.0	3.0
Congo, Rep.	2.8	2.8	3.5	2.5	2.5	2.8	3.5	2.5	2.5
Côte d'Ivoire	2.5	1.8	2.5	2.0	1.0	3.2	3.5	3.0	3.0
Djibouti	3.1	2.8	3.5	2.5	2.5	3.5	4.0	3.5	3.0
Equatorial Guinea[c]	..	..	..	..	..	..	..	..	..
Eritrea	2.5	2.2	2.0	2.0	2.5	1.8	1.5	2.0	2.0
Ethiopia	3.4	3.5	3.0	4.0	3.5	3.2	3.0	3.0	3.5
Gabon[c]	..	..	..	..	..	..	..	..	..
Gambia, The	3.1	3.0	3.5	3.0	2.5	3.3	4.0	3.0	3.0
Ghana	3.9	4.2	4.0	4.5	4.0	3.8	4.0	3.5	4.0
Guinea	2.9	2.7	2.5	3.0	2.5	3.5	4.5	3.0	3.0
Guinea-Bissau	2.6	2.0	2.0	2.5	1.5	3.2	4.0	3.0	2.5
Kenya	3.7	4.2	4.5	4.0	4.0	3.8	4.0	3.5	4.0
Lesotho	3.5	4.0	4.0	4.0	4.0	3.3	3.5	3.5	3.0
Liberia[d]	..	..	..	..	..	..	..	..	..
Madagascar	3.6	3.5	4.0	3.0	3.5	3.8	4.0	3.5	4.0
Malawi	3.4	3.2	3.5	3.0	3.0	3.5	4.0	3.0	3.5
Mali	3.7	4.3	4.5	4.0	4.5	3.5	4.0	3.0	3.5
Mauritania	3.3	3.3	3.0	3.0	4.0	3.5	4.5	2.5	3.5
Mauritius[c]	..	..	..	..	..	3.5	4.5	3.0	3.0
Mozambique	3.5	4.2	4.0	4.0	4.5	3.5	4.5	3.0	3.0
Namibia[c]	..	..	..	..	..	..	..	..	..
Niger	3.3	3.7	4.0	3.5	3.5	3.3	4.0	3.0	3.0
Nigeria	3.2	4.0	4.0	4.0	4.0	3.0	3.0	3.0	3.0
Rwanda	3.6	3.8	4.0	4.0	3.5	3.5	3.5	3.5	3.5
São Tomé and Principe	3.0	2.8	3.0	3.0	2.5	3.2	4.0	2.5	3.0
Senegal	3.7	4.0	4.0	4.0	4.0	3.7	4.0	3.5	3.5
Seychelles[c]	..	..	..	..	..	..	..	..	..
Sierra Leone	3.1	3.7	4.0	3.5	3.5	3.0	3.5	3.0	2.5
Somalia[d]	..	..	..	..	..	..	..	..	..
South Africa[c]	..	..	..	..	..	..	..	..	..
Sudan	2.5	2.7	3.5	3.0	1.5	2.8	2.5	3.0	3.0
Swaziland[c]	..	..	..	..	..	..	..	..	..
Tanzania	3.9	4.5	5.0	4.5	4.0	3.7	4.0	3.5	3.5
Togo	2.5	2.0	2.5	2.0	1.5	3.2	4.0	2.5	3.0
Uganda	3.9	4.5	4.5	4.5	4.5	3.8	4.0	3.5	4.0
Zambia	3.4	3.7	4.0	3.5	3.5	3.3	4.0	3.0	3.0
Zimbabwe	1.8	1.0	1.0	1.0	1.0	2.2	2.0	2.5	2.0
NORTH AFRICA									
Algeria[c]	..	..	..	..	..	..	..	..	..
Egypt, Arab Rep.[c]	..	..	..	..	..	..	..	..	..
Libya[c]	..	..	..	..	..	..	..	..	..
Morocco[c]	..	..	..	..	..	..	..	..	..
Tunisia[c]	..	..	..	..	..	..	..	..	..

Note: The rating scale for each indicator ranges from 1 (low) to 6 (high).
a. Calculated as the average of the average ratings of each cluster.
b. All criteria are weighted equally.
c. Not an IDA member.
d. Not rated in the 2006 International Development Association (IDA) resource allocation index.

Policies for social inclusion and equity						Public sector management and institutions					
Average[b] 2006	Gender equality 2006	Equity of public resource use 2006	Building human resources 2006	Social protection and labor 2006	Policies and institutions for environmental sustainability 2006	Average[b] 2006	Property rights and rule-based governance 2006	Quality of budgetary and financial management 2006	Quality of public administration 2006	Efficiency of revenue mobilization 2006	Transparency, accountability, and corruption in public sector 2006
2.7	3.0	2.5	2.5	2.5	3.0	2.4	2.0	2.5	2.5	2.5	2.5
3.2	3.0	3.0	3.5	3.0	3.5	3.3	3.0	3.5	3.0	3.5	3.5
..	..	..	..	..	..	..	..	..	..	..	..
3.6	3.5	4.0	3.5	3.5	3.5	3.5	3.5	4.0	3.5	3.5	3.0
3.1	3.5	3.0	3.0	3.0	3.0	2.7	2.5	3.0	2.5	3.0	2.5
3.2	3.5	3.0	3.5	3.0	3.0	3.0	2.5	3.5	3.0	3.5	2.5
4.3	4.5	4.5	4.5	4.5	3.5	3.9	4.0	3.5	4.0	3.5	4.5
2.2	2.5	2.0	2.0	2.0	2.5	2.2	2.0	2.0	2.0	2.5	2.5
2.6	2.5	3.0	2.5	2.5	2.5	2.4	2.0	2.5	3.0	2.5	2.0
2.7	3.0	3.0	3.0	2.5	2.0	2.2	2.5	1.5	2.0	2.5	2.5
2.9	3.0	3.0	3.0	3.0	2.5	2.3	2.0	2.5	2.5	2.5	2.0
2.7	3.0	2.5	3.0	2.5	2.5	2.7	2.5	3.0	2.5	3.0	2.5
2.3	2.5	1.5	2.0	2.5	3.0	2.5	2.0	2.5	2.0	4.0	2.0
3.1	3.0	3.0	3.5	3.0	3.0	2.8	2.5	3.0	2.5	3.5	2.5
..	..	..	..	..	..	..	..	..	..	..	..
3.0	3.5	3.0	3.5	3.0	2.0	2.8	2.5	2.5	3.0	3.5	2.5
3.6	3.0	4.5	3.5	3.5	3.5	3.3	3.0	4.0	3.0	4.0	2.5
..	..	..	..	..	..	..	..	..	..	..	..
3.1	3.5	3.0	3.5	2.5	3.0	2.9	3.5	2.5	3.0	3.5	2.0
3.8	4.0	4.0	4.0	3.5	3.5	3.9	3.5	4.0	3.5	4.5	4.0
3.0	3.5	3.0	3.0	3.0	2.5	2.6	2.0	2.5	3.0	3.0	2.5
2.6	2.5	3.0	2.5	2.5	2.5	2.6	2.5	2.5	2.5	3.0	2.5
3.2	3.0	3.5	3.5	3.0	3.0	3.4	3.0	3.5	3.5	4.0	3.0
3.4	4.0	3.0	3.5	3.0	3.5	3.4	3.5	3.0	3.0	4.0	3.5
..	..	..	..	..	..	..	..	..	..	..	..
3.6	3.5	3.5	3.5	3.5	4.0	3.4	3.5	3.0	3.5	3.5	3.5
3.5	3.5	3.5	3.5	3.5	3.5	3.4	3.5	3.0	3.5	4.0	3.0
3.4	3.5	3.5	3.5	3.5	3.0	3.5	3.5	3.5	3.0	4.0	3.5
3.4	3.5	3.5	3.5	3.0	3.5	2.9	3.0	2.5	3.0	3.5	2.5
..	..	..	..	..	..	..	..	..	..	..	..
3.3	3.5	3.5	3.5	3.0	3.0	3.1	3.0	3.5	2.5	3.5	3.0
..	..	..	..	..	..	..	..	..	..	..	..
3.0	2.5	3.5	3.0	3.0	3.0	3.2	3.0	3.5	3.0	3.5	3.0
3.1	3.0	3.5	3.0	3.0	3.0	2.8	2.5	3.0	2.5	3.0	3.0
3.8	3.5	4.5	4.5	3.5	3.0	3.4	3.0	4.0	3.5	3.5	3.0
2.8	3.0	3.5	2.5	2.5	2.5	3.0	2.5	2.5	3.0	3.5	3.5
3.4	3.5	3.5	3.5	3.0	3.5	3.6	3.5	3.5	3.5	4.5	3.0
..	..	..	..	..	..	..	..	..	..	..	..
2.8	3.0	3.0	3.0	3.0	2.0	2.9	2.5	3.5	3.0	3.0	2.5
..	..	..	..	..	..	..	..	..	..	..	..
..	..	..	..	..	..	..	..	..	..	..	..
2.3	2.0	2.5	2.5	2.0	2.5	2.3	2.0	2.0	2.5	3.0	2.0
..	..	..	..	..	..	..	..	..	..	..	..
3.8	4.0	4.0	4.0	3.5	3.5	3.8	3.5	4.5	3.5	4.0	3.5
2.6	3.0	2.0	3.0	2.5	2.5	2.2	2.5	2.0	2.0	2.5	2.0
3.9	3.5	4.5	4.0	3.5	4.0	3.3	3.5	4.0	3.0	3.0	3.0
3.4	3.5	3.5	3.5	3.0	3.5	3.2	3.0	3.5	3.0	3.5	3.0
2.0	2.5	1.5	2.0	1.5	2.5	1.9	1.0	2.0	2.0	3.5	1.0
..	..	..	..	..	..	..	..	..	..	..	..
..	..	..	..	..	..	..	..	..	..	..	..
..	..	..	..	..	..	..	..	..	..	..	..
..	..	..	..	..	..	..	..	..	..	..	..

14.1 Burkina Faso household survey, 2003

Indicator	National total	Rural						Urban					
		All	Q1	Q2	Q3	Q4	Q5	All	Q1	Q2	Q3	Q4	Q5
Demographic indicators													
Sample size (households)	8,494	5,894	618	853	1,020	1,278	2,125	2,600	253	326	387	573	1,061
Total population (thousands)	11,385	9,317	1,387	1,672	1,804	1,947	2,506	2,068	319	349	390	458	554
Age dependency ratio	1.0	1.1	1.3	1.2	1.2	1.1	0.8	0.6	0.9	0.8	0.7	0.6	0.5
Average household size	6.4	6.6	9.8	8.4	7.5	6.5	4.7	5.6	8.4	7.4	6.8	5.5	3.9
Marital status of head of household (%)													
Monogamous male	4	3	0	1	1	2	5	10	1	3	4	5	21
Polygamous male	60	59	44	50	57	60	68	63	60	59	67	68	62
Single male	29	33	53	44	37	33	21	13	24	25	18	12	5
De facto female	0	0	0	0	..	..	0	0	..	..	..	..	0
De jure female	7	5	3	4	4	5	6	13	14	13	12	14	12
MDG 1: extreme poverty and hunger													
Mean monthly expenditure (CFA francs)	75,614	65,140	36,960	46,013	58,598	71,470	112,679	129,090	55,311	81,398	106,453	146,524	256,278
Mean monthly share on food (%)	58	65	72	70	69	65	57	42	54	51	48	44	34
Mean monthly share on health (%)	5	5	2	3	3	3	9	6	3	2	6	7	8
Mean monthly share on education (%)	3	1	2	1	2	1	1	8	4	8	8	7	8
MDGs 2 and 3: education and literacy; gender equality													
Primary school within 30 minutes (% of households)	63	55	56	58	58	54	53	91	87	86	89	93	93
Net primary enrollment rate (% of relevant age group)													
Total	93	91	87	90	92	91	93	96	95	95	94	97	97
Male	93	91	88	90	94	90	93	96	95	93	96	96	98
Female	92	91	84	90	90	92	94	95	94	97	93	97	95
Net secondary enrollment rate (% of relevant age group)													
Total	34	21	16	20	17	23	27	48	24	36	42	52	68
Male	32	21	19	18	14	26	29	47	26	34	41	51	70
Female	36	21	9	24	24	19	23	48	23	38	43	53	66
Tertiary enrollment rate (per 10,000)													
Adult literacy rate (%)													
Total	22	13	9	11	10	12	17	56	34	43	49	57	76
Male	29	19	14	18	17	17	23	66	44	54	58	67	83
Female	15	7	4	5	5	7	11	47	25	33	39	49	69
Youth literacy rate (% ages 15–24)													
Total	31	19	15	20	19	18	20	71	53	70	70	74	80
Male	38	26	22	26	26	24	28	78	58	76	75	83	90
Female	25	13	8	13	12	13	14	65	47	62	63	67	72
MDGs 4 and 5: child mortality; maternal health													
Health center less than 1 hour away (% of population)	65	57	56	55	55	57	59	95	91	89	94	95	97
Morbidity (% of population)	6	6	3	4	6	6	8	7	5	4	6	7	10
Health care provider consulted when sick (%)	64	62	44	49	56	65	71	71	55	54	72	77	77
Type of health care provider consulted (% of total)													
Public	70	72	57	62	67	70	79	62	66	67	57	64	61
Private, modern medicine	7	2	1	4	2	2	2	25	8	13	27	25	31
Private, traditional healers	17	20	39	28	25	18	14	8	22	14	12	6	3
Missionary or nongovernmental organization	..	..	..	..	..	..	..	..	..	..	..	..	..
Child survival and malnutrition (%)													
Birth assisted by trained staff	52	43	32	42	43	46	50	94	86	94	93	96	98
Immunization coverage, 1-year-olds	..	..	..	..	..	..	..	..	..	..	..	..	..
Measles immunization coverage, 1-year-olds	..	..	..	..	..	..	..	..	..	..	..	..	..
Stunting (6–59 months)	43	46	45	46	47	44	47	33	34	29	36	36	31
Wasting (6–59 months)	31	32	35	32	33	32	30	28	24	33	33	28	24
Underweight (6–59 months)	47	50	52	51	51	49	48	35	31	38	43	38	28
MDG 7: environmental sustainability													
Access to sanitation facilities (% of population)	35	20	12	16	18	20	25	91	70	85	92	95	97
Water source less than 1 hour away (% of population)	90	88	88	90	90	88	85	98	98	97	97	97	98
Market less than 1 hour away (% of population)	83	80	80	80	80	81	79	97	94	96	96	96	98
Access to improved water source (% of population)													
Total[a]	27	15	14	16	15	15	16	72	52	63	75	76	77
Own tap	19	5	4	5	4	5	6	70	44	59	71	74	76
Other piped	..	..	..	..	..	..	..	..	..	..	..	..	..
Well, protected	9	10	10	11	11	11	10	3	8	4	5	2	1
Traditional fuel use (%)													
Total[a]	95	98	99	99	99	99	96	85	99	99	98	93	67
Firewood	91	96	97	98	98	97	94	73	99	94	93	82	47
Charcoal	4	2	2	1	1	2	3	12	1	5	5	11	21

a. Components may not sum to total because of rounding.

Table **14.2** Cameroon household survey, 2001

Indicator	National total	Expenditure quintile											
		Rural						Urban					
		All	Q1	Q2	Q3	Q4	Q5	All	Q1	Q2	Q3	Q4	Q5
Demographic indicators													
Sample size (households)	10,992	6,017	646	764	1,026	1,217	2,364	4,975	759	786	886	1,061	1,483
Total population (thousands)	15,473	10,089	2,019	2,016	2,019	2,018	2,018	5,383	1,077	1,076	1,076	1,076	1,078
Age dependency ratio	0.9	1.0	1.4	1.3	1.1	0.9	0.6	0.7	1.0	0.8	0.7	0.5	0.4
Average household size	5.0	5.0	7.2	6.8	5.5	5.0	3.0	4.9	7.3	6.3	5.7	4.5	3.1
Marital status of head of household (%)													
Monogamous male	44	46	50	50	50	48	40	40	47	49	46	38	32
Polygamous male	14	16	22	22	16	17	11	9	16	11	10	9	6
Single male	18	15	5	6	11	11	26	25	15	15	17	26	38
De facto female	4	4	5	5	5	4	3	4	5	4	5	4	4
De jure female	19	19	18	17	18	20	20	21	17	20	22	23	21
MDG 1: extreme poverty and hunger													
Mean monthly expenditure (CFA francs)	30,619	22,063	6,609	10,217	13,705	18,951	40,025	46,540	11,847	18,846	25,889	37,099	93,334
Mean monthly share on food (%)	59	69	68	71	70	69	68	42	48	45	44	42	36
Mean monthly share on health (%)	7	7	7	6	7	7	8	7	6	6	7	7	8
Mean monthly share on education (%)	4	3	3	3	3	3	3	6	6	7	7	6	5
MDGs 2 and 3: education and literacy; gender equality													
Primary school within 30 minutes (% of households)	85	79	75	77	79	77	83	96	96	96	96	95	96
Net primary enrollment rate (% of relevant age group)													
Total	93	92	92	91	93	93	92	94	94	95	95	93	89
Male	93	93	93	92	94	93	90	94	94	95	95	94	91
Female	92	92	90	90	93	93	93	93	94	96	95	92	87
Net secondary enrollment rate (% of relevant age group)													
Total	40	29	14	22	28	33	48	57	38	53	59	64	72
Male	39	29	15	22	28	33	49	55	35	49	59	64	73
Female	41	28	12	21	27	33	47	58	40	57	59	64	71
Tertiary enrollment rate (per 10,000)	89	..	..	..	..	..	..	..	..	..	..	..	..
Adult literacy rate (%)													
Total	68	56	50	50	55	58	62	88	76	85	89	92	94
Male	77	67	61	60	66	69	72	92	83	91	94	96	96
Female	60	47	42	42	46	49	51	83	70	80	84	88	92
Youth literacy rate (% ages 15–24)													
Total	82	73	69	69	76	74	78	94	89	93	95	96	97
Male	88	82	76	78	85	84	85	96	90	95	97	97	98
Female	77	66	62	61	69	67	71	93	87	91	93	95	95
MDGs 4 and 5: child mortality; maternal health													
Health center less than 1 hour away (% of population)	90	84	77	83	84	84	88	100	99	100	100	100	100
Morbidity (% of population)	31	31	28	29	31	33	35	31	30	31	31	30	33
Health care provider consulted when sick (%)	..	..	..	..	..	..	..	..	..	..	..	..	..
Type of health care provider consulted (% of total)													
Public	53	55	53	53	53	59	58	48	44	49	51	49	48
Private, modern medicine	13	7	6	5	7	8	9	23	19	20	20	24	31
Private, traditional healers	15	18	18	21	21	15	14	11	18	12	9	7	6
Other	2	3	2	3	4	3	4	1	1	0	1	1	1
Child survival and malnutrition (%)													
Birth assisted by trained staff	..	..	..	..	..	..	..	..	..	..	..	..	..
Immunization coverage, 1-year-olds	..	..	..	..	..	..	..	..	..	..	..	..	..
Measles immunization coverage, 1-year-olds	..	..	..	..	..	..	..	..	..	..	..	..	..
Stunting (6–59 months)	..	..	..	..	..	..	..	..	..	..	..	..	..
Wasting (6–59 months)	..	..	..	..	..	..	..	..	..	..	..	..	..
Underweight (6–59 months)	..	..	..	..	..	..	..	..	..	..	..	..	..
MDG 7: environmental sustainability													
Access to sanitation facilities (% of population)	43	26	13	15	21	29	36	75	58	68	75	79	84
Water source less than 1 hour away (% of population)	68	75	71	80	73	74	76	56	56	59	61	57	50
Market less than 1 hour away (% of population)	90	85	82	85	84	86	88	99	99	99	99	100	99
Access to improved water source (% of population)													
Total[a]	66	50	47	44	47	48	58	96	88	94	97	97	98
Own tap	15	6	3	4	4	5	10	32	11	17	24	35	49
Other piped	27	14	12	11	11	13	17	52	58	62	59	51	41
Well, protected	24	31	32	30	32	30	31	12	19	15	14	10	8
Traditional fuel use (%)													
Total[a]	75	94	99	99	97	96	86	41	75	58	51	34	17
Firewood	75	93	99	99	96	96	85	40	75	58	49	33	16
Charcoal	0	0	..	..	0	0	0	1	0	1	2	1	1

a. Components may not sum to total because of rounding.

14.3 Ethiopia household survey, 2000

Indicator	National total	Rural All	Rural Q1	Rural Q2	Rural Q3	Rural Q4	Rural Q5	Urban All	Urban Q1	Urban Q2	Urban Q3	Urban Q4	Urban Q5
Demographic indicators													
Sample size (households)	16,672	8,459	1,469	1,382	1,519	1,678	2,411	8,213	1,118	1,358	1,506	1,883	2,348
Total population (thousands)	54,756	47,531	9,502	9,513	9,504	9,507	9,505	7,225	1,446	1,443	1,446	1,445	1,445
Age dependency ratio	1.0	1.1	1.3	1.2	1.1	1.0	0.8	0.7	1.0	0.9	0.8	0.6	0.5
Average household size	4.9	4.9	5.9	5.4	5.2	4.8	3.8	4.5	5.6	5.1	4.7	4.3	3.5
Marital status of head of household (%)													
Monogamous male	68	71	75	72	74	74	64	48	53	50	50	49	41
Polygamous male	1	1	1	1	1	0	1	0	0	0	0	0	0
Single male	6	5	3	4	3	4	8	11	6	4	7	10	23
De facto female	1	1	1	1	1	0	1	3	2	4	4	3	2
De jure female	25	23	20	22	21	22	27	38	39	42	39	38	34
MDG 1: extreme poverty and hunger													
Mean monthly expenditure (birr)	103	93	42	60	75	95	161	162	49	76	103	147	346
Mean monthly share on food (%)	66	68	72	71	69	68	62	55	66	62	59	53	43
Mean monthly share on health (%)	1	1	1	1	1	1	1	1	1	1	1	1	1
Mean monthly share on education (%)	1	0	0	0	0	0	0	2	2	1	2	2	2
MDGs 2 and 3: education and literacy; gender equality													
Primary school within 30 minutes (% of households)	..	..	..	..	..	..	..	..	..	..	..	..	..
Net primary enrollment rate (% of relevant age group)													
Total	30	25	19	23	29	25	32	75	66	70	76	84	85
Male	32	27	20	25	30	27	35	75	68	68	75	85	86
Female	29	22	18	20	28	21	29	75	64	71	77	82	84
Net secondary enrollment rate (% of relevant age group)													
Total	9	3	2	3	3	3	5	40	30	36	41	50	47
Male	10	4	4	3	3	5	7	43	29	38	47	54	54
Female	8	2	1	2	2	2	3	38	30	35	36	46	42
Tertiary enrollment rate (per 10,000)	10	..	..	..	..	..	..	..	..	..	..	..	..
Adult literacy rate (%)													
Total	28	21	15	19	20	23	25	67	54	59	66	71	79
Male	41	34	26	32	33	39	39	81	70	75	80	86	91
Female	17	9	6	8	8	9	11	56	43	47	56	61	69
Youth literacy rate (% ages 15–24)													
Total	39	29	24	32	29	30	31	84	80	81	86	87	86
Male	50	43	35	47	43	45	42	90	84	86	91	95	95
Female	28	17	12	17	16	16	20	80	76	78	82	81	81
MDGs 4 and 5: child mortality; maternal health													
Health center less than 5 km away (% of population)	47	38	37	39	40	37	37	98	97	98	99	99	98
Morbidity (% of population)	26	27	27	27	27	26	31	20	20	20	20	19	20
Health care provider consulted when sick (%)	41	39	30	36	40	41	46	67	60	65	68	70	71
Type of health care provider consulted (% of total)													
Public	45	44	44	49	45	42	41	52	56	59	52	49	43
Private, modern medicine	45	45	46	40	46	46	48	42	36	36	41	43	51
Private, traditional healers	1	1	0	0	1	1	1	1	0	0	1	2	1
Other	6	7	6	7	5	9	7	4	4	3	4	3	4
Child survival and malnutrition (%)													
Birth assisted by trained staff	..	..	..	..	..	..	..	..	..	..	..	..	..
Immunization coverage, 1-year-olds	45	41	35	48	42	38	45	85	81	81	84	96	88
Measles immunization coverage, 1-year-olds	51	47	44	50	47	49	46	90	84	88	90	98	94
Stunting (6–59 months)	59	61	64	60	61	61	55	47	56	51	49	43	29
Wasting (6–59 months)	11	11	12	11	11	9	11	7	8	9	6	4	7
Underweight (6–59 months)	45	46	53	46	48	41	43	27	36	30	27	22	14
MDG 7: environmental sustainability													
Access to sanitation facilities (% of population)	17	9	7	8	7	9	11	71	48	63	72	78	86
Water source less than 5 km away (% of population)	90	99	90	89	88	90	87	98	97	98	98	98	99
Market less than 5 km away (% of population)	58	52	54	52	52	52	50	98	98	98	99	99	97
Access to improved water source (% of population)													
Total[a]	29	19	15	18	18	19	21	92	83	91	93	92	96
Own tap	0	0	0	0	0	0	0	1	1	1	1	2	2
Other piped	17	7	7	7	6	6	8	82	74	79	84	83	88
Well, protected	11	12	8	11	12	13	13	8	9	11	8	7	6
Traditional fuel use (%)													
Total[a]	77	78	82	78	77	78	77	66	80	74	70	65	51
Firewood	75	78	82	78	77	78	77	58	75	67	61	57	40
Charcoal	1	0	0	..	..	..	0	8	5	7	9	8	11

a. Components may not sum to total because of rounding.

HOUSEHOLD WELFARE

Table 14.4

Table 14.4 Malawi household survey, 2004

Indicator	National total	Rural All	Q1	Q2	Q3	Q4	Q5	Urban All	Q1	Q2	Q3	Q4	Q5
Demographic indicators													
Sample size (households)	11,280	9,840	1,495	1,747	1,924	2,106	2,568	1,440	249	246	283	335	327
Total population (thousands)	12,505	11,075	2,187	2,186	2,200	2,219	2,282	1,429	279	281	280	287	299
Age dependency ratio	1.0	1.0	1.4	1.2	1.1	1.0	0.7	0.7	1.1	0.9	0.8	0.6	0.4
Average household size	4.5	4.6	5.9	5.2	4.7	4.2	3.5	4.3	5.3	4.9	4.5	3.7	3.5
Marital status of head of household (%)													
Monogamous male	63	62	62	63	63	64	58	69	69	81	76	68	57
Polygamous male	8	9	9	11	10	8	8	3	6	3	2	2	2
Single male	6	5	1	1	2	5	13	13	1	4	8	17	27
De facto female	2	2	3	3	2	2	2	1	3	1	2	0	1
De jure female	21	22	25	21	22	21	19	14	20	11	12	12	14
MDG 1: extreme poverty and hunger													
Mean monthly expenditure (kwacha)	85	72	31	44	58	78	148	184	42	68	98	143	565
Mean monthly share on food (%)	75	76	79	79	78	76	69	64	76	73	67	61	42
Mean monthly share on health (%)	3	3	3	3	3	3	4	3	3	3	3	3	4
Mean monthly share on education (%)	1	1	1	1	1	1	1	2	2	1	2	3	4
MDGs 2 and 3: education and literacy; gender equality													
Primary school within 30 minutes (% of households)	..	..	..	..	..	..	..	..	..	..	..	..	..
Net primary enrollment rate (% of relevant age group)													
Total	65	64	57	60	64	69	73	78	71	78	86	79	81
Male	64	63	57	59	63	68	72	78	71	78	86	75	79
Female	66	65	58	61	65	70	74	79	71	78	86	83	83
Net secondary enrollment rate (% of relevant age group)													
Total	7	5	2	3	3	6	10	20	4	12	16	30	37
Male	7	5	2	3	3	6	10	20	3	14	16	33	35
Female	6	5	2	2	3	6	10	20	4	10	15	28	39
Tertiary enrollment rate (per 10,000)	..	..	..	..	..	..	..	..	..	..	..	..	..
Adult literacy rate (%)													
Total	29	29	14	13	13	13	13	17	17	17	15	16	20
Male	43	16	17	16	16	17	15	18	20	17	17	18	18
Female	15	10	10	9	9	9	11	16	13	17	13	13	21
Youth literacy rate (% ages 15–24)													
Total	35	34	36	35	34	33	32	40	45	42	35	37	41
Male	43	42	44	43	44	45	38	46	52	48	46	50	40
Female	27	26	29	28	26	23	26	33	38	37	25	25	42
MDGs 4 and 5: child mortality; maternal health													
Health center less than 5 km away (% of population)	..	..	..	..	..	..	..	..	..	..	..	..	..
Morbidity (% of population)	28	29	22	27	29	32	33	17	18	16	18	17	16
Health care provider consulted when sick (%)	87	87	83	86	86	89	88	90	84	90	93	92	89
Type of health care provider consulted (% of total)													
Public	36	35	39	38	35	32	32	44	41	51	44	50	31
Private, modern medicine	52	52	48	51	53	54	54	51	51	45	48	45	66
Private, traditional healers	5	5	6	4	5	6	3	3	5	2	3	2	1
Missionary or nongovernmental organization	4	4	3	3	3	4	7	2	1	2	4	1	1
Other	4	4	4	3	4	4	3	1	2	..	1	1	2
Child survival and malnutrition (%)													
Birth assisted by trained staff	..	..	..	..	..	..	..	..	..	..	..	..	..
Immunization coverage, 1-year-olds	..	..	..	..	..	..	..	..	..	..	..	..	..
Measles immunization coverage, 1-year-olds	..	..	..	..	..	..	..	..	..	..	..	..	..
Stunting (6–59 months)	39	39	39	39	41	39	36	35	43	36	30	39	19
Wasting (6–59 months)	2	2	3	3	2	2	2	2	2	4	2	0	2
Underweight (6–59 months)	16	16	18	17	15	14	16	15	19	18	12	11	14
MDG 7: environmental sustainability													
Access to sanitation facilities (% of population)	18	9	6	7	9	9	11	66	57	68	68	73	65
Water source less than 5 km away (% of population)	..	..	..	..	..	..	..	..	..	..	..	..	..
Market less than 5 km away (% of population)	..	..	..	..	..	..	..	..	..	..	..	..	..
Access to improved water source (% of population)													
Total[a]	67	64	64	63	64	62	67	88	69	86	86	92	97
Own tap	5	2	1	1	1	2	4	28	6	13	16	30	61
Other piped	15	11	10	10	11	9	13	49	42	55	60	56	33
Well, protected	47	51	53	53	52	51	50	11	21	18	10	7	3
Traditional fuel use (%)													
Total[a]	97	98	99	99	99	98	98	87	99	95	96	89	62
Firewood	90	97	99	98	98	97	94	38	71	50	40	29	16
Charcoal	7	1	..	0	0	1	3	49	28	45	56	61	47

Note: Data are provisional.

a. Components may not sum to total because of rounding.

14.5 Niger household survey, 2005

Indicator	National total	Rural						Urban					
		All	Q1	Q2	Q3	Q4	Q5	All	Q1	Q2	Q3	Q4	Q5
Demographic indicators													
Sample size (households)	6,690	4,670	682	775	869	1,024	1,320	2,020	277	308	361	453	621
Total population (thousands)	12,627	10,510	2,101	2,103	2,102	2,101	2,102	2,116	424	422	422	423	423
Age dependency ratio	1.1	1.2	1.4	1.1	1.1	0.9	0.8	0.9	1.4	1.2	1.0	0.9	0.7
Average household size	8.4	8.4	10.1	9.4	8.5	7.6	6.4	8.4	9.3	9.4	9.1	8.2	6.1
Marital status of head of household (%)													
Monogamous male	68	69	72	73	73	67	54	64	60	69	67	64	57
Polygamous male	22	22	12	19	22	28	42	18	9	17	19	24	33
Single male	3	3	5	3	2	2	1	4	6	4	3	4	2
De facto female	1	0	1	0	0	0	1	1	1	1	1	0	1
De jure female	7	5	11	4	4	3	2	13	24	10	10	9	8
MDG 1: extreme poverty and hunger													
Mean monthly expenditure (CFA francs)	65,877	59,669	23,443	38,353	48,786	61,670	126,084	96,715	36,492	62,921	87,469	112,844	183,902
Mean monthly share on food (%)	85	86	81	84	87	88	89	81	83	85	82	81	75
Mean monthly share on health (%)	1	0	0	0	0	0	0	2	1	1	2	3	3
Mean monthly share on education (%)	0	0	0	0	0	0	0	0	0	0	0	1	1
MDGs 2 and 3: education and literacy; gender equality													
Primary school within 30 minutes (% of households)	..	..	..	..	..	..	..	..	..	..	..	..	..
Net primary enrollment rate (% of relevant age group)													
Total	27	24	20	20	24	24	30	47	36	38	46	54	61
Male	30	28	23	25	28	27	34	47	36	38	48	56	58
Female	24	20	17	15	20	21	26	47	37	39	43	52	64
Net secondary enrollment rate (% of relevant age group)													
Total	7	3	2	2	3	3	5	22	8	15	19	24	37
Male	9	5	4	5	5	5	6	21	5	13	15	25	40
Female	6	2	0	0	2	2	3	22	11	18	23	23	34
Tertiary enrollment rate (per 10,000)	..	..	..	..	..	..	..	..	..	..	..	..	..
Adult literacy rate (%)													
Total	31	23	21	21	25	23	31	53	30	32	43	57	65
Male	45	38	35	36	38	39	46	65	41	42	57	71	76
Female	17	9	6	6	11	7	15	41	19	23	30	42	54
Youth literacy rate (% ages 15–24)													
Total	39	29	26	28	35	23	36	66	45	39	63	76	74
Male	52	44	41	46	52	35	52	72	47	42	68	86	83
Female	26	14	11	9	18	10	21	60	43	36	58	66	66
MDGs 4 and 5: child mortality; maternal health													
Health center less than 1 hour away (% of population)	..	..	..	..	..	..	..	..	..	..	..	..	..
Morbidity (% of population)	11	11	10	13	14	14	13	9	7	9	9	7	10
Health care provider consulted when sick (%)	8	8	7	10	10	11	11	7	5	7	7	6	10
Type of health care provider consulted (% of total)													
Public	61	60	55	65	82	53	62	62	63	73	51	73	59
Private, modern medicine	22	19	24	16	7	3	20	33	34	21	44	24	36
Private, traditional healers	17	21	22	20	11	44	18	4	3	6	5	3	5
Missionary or nongovernmental organization	..	..	..	..	..	..	..	..	..	..	..	..	..
Other	..	..	..	..	..	..	..	..	..	..	..	..	..
Child survival and malnutrition (%)													
Birth assisted by trained staff	..	..	..	..	..	..	..	..	..	..	..	..	..
Immunization coverage, 1-year-olds	..	..	..	..	..	..	..	..	..	..	..	..	..
Measles immunization coverage, 1-year-olds	..	..	..	..	..	..	..	..	..	..	..	..	..
Stunting (6–59 months)	..	..	..	..	..	..	..	..	..	..	..	..	..
Wasting (6–59 months)	..	..	..	..	..	..	..	..	..	..	..	..	..
Underweight (6–59 months)	..	..	..	..	..	..	..	..	..	..	..	..	..
MDG 7: environmental sustainability													
Access to sanitation facilities (% of population)	21	10	8	9	11	10	14	75	59	72	72	82	91
Water source less than 1 hour away (% of population)	..	..	..	..	..	..	..	..	..	..	..	..	..
Market less than 1 hour away (% of population)	..	..	..	..	..	..	..	..	..	..	..	..	..
Access to improved water source (% of population)													
Total[a]	51	44	47	45	43	41	43	84	89	83	80	84	86
Own tap	8	3	4	3	2	3	3	32	11	15	23	45	64
Other piped	26	21	23	22	22	19	22	51	75	65	55	37	20
Well, protected	17	19	20	20	20	20	18	2	3	3	2	2	2
Traditional fuel use (%)													
Total[a]	97	97	96	97	98	97	98	96	97	98	96	97	92
Firewood	96	96	95	96	97	97	97	95	97	97	94	96	90
Charcoal	1	1	1	0	0	0	1	1	1	1	2	2	2

Note: Data are provisional.

a. Components may not sum to total because of rounding.

Table 14.6 Nigeria household survey, 2004

Indicator	National total	Expenditure quintile											
		Rural						Urban					
		All	Q1	Q2	Q3	Q4	Q5	All	Q1	Q2	Q3	Q4	Q5
Demographic indicators													
Sample size (households)	19,158	14,512	2,321	2,446	2,717	3,120	3,908	4,646	783	779	834	988	1,262
Total population (thousands)	126,305	70,599	14,115	14,127	14,116	14,122	14,118	55,706	11,144	11,138	11,140	11,131	11,153
Age dependency ratio	0.8	0.9	1.1	1.0	0.9	0.8	0.6	0.8	0.8	0.9	0.8	0.7	0.5
Average household size	4.7	4.8	6.5	6.0	5.2	4.5	3.4	4.6	5.6	5.7	5.1	4.4	3.3
Marital status of head of household (%)													
Monogamous male	58	58	54	63	65	62	51	57	56	61	59	59	51
Polygamous male	15	18	32	26	20	14	8	12	16	17	15	10	7
Single male	11	9	4	3	5	8	19	14	10	7	8	13	25
De facto female	3	2	2	2	2	2	3	3	4	3	4	3	3
De jure female	13	12	8	7	9	14	19	14	13	12	14	16	14
MDG 1: extreme poverty and hunger													
Mean monthly expenditure (Nigerian naira)	11,635	9,924	3,922	6,391	8,008	9,939	16,272	13,705	4,548	8,809	11,580	14,279	22,892
Mean monthly share on food (%)	54	61	57	65	65	64	54	45	36	51	51	50	41
Mean monthly share on health (%)	8	8	3	4	5	7	16	7	4	5	6	6	13
Mean monthly share on education (%)	5	3	4	3	3	3	3	8	11	7	8	7	7
MDGs 2 and 3: education and literacy; gender equality													
Primary school within 30 minutes (% of households)	..	..	..	..	..	..	..	..	..	..	..	..	..
Net primary enrollment rate (% of relevant age group)	..	..	..	..	..	..	..	..	..	..	..	..	..
Total	..	..	..	..	..	..	..	..	..	..	..	..	..
Male	..	..	..	..	..	..	..	..	..	..	..	..	..
Female	..	..	..	..	..	..	..	..	..	..	..	..	..
Net secondary enrollment rate (% of relevant age group)													
Total	..	..	..	..	..	..	..	..	..	..	..	..	..
Male	..	..	..	..	..	..	..	..	..	..	..	..	..
Female	..	..	..	..	..	..	..	..	..	..	..	..	..
Tertiary enrollment rate (per 10,000)	..	..	..	..	..	..	..	..	..	..	..	..	..
Adult literacy rate (%)													
Total	62	50	38	42	48	55	63	75	71	68	73	80	83
Male	69	57	44	49	55	62	71	83	78	77	81	86	89
Female	54	43	31	36	41	49	54	68	65	59	65	73	75
Youth literacy rate (% ages 15–24)													
Total	78	68	55	60	66	72	81	88	84	86	89	93	89
Male	82	74	60	67	75	81	86	90	85	88	92	96	92
Female	73	62	50	53	58	65	77	86	82	84	85	90	87
MDGs 4 and 5: child mortality; maternal health													
Health center less than 1 hour away (% of population)	..	..	..	..	..	..	..	..	..	..	..	..	..
Morbidity (% of population)	12	12	8	10	11	14	21	11	7	9	10	11	17
Health care provider consulted when sick (%)	57	57	31	41	50	62	74	57	30	50	56	58	71
Type of health care provider consulted (% of total)													
Public	38	37	27	26	31	32	47	40	36	41	41	39	40
Private, modern medicine	57	58	69	69	63	64	49	55	58	54	56	56	53
Private, traditional healers	2	2	1	1	2	1	2	1		2	0	1	2
Other	3	3	3	4	4	3	3	4	6	4	3	4	4
Child survival and malnutrition (%)													
Birth assisted by trained staff	..	..	..	..	..	..	..	..	..	..	..	..	..
Immunization coverage, 1-year-olds	..	..	..	..	..	..	..	..	..	..	..	..	..
Measles immunization coverage, 1-year-olds	..	..	..	..	..	..	..	..	..	..	..	..	..
Stunting (6–59 months)	..	..	..	..	..	..	..	..	..	..	..	..	..
Wasting (6–59 months)	..	..	..	..	..	..	..	..	..	..	..	..	..
Underweight (6–59 months)	..	..	..	..	..	..	..	..	..	..	..	..	..
MDG 7: environmental sustainability													
Access to sanitation facilities (% of population)	60	50	47	48	50	50	52	72	73	71	71	72	75
Water source less than 1 hour away (% of population)	..	..	..	..	..	..	..	..	..	..	..	..	..
Market less than 1 hour away (% of population)	..	..	..	..	..	..	..	..	..	..	..	..	..
Access to improved water source (% of population)													
Total[a]	61	42	41	41	43	41	43	83	81	82	82	86	84
Own tap	13	4	3	3	4	3	5	23	18	21	23	24	28
Other piped	11	4	3	4	5	4	5	18	24	18	17	17	16
Well, protected	38	34	35	35	35	34	33	42	39	43	42	45	40
Traditional fuel use (%)													
Total[a]	65	88	92	93	91	89	79	38	44	52	43	36	24
Firewood	64	87	92	93	90	89	79	37	42	51	42	35	23
Charcoal	1	0	0	0	1	0	1	1	2	1	1	1	2

Note: Data are provisional.

a. Components may not sum to total because of rounding.

14.7 São Tomé and Principe household survey, 2000

Indicator	National total	Rural All	Rural Q1	Rural Q2	Rural Q3	Rural Q4	Rural Q5	Urban All	Urban Q1	Urban Q2	Urban Q3	Urban Q4	Urban Q5
Demographic indicators													
Sample size (households)	2,416	1,173	179	197	215	244	338	1,243	187	202	242	264	348
Total population (thousands)	128	57	11	11	11	11	11	71	14	14	14	14	14
Age dependency ratio	0.9	1.0	1.3	1.1	1.0	1.0	0.6	0.8	1.1	1.0	0.8	0.8	0.6
Average household size	4.6	4.5	6.3	5.7	4.9	4.2	3.0	4.6	6.2	5.5	4.9	4.4	3.3
Marital status of head of household (%)													
Monogamous male	51	53	62	66	66	48	37	50	51	50	46	56	46
Polygamous male	..	..	..	..	..	..	..	..	..	..	..	..	..
Single male	16	18	9	5	10	16	36	15	4	9	12	14	26
De facto female	7	6	5	5	5	8	7	8	7	11	12	5	8
De jure female	25	23	25	24	19	27	20	27	37	29	30	25	20
MDG 1: extreme poverty and hunger													
Mean monthly expenditure (dobras)	451,490	318,313	80,362	128,371	175,196	243,054	679,373	560,829	108,471	179,366	252,850	359,041	1,403,366
Mean monthly share on food (%)	72	75	78	77	78	76	71	69	76	74	69	68	62
Mean monthly share on health (%)	3	3	3	3	2	3	3	4	3	3	4	3	5
Mean monthly share on education (%)	2	2	2	2	2	2	1	3	2	3	3	3	2
MDGs 2 and 3: education and literacy; gender equality													
Primary school within 30 minutes (% of households)	34	33	46	44	37	35	16	35	51	39	35	38	23
Net primary enrollment rate (% of relevant age group)													
Total	70	67	68	68	63	68	67	73	71	73	78	73	74
Male	71	70	67	75	62	71	70	73	72	71	75	80	66
Female	69	64	68	60	63	64	63	73	69	75	81	65	79
Net secondary enrollment rate (% of relevant age group)													
Total	43	29	13	26	23	34	50	52	32	39	64	62	64
Male	43	29	15	24	24	42	47	52	30	41	65	66	66
Female	42	28	11	28	22	25	51	52	35	37	62	59	63
Tertiary enrollment rate (per 10,000)	..	..	..	..	..	..	..	..	..	..	..	..	..
Adult literacy rate (%)													
Total	83	80	76	82	79	77	85	86	78	83	85	89	91
Male	92	89	87	89	89	87	92	94	90	92	92	95	97
Female	76	72	67	76	69	69	77	79	68	75	80	84	84
Youth literacy rate (% ages 15–24)													
Total	94	92	90	92	91	91	95	96	91	94	98	98	96
Male	95	93	95	91	90	94	96	96	94	96	97	98	98
Female	93	91	86	92	92	88	95	95	88	92	98	98	95
MDGs 4 and 5: child mortality; maternal health													
Health center less than 1 hour away (% of population)	84	81	77	74	81	82	85	87	86	90	85	89	87
Morbidity (% of population)	18	15	12	14	14	17	20	19	12	19	19	22	24
Health care provider consulted when sick (%)	48	45	41	45	40	50	47	50	38	44	50	56	57
Type of health care provider consulted (% of total)													
Public	70	81	94	88	78	83	68	64	80	78	68	62	53
Private, modern medicine	25	14	4	9	16	10	27	31	15	18	29	32	43
Private, traditional healers	3	2	..	3	..	3	4	4	5	1	3	6	2
Other	1	2	2	..	6	3	1	1	..	3	..	..	2
Child survival and malnutrition (%)													
Birth assisted by trained staff	..	..	..	..	..	..	..	..	..	..	..	..	..
Immunization coverage, 1-year-olds	..	..	..	..	..	..	..	..	..	..	..	..	..
Measles immunization coverage, 1-year-olds	..	..	..	..	..	..	..	..	..	..	..	..	..
Stunting (6–59 months)	..	..	..	..	..	..	..	..	..	..	..	..	..
Wasting (6–59 months)	..	..	..	..	..	..	..	..	..	..	..	..	..
Underweight (6–59 months)	..	..	..	..	..	..	..	..	..	..	..	..	..
MDG 7: environmental sustainability													
Access to sanitation facilities (% of population)	28	21	18	12	20	20	27	35	14	26	36	41	46
Water source less than 1 hour away (% of population)	88	93	93	94	93	95	92	84	82	80	87	86	85
Market less than 1 hour away (% of population)	87	81	74	73	80	86	86	92	90	88	91	93	94
Access to improved water source (% of population)													
Total[a]	77	67	74	70	64	70	63	84	82	79	81	89	88
Own tap	20	10	7	9	7	13	12	27	12	20	26	29	40
Other piped	8	13	19	15	15	11	10	4	4	3	5	5	4
Well, protected	49	44	48	46	42	46	41	53	65	56	49	56	43
Traditional fuel use (%)													
Total[a]	84	95	100	98	99	94	88	75	96	83	81	72	57
Firewood	73	91	98	96	97	90	82	59	88	74	63	50	36
Charcoal	11	4	1	2	2	4	6	16	8	9	18	22	20

a. Components may not sum to total because of rounding.

HOUSEHOLD WELFARE

Table

14.8 Sierra Leone household survey, 2002/03

Indicator	National total	Expenditure quintile											
		Rural						Urban					
		All	Q1	Q2	Q3	Q4	Q5	All	Q1	Q2	Q3	Q4	Q5
Demographic indicators													
Sample size (households)	3,713	2,396	412	451	453	511	569	1,317	223	246	277	276	295
Total population (thousands)	5,337	3,440	688	689	688	688	688	1,897	379	379	380	379	380
Age dependency ratio	0.9	1.0	1.1	1.0	1.0	0.9	0.9	0.8	1.0	1.0	0.8	0.7	0.6
Average household size	7.4	7.3	8.2	7.6	7.5	6.8	6.3	7.5	8.4	7.6	7.1	7.2	7.4
Marital status of head of household (%)													
Monogamous male	61	60	52	56	61	65	64	63	56	62	66	67	64
Polygamous male	19	23	31	28	26	19	15	10	13	13	13	8	6
Single male	4	3	2	2	3	3	4	6	2	3	3	7	14
De facto female	2	2	3	1	1	2	2	2	1	3	2	2	1
De jure female	14	12	12	13	10	11	15	19	27	19	16	16	16
MDG 1: extreme poverty and hunger													
Mean monthly expenditure (leones)	294,515	239,364	103,175	150,703	197,851	237,999	438,780	378,978	154,151	242,246	322,612	385,918	685,453
Mean monthly share on food (%)	52	59	60	61	62	61	53	42	49	46	45	43	32
Mean monthly share on health (%)	10	2	6	9	7	10	14	13	9	10	12	12	19
Mean monthly share on education (%)	4	2	3	2	2	2	2	6	5	6	6	6	5
MDGs 2 and 3: education and literacy; gender equality													
Primary school within 30 minutes (% of households)													
Net primary enrollment rate (% of relevant age group)													
Total	73	67	62	64	67	69	75	86	78	85	89	87	91
Male	72	66	58	65	66	70	72	85	78	83	88	88	93
Female	74	68	66	63	68	67	77	86	78	87	90	87	89
Net secondary enrollment rate (% of relevant age group)													
Total	19	10	7	7	11	10	18	33	27	23	24	37	51
Male	22	13	9	10	12	13	22	36	31	28	24	47	48
Female	17	7	4	3	9	7	13	30	23	18	24	27	54
Tertiary enrollment rate (per 10,000)	..	..	..	..	..	..	..	..	..	..	..	..	..
Adult literacy rate (%)													
Total	27	13	11	10	11	14	20	49	32	37	41	52	75
Male	35	20	17	17	17	21	27	58	43	50	49	59	81
Female	19	8	6	5	6	8	14	40	24	26	33	46	68
Youth literacy rate (% ages 15–24)													
Total	40	23	18	17	17	28	35	62	49	51	56	62	81
Male	47	31	26	24	25	36	42	68	59	62	64	65	85
Female	33	16	12	11	11	20	27	55	39	42	48	60	78
MDGs 4 and 5: child mortality; maternal health													
Health center less than 1 hour away (% of population)	..	..	..	..	..	..	..	..	..	..	..	..	..
Morbidity (% of population)	44	42	34	40	42	42	49	45	37	44	45	45	54
Health care provider consulted when sick (%)	59	65	49	64	67	68	75	56	41	50	49	58	75
Type of health care provider consulted (% of total)													
Public	53	55	50	39	53	51	61	51	51	52	49	55	51
Private, modern medicine	30	27	16	31	27	33	25	36	18	32	28	31	48
Private, traditional healers	9	11	23	16	12	8	9	4	6	5	12	5	
Other	8	7	11	14	8	9	5	8	25	11	12	10	2
Child survival and malnutrition (%)													
Birth assisted by trained staff	..	..	..	..	..	..	..	..	..	..	..	..	..
Immunization coverage, 1-year-olds	72	72	74	57	64	71	96	73	70	75	71	63	87
Measles immunization coverage, 1-year-olds	16	16	16	24	15	13	8	18	19	17	21	21	9
Stunting (6–59 months)	..	..	..	..	..	..	..	..	..	..	..	..	..
Wasting (6–59 months)	..	..	..	..	..	..	..	..	..	..	..	..	..
Underweight (6–59 months)	..	..	..	..	..	..	..	..	..	..	..	..	..
MDG 7: environmental sustainability													
Access to sanitation facilities (% of population)	4	2	2	2	1	2	4	7	1	2	4	5	23
Water source less than 1 hour away (% of population)	..	..	..	..	..	..	..	..	..	..	..	..	..
Market less than 1 hour away (% of population)	..	..	..	..	..	..	..	..	..	..	..	..	..
Access to improved water source (% of population)													
Total[a]	37	25	24	25	23	22	31	59	40	51	52	67	79
Own tap	7	1	0	1	1	0	4	18	0	3	10	20	49
Other piped	12	5	6	8	5	3	5	24	19	23	19	33	23
Well, protected	18	19	18	17	17	20	22	17	21	24	22	15	7
Traditional fuel use (%)													
Total[a]	97	99	99	99	99	99	98	95	99	98	98	95	86
Firewood	93	98	98	98	98	98	97	83	98	96	91	83	55
Charcoal	5	1	1	1	1	0	1	12	1	2	7	12	32

Note: Data are provisional.

a. Components may not sum to total because of rounding.

14.9 Uganda household survey, 2002/03

Indicator	National total	Rural All	Rural Q1	Rural Q2	Rural Q3	Rural Q4	Rural Q5	Urban All	Urban Q1	Urban Q2	Urban Q3	Urban Q4	Urban Q5
Demographic indicators													
Sample size (households)	9,710	5,648	937	1,019	1,036	1,182	1,474	4,062	894	877	766	701	824
Total population (thousands)	25,273	21,795	4,359	4,358	4,358	4,363	4,357	3,477	695	696	696	696	695
Age dependency ratio	1.2	1.3	1.7	1.5	1.4	1.2	0.9	0.8	1.3	1.1	0.8	0.6	0.4
Average household size	5.1	5.3	6.4	5.9	5.8	5.3	4.0	4.1	5.7	4.6	4.3	4.0	3.0
Marital status of head of household (%)													
Monogamous male	54	56	56	61	60	57	50	45	52	53	45	45	37
Polygamous male	12	13	13	12	14	14	12	7	9	8	7	8	3
Single male	8	7	3	3	4	6	15	12	5	6	13	14	18
De facto female	8	8	10	9	8	8	7	9	8	8	6	7	12
De jure female	18	16	18	15	14	15	17	27	25	25	28	27	30
MDG 1: extreme poverty and hunger													
Mean monthly expenditure (Ugandan shillings)	1,523	1,322	593	854	1,121	1,393	2,175	2,499	864	1,208	1,689	2,281	4,926
Mean monthly share on food (%)	56	58	60	62	61	59	52	43	52	49	45	42	34
Mean monthly share on health (%)	4	4	2	3	3	4	6	7	5	6	6	6	9
Mean monthly share on education (%)	4	4	4	3	4	4	5	4	3	3	5	4	3
MDGs 2 and 3: education and literacy; gender equality													
Primary school within 30 minutes (% of households)	..	..	..	..	..	..	..	..	..	..	..	..	..
Net primary enrollment rate (% of relevant age group)													
Total	63	62	50	59	63	67	73	73	64	69	80	75	82
Male	62	61	51	58	63	65	72	71	63	65	77	75	78
Female	64	63	50	60	64	68	74	75	64	73	82	75	86
Net secondary enrollment rate (% of relevant age group)													
Total	13	11	2	5	10	15	22	26	15	19	27	30	40
Male	13	11	1	4	7	19	21	26	13	23	26	29	39
Female	14	12	2	5	14	11	23	27	17	16	28	31	41
Tertiary enrollment rate (per 10,000)	3	..	..	..	..	..	..	..	..	..	..	..	..
Adult literacy rate (%)													
Total	70	66	49	61	66	71	79	87	72	83	86	92	95
Male	80	77	66	75	75	81	85	91	80	91	90	93	95
Female	61	56	34	48	58	62	73	84	65	77	82	92	94
Youth literacy rate (% ages 15–24)													
Total	80	78	62	73	79	81	86	90	78	89	88	94	95
Male	85	83	72	84	83	86	88	91	80	92	88	93	96
Female	76	73	52	63	76	77	84	89	77	86	88	94	95
MDGs 4 and 5: child mortality; maternal health													
Health center less than 1 hour away (% of population)	..	..	..	..	..	..	..	..	..	..	..	..	..
Morbidity (% of population)	29	29	28	28	28	29	33	28	25	29	29	28	28
Health care provider consulted when sick (%)	93	92	87	91	94	94	95	94	91	91	96	96	97
Type of health care provider consulted (% of total)													
Public	30	32	44	36	29	25	26	18	28	23	18	15	10
Private, modern medicine	64	62	51	59	63	67	65	76	66	72	77	78	84
Private, traditional healers	1	1	1	1	2	1	1	1	2	1	0	0	0
Missionary or nongovernmental organization	5	5	4	3	5	6	7	5	4	3	5	7	4
Other	0	0	0	1	0	0	1	1	0	0	0	..	2
Child survival and malnutrition (%)													
Birth assisted by trained staff	..	..	..	..	..	..	..	..	..	..	..	..	..
Immunization coverage, 1-year-olds	..	..	..	..	..	..	..	..	..	..	..	..	..
Measles immunization coverage, 1-year-olds	..	..	..	..	..	..	..	..	..	..	..	..	..
Stunting (6–59 months)	..	..	..	..	..	..	..	..	..	..	..	..	..
Wasting (6–59 months)	..	..	..	..	..	..	..	..	..	..	..	..	..
Underweight (6–59 months)	..	..	..	..	..	..	..	..	..	..	..	..	..
MDG 7: environmental sustainability													
Access to sanitation facilities (% of population)	76	72	50	67	74	77	84	95	86	94	96	98	99
Water source less than 1 hour away (% of population)	..	..	..	..	..	..	..	..	..	..	..	..	..
Market less than 1 hour away (% of population)	..	..	..	..	..	..	..	..	..	..	..	..	..
Access to improved water source (% of population)													
Total[a]	60	56	57	55	55	56	57	81	77	79	81	82	85
Own tap	..	..	..	..	..	..	..	..	..	..	..	..	..
Other piped	9	2	1	1	1	2	5	48	22	34	46	58	65
Well, protected	51	54	56	54	54	54	52	34	55	45	35	24	20
Traditional fuel use (%)													
Total[a]	97	98	99	99	99	99	97	89	99	97	93	93	73
Firewood	79	90	97	96	97	92	76	22	54	33	19	12	7
Charcoal	18	8	1	3	3	8	20	67	45	64	74	81	66

Note: The survey did not collect data in the Kitgum, Gulu, Kasese, and Bundibugio districts.

a. Components may not sum to total because of rounding.

HOUSEHOLD WELFARE

Technical notes

General notes

.. means that data are not available or that aggregates cannot be calculated because of missing data in the years shown

$ means U.S. dollars

A blank means not applicable or, for an aggregate, not analytically meaningful.

A billion is 1,000 million.

1. Basic indicators

TABLE 1.1. BASIC INDICATORS

Population is World Bank estimates, usually projected from the most recent population censuses or surveys (mostly from 1980–2005). Refugees not permanently settled in the country of asylum are generally considered to be part of the population of their country of origin.

Land area is the land surface area of a country, excluding inland waters, national claims to continental shelf, and exclusive economic zones.

Gross national income (GNI) per capita is the total domestic and foreign value added claimed by residents, which comprises gross domestic product plus net factor income from abroad (the income residents receive from abroad for factor services including labor and capital) less similar payments made to nonresidents who contribute to the domestic economy, divided by midyear population. It is calculated using the World Bank Atlas method with constant 2000 exchange rates (box 1). Growth rates are shown in real terms. They have been calculated by the least-squares method using constant 2000 GNI per capita dollars (see also table 2.8).

Life expectancy at birth is the number of years a newborn infant would live if prevailing patterns of mortality at the time of its birth were to remain the same throughout its life. Data are World Bank estimates based on data from the United Nations Population Division, the United Nations Statistics Division, and national statistical offices.

Box 1	The *World Bank Atlas* method for converting gross national income to a common denominator

The *World Bank Atlas* method uses a three-year average of conversion factors to convert gross national income (GNI) data, expressed in different national currencies, to a common denomination, conventionally U.S. dollars. The *Atlas* conversion factor for any year is the average of the official exchange rate or alternative conversion factor for that year and for the two preceding years, after adjusting them for differences in relative inflation between that country and the United States. This three-year average smoothes fluctuations in prices and exchange rates for each country. The resulting GNI in U.S. dollars is divided by the midyear population for the latest of the three years to derive GNI per capita.

The following formulas describe the procedures for computing the conversion factor for year t:

$$e^{*}_{t-2,t} = \frac{1}{3}\left[e_{t-2}\left(\frac{P_t}{P_{t-2}} \bigg/ \frac{P^{\$}_t}{P^{\$}_{t-2}}\right) + e_{t-1}\left(\frac{P_t}{P_{t-1}} \bigg/ \frac{P^{\$}_t}{P^{\$}_{t-1}}\right) + e_t\right]$$

and for calculating per capita GNI in U.S. dollars for year t:

$$Y^{\$}_t = (Y_t/N_t) + e^{*}_{t-2,t}$$

where Y_t is current GNI (local currency) for year t, P_t is the GNI deflator for year t, N_t is midyear population for year t, and $P^{\$}_t$ is the U.S. GNI deflator for year t.

Under-five mortality rate is the probability that a newborn baby will die before reaching age 5, if subject to current age-specific mortality rates. The probability is expressed as a rate per 1,000.

Gini coefficient is the most commonly used measure of inequality. The coefficient ranges from 0, which reflects complete equality, to 1, which indicates complete inequality (one person has all the income or consumption, all others have none). Graphically, the Gini coefficient can be easily represented by the area between the Lorenz curve and the line of equality.

Adult literacy rate is the percentage of adults ages 15 and older who can, with understanding, read and write a short, simple statement on their everyday life.

Net official development assistance per capita is net disbursements of loans and grants from all official sources on concessional financial terms divided by the midyear population for the corresponding year

Regional aggregates for GNI per capita, life expectancy at birth, and adult literacy rates are weighted by population.

Source: Data on population, land area, GNI per capita, life expectancy at birth, under-five mortality, Gini coefficient, and adult literacy are from the World Bank's World Development Indicators database. Data on aid flows are from the Organisation for Economic Co-operation and Development's Geographic Distribution of Aid Flows to Developing Countries database.

2. National accounts

TABLE 2.1. GROSS DOMESTIC PRODUCT, NOMINAL
Gross domestic product (GDP), nominal, is the total output of goods and services for final use produced by residents and non-residents, regardless of the allocation to domestic and foreign claims. It is calculated without making deductions for depreciation of fabricated capital assets or depletion and degradation of natural resources. GDP figures are shown at market prices (also known as purchaser values) and converted from national currency GDP series in current prices to U.S. dollars at official annual exchange rates.

The sum of the components of GDP by industrial origin (presented here as value added) will not normally equal total GDP for several reasons. First, components of GDP by expenditure are individually rescaled and summed to provide a partially rebased series for total GDP. Second, total GDP is shown at purchaser value, while value added components are conventionally reported at producer prices. As explained above, purchaser values exclude net indirect taxes, while producer prices include indirect taxes. Third, certain items, such as imputed bank charges, are added in total GDP.

Source: World Bank country desk data.

TABLE 2.2. GROSS DOMESTIC PRODUCT, REAL
Gross domestic product (GDP), real, is obtained by converting national currency GDP series to U.S. dollars using constant (2000) exchange rates. For countries where the official exchange rate does not effectively reflect the rate applied to actual foreign exchange transactions, an alternative currency conversion factor has been used.

Source: World Bank country desk data.

TABLE 2.3. GROSS DOMESTIC PRODUCT GROWTH
Gross domestic product (GDP) growth is the average annual growth rate of real GDP (table 2.2) at market prices based on constant local currency. Aggregates are based on constant 2000 U.S. dollars.

Source: World Bank country desk data.

TABLE 2.4. GROSS DOMESTIC PRODUCT PER CAPITA, REAL
Gross domestic product (GDP) per capita, real, is calculated by dividing real GDP (table 2.2) by corresponding midyear population.

Source: World Bank country desk data.

TABLE 2.5. GROSS DOMESTIC PRODUCT PER CAPITA GROWTH
Gross domestic product (GDP) per capita growth is the average annual growth rate of real GDP per capita (table 2.4).

Source: World Bank country desk data.

TABLE 2.6. GROSS NATIONAL INCOME, NOMINAL

Gross national income, nominal, is the sum of value added by all resident producers plus any product taxes (less subsidies) not included in the valuation of output plus net receipts of primary income (compensation of employees and property income) from abroad. Data are converted from national currency in current prices to U.S. dollars at official annual exchange rates. See box 2 for a discussion of the differences between gross domestic product and gross national income.

Source: World Bank and Organisation for Economic Co-operation and Development (OECD) national accounts data.

TABLE 2.7. GROSS NATIONAL INCOME, REAL

Gross national income, real, is obtained by converting national currency gross national income series to U.S. dollars using constant (2000) exchange rates.

Source: World Bank and OECD national accounts data.

TABLE 2.8. GROSS NATIONAL INCOME PER CAPITA

Gross national income (GNI) per capita is calculated using the *World Bank Atlas* method (see box 1). It similar in concept to GNI per capita in current prices, except that the use of three-year averages of exchange rates smoothes out sharp fluctuations from year to year.

Source: World Bank country desk data.

TABLE 2.9. GROSS DOMESTIC PRODUCT DEFLATOR (LOCAL CURRENCY SERIES)

Gross domestic product (GDP) deflator (local currency series) is nominal GDP in current local currency divided by real GDP in constant 2000 local currency, expressed as an index with base year 2000.

Source: World Bank country desk data.

TABLE 2.10. GROSS DOMESTIC PRODUCT DEFLATOR (U.S. DOLLAR SERIES)

Gross domestic product (GDP) deflator (U.S. dollar series) is nominal GDP in current U.S. dollars (table 2.1) divided by real GDP in constant 2000 U.S. dollars (table 2.2), expressed as an index with base year 2000. The series shows the effects of domestic price changes and exchange rate variations.

Source: World Bank country desk data.

TABLE 2.11. GROSS DOMESTIC SAVINGS

Gross domestic savings is calculated by deducting total consumption (table 2.13) from nominal gross domestic product (table 2.1).

Source: World Bank country desk data.

TABLE 2.12. GROSS NATIONAL SAVINGS

Gross national savings is the sum of gross domestic savings (table 2.11), net factor income from abroad, and net private transfers from abroad. The estimate here also includes net public transfers from abroad.

Source: World Bank country desk data.

TABLE 2.13. GENERAL GOVERNMENT FINAL CONSUMPTION

General government consumption is all current expenditure for purchases of goods and services by all levels of government, including capital expenditure on national defense and security. Other capital expenditure by government is included in capital formation.

Source: World Bank country desk data.

TABLE 2.14. FINAL CONSUMPTION EXPENDITURE

Final consumption expenditure (formerly total consumption) is the sum of household final consumption expenditure (private consumption) and general government final consumption expenditure (table 2.13), shown as a share of gross domestic product. This estimate includes any statistical discrepancy in the use of resources relative to the supply of resourcesPrivate consumption, not separately shown here, is the value of all goods and services purchased or received as income in kind by households and nonprofit institutions. It excludes purchases of dwellings, but includes imputed rent for owner-occupied dwellings. In practice, it includes any statistical discrepancy in the use of resources.

Source: World Bank country desk data.

| Box 2 | Gross domestic product and gross national product |

Gross domestic product (GDP) is the broadest quantitative measure of a nation's total economic activity. It measures, in market prices, the value of economic activity within a country's geographic borders, including all final goods and services produced over a period of time (usually a year). There are two ways of calculating GDP. The expenditure approach sums consumption, investment, government expenditure, and net exports. The income approach sums wages, rents, interests, profits, nonincome charges, and net foreign factor income earned. Both methods should yield the same results because total expenditure on goods and services by definition must equal the value of goods and services produced, which must equal the total income paid to the factors that produced the goods and services.

GDP is just one way of measuring the total output of an economy. Gross national product (GNP) is another. It measures the value of all goods and services produced by permanent residents of a country regardless of their location. For example, the income of a U.S. citizen working in Paris would count toward U.S. GNP—but also French GDP. To take another example, revenue from activities of Euro Disney in Paris would count toward U.S. GNP because the Walt Disney Company is a U.S.-owned company, but because the activities take place in Paris, it would count toward French GDP.

The distinction between GDP and GNP is the difference in how production by foreigners in a country and by nationals outside of a country is counted. For GDP production by foreigners within a country is included and production by nationals outside a country is not. For GNP production by foreigners within a country is not included but production by nationals outside a country is. Thus, while GDP is the value of goods and services produced within a country, GNP is the value of goods and services produced by citizens of a country.

This distinction matters little for countries such as the United States, where payments to U.S. residents, including U.S.-based firms, from their activities in the rest of the world are roughly the same as payments to foreign residents from their activities in the United States. But for developing countries GDP may be a poor indicator of financial performance. For example, a country with large amounts of foreign direct investment, the profits of which are repatriated, will have a high GDP but will not see a commensurate raise in available capital or living standards. A similar situation occurs in oil-producing developing countries; a large share of oil profits is repatriated by foreign oil companies.

Figure 1 shows how new foreign direct investment is rapidly flowing to mineral exporters in Africa. Figure 2 shows the difference between GDP and GNP for African economies that rely heavily on foreign direct investment. This comparison is important because it shows the difference between how much income is generated in a particular country and how much income is repatriated.

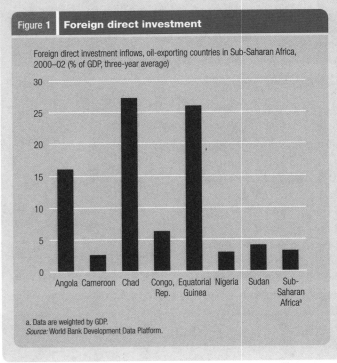

Figure 1 Foreign direct investment

Foreign direct investment inflows, oil-exporting countries in Sub-Saharan Africa, 2000–02 (% of GDP, three-year average)

a. Data are weighted by GDP.
Source: World Bank Development Data Platform.

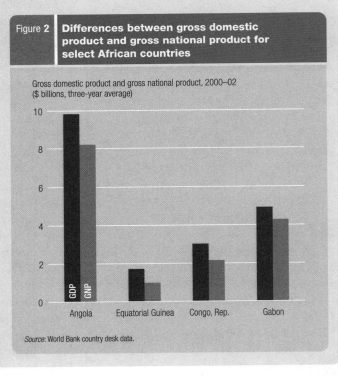

Figure 2 Differences between gross domestic product and gross national product for select African countries

Gross domestic product and gross national product, 2000–02 ($ billions, three-year average)

Source: World Bank country desk data.

TABLE 2.15. FINAL CONSUMPTION EXPENDITURE PER CAPITA

Final consumption expenditure per capita is final consumption expenditure in current U.S. dollars (table 2.14) divided by midyear population.

Source: World Bank country desk data.

Table 2.16. Agriculture value added

Agriculture value added is the gross output of forestry, hunting, and fishing less the value of their intermediate inputs. It is shown at factor cost for most countries, but it is shown at market prices, that is, including intermediate inputs, for Botswana, Cameroon, Chad, Democratic Republic of Congo, Republic of Congo, Gabon, Guinea, Madagascar, Mali, Morocco, Niger, Rwanda, Senegal, Togo, and Zambia.

Source: World Bank country desk data.

Table 2.17. Industry value added

Industry value added is the gross output of mining, manufacturing, construction, electricity, water, and gas, less the value of their intermediate inputs. It is shown at factor cost for most countries, but it is shown at market prices, that is, including intermediate inputs, for Botswana, Cameroon, Chad, Democratic Republic of Congo, Republic of Congo, Gabon, Guinea, Madagascar, Mali, Morocco, Niger, Rwanda, Senegal, Togo, and Zambia.

Source: World Bank country desk data.

Table 2.18. Services value added

Services value added is the gross output of all other branches of economic activity, including government, less the value of their intermediate inputs. It is shown at factor cost for most countries, but it is shown at market prices, that is, including intermediate inputs, for Botswana, Cameroon, Chad, Democratic Republic of Congo, Republic of Congo, Gabon, Guinea, Madagascar, Mali, Morocco, Niger, Rwanda, Senegal, Togo, and Zambia. Other items, such as imputed bank service charges (which are difficult to assess in the same fashion for all countries) and any corrections for statistical discrepancies, are not included.

Source: World Bank country desk data.

Table 2.19. Gross fixed capital formation

Gross fixed capital formation consists of gross domestic fixed capital formation plus net changes in the level of inventories. Gross capital formation comprises outlays by the public sector (table 2.20) and the private sector (table 2.21). Examples include improvements in land, dwellings, machinery, and other equipment. For some countries the sum of gross private investment and gross public investment does not total gross domestic investment due to statistical discrepancies.

Source: World Bank country desk data.

Table 2.20. General government fixed capital formation

General government fixed capital formation is gross domestic fixed capital formation (see table 2.19) for the public sector.

Source: World Bank country desk data.

Table 1	Method used to calculate regional aggregates and period averages in section 2 tables					
Table	**Method 1**	**Method 2**	**Method 3**	**Method 4**	**Method 5**	**Method 6**
2.1 Gross domestic product, nominal	×			×		
2.2 Gross domestic product, real	×				×	
2.3 Gross domestic product growth	×				×	
2.4 Gross domestic product per capita, real		×			×	
2.5 Gross domestic product per capita, growth	×			×		
2.6 Gross national income, nominal	×			×		
2.7 Gross national income, real	×				×	
2.8 Gross national income per capita		×		×		
2.9 Gross domestic product deflator (local currency series)		×				×
2.10 Gross domestic product deflator (U.S. series)		×		×		
2.11 Gross domestic savings		×		×		
2.12 Gross national savings		×		×		
2.13 General government final consumption		×		×		
2.14 Final consumption expenditure		×		×		
2.15 Final consumption expenditure per capita		×		×		
2.16 Agriculture value added	×				×	
2.17 Industry value added	×				×	
2.18 Services value added	×				×	
2.19 Gross fixed capital formation		×		×		
2.20 General government fixed capita formation		×		×		
2.21 Private sector fixed capital formation		×		×		
2.22 Resource balance (exports minus imports)			×	×		
2.23 Exports of goods and services, nominal	×			×		
2.24 Imports of goods and services, nominal	×			×		
2.25 Exports of goods and services, real	×				×	
2.26 Imports of goods and services, real	×				×	

Note: Method 1 is the simple total of the gap-filled indicator; method 2 is the simple total of the gap-filled main indicator divided by the simple total of the gap-filled secondary indicator; method 3 is the simple total of the first gap-filled main indicator minus the simple total of the second gap-filled main indicator, divided by the simple total of the secondary indicator; method 4 is the arithmetic mean (using the same series as shown in the table; that is, ratio if the rest of the table is shown as ratio, level if the rest of the table is shown as level, growth rate if the rest is shown as growth rate, and so on); method 5 is the least-squares growth rate (using the main indicator); method 6 is the median.

TABLE 2.21. PRIVATE SECTOR FIXED CAPITAL
FORMATION
Private sector fixed capital formation is gross
domestic fixed capital formation (see table
2.19) for the private sector.

Source: World Bank country desk data.

TABLE 2.22. RESOURCE BALANCE (EXPORTS
MINUS IMPORTS)
Resource balance is the difference between free
on board exports (table 2.23) and cost, insurance, and freight imports (table 2.24) of goods
and services (or the difference between gross
domestic savings and gross capital formation).
The resource balance is shown as a share of
nominal gross domestic product (table 2.1).

Source: World Bank country desk data.

TABLES 2.23 AND 2.24. EXPORTS AND IM-
PORTS OF GOODS AND SERVICES, NOMINAL
*Exports and imports of goods and services,
nominal,* comprise all transactions between
residents of an economy and the rest of the
world involving a change in ownership of
general merchandise, goods sent for processing and repairs, nonmonetary gold, and services expressed in current U.S dollars.

Source: World Bank country desk data.

TABLES 2.25 AND 2.26. EXPORTS AND IM-
PORTS OF GOODS AND SERVICES, REAL
Exports and imports of goods and services, real,
are defined as in tables 2.23 and 2.24, but expressed in constant 2000 U.S. dollars.

Source: World Bank country desk data.

3. Millennium Development Goals

TABLE 3.1. MILLENNIUM DEVELOPMENT
GOAL 1: ERADICATE EXTREME POVERTY AND
HUNGER
*Share of population below national poverty line
(poverty headcount ratio)* is the percentage
of the population living below the national
poverty line. National estimates are based
on population-weighted subgroup estimates
from household surveys. See box 3 for a
discussion of cross-country comparisons of
poverty and box 4 for a discussion of objective and subjective measures of poverty.

*Share of population below purchasing power
parity (PPP) $1 a day* is the percentage of the
population living on less than $1.08 a day at
1993 international prices. As a result of revisions in PPP exchange rates, poverty rates for
individual countries cannot be compared with
poverty rates reported in earlier editions.

Poverty gap ratio at $1 a day is the mean
shortfall from the poverty line (counting the
nonpoor as having zero shortfall), expressed
as a percentage of the poverty line. This measure reflects the depth of poverty as well as
its incidence.

*Share of poorest quintile in national consump-
tion or income* is the share of consumption, or
in some cases income, that accrues to the
poorest 20 percent of the population.

*Prevalence of child malnutrition, under-
weight,* is the percentage of children under
age 5 whose weight for age is more than two
standard deviations below the median for the
international reference population ages 0–59
months. The reference population, adopted
by the World Health Organization in 1983,
is based on children from the United States,
who are assumed to be well nourished.

*Population below minimum dietary energy
consumption* (also referred to as prevalence of
undernourishment) is the population whose
food intake is insufficient to meet dietary energy requirements continuously.

Source: Data on poverty measures are
prepared by the World Bank's Development
Research Group. The national poverty lines
are based on the World Bank's country poverty assessments. The international poverty
lines are based on nationally representative
primary household surveys conducted by
national statistical offices or by private agencies under the supervision of government
or international agencies and obtained from
government statistical offices and World
Bank country departments. The World Bank
has prepared an annual review of its poverty
work since 1993. For details on data sources and methods used in deriving the World
Bank's latest estimates, see Chen and Raval-
lion (2004).

Data have been compiled by World Bank
staff from primary and secondary sources.
Efforts have been made to harmonize these
data series with those published on the United Nations Millennium Development Goals

Three things are needed to measure poverty in a country: an indicator of well-being or welfare, such as consumption per capita or per equivalent adult; a threshold, or poverty line, to which each household's welfare can be compared; and a poverty measure that aggregates the information on poverty obtained for each household into meaningful statistics for a country as a whole. Different poverty estimates can result depending on the indicator, threshold, or poverty measure used. Standard measures used to monitor global poverty trends, such as the share of the population living on less than $1 or $2 a day, are typically not used for country-specific work. It is indeed better for country work to adapt the methodology used for estimating poverty to country specifics, be it to country characteristics or data quality. Still, this does not mean that cross-country comparisons are not useful. They can be used to suggest revisions in poverty estimates, as in the CFA franc zone.

The table and figure show World Bank poverty estimates from a series of recent poverty assessments for countries of the CFA franc zone. Poverty comparisons between the countries are facilitated by the countries' shared currency, similar inflation rates, and free trade between member countries. Each country has a slightly different methodology for estimating poverty. Most use a poverty line based on the cost of basic needs method, although they differ in whether they use consumption per capita or per equivalent adult and in the caloric requirement norm used to determine what households should be able to purchase. The surveys used in each country also differ. But an inverse relationship clearly exists between the natural log of GDP per capita and the share of the population living in poverty.[1] The curve fitted through the scatter plot in the figure gives a very rough idea of the poverty level expected for a given GDP per capita. Divergence from this curve may stem from issues of data quality or from different levels of inequality between countries, for example.

These simple comparisons of poverty levels between countries have actually been used to suggest changes in methodologies for measuring poverty at the country level in the CFA franc zone. Preliminary estimates for Togo presented at a February 2007 workshop were much higher than those reported in the table and suggested that Togo had by far the highest poverty rate in the CFA franc zone—a surprising finding given the country's relative GDP per capita. The data in the table led to a downward revision of Togo's poverty estimates. Similarly, previous estimates suggested that Mali had a much higher poverty rate than shown in the table. The data helped in suggesting alternative poverty estimates at a September 2007 workshop in Bamako. Obviously, caution should be exercised in making cross-country poverty comparisons. But given the different assumptions that countries use to estimate poverty and their debatable strengths and weaknesses, it is often useful to use simple cross-country comparisons to help inform the methodological choices made for poverty measurement in any given country.

1. GDP per capita is expressed in U.S. dollars for simplicity, despite the fact that the CFA franc appreciated against the dollar in recent years.

Poverty in the CFA Franc zone: Estimates by country

Country	Household survey year	GDP per capita ($)	Natural log of GDP per capita divided by 100	Method for measuring poverty	Share of population in poverty (%)	Gini index
Benin	2003	325	1.18	Relative	39.0	0.36
Burkina Faso	2003	247	0.90	Cost of basic needs	46.4	0.46
Cameroon	2001	695	1.94	Cost of basic needs	40.2	0.41
Central African Republic	2003	225	0.81	Cost of basic needs	67.2	0.44
Chad	2003	211	0.75	Cost of basic needs	55.0	0.37
Congo, Rep.	2005	994	2.30	Cost of basic needs	50.7	0.46
Côte d'Ivoire	2002	592	1.78	Relative	38.4	0.50
Gabon	2005	3,991	3.69	Cost of basic needs	33.2	0.44
Guinea-Bissau	2002	138	0.33	$1 a day	65.7	0.36
Mali	2001	226	0.82	Cost of basic needs	55.6	0.38
Niger	2005	158	0.45	Cost of basic needs	62.1	0.47
Senegal	2001	442	1.49	Cost of basic needs	57.1	0.34
Togo	2006	238	0.87	Cost of basic needs	61.7	0.32

Note: Recent household survey data are not available for Equatorial Guinea.
Source: Wodon 2007b.

Poverty and per capita GDP

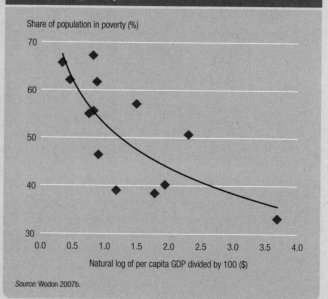

Source: Wodon 2007b.

Box 4 | Comparing objective and subjective measures of poverty

Several African countries have succeeded at increasing their economic growth rate, translating into substantial poverty reduction. At the same time people have not felt their poverty situation improving, a source of concern to elected policymakers. To what extent is there a divergence between objective and subjective measures of poverty, and what explains it?

Data from household surveys can help answer this question. The table below provide poverty estimates from selected World Bank poverty assessments in countries with high growth rates between repeated household surveys with consumption data. (Growth vanished in Guinea and slowed down in Cameroon after 2001–02). The table also provides data on poverty as measured in the household surveys and on subjective perceptions regarding poverty trends. In all four countries growth significantly reduced poverty, often with an elasticity of poverty reduction to growth of –1. Inequality increased in some countries but decreased in others, suggesting no general pattern. But perceptions regarding poverty were not as favorable: a majority of respondents declared that poverty had worsened in their country or community. Even for Senegal in 2001–06, a larger share of the population cited a deteriorating poverty situation in their community (although perceptions seem to have improved over those for 1994–2001).

Four tentative explanations can explain this apparent disconnect between a substantial decline in objective poverty measures and perceptions of a deterioration in the countries' or communities' poverty situation. First, when assessing trends in poverty subjectively, households may be influenced by persistent and in some cases increasing inequality. In a relative deprivation framework growth without a reduction in inequality may lead to higher feelings of deprivation over time. Second, even if many households benefit from higher consumption levels over time, their vulnerability to shocks remains very high. West African countries, among others, have been subjected to weather and commodity price shocks in recent years. Third, subjective

Measure or perception of poverty	Cameroon 1996–2001	Guinea 1994–2002	Mauritania 1990–2000	Senegal 1994–2001	Senegal 2001–06
Growth and objective poverty					
Cumulative growth in GDP per capita (1)	12.7	16.7	16.8	18.9	9.3
Initial poverty incidence (2)	53.3	62.6	56.6	67.8	57.1
Final poverty incidence (3)	40.2	49.1	46.7	57.1	50.8
Poverty reduction (4) = [(3)−(2)]/(2)	−0.246	−0.216	−0.175	−0.158	−0.110
Elasticity of poverty to GDP growth (4)/(1)	−1.94	−1.19	−1.04	−0.84	−1.19
Gini index of inequality					
Initial Gini index	40.6	45.8	33.8[a]	32.6	34.1
Final Gini index	40.8	41.0	39.0	34.2	32.0
Perception regarding poverty					
Deterioration	54.1	23.1	30.9	64.3	43.9
No change	17.4	49.5	40.8	12.8	22.1
Improvement	17.3	24.5	28.3	19.0	31.2
No opinion	11.2	2.9	—	4.0	2.8

a. Data are for 1996.
Source: Wodon 2007a.

perceptions of poverty may also account for nonmonetary aspects of well-being. Low levels of satisfaction with publicly provided services for education, health, and basic infrastructure may affect negatively perceptions in most countries. Fourth, even if the share of the population living in poverty is reduced over time, the number of the poor is increasing due to high population growth.

website (www.un.org/millenniumgoals), but some differences in timing, sources, and definitions remain.

Data on child malnutrition and population below minimum dietary energy consumption are from the Food and Agriculture Organization (see www.fao.org/faostat/foodsecurity/index_en.htm).

TABLE 3.2. MILLENNIUM DEVELOPMENT GOAL 2: ACHIEVE UNIVERSAL PRIMARY EDUCATION
Primary education provides children with basic reading, writing, and mathematics skills along with an elementary understanding of such subjects as history, geography, natural science, social science, art, and music.

Net primary enrollment ratio is the ratio of children of official primary school age based on the International Standard Classification of Education 1997 who are enrolled in primary school to the population of the corresponding official primary school age.

Primary completion rate is the percentage of students completing the last year of primary school. It is calculated as the total number of students in the last grade of primary school minus the number of repeaters in that grade divided by the total number of children of official graduation age.

Share of cohort reaching grade 5 is the percentage of children enrolled in grade 1 of primary school who eventually reach grade 5.

The estimate is based on the reconstructed cohort method.

Youth literacy rate is the percentage of people ages 15–24 who can, with understanding, both read and write a short, simple statement about their everyday life.

Source: Data are from the United Nations Educational, Scientific, and Cultural Organization Institute for Statistics. Data have been compiled by World Bank staff from primary and secondary sources. Efforts have been made to harmonize these data series with those published on the United Nations Millennium Development Goals website (www.un.org/millenniumgoals), but some differences in timing, sources, and definitions remain.

TABLE 3.3. MILLENNIUM DEVELOPMENT GOAL 3: PROMOTE GENDER EQUALITY AND EMPOWER WOMEN

Ratio of girls to boys in primary and secondary school is the ratio of female to male gross enrollment rate in primary and secondary school.

Ratio of young literate women to men is the ratio of the female to male youth literacy rate.

Women in national parliament are the percentage of parliamentary seats in a single or lower chamber occupied by women.

Share of women employed in the nonagricultural sector is women wage employees in the nonagricultural sector as a share of total nonagricultural employment.

Source: Data on net enrollment and literacy are from the United Nations Educational, Scientific, and Cultural Organization Institute for Statistics. Data on women in national parliaments are from the Inter-Parliamentary Union. Data on women's employment are from the International Labour Organization's Key Indicators of the Labour Market, fourth edition.

TABLE 3.4. MILLENNIUM DEVELOPMENT GOAL 4: REDUCE CHILD MORTALITY

Under-five mortality rate is the probability that a newborn baby will die before reaching age 5, if subject to current age-specific mortality rates. The probability is expressed as a rate per 1,000.

Infant mortality rate is the number of infants dying before reaching one year of age, per 1,000 live births.

Child immunization rate, measles, is the percentage of children ages 12–23 months who received vaccinations for measles before 12 months or at any time before the survey. A child is considered adequately immunized against measles after receiving one dose of vaccine.

Source: Data on under-five and infant mortality are the harmonized estimates of the World Health Organization, United Nations Children's Fund (UNICEF), and the World Bank, based mainly on household surveys, censuses, and vital registration, supplemented by the World Bank's estimates based on household surveys and vital registration. Other estimates are compiled and produced by the World Bank's Human Development Network and Development Data Group in consultation with its operational staff and country offices. Data on child immunization are from the World Health Organization and UNICEF estimates of national immunization coverage.

TABLE 3.5. MILLENNIUM DEVELOPMENT GOAL 5: IMPROVE MATERNAL HEALTH

Maternal mortality ratio, modeled estimate, is the number of women who die from pregnancy-related causes during pregnancy and childbirth, per 100,000 live births.

Births attended by skilled health staff are the percentage of deliveries attended by personnel trained to give the necessary supervision, care, and advice to women during pregnancy, labor, and the postpartum period; to conduct deliveries on their own; and to care for newborns.

Source: Data on maternal mortality are from AbouZahr and Wardlaw (2003). Data on births attended by skilled health staff are from the United Nations Children's Fund's State of the World's Children 2006 and Childinfo, and Demographic and Health Surveys by Macro International.

TABLE 3.6. MILLENNIUM DEVELOPMENT GOAL 6: COMBAT HIV/AIDS, MALARIA, AND OTHER DISEASES

Prevalence of HIV is the percentage of people ages 15–49 who are infected with HIV.

Contraceptive prevalence rate is the percentage of women who are practicing, or whose sexual partners are practicing, any form of contraception. It is usually measured for married women ages 15–49 only.

Deaths due to malaria is the number of malaria deaths per 100,000 people.

Share of children under age 5 sleeping under insecticide-treated bednets is the percentage of children under age 5 with access to an insecticide-treated bednet to prevent malaria.

Incidence of tuberculosis is the estimated number of new tuberculosis cases (pulmonary, smear positive, and extrapulmonary), per 100,000 people.

Tuberculosis cases detected under DOTS is the percentage of estimated new infectious tuberculosis cases detected under DOTS, the internationally recommended tuberculosis control strategy.

Source: Data on HIV prevalence are from the Joint United Nations Programme on HIV/AIDS and the World Health Organization's (WHO) 2006 Report on the Global AIDS Epidemic. Data on contraceptive prevalence are from household surveys, including Demographic and Health Surveys by Macro International and Multiple Indicator Cluster Surveys by the United Nations Children's Fund (UNICEF). Data on deaths due to malaria are from the WHO. Data on insecticide-treated bednet use are from UNICEF's State of the World's Children 2006 and Childinfo, and Demographic and Health Surveys by Macro International. Data on tuberculosis are from the WHO's Global Tuberculosis Control Report 2006.

TABLE 3.7. MILLENNIUM DEVELOPMENT GOAL 7: ENSURE ENVIRONMENT SUSTAINABILITY

Forest area is land under natural or planted stands of trees, whether productive or not.

Nationally protected areas are totally or partially protected areas of at least 1,000 hectares that are designated as scientific reserves with limited public access, national parks, natural monuments, nature reserves or wildlife sanctuaries, and protected landscapes. Marine areas, unclassified areas, and litoral (intertidal) areas are not included. The data also do not include sites protected under local or provincial law.

Gross domestic product (GDP) per unit of energy use is the GDP in purchasing power parity (PPP) U.S. dollars per kilogram of oil equivalent of energy use. PPP GDP is gross domestic product converted to 2000 constant international dollars using purchasing power parity rates. An international dollar has the same purchasing power over GDP as a U.S. dollar has in the United States.

Carbon dioxide emissions are those stemming from the burning of fossil fuels and the manufacture of cement. They include carbon dioxide produced during consumption of solid, liquid, and gas fuels and gas flaring.

Solid fuel use is the percentage of the population using solid fuels as opposed to modern fuels. Solid fuels are defined to include fuel wood, straw, dung, coal, and charcoal. Modern fuels are defined to include electricity, liquefied petroleum gas, natural gas, kerosene, and gasoline.

Population with sustainable access to an improved water source is the percentage of the population with reasonable access to an adequate amount of water from an improved source, such as a household connection, public standpipe, borehole, protected well or spring, or rainwater collection. Unimproved sources include vendors, tanker trucks, and unprotected wells and springs. Reasonable access is defined as the availability of at least 20 liters a person a day from a source within 1 kilometer of the dwelling.

Population with sustainable access to improved sanitation is the percentage of the population with at least adequate access to excreta disposal facilities that can effectively prevent human, animal, and insect contact with excreta. Improved facilities range from simple but protected pit latrines to flush toilets with a sewerage connection. The excreta disposal system is considered adequate if it is private or shared (but not public) and if it hygienically separates human excreta from human contact. To be effective, facilities must be correctly constructed and properly maintained.

Source: Data on forest area are from the Food and Agricultural Organization's Global Forest Resources Assessment. Data on nationally protected areas are from the United Nations Environment Programme and the World Conservation Monitoring Centre.

Data on energy use are from electronic files of the International Energy Agency. Data on carbon dioxide emissions are from the Carbon Dioxide Information Analysis Center, Environmental Sciences Division, Oak Ridge National Laboratory, in the U.S. state of Tennessee. Data on solid fuel use are from household survey data, supplemented by World Bank estimates. Data on access to water and sanitation are from the World Health Organization and United Nations Children's Fund's Meeting the MDG Drinking Water and Sanitation Target (www.unicef.org/wes/mdgreport).

TABLE 3.8. MILLENNIUM DEVELOPMENT GOAL 8: DEVELOP A GLOBAL PARTNERSHIP FOR DEVELOPMENT

Heavily Indebted Poor Countries (HIPC) Debt Initiative decision point is the date at which a HIPC with an established track record of good performance under adjustment programs supported by the International Monetary Fund (IMF) and the World Bank commits to undertake additional reforms and to develop and implement a poverty reduction strategy.

HIPC completion point is the date at which the country successfully completes the key structural reforms agreed on at the decision point, including developing and implementing its poverty reduction strategy. The country then receives the bulk of debt relief under the HIPC Initiative without further policy conditions.

Debt service relief committed is the amount of debt service relief, calculated at the Enhanced HIPC Initiative decision point, that will allow the country to achieve debt sustainability at the completion point.

Public and publicly guaranteed debt service is the sum of principal repayments and interest actually paid on total long-term debt (public and publicly guaranteed and private nonguaranteed), use of IMF credit, and interest on short-term debt.

Youth unemployment rate is the percentage of the labor force ages 15–24 without work but available for and seeking employment. Definitions of labor force and unemployment may differ by country.

Fixed-line and mobile telephone subscribers are subscribers to a fixed-line telephone service, which connects a customer's equipment to the public switched telephone network, or to a public mobile telephone service, which uses cellular technology.

Personal computers are self-contained computers designed for use by a single individual.

Internet users are people with access to the worldwide network.

Source: Data on HIPC countries are from the IMF's March 2006 "HIPC Status Reports." Data on external debt are mainly from reports to the World Bank through its Debtor Reporting System from member countries that have received International Bank for Reconstruction and Development loans or International Development Association credits, as well as World Bank and IMF files. Data on youth unemployment are from the International Labour Organization's Key Indicators of the Labour Market, fourth edition. Data on phone subscribers, personal computers, and Internet users are from the International Telecommunication Union's (ITU) World Telecommunication Development Report database and World Bank estimates.

4. Paris Declaration indicators

TABLE 4.1. STATUS OF PARIS DECLARATION INDICATORS

The Paris Declaration is the outcome of the 2005 Paris High-Level Forum on Aid Effectiveness. In the Declaration 60 partner countries, 30 donor countries, and 30 development agencies committed to specific actions to further country ownership, harmonization, alignment, managing for development results, and mutual accountability for the use of aid. Participants agreed on 12 indicators of aid effectiveness. These indicators include good national development strategies, reliable country systems for procurement and public financial management, the development and use of results frameworks, and mutual assessment of progress. Qualitative desk reviews by the Organisation for Economic Co-operation and Development's Development Assistance Committee and the World Bank and a survey questionnaire for governments and donors are used to calculate the indicators. Table 4.1 includes five of these indicators.

Operational development strategies measure the extent to which a country has an operational development strategy to guide the aid coordination effort and the country's overall development. The score is based on the World Bank's 2005 Comprehensive Development Framework Progress Report. An operational strategy calls for a coherent long-term vision and a medium-term strategy derived from it; specific targets serving a holistic, balanced and well sequenced development strategy; and capacity and resources for its implementation.

Reliable public financial management is the World Bank's annual Country Policy and Institutional Assessment rating for the quality of public financial management. Measured on a scale of 1 (worst) to 5 (best), its focus is on how much existing systems adhere to broadly accepted good practices and whether a reform program is in place to promote improved practices.

Avoidance of parallel project implementation units (PIUs) is the number of parallel project implementation units. "Parallel" indicates that the units were created outside existing country institutional structures. The survey guidance distinguishes between PIUs and executing agencies and describes three typical features of parallel PIUs: they are accountable to external funding agencies rather than to country implementing agencies (ministries, departments, agencies, and the like), most of the professional staff are appointed by the donor, and the personnel salaries often exceeds those of civil service personnel. Interpretation of the Paris Declaration survey question on this subject was controversial in a number of countries. It is unclear that within countries all donors applied the same criteria with the same degree of rigor or that across countries the same standards were used. In several cases the descriptive part of the survey results indicates that some donors applied a legalistic criterion of accountability to the formal executing agency, whereas the national coordinator and other donors would have preferred greater recognition of the substantive reality of accountability to the donor. Some respondents may have confused the definitional question ("Is the unit 'parallel'?") with the aid management question ("Is the parallelism justified in terms of the developmental benefits and costs?").

Monitorable performance assessment frameworks measure the extent to which a country's commitment to establishing performance frameworks has been realized. The indicator relies on the scorings of the 2005 Comprehensive Development Framework Progress Report and considers three criteria: the quality of development information, stakeholder access to development information, and coordinated country-level monitoring and evaluation. The assessments therefore reflect both the extent to which sound data on development outputs, outcomes, and impacts are collected, and various aspects of the way information is used, disseminated among stakeholders, and fed back into policy.

Mutual accountability indicates whether there is a mechanism for mutual review of progress on aid effectiveness commitments. This is an important innovation of the Paris Declaration because it develops the idea that aid is more effective when both donors and partner governments are accountable to their constituents for the use of resources to achieve development results and when they are accountable to each other. The specific focus is mutual accountability for the implementation of the partnership commitments included in the Paris Declaration and any local agreements on enhancing aid effectiveness.

Source: Overview of the Results 2006 Survey on Monitoring the Paris Declaration and World Bank data.

5. Private sector development

TABLE 5.1. BUSINESS ENVIRONMENT
Number of startup procedures to register a business is the number of procedures required to start a business, including interactions to obtain necessary permits and licenses and to complete all inscriptions, verifications, and notifications to start operations.

Time to start a business is the number of calendar days needed to complete the procedures to legally operate a business. If a procedure can be speeded up at additional cost, the fastest procedure, independent of cost, is chosen.

Cost to start a business is normalized by presenting it as a percentage of gross national income (GNI) per capita.

Number of procedures to register property is the number of procedures required for a business to secure rights to property.

Time to register property is the number of calendar days needed for a business to secure rights to property.

Number of procedures to enforce a contract is the number of independent actions, mandated by law or courts, that demand interaction between the parties of a contract or between them and the judge or court officer.

Time to enforce a contract is the number of calendar days from the filing of the lawsuit in court until the final determination and, in appropriate cases, payment.

Protecting investors disclosure index measures the degree to which investors are protected through disclosure of ownership and financial information.

Time to resolve insolvency is the number of years from the filing for insolvency in court until the resolution of distressed assets.

Rigidity of employment index measures the regulation of employment, specifically the hiring and firing of workers and the rigidity of working hours. This index is the average of three subindexes: a difficulty of hiring index, a rigidity of hours index, and a difficulty of firing index.

Source: Data are from the World Bank's Doing Business project (http://rru.worldbank.org/DoingBusiness/).

TABLE 5.2. INVESTMENT CLIMATE

Private investment is private sector fixed capital formation (table 2.21) divided by nominal gross domestic product (table 2.1).

Net foreign direct investment is investment by residents of the Organisation for Economic Co-operation and Development's (OECD) Development Assistance Committee (DAC) member countries to acquire a lasting management interest (at least 10 percent of voting stock) in an enterprise operating in the recipient country. The data reflect changes in the net worth of subsidiaries in recipient countries whose parent company is in the DAC source country. See box 5 for a discussion of the availability and accuracy of statistics on foreign direct investment.

Domestic credit to private sector is financial resources provided to the private sector, such as through loans, purchases of nonequity securities, and trade credits and other accounts receivable, that establish a claim for repayment. For some countries these claims include credit to public enterprises.

Policy uncertainty is the share of senior managers who ranked economic and regulatory policy uncertainty as a major or very severe constraint. See box 6 for a discussion of how good policies matter more for the business climate than natural resources or geography, a finding of *Africa Competitiveness Report 2007.*

Corruption is the share of senior managers who ranked corruption as a major or very severe constraint.

Courts are the share of senior managers who ranked courts and dispute resolution systems as a major or very severe constraint.

Lack of confidence in courts to uphold property rights is the share of senior managers who do not agree with the statement: "I am confident that the judicial system will enforce my contractual and property rights in business disputes."

Crime is the share of senior managers who ranked crime, theft, and disorder as a major or very severe constraint.

Tax rates are the share of senior managers who ranked tax rates as a major or very severe constraint.

Finance is the share of senior managers who ranked access to finance or cost of finance as a major or very severe constraint.

Electricity is the share of senior managers who ranked electricity as a major or severe constraint.

Labor regulation is the share of senior managers who ranked labor regulations as a major or severe constraint.

Labor skills are the share of senior managers who ranked skills of available workers as a major or severe constraint.

Number of tax payments is the number of taxes paid by businesses, including electronic filing. The tax is counted as paid once a year even if payments are more frequent.

Time to prepare, file, and pay taxes is the number of hours it takes to prepare, file, and pay (or withhold) three major types of taxes: the corporate income tax, the value added or sales tax, and labor taxes, including payroll taxes and social security contributions.

Total tax payable is the total amount of taxes payable by the business (except for labor taxes) after accounting for deductions and exemptions as a percentage of profit. For further details on the method used for assessing the total tax payable.

With foreign direct investment (FDI) flows to African countries becoming an important source of foreign capital and technologies, reliable and accurate statistics are crucial for sound FDI policies. Despite major achievements around the world in gathering FDI data, the availability and quality of FDI data remain an issue in developing countries, including African countries.

The main source of data for estimating aggregate levels of FDI for most countries are central bank foreign exchange records, which are collected as part of balance of payments data. FDI statistics based on balance of payments data are becoming increasingly standardized as the International Monetary Fund's *Balance of Payments Manual* and the Organisation for Economic Co-operation and Development's *Benchmark Definition of Foreign Direct Investment* are used as the main sources.

However, balance of payments data often fail to capture foreign residents' investment activities that do not involve direct cross-border capital transactions—for example, reinvested earnings, where investment in a company is based on its own profits made from past investments in the same host country. Other examples are equity in the form of machinery (investment in kind) and intracompany debt.

More countries—but not all—have begun incorporating these elements of FDI. Only a few countries in Africa do. According to a recent survey by the United Nations Conference on Trade and Development (UNCTAD 2005), only Botswana and Nigeria report all these elements, and South Africa and Tunisia report reinvested earnings.

Failure to include these elements has resulted in discrepancies in FDI data. For example, in theory total worldwide FDI inflows should equal total worldwide FDI outflows. But a significant discrepancy between them exists because of the omission of these components (see figure).

Another source of FDI data is government administrative records, such as approval data of investment projects by foreign companies. The advantage of this source is that it incorporates sectoral and geographical information (origins and destinations) of foreign investments, which is useful information for microeconomic analysis of implications of FDI in countries' economic and industrial growth.

But only a few countries publish sectoral and geographical distributions of their FDI inflows and outflows. Availability of such data in African countries is particularly limited; only five countries report their FDI inflows by origin, and only three report inflows by sector (UNCTAD 2005). Availability of cross-sectional information of sectoral and geographical distributions of FDI flows is limited mostly to developed countries.

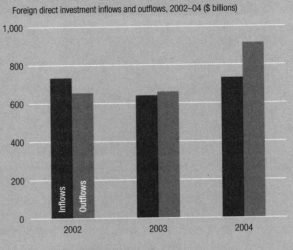

World foreign direct investment

Foreign direct investment inflows and outflows, 2002–04 ($ billions)

Source: World Bank World Development Indicators database.

Another problem with the administrative source–based estimation is that many countries lack the details required to match international standards, which leads to inconsistency across countries in compiling FDI data. Also, administrative source–based FDI data often have some flaws in valuing investment projects due to the time gap between project approval and actual investment activity.

Some countries have implemented firm-level investor surveys, such as censuses, to supplement their balance of payments– and administrative data–based FDI statistics and improve the overall quality of their FDI statistics. These surveys can collect data on reinvested earnings and depreciation of FDI stocks. The downside of this approach, however, is the extreme difficulty in tracking all firms that conduct FDI transactions. The process is also so costly that only a handful countries have implemented them.

Many countries in Africa lack sufficient human and institutional capacity to address the availability and quality of FDI data. Capacity building at the national level is very much needed in FDI statistics. Collaboration among agencies—the ministry of finance, ministry of commerce, ministry of industries, central banks, fiscal and tax authorities, and investment promotion agencies—is also important.

Source: IMF 2003; UNCTAD 2005.

Highest marginal tax rate, corporate, is the highest rate shown on the schedule of tax rates applied to the taxable income of corporations.

Time dealing with officials is the average percentage of senior management's time that is spent in a typical week dealing with requirements imposed by government regulations (for example, taxes, customs, labor regulations, licensing, and registration), including dealings with officials, completing forms, and the like.

Box 6 | **Findings of *Africa Competitiveness Report 2007***

The first message of *Africa Competitiveness Report 2007* (World Economic Forum 2007) is that good policies matter more for the investment climate than resource abundance or sea access. By combining different variables representative of the business climate into one composite indicator, the report shows that resource-endowed countries have a similar quality of business climate as resource-scarce countries. So do landlocked countries and countries with sea access. For improving the investment climate, geography and geology count less than good policies (figure 1).

The World Bank's Enterprise Survey questionnaire asks respondents to rank a list of issues based on how constraining they are to the operations and growth of their business. Although substantial country variation exists, access to finance, infrastructure, institutions, and skills are the constraints most often reported as "major" or "very severe" by entrepreneurs, both male and female, across Africa (figure 2).

Half of respondents report access to finance as a top constraint. Across countries access to finance appears more acute in resource rich countries and low-income countries. Within countries access to finance is problematic for small firms and locally owned enterprises. In addition, expanding firms are 10 percent more likely to report access to finance as a major constraint. Performance indicators show that better access to finance is associated with both higher productivity and employment growth.

Infrastructure remains one of the tightest bottlenecks to businesses in Africa. In low-income countries electricity is the top reported constraint. Moreover, unreliable power supply is a constraint that affects all firms, regardless of size. Transportation, by contrast, affects landlocked countries and small and medium-size firms more. Firms in Africa report losing as much as 8 percent of sales due to power outages and 3 percent due to transportation

delays. Improvements in infrastructure would have a substantial impact on firm competitiveness, increasing total factor productivity by 5 percent and employment by 7 percent.

Quality of public institutions comprises law and order, corruption, court efficiency, and quality in the provision of public services. Across African countries corruption in particular remains a serious obstacle—viewed as one of the top five overall constraints among business owners, irrespective of gender and firm size. Performance indicators show that a 10 percent improvement in the

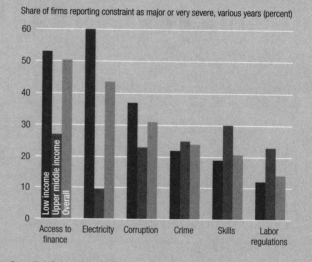

Figure 2 | **Top constraints to business operations growth in Africa**

Share of firms reporting constraint as major or very severe, various years (percent)

Source: World Economic Forum 2007.

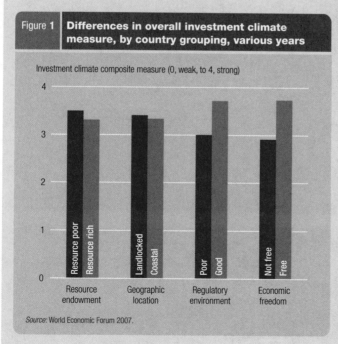

Figure 3 | **Skills and labor regulation constraints, by size of firm**

Share of firms reporting constraint as major or very severe, various years (percent)

Source: World Economic Forum 2007.

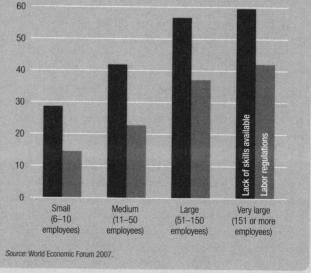

Figure 1 | **Differences in overall investment climate measure, by country grouping, various years**

Investment climate composite measure (0, weak, to 4, strong)

Source: World Economic Forum 2007.

(continued)

Box 6 | Findings of *Africa Competitiveness Report 2007* (continued)

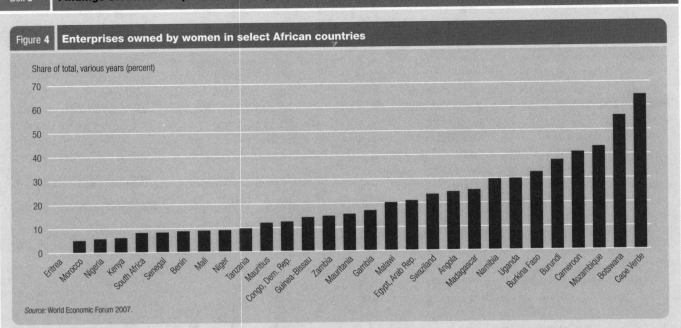

Figure 4 | **Enterprises owned by women in select African countries**

Share of total, various years (percent)

Source: World Economic Forum 2007.

objective measure of corruption and regulation is associated with about a 2 percent increase in productivity.

Lack of skills remains a critical problem in Africa. Large firms are almost 60 percent more likely to report skills availability and labor regulations as constraining factors (figure 3). With larger workforces and more stringent hiring and firing requirements, this is not surprising. Increasing the supply of skilled workers has shown a positive impact on employment growth. A 10 percent improvement in the objective measure of the supply of skilled workers will increase employment by 1 percent.

The report identifies increased entrepreneurial participation of women as Africa's hidden growth potential. Albeit with large variation across countries, female entrepreneurs in Africa remain a minority compared with their male counterparts in most African countries (figure 4). The report suggests that there is no clear gender-distinct pattern of constraints faced by firms across Africa. But female entrepreneurs tend to be younger, less likely to be married, and more likely to be engaged in family enterprises.

The report concludes that once a firm is in business, enterprises managed by women are as productive as those run by men, based on productivity indicators such as value added per worker and total factor productivity (figure 5). This finding highlights the considerable hidden growth potential of women-owned enterprises once entry barriers to women's entrepreneurial participation are removed.

The report also compares Africa's four largest economies, Algeria, Egypt, Nigeria, and South Africa, with Brazil, China, India, and Russia., four of the largest developing and transition economies It argues that the four African economies together have the size and scale to become drivers of Africa's economic growth. But key obstacles to competitiveness in their investment climates and very low intra-African trade hinder their capacities to act as effective growth poles (figure 6).

Finally, the report highlights the critical importance of information and communication technologies for boosting efficiency, boosting skill, and technology levels and moving into higher value products. It recognizes African governments' shifting role in information and communication technologies from owning and operating to promoting competitiveness by establishing a sound policy framework and stable institutions—particularly in the mobile telephone market. This has substantially transformed the structure of the mobile telephone market in Africa over the last decade (figure 7).

These efforts have resulted in strong growth in African markets—particularly in mobile telephone technologies (figure 8).

Figure 5 | **Performance of men- and women-owned enterprises**

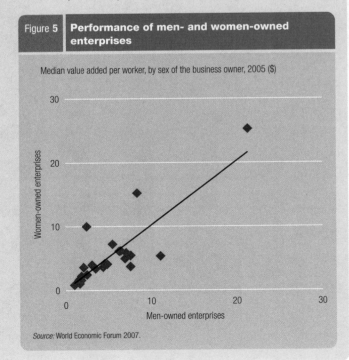

Median value added per worker, by sex of the business owner, 2005 ($)

Source: World Economic Forum 2007.

Findings of *Africa Competitiveness Report 2007* (continued)

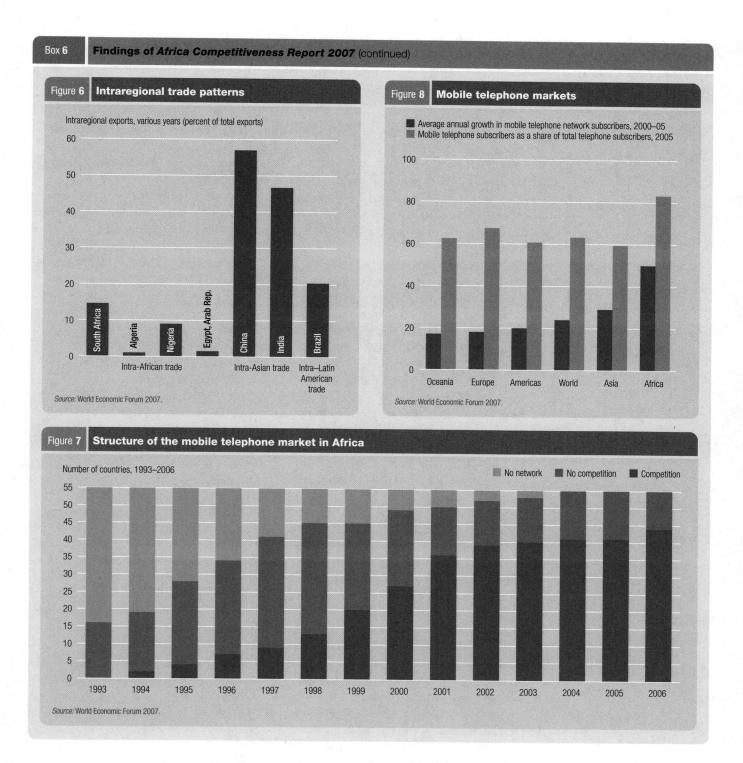

Figure 6 | **Intraregional trade patterns**

Intraregional exports, various years (percent of total exports)

Source: World Economic Forum 2007.

Figure 8 | **Mobile telephone markets**

- Average annual growth in mobile telephone network subscribers, 2000–05
- Mobile telephone subscribers as a share of total telephone subscribers, 2005

Source: World Economic Forum 2007.

Figure 7 | **Structure of the mobile telephone market in Africa**

Number of countries, 1993–2006

No network   No competition   Competition

Source: World Economic Forum 2007.

Average time to clear customs is the number of days to clear an imported good through customs.

Bank branches are deposit money bank branches.

Interest rate spread is the interest rate charged by banks on loans to prime customers minus the interest rate paid by commercial or similar banks for demand, time, or savings deposits.

Listed domestic companies are domestically incorporated companies listed on a country's stock exchanges at the end of the year. They exclude investment companies, mutual funds, and other collective investment vehicles.

Market capitalization of listed companies, also known as market value, is the share price of a listed domestic company's stock times the number of shares outstanding.

Turnover ratio for traded stocks is the total value of shares traded during the period divided by the average market capitalization for the period. Average market capitalization is calculated as the average of the end-of-period values for the current period and the previous period.

Source: Data on private investment are from the World Bank's World Development Indicators database. Data on net foreign direct investment are from the World Bank's World Development Indicators database. Data on domestic credit to the private sector are from the International Monetary Fund's International Financial Statistics database and data files, World Bank and OECD gross domestic product (GDP) estimates, and the World Bank's World Development Indicators database. Data on investment climate constraints to firms are based on enterprise surveys conducted by the World Bank and its partners during 2001–05 (http://rru.worldbank.org/EnterpriseSurveys). Data on regulation and tax administration and highest marginal corporate tax rates are from the World Bank's Doing Business project (http://rru.worldbank.org/DoingBusiness). Data on time dealing with officials and average time to clear customs are from World Bank Enterprise Surveys (http://rru.worldbank.org/EnterpriseSurveys/). Data on bank branches are from surveys of banking and regulatory institutions by the World Bank's Research Department and Financial Sector and Operations Policy Department and the World Development Indicators database. Data on interest rate spreads are from the IMF's International Financial Statistics database and data files and the World Bank's World Development Indicators database. Data on listed domestic companies and turnover ratios for traded stocks are from Standard & Poor's *Emerging Stock Markets Factbook* and supplemental data and the World Bank's World Development Indicators database. Data on market capitalization of listed companies are from Standard & Poor's *Emerging Stock Markets Factbook* and supplemental data, World Bank and OECD estimates of GDP, and the World Bank's World Development Indicators database.

6. Trade

TABLE 6.1. INTERNATIONAL TRADE AND TARIFF BARRIERS

Merchandise trade is the sum of imports and exports of divided by nominal gross domestic product.

Exports and *imports* comprise all transactions between residents of an economy and the rest of the world involving a change in ownership of general merchandise, goods sent for processing and repairs, and nonmonetary gold. Data are shown in current U.S. dollars. Exports and imports as a share of gross domestic product (GDP) are calculated as merchandise exports and imports divided by nominal GDP. Annual growth of exports and imports is calculated using the real imports and exports series in tables 2.25 and 2.26. See box 7 for a discussion of the importance of cross-border trade for Rwanda's exports and imports.

Terms of trade index measures the relative movement of export and import prices. This series is calculated as the ratio of a country's export unit values or prices to its import unit values or prices shows changes over a base year (2000) in the level of export unit values as a percentage of import unit values.

Structure of merchandise exports and *imports* components may not sum to 100 percent because of unclassified trade.

Food comprises the commodities in Standard International Trade Classification (SITC) sections 0 (food and live animals), 1 (beverages and tobacco), and 4 (animal and vegetable oils and fats) and SITC division 22 (oil seeds, oil nuts, and oil kernels).

Agricultural raw materials comprise the commodities in SITC section 2 (crude materials except fuels), excluding divisions 22, 27 (crude fertilizers and minerals excluding coal, petroleum, and precious stones), and 28 (metalliferous ores and scrap).

Fuels comprise SITC section 3 (mineral fuels).

Ores and metals comprise the commodities in SITC sections 27, 28, and 68 (nonferrous metals).

Manufactures comprise the commodities in SITC sections 5 (chemicals), 6 (basic manufactures), 7 (machinery and transport equipment), and 8 (miscellaneous manufactured goods), excluding division 68.

Cross-border trade in Rwanda—an important source of income for less well-off households—has been growing over the last decade (tables 1 and 2). Cross-border trade is trade between Rwanda and its immediate neighbors (Burundi, Democratic Republic of Congo, Tanzania, and Uganda). The income earned by a large number of small traders and family-operated ventures augments household income and agricultural production (through the provision of fertilizers and livestock feed), thereby helping reduce poverty. Cross-border activities also support regional food security.

Cross-border trade is also an important source of government revenue. Overall, the customs post at Gikongo, in Kigali, which clears 90–95 percent of imports, accounts for 90 percent of total customs duties. The airport custom post accounts for 7.5 percent of customs duties, and border customs posts account for 2.5 percent of customs duties.

Most cross-border trade in Rwanda takes place between Kigali and neighboring countries. According to a 2001/02 National Bank of Rwanda survey, these transactions account for about 99 percent of cross-border exchanges. Transactions between customs posts and neighboring countries account for the remaining 1 percent of cross-border transactions.

The main goods traded are agricultural commodities (maize, sugar, milk, rice, wheat, and flour), industrial goods (petroleum products, machinery, cement, shoes, plate, lamp, and pan), water resources (fish), forest resources (cassiterite), and services (mobile telephony, human skills, and banking activities). Rwanda also re-exports some goods, including secondhand clothes and fuel for

Table 1	Exports and imports and cross-border trade as a share of GDP, 2001–04 (percent)			
Year	Exports of goods	Imports of goods	Cross-border trade[a]	
			Exports	Imports
2001	4.83	12.69	0.28	0.69
2002	3.18	11.03	0.46	0.98
2003	2.77	10.21	0.46	1.68
2004	4.41	11.62	0.58	2.06
Average, 2001–04	3.80	11.39	0.50	1.58

a. Value of included transactions exceeded 200,000 francs ($370).
Source: World Bank 2007 and National Bank of Rwanda.

Table 2	Growth rates of exports and imports as a share of GDP, 2001–04 (percent)		
Exports of goods and services	Imports of goods and services	Cross-border trade[a]	
		Exports	Imports
4.04	−2.23	30.85	45.45

a. Value of included transactions exceeded 200,000 francs ($370).
Source: World Bank 2007 and National Bank of Rwanda.

airplanes and vehicles to Burundi and the Democratic Republic of Congo.

Source: Coulibaly, Ezemenari, and Maburuki 2007.

Export diversification index measures the extent to which exports are diversified. It is constructed as the inverse of a Herfindahl index, using disaggregated exports at four digits (following the SITC3). A higher index indicates more export diversification.

Competitiveness indicator has two aspects: sectoral effect and global competitiveness effect. To calculate both indicators, growth of exports is decomposed into three components: the growth rate of total international trade over the reference period (2001–05); the *sectoral effect,* which measures the contribution to a country's export growth of the dynamics of the sectoral markets in which the country sells its products, assuming that sectoral market shares are constant; and the *competitiveness effect,* which measures the contribution of changes in sectoral market shares to a country's export growth.

Binding coverage is the percentage of product lines with an agreed bound rate.

Simple mean bound rate is the unweighted average of all the lines in the tariff schedule in which bound rates have been set.

Simple mean tariff is the unweighted average of effectively applied rates or most favored nation rates for all products subject to tariffs calculated for all traded goods.

Weighted mean tariff is the average of effectively applied rates or most favored nation rates weighted by the product import shares corresponding to each partner country.

Share of lines with international peaks is the share of lines in the tariff schedule with tariff rates that exceed 15 percent.

Share of lines with specific rates is the share of lines in the tariff schedule that are set on a per unit basis or that combine ad valorem and per unit rates.

Primary products are commodities classified in SITC revision 2 sections 0–4 plus division 68.

Manufactured products are commodities classified in SITC revision 2 sections 5–8 excluding division 68.

Tariff barriers are a form of duty based on the value of the import.

Average cost to ship 20 ft container from port to destination is the cost of all operations associated with moving a container from onboard a ship to the considered economic center, weighted based on container traffic for each corridor.

Average time to clear customs is the number of days to clear an imported good through customs.

Source: All indicators in the table were calculated by World Bank staff using the World Integrated Trade Solution system. Data on the export diversification index and the competitiveness indicator are from the Organisation for Economic Co-operation and Development. Data on tariffs are from the United Nations Conference on Trade and Development and the World Trade Organization. Data on global imports are from the United Nations Statistics Division's COMTRADE database. Data on merchandise exports and imports are from World Bank country desks. Data on shipping costs are from the World Bank's Sub-Saharan Africa Transport Policy Program (SSATP). Data on average time to clear customs are from World Bank Enterprise Surveys (http://rru.worldbank.org/EnterpriseSurveys/).

TABLE 6.2 TOP THREE EXPORTS AND SHARE IN TOTAL EXPORTS, 2005
Top exports and *share of total exports* are based on exports disaggregated at the four-digit level (following the Standard International Trade Classification Revision 3).

Number of exports accounting for 75 percent of total exports is the number of exports in a country that account for 75 percent of the country's exports.

Source: All indicators in the table are from the Organisation for Economic Co-operation and Development.

TABLE 6.3 REGIONAL INTEGRATION, TRADE BLOCS
Merchandise exports within bloc are the sum of merchandise exports by members of a trade bloc to other members of the bloc. They are shown both in U.S. dollars and as a percentage of total merchandise exports by the bloc.

Source: Data on merchandise trade flows are published in the International Monetary Fund's (IMF) *Direction of Trade Statistics Yearbook* and *Direction of Trade Statistics Quarterly*. The data in the table were calculated using the IMF's Direction of Trade database. The United Nations Conference on Trade and Development publishes data on intraregional trade in its *Handbook of International Trade and Development Statistics*. The information on trade bloc membership is from World Bank (2000), the World Bank's *Global Economic Prospects 2005*, and the World Bank's International Trade Unit.

7. Infrastructure

TABLE 7.1. WATER AND SANITATION
Internal fresh water resources per capita is the sum of total renewable resources, which include internal flows of rivers and groundwater from rainfall in the country, and river flows from other countries.

Population with sustainable access to an improved water source is the percentage of population with reasonable access to an adequate amount of water from an improved source, such as a household connection, public standpipe, borehole, protected well or spring, or rainwater collection. Unimproved sources include vendors, tanker trucks, and unprotected wells and springs. Reasonable access is defined as the availability of at least 20 liters a person a day from a source within 1 kilometer of the user's dwelling.

Population with sustainable access to improved sanitation is the percentage of the population with at least adequate access to excreta disposal facilities that can effectively prevent human, animal, and insect contact with excreta. Improved facilities range from simple but protected pit latrines to flush toilets with a sewerage connection. The excreta disposal system is considered adequate if it is private or shared (but not public) and if it hygienically separates human excreta from human contact. To be effective, facilities must be correctly constructed and properly maintained.

Water supply failure for firms receiving water is the average number of days per year that firms experienced insufficient water supply for production.

Committed nominal investment in water projects with private participation is annual committed investment in water projects with private investment, including projects for potable water generation and distribution and sewerage collection and treatment projects.

Average annual official development assistance (ODA) disbursements for water and sanitation are average annual ODA for water and sanitation, including bilateral, multilateral, and other donors.

Source: Data on fresh water resources are from the World Bank's World Development Indicators database. Data on access to water and sanitation are from the World Health Organization and United Nations Children's Fund's Meeting the MDG Drinking Water and Sanitation Target (www.unicef.org/wes/mdgreport). Data on water supply failure are from World Bank Investment Climate Surveys. Data on committed nominal investment in potable water projects with private participation are from the World Bank's Private Participation in Infrastructure database. Data on ODA disbursements are from the Organisation for Economic Co-operation and Development.

TABLE 7.2. TRANSPORTATION

Road network is the length of motorways, highways, main or national roads, secondary or regional roads, and other roads.

Rail lines are the length of railway route available for train service, irrespective of the number of parallel tracks.

Road density, ratio to arable land is the total length of national road network per 1,000 square kilometers of arable land area. The use of arable land area in the denominator focuses on inhabited sectors of total land area by excluding wilderness areas.

Road density, ratio to total land is the total length of national road network per 1,000 square kilometers of total land area.

Rural access is the percentage of the rural population who live within 2 kilometers of an all-season passable road as a share of the total rural population.

Vehicle fleet is motor vehicles, including cars, buses, and freight vehicles but not two-wheelers.

Commercial vehicles are the number of commercial vehicles that use at least 24 liters of diesel fuel per 100 kilometers.

Passenger vehicles are road motor vehicles, other than two-wheelers, intended for the carriage of passengers and designed to seat no more than nine people (including the driver).

Road network in good or fair condition is the length of the national road network, including the interurban classified network without the urban and rural network, that is in good or fair condition, as defined by each country's road agency.

Ratio of paved to total roads is the length of paved roads—which are those surfaced with crushed stone (macadam) and hydrocarbon binder or bituminized agents, with concrete, or with cobblestones—as a percentage of all the country's roads.

Average time to ship 20 ft container from port to final destination is the time in days from when the ship is available for unloading (be it moored at the berth or offshore) until the content of the container is made available to the final customer at the destination in the considered economic center, weighted based on container traffic for each corridor.

Average cost to ship 20 ft container from port to final destination is the costs of all operations associated with bringing a container from onboard a ship to the considered economic center, weighted based on container traffic for each corridor.

Price of diesel fuel and *super gasoline* is the price as posted at filling stations in a country's capital city. When several fuel prices for major cities were available, the unweighted average is used. Since super gasoline (95 octane/A95/premium) is not available everywhere, it is sometime replaced by regular gasoline (92 octane/A92), premium plus gasoline (98 octane/A98), or an average of the two.

Committed nominal investment in transport projects with private participation is annual committed investment in transport projects with private investment, including projects for airport runways and terminals, railways (including fixed assets, freight, intercity passenger, and local passenger), toll roads, bridges, and tunnels.

Average annual official development assistance (ODA) disbursements for transportation and storage are average annual ODA for transportation and storage, including bilateral, multilateral, and other donors.

Source: Data on length of road network and size of vehicle fleet are from the International Road Federation's *World Road Statistics.* Data on rail lines and ratio of paved to total roads are from the World Bank's World Development Indicators database. Data on road density and rural access to roads are from the World Bank's Sub-Saharan Africa Transport Policy Program (SSATP) and World Development Indicators database. Data on length of national network in good or fair condition and average time and costs are from the World Bank's SSATP. Data on fuel and gasoline prices are from the German Society for Technical Cooperation (GTZ). Data on committed nominal investment in transport projects with private participation are from the World Bank's Private Participation in Infrastructure database. Data on ODA disbursements are from the Organisation for Economic Co-operation and Development.

TABLE 7.3. INFORMATION AND COMMUNICATION TECHNOLOGY

Telephone subscribers are subscribers to a main telephone line service, which connects a customer's equipment to the public switched telephone network, or to a cellular telephone service, which uses cellular technology.

Households with own telephone is the percentage of households possessing a telephone.

Average delay for firm in obtaining a telephone connection is the average actual delay in days that firms experience when obtaining a telephone connection, measured from the day the establishment applied to the day it received the service or approval.

Internet users are people with access to the worldwide network.

Duration of telephone outages is the average duration in hours of instances of telephone unavailability related to production.

Telephone faults are the total number of reported faults for the year divided by the total number of mainlines in operation multiplied by 100. The definition of fault can vary. Some countries include faulty customer equipment; others distinguish between reported and actual found faults. There is also sometimes a distinction between residential and business lines. Another consideration is the time period: some countries report this indicator on a monthly basis; in these cases data are converted to yearly estimates.

Price basket for Internet is calculated based on the cheapest available tariff for accessing the Internet 20 hours a month (10 hours peak and 10 hours off-peak). The basket does not include telephone line rental but does include telephone usage charges if applicable. Data are compiled in the national currency and converted to U.S. dollars using the annual average exchange rate.

Cost of 3 minute local phone call during peak hours is the cost of a three-minute local call during peak hours. Local call refers to a call within the same exchange area using the subscriber's own terminal (that is, not from a public telephone).

Cost of 3 minute cellular local call during off-peak hours is the cost of a three-minute cellular local call during off-peak hours.

Cost of 3 minute phone call to the United States (US) during peak hours is the cost of a three-minute call to the United States during peak hours.

Annual investment in telephone service is the annual investment in equipment for fixed telephone service.

Annual investment in mobile communication is the capital investment on equipment for mobile communication networks.

Annual investment in telecommunications is the expenditure associated with acquiring the ownership of telecommunication equipment infrastructure (including supporting land and buildings and intellectual and non-tangible property such as computer software). It includes expenditure on initial installations and on additions to existing installations.

Committed nominal investment in telecommunication projects with private participation is annual committed investment in telecommunication projects with private investment, including projects for fixed or mobile local telephony, domestic long-distance telephony, and international long-distance telephony.

Average annual official development assistance (ODA) disbursements for communications are average annual ODA for communications, including bilateral, multilateral, and other donors.

Source: Data on telephone subscribers, reported phone faults, cost of local and cellular calls, and investment in telephone service, mobile communication, and telecommunications are from the International

Telecommunications Union. Data on households with own telephone are from Demographic and Health Surveys. Data on delays for firms in obtaining a telephone connection and duration of telephone outages, are from World Bank Investment Climate Assessments. Data on Internet users and pricing are from the International Telecommunication Union, *World Telecommunication Development Report* and database, and World Bank estimates. Data on cost of a call to the United States are from the World Bank's Global Development Finance and World Development Indicator databases. Data on committed nominal investment are from the World Bank's Private Participation in Infrastructure database. Data on ODA disbursements are from the Organisation for Economic Co-operation and Development.

TABLE 7.4. ENERGY

Electric power consumption is the production of power plants and combined heat and power plants, less distribution losses and own use by heat and power plants.

GDP per unit of energy use is nominal GDP in purchasing power parity (PPP) U.S. dollars divided by apparent consumption, which is equal to indigenous production plus imports and stock changes minus exports and fuels supplied to ships and aircraft engaged in international transport.

Access to electricity is the percentage of the population living in households with access to electricity.

Solid fuels use is the percentage of the population using solid fuels as opposed to modern fuels. Solid fuels include fuel wood, straw, dung, coal, and charcoal. Modern fuels include electricity, liquefied petroleum gas, natural gas, kerosene, and gasoline.

Average delay for firm in obtaining electrical connection is the average actual delay in days that firms experience when obtaining an electrical connection, measured from the day the establishment applied to the day it received the service or approval.

Electric power transmission and distribution losses are technical and nontechnical losses, including electricity losses due to operation of the system and the delivery of electricity as well as those caused by unmetered supply. This comprises all losses due to transport and distribution of electrical energy and heat.

Electrical outages of firms are the average number of days per year that establishments experienced power outages or surges from the public grid.

Firms that share or own their own generator is the percentage of firms that responded "Yes" to the following question: "Does your establishment own or share a generator?"

Firms identifying electricity as major or very severe obstacle to business operation and growth is the percentage of firms that responded "major" or "very severe" obstacle to the following question: "Please tell us if any of the following issues are a problem for the operation and growth of your business. If an issue (infrastructure, regulation, and permits) poses a problem, please judge its severity as an obstacle on a five-point scale that ranges from 0 = no obstacle to 5 = very severe obstacle."

Committed nominal investment in energy projects with private participation is annual committed investment in energy projects with private investment, including projects for electricity generation, transmission, and distribution as well as natural gas transmission and distribution.

Average annual official development assistance (ODA) disbursements for energy are average annual overseas ODA for energy, including bilateral, multilateral, and other donors).

Source: Data on electric power consumption and PPP GDP per unit of energy use are from the World Bank's World Development Indicators database. Data on access to electricity and solid fuels use are from household survey data, supplemented by World Bank Project Appraisal Documents. Data on delays for firms in obtaining an electrical connection, electrical outages of firms, firms that share or own their own generator, and firms identifying electricity as a major or very severe obstacle to business operation and growth are from World Bank Investment Climate Assessments. Data on transmission and distribution losses are from the World Bank's World Development Indicators database, supplemented by World Bank Project Appraisal Documents. Data on committed nominal investment are from the World Bank's Private Participation in Infrastructure database. Data on ODA disbursements are from the Organisation for Economic Co-operation and Development.

TABLE 7.5. FINANCIAL SECTOR INFRASTRUCTURE

Sovereign ratings are long- and short-term foreign currency ratings.

Gross national savings are the sum of gross domestic savings (table 2.12) and net factor income and net private transfers from abroad. The estimate here also includes net public transfers from abroad.

Money and quasi money (M2) are the sum of currency outside banks, demand deposits other than those of the central government, and the time, savings, and foreign currency deposits of resident sectors other than the central government. This definition of money supply is frequently called M2 and corresponds to lines 34 and 35 in the IMF's *International Financial Statistics*.

Real interest rate is the lending interest rate adjusted for inflation as measured by the gross domestic product (GDP) deflator.

Domestic credit to private sector is financial resources provided to the private sector, such as through loans, purchases of nonequity securities, and trade credits and other accounts receivable, that establish a claim for repayment. For some countries these claims include credit to public enterprises.

Interest rate spread is the interest rate charged by banks on loans to prime customers minus the interest rate paid by commercial or similar banks for demand, time, or savings deposits.

Ratio of bank nonperforming loans to total gross loans is the value of nonperforming loans divided by the total value of the loan portfolio (including nonperforming loans before the deduction of specific loan-loss provisions). The loan amount recorded as nonperforming should be the gross value of the loan as recorded on the balance sheet, not just the amount that is overdue.

Bank branches are deposit money bank branches. See box 8 for a discussion of informal finance.

Listed domestic companies are domestically incorporated companies listed on a country's stock exchanges at the end of the year. They exclude investment companies, mutual funds, and other collective investment vehicles.

Market capitalization of listed companies, also known as market value, is the share price of a listed domestic company's stock times the number of shares outstanding.

Turnover ratio for traded stocks is the total value of shares traded during the period divided by the average market capitalization for the period. Average market capitalization is calculated as the average of the end-of-period values for the current period and the previous period.

Source: Data on sovereign ratings are from Fitch Ratings. Data on gross national savings are from World Bank country desks. Data on money and quasi money and domestic credit to the private sector are from the IMF's International Financial Statistics database and data files, World Bank and OECD estimates of GDP, and the World Bank's World Development Indicators database. Data on real interest rates are from the IMF's International Financial Statistics database and data files using World Bank data on the GDP deflator and the World Bank's World Development Indicators database. Data on interest rate spreads are from the IMF's International Financial Statistics database and data files and the World Bank's World Development Indicators database. Data on ratios of bank nonperforming loans to total are from the IMF's *Global Financial Stability Report* and the World Bank's World Development Indicators database. Data on bank branches are from surveys of banking and regulatory institutions by the World Bank's Research Department and Financial Sector and Operations Policy Department and the World Development Indicators database. Data on listed domestic companies and turnover ratios for traded stocks are from Standard & Poor's *Emerging Stock Markets Factbook* and supplemental data and the World Bank's World Development Indicators database. Data on market capitalization of listed companies are from Standard & Poor's *Emerging Stock Markets Factbook* and supplemental data, World Bank and OECD estimates of GDP, and the World Bank's World Development Indicators database.

8. Human development

TABLE 8.1. EDUCATION

Youth literacy rate is the percentage of people ages 15–24 who can, with understanding, both read and write a short, simple statement about their everyday life.

| Box 8 | **What is informal finance?** |

Financial services such as payment, savings, credit, and insurance services are an important lubricant for a vibrant market-based economy. By facilitating the exchange of goods and services between people and over time, pooling savings and intermediating them to investment projects, and insuring people against shocks and allowing them to save for retirement, financial institutions and markets are important drivers of economic development. They are especially important in Africa's fight to reach the Millennium Development Goal target of halving poverty by 2015. While academics and policymakers are typically concerned with formal finance—with financial institutions and markets that are regulated and supervised by government authorities—a wide array of informal and semiformal institutions and markets also provide important services.

Informal finance is a broad concept, encompassing a wide variety of services and relationships ranging from loans from friends and family to informal savings and credit clubs to moneylenders. Informal does not necessarily mean illegal, but rather financial service provision outside the oversight of any government authority. This includes professional money lenders, credit linked to trade or rent agreements, deposit collectors (also known as *susu* or *esusu* collectors in West Africa), informal burial societies, *hawala* and other ethnically based international money transfer businesses, and a variety of savings and credit associations, including rotating credit and savings associations, *stokvels*, and *tontines.* Unlike most formal financial relationships, informal finance is based on personal relationships and socioeconomic proximity. Most providers focus on only one service—savings, credit, payment, or insurance rather than offering a bundle of services as many formal financial providers do. The relative importance of different informal financial providers varies across countries and regions.

The line between formal and informal finance, however, is not clear cut. A number of financial institutions could be described as semiformal, such as savings and credit cooperative societies or microcredit projects that have to register with public authorities, but are not subject to any regulation or supervision.

Informal finance is an important stage in the development process. In 19th century Western Europe informal financial arrangement flourished in a wide range of institutional forms. In France, for example, notaries were financial intermediaries for the nascent manufacturing and trade sectors (Cull and others 2006). But even today, unregistered (and therefore usually illegal) moneylenders continue to operate in deprived neighborhoods of even the richest economies. While precise data are missing, anecdotal evidence suggests that the importance of informal finance decreases as economies develop; the formal financial system becomes more efficient in reaching out and formal financial services become more affordable to larger shares of the population. Also, some informal financial providers will become formal and thus subject to regulatory and supervisory frameworks.

Collecting data

While aggregate data on formal financial institutions and markets are readily available, they are not for informal financial institutions. It is thus impossible to quantify the importance of informal compared with formal finance. Data on access to and use of formal financial services have only recently become available, and data on use of informal financial services are still limited to a few individual countries. But estimates suggest that in many Sub-Saharan countries less than 20 percent of the population have access to formal financial services, leaving some 80 percent of the population to use at least one informal financial service. While surveys of small formal enterprises indicate that less than 10 percent of working capital and new investment is financed with resources from informal lenders and friends and families, this share is likely higher for informal enterprises, though, there is significant overlap between the clientele of formal and informal financial service providers.

While household and firm-level surveys can give a good cross-sectional snapshot of how much of the population uses formal and informal financial services, financial diaries can document the financial life of low-income people over time (see, for example, www.financialdiaries.com). In South Africa diaries have shown that low-income people use an average of 4 savings, 2 insurance, and 11 credit instruments and a mix of formal and informal providers. Diaries can also help explain the needs for financial services and advice to help policymakers and commercial financial institutions develop policies and products.

Overcoming data challenges

An array of data collection efforts is needed to provide a better picture of who has access to and uses which financial services. While investment climate surveys have gone far as a consistent cross-country source of firm financing data, a similar instrument is still in development on the household side. Micro studies are time- and cost-intensive and typically cannot be undertaken frequently. But combining household- or firm-level data with aggregate data such as deposit or loan accounts can help track countries more frequently and allow cross-country comparisons.

While cross-country comparisons are important, country-specific details must be taken into account, including barriers that impede clients from accessing formal financial services. This is important for policymakers because formal financial services, able to reach out beyond limited sociogeographic areas, are generally more efficient. Also, little information is available on costs and interest rates in informal finance beyond the anecdotal evidence that moneylenders charge very high interest rates, while friends and family often charge no interest.

Adult literacy rate is the proportion of adults ages 15 and older who can, with understanding, read and write a short, simple statement on their everyday life.

Primary education provides children with basic reading, writing, and mathematics skills along with an elementary understanding of such subjects as history, geography, natural science, social science, art, and music.

Secondary education completes the provision of basic education that began at the primary level and aims to lay the foundations for lifelong learning and human development by offering more subject- or skill-oriented instruction using more specialized teachers.

Tertiary education, whether or not at an advanced research qualification, normally requires, as a minimum condition of admission, the successful completion of education at the secondary level.

Gross enrollment ratio is the ratio of total enrollment, regardless of age, to the population of the age group that officially corresponds to the level of education shown.

Net enrollment ratio is the ratio of children of official school age based on the International Standard Classification of Education 1997 who are enrolled in school to the population of the corresponding official school age.

Student-teacher ratio is the number of students enrolled in school divided by the number of teachers, regardless of their teaching assignment.

Public spending on education is current and capital public expenditure on education plus subsidies to private education at the primary, secondary, and tertiary levels by local, regional, and national government, including municipalities. It excludes household contributions.

Source: United Nations Educational, Scientific, and Cultural Organization Institute for Statistics.

TABLE 8.2. HEALTH
Life expectancy at birth is the number of years a newborn infant would live if prevailing patterns of mortality at the time of its birth were to remain the same throughout its life. Data are World Bank estimates based on data from the United Nations Population Division, the United Nations Statistics Division, and national statistical offices.

Under-five mortality rate is the probability that a newborn baby will die before reaching age 5, if subject to current age-specific mortality rates. The probability is expressed as a rate per 1,000.

Infant mortality rate is the number of infants dying before reaching one year of age, per 1,000 live births.

Maternal mortality ratio, modeled estimate, is the number of women who die from pregnancy-related causes during pregnancy and childbirth, per 100,000 live births.

Prevalence of HIV is the percentage of people ages 15–49 who are infected with HIV.

Incidence of tuberculosis is the number of tuberculosis cases (pulmonary, smear positive, and extrapulmonary) in a population at a given point in time, per 100,000 people. This indicator is sometimes referred to as "point prevalence." Estimates include cases of tuberculosis among people with HIV.

Deaths due to malaria is the number of malaria deaths per 100,000 people.

Child immunization rate is the percentage of children ages 12–23 months who received vaccinations before 12 months or at any time before the survey for four diseases—measles and diphtheria, pertussis (whooping cough), and tetanus (DPT). A child is considered adequately immunized against measles after receiving one dose of vaccine and against DPT after receiving three doses.

Stunting is the percentage of children under age 5 whose height for age is more than two standard deviations below the median for the international reference population ages 0–59 months. For children up to two years of age height is measured by recumbent length. For older children height is measured by stature while standing. The reference population adopted by the World Health Organization in 1983 is based on children from the United States, who are assumed to be well nourished.

Underweight is the percentage of children under age 5 whose weight for age is more than two standard deviations below the median reference standard for their age as established by the World Health Organization, the U.S. Centers for Disease Control and Prevention, and the U.S. National Center for Health Statistics. Data are based on children under age 3, 4, or 5, depending on the country.

Births attended by skilled health staff are the percentage of deliveries attended by personnel trained to give the necessary supervision, care, and advice to women during pregnancy, labor, and the postpartum period; to conduct deliveries on their own; and to care for newborns.

Contraceptive prevalence rate is the percentage of women who are practicing, or whose sexual partners are practicing, any form of contraception. It is usually measured for married women ages 15–49 only.

Children sleeping under insecticide-treated bednets is the percentage of children under age 5 with access to an insecticide-treated bednet to prevent malaria.

Tuberculosis cases detected under DOTS are the percentage of estimated new infectious tuberculosis cases detected under DOTS, the internationally recommended tuberculosis control strategy.

Tuberculosis treatment success rate is the percentage of new smear-positive tuberculosis cases registered under DOTS in a given year that successfully completed treatment, whether with bacteriologic evidence of success ("cured") or without ("treatment completed").

Children with fever receiving antimalarial drugs are the percentage of children under age 5 in malaria-risk areas with fever being treated with effective antimalarial drugs.

Population with sustainable access to an improved water source is the percentage of the population with reasonable access to an adequate amount of water from an improved source, such as a household connection, public standpipe, borehole, protected well or spring, or rainwater collection. Unimproved sources include vendors, tanker trucks, and unprotected wells and springs. Reasonable access is defined as the availability of at least 20 liters a person a day from a source within 1 kilometer of the dwelling. See box 9 for a discussion of using Demographic and Health Surveys to measure access to infrastructure, including water and sanitation infrastructure.

Population with sustainable access to improved sanitation is the percentage of the population with at least adequate access to excreta disposal facilities that can effectively prevent human, animal, and insect contact with excreta. Improved facilities range from simple but protected pit latrines to flush toilets with a sewerage connection. The excreta disposal system is considered adequate if it is private or shared (but not public) and if it hygienically separates human excreta from human contact. To be effective, facilities must be correctly constructed and properly maintained.

Physicians are the number of physicians, including generalists and specialists.

Nurses are the number of nurses, including professional nurses, auxiliary nurses, enrolled nurses, and other nurses, such as dental nurses and primary care nurses.

Midwives are the number of midwives, including professional midwives, auxiliary midwives, and enrolled midwives. Traditional birth attendants, who are counted as community health workers, are not included.

Total health expenditure is the sum of public and private health expenditure. It covers the provision of health services (preventive and curative), family planning activities, nutrition activities, and emergency aid designated for health but does not include provision of water and sanitation.

Public health expenditure consists of recurrent and capital spending from government (central and local) budgets, external borrowing and grants (including donations from international agencies and nongovernmental organizations), and social (or compulsory) health insurance funds.

Private health expenditure includes direct household (out-of-pocket) spending, private insurance, charitable donations, and direct service payments by private corporations.

Out-of-pocket health expenditure is any direct outlay by households, including gratuities and in-kind payments, to health practitioners and suppliers of pharmaceuticals, therapeutic appliances, and other goods and services whose primary intent is to contribute to the restoration or enhancement of the health status of individuals or population groups. It is a part of private health expenditure.

Health expenditure per capita is the total health expenditure is the sum of public and private health expenditures as a ratio of total population. It covers the provision of health services (preventive and curative), family planning activities, nutrition activities, and emergency aid designated for health but does

Household surveys have long been used to estimate poverty and inequality trends but not to the same extent to assess trends in access to infrastructure. A recent study in Africa used Demographic and Health Surveys from 22 countries that have conducted at least two surveys between 1990 and 2005 to collect comparable information across countries on access to water, electricity, and sanitation over time. To conduct a distributional analysis of access, an asset index was constructed using principal components analysis, and households were divided into five quintiles of population by their level of wealth or assets.

The difficulty in estimating the Africawide trend in access rates stems from the fact that the panel of countries or surveys is not balanced. Countries have observations for different years. So three alternative methods were used to estimate overall access trends. The first method includes only the 11 countries for which there are data for three time periods, 1990–95, 1996–2000, and 2001–05. The second method includes countries with data for only one or two time periods. For countries with data for only one time period the data are used for all three time periods, assuming no change over time in access. If data are available for two periods, the annual growth rate in coverage between the two periods is used to estimate the rate for the third period. The third method is similar but assumes that access rates cannot fall more than population growth. If access rates in the third period drop by more than what would be observed assuming no growth in the total number of connections, the survey data for the third period are replaced with the coverage rate in the second period times the ratio of the population in the second period divided by the population in the third period.

Issues of comparability between surveys in some countries and the need to correct for some outliers mean that the preferred estimates for this analysis are from the third method.

The results from all three methods suggest that access rates for electricity and a flush toilet have improved slightly over time but that rates for access to piped water have not (see table). Access rates within urban and rural areas have not changed much (except for countries with rural electrification projects), which suggests that migration from rural to urban areas has contributed to the higher access rates. Finally, the gains in access to electricity have been better shared across wealth groups (except for the very poor) than have the gains in access to flush toilets, which tend to have benefited the richest households the most. Among the poorest quintile access to all three basic infrastructure services remains virtually inexistent.

Trends in access to basic infrastructure services in Africa, 1990–2005 (percent)

Subgroup and method	Piped water		2001–05	Electricity		2001–05	Flush toilet		2001–05
National									
Method 1	12	13	10	19	29	34	7	8	10
Method 2	17	17	15	23	28	31	10	10	11
Method 3	17	17	16	23	28	29	10	10	12
Urban									
Method 1	38	34	25	67	72	72	26	27	26
Method 2	49	44	37	70	70	70	35	32	30
Method 3	49	44	40	70	70	70	35	32	30
Rural									
Method 1	4	4	4	5	13	16	1	2	3
Method 2	4	4	4	6	10	13	1	1	2
Method 3	4	4	4	6	10	13	1	1	2
Poorest quintile									
Method 1	0	0	0	0	1	5	0	0	0
Method 2	0	0	0	0	2	3	0	0	0
Method 3	0	0	0	0	2	3	0	0	0
Second quintile									
Method 1	1	2	1	2	8	19	0	0	1
Method 2	3	4	3	2	8	32	1	1	1
Method 3	3	4	4	2	8	32	1	1	1
Third quintile									
Method 1	3	3	4	6	20	22	2	1	2
Method 2	9	8	19	12	19	25	4	4	13
Method 3	9	8	20	12	19	25	4	4	13
Fourth quintile									
Method 1	14	12	13	24	41	45	7	5	7
Method 2	33	19	19	27	36	40	15	12	17
Method 3	33	19	20	27	36	40	15	12	17
Richest quintile									
Method 1	42	46	35	63	73	77	27	36	41
Method 2	47	48	42	65	69	71	31	34	36
Method 3	47	48	48	65	69	71	31	34	36

Source: Banerjee and others 2007.

not include provision of water and sanitation. Data are in current U.S. dollars.

Source: Data are from the latest Core Health Indicators from World Health Organization sources, including *World Health Statistics 2006* and *World Health Report 2006* (http:// www3.who.int/whosis/core/core_select.cfm ?path=whosis,core&language=english). Data on health expenditure are from the World Health Organization' *World Health Report* and updates and from the Organisation for Economic Co-operation and Development for its member countries, supplemented by World

Bank poverty assessments and country and sector studies, and household surveys conducted by governments or by statistical or international organizations.

9. Agriculture, rural development, and environment

TABLE 9.1. RURAL DEVELOPMENT

Rural population is the difference between the total population and the urban population.

Rural population density is the rural population divided by the arable land area. Arable land includes land defined by the Food and Agriculture Organization (FAO) as land under temporary crops (double-cropped areas are counted once), temporary meadows for mowing or for pasture, land under market or kitchen gardens, and land temporarily fallow. Land abandoned as a result of shifting cultivation is excluded.

Rural population below the national poverty line is the percentage of the rural population living below the national poverty line.

Share of rural population with sustainable access to an improved water source is the percentage of the rural population with reasonable access to an adequate amount of water from an improved source, such as a household connection, public standpipe, borehole, protected well or spring, or rainwater collection. Unimproved sources include vendors, tanker trucks, and unprotected wells and springs. Reasonable access is defined as the availability of at least 20 liters a person a day from a source within 1 kilometer of the dwelling.

Share of rural population with sustainable access to improved sanitation facilities is the percentage of the rural population with at least adequate access to excreta disposal facilities that can effectively prevent human, animal, and insect contact with excreta. Improved facilities range from simple but protected pit latrines to flush toilets with a sewerage connection. The excreta disposal system is considered adequate if it is private or shared (but not public) and if it hygienically separates human excreta from human contact. To be effective, facilities must be correctly constructed and properly maintained.

Share of rural population with access to electricity is the percentage of the rural population living in households with access to electricity.

Share of rural population with access to transportation is the percentage of the rural population who live within 2 kilometers of an all-season passable road as a share of the total rural population.

Share of rural households with access to a landline telephone is the percentage of rural households possessing a telephone.

Source: Data on rural population are calculated from urban population shares from the United Nations Population Division's *World Urbanization Prospects* and from total population figures from the World Bank. Data on rural population density are from the FAO and World Bank population estimates. Data on rural population below the poverty line are national estimates based on population-weighted subgroup estimates from household surveys. Data on rural population with access to water and rural population with access to sanitation are from World Health Organization and United Nations Children's Fund's *Meeting the MDG Water and Sanitation Target* (www.unicef.org/wes/mdgreport). Data on rural population with access to electricity are from household survey data, supplemented by World Bank Project Appraisal Documents. Data on rural population with access to transport are from the World Bank's Sub-Saharan Africa Transport Policy Program (SSATP). Data on rural households with own telephone are from Demographic and Health Surveys.

TABLE 9.2. AGRICULTURE

Agriculture value added is shown at factor cost in current U.S. dollars divided by nominal gross domestic product. Value added in agriculture comprises the gross output of forestry, hunting, and fishing less the value of their intermediate inputs. However, for Botswana, Cameroon, Chad, Democratic Republic of Congo, Republic of Congo, Gabon, Guinea, Madagascar, Mali, Morocco, Niger, Rwanda, Senegal, Togo, and Zambia, it is shown at market prices, that is, including intermediate inputs.

Crop production index shows agricultural production for each year relative to the base period 1999–2001. It includes all crops except fodder crops. Regional and income group aggregates for the Food and Agriculture Organization's (FAO) production indexes are calculated from the underlying values in international dollars, normalized to the base period 1999–2001.

Food production index covers food crops that are considered edible and that contain nutrients. Coffee and tea are excluded because, although edible, they have no nutritive value.

Livestock production index includes meat and milk from all sources, dairy products such as cheese, and eggs, honey, raw silk, wool, and hides and skins.

Cereal production is crops harvested for dry grain only. Cereals include wheat, rice, maize, barley, oats, rye, millet, sorghum, buckwheat, and mixed grains. Cereal crops harvested for hay or harvested green for food, feed, or silage and those used for grazing are excluded.

Agricultural exports and *imports* are expressed in current U.S. dollars at free on board prices. The term agriculture in trade refers to both food and agriculture and does not include forestry and fishery products.

Food exports and *imports* are expressed in current U.S. dollars at free on board prices.

Permanent cropland is land cultivated with crops that occupy the land for long periods and need not be replanted after each harvest, such as cocoa, coffee, and rubber. It includes land under flowering shrubs, fruit trees, nut trees, and vines, but excludes land under trees grown for wood or timber.

Cereal cropland refers to harvested area, although some countries report only sown or cultivated area.

Irrigated land is areas equipped to provide water to the crops, including areas equipped for full and partial control irrigation, spate irrigation areas, and equipped wetland or inland valley bottoms.

Fertilizer consumption is the aggregate of nitrogenous, phosphate, and potash fertilizers.

Agricultural machinery refers to the number of wheel and crawler tractors (excluding garden tractors) in use in agriculture at the end of the calendar year specified or during the first quarter of the following year. Arable land includes land defined by the FAO as land under temporary crops (double-cropped areas are counted once), temporary meadows for mowing or for pasture, land under market or kitchen gardens, and land temporarily fallow. Land abandoned as a result of shifting cultivation is excluded.

Agricultural employment includes people who work for a public or private employer and who receive remuneration in wages, salary, commission, tips, piece rates, or pay in kind. Agriculture corresponds to division 1 (International Standard Industrial Classification, ISIC, revision 2) or tabulation categories A and B (ISIC revision 3) and includes hunting, forestry, and fishing.

Incidence of drought shows whether a country experienced a significant shortage of rain that unfavorably affected agricultural production.

Agriculture value added per worker is the output of the agricultural sector (ISIC divisions 1–5) less the value of intermediate inputs. Agriculture comprises value added from forestry, hunting, and fishing as well as cultivation of crops and livestock production. Data are in constant 2000 U.S. dollars.

Cereal yield is includes wheat, rice, maize, barley, oats, rye, millet, sorghum, buckwheat, and mixed grains. Production data on cereals relate to crops harvested for dry grain only. Cereal crops harvested for hay or harvested green for food, feed, or silage and those used for grazing are excluded.

Source: Data on agriculture value added are from World Bank country desks. Data on crop, food, livestock, and cereal production, agricultural exports and imports, permanent cropland, cereal cropland, and agricultural machinery are from the FAO. Data on irrigated land are from the FAO's *Production Yearbook* and data files. Data on fertilizer consumption are from the FAO database for the *Fertilizer Yearbook*. Data on agricultural employment are from the International Labour Organization. Data on incidence of drought are from the Southern Africa Flood and Drought Network and East Africa Drought (CE). Data on agriculture value added per worker are from World Bank national accounts files and the FAO's *Production Yearbook* and data files.

TABLE 9.3. ENVIRONMENT

Forest area is land under natural or planted stands of trees, whether productive or not.

Average annual deforestation refers to the permanent conversion of natural forest area to other uses, including shifting cultivation, permanent agriculture, ranching, settlements, and infrastructure development. Deforested areas do not include areas logged but intended for regeneration or areas degraded by fuelwood gathering, acid precipitation, or forest fires. Negative numbers indicate an increase in forest area.

Renewable internal fresh water resources refer to internal renewable resources (internal river flows and groundwater from rainfall) in the country.

Annual fresh water withdrawals refer to total water withdrawals, not counting evaporation losses from storage basins. Withdrawals also include water from desalination plants in countries where they are a significant source. Withdrawals can exceed 100 percent of total renewable resources where extraction from nonrenewable aquifers or desalination plants is considerable or where there is significant water reuse. Withdrawals for agriculture and industry are total withdrawals for irrigation and livestock production and for direct industrial use (including withdrawals for cooling thermoelectric plants). Withdrawals for domestic uses include drinking water, municipal use or supply, and use for public services, commercial establishments, and homes.

Water productivity is calculated as gross domestic product in constant prices divided by annual total water withdrawal. Sectoral water productivity is calculated as annual value added in agriculture or industry divided by water withdrawal in each sector.

Emissions of organic water pollutants are measured in terms of biochemical oxygen demand, which refers to the amount of oxygen that bacteria in water will consume in breaking down waste. This is a standard water-treatment test for the presence of organic pollutants.

Energy production refers to forms of primary energy—petroleum (crude oil, natural gas liquids, and oil from nonconventional sources), natural gas, solid fuels (coal, lignite, and other derived fuels), and combustible renewables and waste—and primary electricity, all converted into oil equivalents.

Energy use refers to use of primary energy before transformation to other end-use fuels, which is equal to indigenous production plus imports and stock changes, minus exports and fuels supplied to ships and aircraft engaged in international transport.

Combustible renewables and waste comprise solid biomass, liquid biomass, biogas, industrial waste, and municipal waste, measured as a percentage of total energy use.

Carbon dioxide emissions are those stemming from the burning of fossil fuels and the manufacture of cement. They include carbon dioxide produced during consumption of solid, liquid, and gas fuels and gas flaring.

Source: Data on forest area and deforestation are from the Food and Agriculture Organization's (FAO) Global Forest Resources Assessment 2005. Data on fresh water resources and withdrawals are from the World Resources Institute, supplemented by the FAO's AQUASTAT data. Data on emissions of organic water pollutants are from the World Bank. Data on energy production and use and combustible renewables and waste are from the International Energy Agency. Data on carbon dioxide emissions are from Carbon Dioxide Information Analysis Center, Environmental Sciences Division, Oak Ridge National Laboratory, in the U.S. state of Tennessee.

10. Labor, migration, and population

TABLE 10.1. LABOR FORCE PARTICIPATION
Labor force is people ages 15 and older who meet the International Labour Organization (ILO) definition of the economically active population. It includes both the employed and the unemployed. While national practices vary in the treatment of such groups as the armed forces and seasonal or part-time workers, the labor force generally includes the armed forces, the unemployed, and first-time job-seekers, but excludes homemakers and other unpaid caregivers and workers in the informal sector. See box 10 for a discussion of employment in the informal sector and informal employment.

Participation rate is the percentage of the population ages 15–64 that is economically active, that is, all people who supply labor for the production of goods and services during a specified period.

Source: International Labour Organization, Global Employment Trends Model 2006, Employment Trends Team.

TABLE 10.2. LABOR FORCE COMPOSITION
Agriculture corresponds to division 1 (International Standard Industrial Classification, ISIC, revision 2) or tabulation categories A

| Box 10 | Employment in the informal sector and informal employment |

The informal sector accounts for the bulk of nonagricultural employment in developing countries and is particularly notable in the poorest countries, where it has grown in recent decades. In Sub-Saharan Africa the informal sector accounts for as much as 78 percent of nonagricultural employment and 41 percent of gross domestic product (ILO 2002), and serves as the main source of job creation. Given its vital role, measuring and describing informal activity have become increasingly important to designing poverty reduction and growth strategies and to understanding labor markets.

Defining and quantifying informality are complicated by the informal sector's high degree of heterogeneity. The concept is intuitively linked to a variety of characteristics that range from operating outside existing labor regulation, not paying payroll taxes, not having a license or registration, not being firmly established, having very low productivity, being owner operated and having few employees, and the like. Some of those characteristics can be seen as pertaining to a firm's operation, and others to the contractual relationship between the employee and the employers. The informal sector could therefore be understood to include those who are self-employed or wage workers in informal firms, workers at formal firms without legal protections or permanent contracts, "homeworkers" (home-based industrial outworkers), apprentices, unpaid family workers, and domestic workers.

The International Labour Organization, in two International Conferences of Labour Statisticians (ICLS 15 and 17), has rationalized the framework for measuring this phenomenon by adopting a resolution on the statistical definition of employment in the informal sector, first, and then broadening the concept to arrive at measures of informal employment. Such definitions might not do justice to the variety of meanings attached to the concept (for example, it has been argued that formality should be seen as a continuum rather than a clearly defined state), but they offer a solid basis for international comparisons. Because people can hold multiple jobs, the unit of measurement for informal employment is jobs rather than employed persons.

Employment in the informal sector is defined as "all jobs in informal sector enterprises or all persons who, during a given reference period, were employed in at least one informal sector enterprises, irrespective of their status in employment and whether it was their main or secondary jobs" (Hussmans 2004).

Informal sector enterprises are those that satisfy four criteria:

- They are private unincorporated enterprises (because they are not separate legal entities it is impossible to separate their activities from other activities of their owner).
- They produce at least some goods meant for sale.
- They are limited in employment size, with the threshold determined by national circumstances (though an expert working group recommended that international comparisons be conducted on the basis of less than five workers).
- They are engaged in nonagricultural activities.

The definition of *informal employment* recognizes that informal jobs may also be found in production units that are not in the informal sector. Thus, in addition to employment in the informal sector, the definition includes informal employment outside the informal sector, characterized as "an employment relation that is, in law or practice, not subject to national labour legislation, income taxation, social protection or entitlement to certain employment benefits" (Hussmanns 2004, p. 6).

In practice, informal employment outside the informal sector comprises employees in formal enterprises or households whose employment relations do not comply with labor regulations, contributing family workers in either formal or informal enterprises (because they typically do not have written contracts of employment), and own-account workers engaged in production of goods for final consumption for the households when such production "represents an important contribution to the total consumption of the household" (Hussmanns 2004, p. 6).

Labor force surveys are the best means for monitoring these indicators, though difficulties arise when employees are unaware of the information used to identify informal firms (such as legal organization, bookkeeping, and registration), when lack of probing leads to productive activities that would be considered informal being reported as formal employment, when information is limited to main jobs, and when information is unavailable for periods longer than a weekly recall, given the seasonal nature of some activities. It is also practically impossible to estimate the number of informal sector enterprises from labor force surveys because the surveys are household based rather than firm based.

Moreover, data on informal workers beyond those working for informal firms (such as homeworkers and casual workers) are quite scarce. Efforts to measure and characterize the informal sector should therefore recognize limitations inherent in the available data and use innovative methods to attempt to capture its heterogeneity.

One example of how to address these issues in practice comes from Ethiopia. The Ethiopian Central Statistical Authority's Labor Force Survey and Urban Employment and Unemployment Survey use a definition of the informal sector based on the characteristics of the firm in which respondents work. They define informal businesses as those that do not keep proper accounts, that do not have a business license, or that have fewer than 10 employees. Because the answers to these questions are not recorded separately,[1] it is impossible to change the criterion for identification (and there is no separate information on size of the firm, for example, which could allow for a fine tuning of the definition or adoption of a different cutoff). This definition leads to an estimate of urban employment in the informal sector of 44 percent of people ages 15 and older (see table). This estimate is considerably lower than the available estimates for Africa as a whole, which is about 60 percent in urban areas.

The surveys do not systematically collect information on the contractual relationship with the employer to fully capture informal employment. Nevertheless additional categories of workers in

Ethiopia: employment in the informal sector and informal employment, urban, ages 15 and older, 2004 (percent)

	Employment in the informal sector[a]	Informal employment[b]
Total	43.5	54.2
Male	39.4	52.1
Female	49.1	57.0

a. Employed in a business that holds no account book, has no license, or employs fewer than 10 employees.
b. Employed in a business that holds no account book, has no license, employs fewer than 10 employees; is an employee domestic, self-employed, apprentice, or unpaid family worker; or paid only in kind.
Note: Data are for employment in the seven days before the survey.
Source: Ethiopia Urban Employment and Unemployment Survey 2004.

informal contractual relationships (or very likely to be) can be identified, such as domestic employees, self-employed people (who appear to be negligible in the survey), apprentices, unpaid family workers, and workers paid only in kind. Adding these categories to bring the measurement closer to the International Labour Organization definition raises the rate of informality to 54 percent of workers. Such a significant increase underscores the need for caution in making cross-country comparisons using nonstandardized data.

Important limitations of these estimates are the surveys' focus on primary jobs only, excluding secondary activities, which are more likely to be informal, and the surveys' likely neglect of migrants, who might not be adequately covered in existing sample frames. Extending sample frames to marginal areas, particularly at times of rapid urbanization, and exploring alternative survey techniques, such as recapture methods, can reach a better understanding of the size of important informal activities such as street vending.

Challenges also typically arise in comparing wages in the formal and informal sectors. In Ethiopia's labor force surveys, for example, wage information is not collected for several categories of informal workers, given the difficulties in accounting for in-kind payments and the lack of complete bookkeeping in informal firms. However, knowing about wages is important for understanding well-being among informal sector workers and thus for guiding policymaking. Complementing data analysis with qualitative work may be the best way to arrive at a more nuanced, country-specific assessment of informality.

1. The questions in the Labor Force Survey were nested so that if the firm did not keep books, respondents were asked if the firm had less than 10 employees; if so, respondents were asked if it had a license. Such questioning restricts the definition to keeping books as the broadest possible criterion.

Source: Hussmans 2004.

and B (ISIC revision 3) and includes hunting, forestry, and fishing.

Industry corresponds to divisions 2–5 (ISIC revision 2) or tabulation categories C–F (ISIC revision 3) and includes mining and quarrying (including oil production), manufacturing, construction, and public utilities (electricity, gas, and water).

Services correspond to divisions 6–9 (ISIC revision 2) or tabulation categories G–P (ISIC revision 3) and include wholesale and retail trade and restaurants and hotels; transport, storage, and communications; financing, insurance, real estate, and business services; and community, social, and personal services.

Wage and salaried workers (employees) are workers who hold the type of jobs defined as paid employment jobs, where incumbents hold explicit (written or oral) or implicit employment contracts that give them a basic remuneration that is not directly dependent on the revenue of the unit for which they work.

Self-employed workers are self-employed workers with employees (employers), self-employed workers with without employees (own-account workers), and members of producer cooperatives. Although the contributing family workers category is technically part of the self-employed according to the classification used by the International Labour Organization (ILO), and could therefore be combined with the other self-employed categories to derive the total self-employed, they are reported here as a separate category in order to emphasize the difference between the two statuses, since the socioeconomic implications associated with each status can be significantly varied. This practice follows that of the ILO's *Key Indicators of the Labour Market.*

Contributing family workers (unpaid workers) are workers who hold self-employment jobs as own-account workers in a market-oriented establishment operated by a related person living in the same household.

Source: Data are from the ILO's *Key Indicators of the Labour Market,* fourth edition.

TABLE 10.3. MIGRATION AND POPULATION

Stock is the number of people born in a country other than that in which they live. It includes refugees.

Net migration is the net average annual number of migrants during the period, that is, the annual number of immigrants less the annual number of emigrants, including both citizens and noncitizens. Data are five-year estimates.

Workers remittances received comprise current transfers by migrant workers and wages and salaries by nonresident workers. See box 11 for a discussion of remittances in Africa.

Population is World Bank estimates, usually projected from the most recent population censuses or surveys (mostly from 1980–2004). Refugees not permanently settled in the country of asylum are generally considered to be part of the population of their country of origin.

Fertility rate is the number of children that would be born to a woman if she were to live to the end of her childbearing years and bear children in accordance with current age-specific fertility rates.

Age composition refers to the percentage of the total population that is in specific age groups.

Dependency ratio is the ratio of dependents—people younger than 15 or older than 64—to the working-age population—those ages 15–64.

Rural population is calculated as the difference between the total population and the urban population.

Urban population is midyear population of areas defined as urban in each country.

Source: World Bank's World Development Indicators database.

11. HIV/AIDS

TABLE 11.1. HIV/AIDS

Estimated number of people living with HIV/AIDS is the number of people in the relevant age group living with HIV.

Estimated prevalence rate is the percentage of the population of the relevant age group who are infected with HIV. Depending on the reliability of the data available, there may be more or less uncertainty surrounding each estimate. Therefore, plausible bounds have been presented for adult rate (low and high estimate).

Deaths due to HIV/AIDS are the estimated number of adults and children that have died in a specific year based in the modeling of HIV surveillance data using standard and appropriate tools.

AIDS orphans are the estimated number of children who have lost their mother or both parents to AIDS before age 17 since the epidemic began in 1990. Some of the orphaned children included in this cumulative total are no longer alive; others are no longer under age 17.

Source: The Joint United Nations Programme on HIV/AIDS and the World Health Organization's *2006 Report on the Global AIDS Epidemic.*

12. Malaria

TABLE 12.1. MALARIA

Population is World Bank estimates, usually projected from the most recent population censuses or surveys (mostly from 1980–2004). Refugees not permanently settled in the country of asylum are generally considered to be part of the population of their country of origin.

Endemic risk of malaria is the percentage of the population living in areas with significant annual transmission of malaria, be it seasonal or perennial.

Epidemic risk of malaria is the percentage of the population living in areas prone to distinct interannual variation, with no transmission taking place at all in some years.

Negligible risk of malaria is the percentage of the population living in areas where malaria is ordinarily not present and where the risk of malaria outbreaks is negligible.

Deaths due to malaria are the number of malaria deaths per 100,000 people.

Under-five mortality rate is the probability that a newborn baby will die before reaching age 5, if subject to current age-specific mortality rates. The probability is expressed as a rate per 1,000.

Children sleeping under insecticide-treated bednets is the percentage of children under age 5 with access to an insecticide-treated bednet to prevent malaria.

Children with fever receiving antimalarial treatment within 24 hours are the percentage

Box 11   Remittances in Africa

Workers remittances have emerged as a major source of external development finance in recent years. Because of the large size of remittances, governments in developing and developed countries have focused on the development impact of remittances and on regulatory issues in sending and receiving remittances. Reliable data on remittances are hard to come by. While the International Monetary Fund publishes statistics on "workers remittances, compensation of employees, and migrants transfers," the data are not comprehensively reported, nor do they capture monetary flows outside formal financial channels.

Issues to consider in quantifying remittances

Workers remittances have been understood to be a migrants' earnings sent from abroad to relatives in their country of origin to meet economic and financial obligations. Interest has been growing in the concept of residence and in information on migrant workers and their associated remittances flows. One problem with measurement is the difficulty of determining actual length of stay and of applying the concept of residency to distinguish between compensation of employees and workers remittances.

A way around this is to use the concept of household to household transactions to capture the component of personal transfers instead. It is important to use broader definitions of remittances, including personal remittances and institutional remittances. The International Monetary Fund recently completed a draft of the sixth edition of the *Balance of Payments and International Investment Position Manual* which introduces the term *personal transfers,* which comprises all current transfers in cash or in kind made or received by resident households to or form other nonresident households (IMF Committee on Balance of Payments Statistics 2006). This term will replace the component *workers' remittances.* The sixth edition will include a new concept of remittances for measuring and analyzing international remittances and resource flows to households and nonprofit institutions serving households. Three categories of remittances would be introduced: personal remittances, total remittances, and total remittances and transfers to nonprofit institutions serving households (IMF 2007).

Countries do not apply the concepts uniformly. Data deficiencies and data omissions further cloud the picture. Data inaccuracy stems from problems associated with knowing the universe of remitters and the intermediaries facilitating the process, enforcing data collection, maintaining a line of communication with intermediaries and other relevant organizations, and possessing the appropriate methodologies to capture the data (Orozco 2005).

Consider Ghana. The Bank of Ghana reports the value of international remittances for 2005 as $99.2 million, but the Ghana minister of finance recently announced that international remittances in 2006 totaled $1.8 billion, leading to confusion. In April the Bank of Ghana reported that it estimated total private transfers made to "nongovernmental organizations, embassies, service providers, individuals, and the like" at $5.8 billion. Only a portion of these transfers are remittances; the rest are payments to service providers,

foreign direct investment, investment income, and portfolio investment (Economist Intelligence Unit 2007). Bank of Ghana officials acknowledged that the flows that they register represent only a fraction of what is probably entering into the country. Their figure does not include all unofficial remittances, which arrive through money-transfer bureaus, transfers such as deposits into personal accounts, and physical movements of cash or goods across borders.

Unrecorded remittances

Official data on remittances are believed to be underestimated, perhaps severely, but there is little agreement on the size of the undercounting. A recent International Monetary Fund study (El-Qorchi, Maimbo and Wilson 2003) estimated that unofficial transfers of remittances to developing countries amount to $10 billion a year. Another study estimates that global remittances are about 2.5 times the size of recorded remittances reported in the International Monetary Fund's balance of payments data (AITE 2005). These estimates differ by a factor of 25. Freund and Spatafora (2005) estimate that informal remittances to Sub-Saharan Africa are relatively high—45–65 percent of formal flows—compared with only about 5–20 percent in Latin America. Adams and Page (2003) and Page and Plaza (2006) also find that unrecorded remittances are large—48 percent worldwide—ranging from 73 percent in Sub-Saharan Africa to a negligible amount in South Asia.[1] Sub-Saharan Africa has the highest share of unrecorded remittances, which may reflect the fact that informal channels are common in many African countries because the formal financial infrastructure is limited (Page and Plaza 2006).

Undercounting arises from two sources. First, most remittance source countries do not require "small" transactions to be reported.[2] Remittances through post offices, exchange bureaus, and other money transfer companies are often not reflected in the official statistics (World Bank 2006).[3] Second, official data do not capture remittance flows through informal channels. Remittances transferred through agents such as informal operators or hand carried by travelers may be nearly as large as remittances through official channels.

A recent World Bank study (Sander and Maimbo 2003) reports that unrecorded flows appear to be high in Africa. In Sudan, for example, informal remittances are estimated at 85 percent of total remittance receipts. Preliminary findings from Mazzucato, van den Boom, and Nsowah-Nuamah (2004) of the Ghana Transnational Networks research program in Amsterdam show that as much as 65 percent of total remittances to Ghana may be sent informally, and the Bank of Ghana estimates that informal flows are at least as high as recorded flows. In South Africa an informal money remittance system exists side by side with the formal system, and the bulk of remittances to neighboring countries flows through informal channels (Genesis Analytics 2003). In Comoros informal transfers account for approximately 80 percent of remittances (da Cruz, Fegler, Schwartzman, 2004). The weakness of the Comoros banking sector—Comoros has only one commercial bank—may account for the wide use of informal channels.

(continued)

Box 11 **Remittances in Africa** (continued)

One example of an informal remittance transfer system is the Somali *xawilaad*. Operated by Somalis and used mainly by Somalis, the *xawilaad* is an informal system of value transfer that operates in almost every part of the world (Horst and Van Hear 2002). Interviews conducted in Virginia, in the United States (one of the areas with the largest Somali migrant population), report that two large companies provide transfers of remittances to the Somali community: Dahbbshil and Amal. (After September 11 one of the largest *xawilaad* companies, Al Barakat, closed down.) The system relies heavily on telecommunications, so *xawiilaad* companies have invested in telephones, mobile radio systems, computer networks, and satellite telecommunications facilities (Montclos and Kagwanja 2000; Gundel 2003). Transfers by *xawiilaad* are fast and efficienct (Montclos 2002). But it is very difficult to estimate the amount of remittances sent through this system to Kenya (the largest refugee site of Somalis) and Somalia.

While some efforts have been made to improve the development impact of remittances in developing countries (such as new definitions in the balance of payments), a need remains to improve data on remittances in Sub-Saharan Africa.

1. The zero estimate for South Asia is a result of the estimating technique. The country observations for which data are available form a portion of the "outer bound" regression plane, and hence their officially recorded remittances are accepted as total remittances. This is not strictly true, but the pattern does conform to the observation that remittances in South Asia increasingly have moved through recorded channels.

2. For example, the reporting threshold (typically per person per day) is $10,000 in the United States, 12,500 euros in Western Europe, and 3 million yen in Japan.

3. The Bank of Ghana is one of the few banks that collect statistics in remittances and require information from registered banks and transfer agencies.

---

of children under age 5 in malaria-risk areas with fever being treated with antimalarial drugs.

Pregnant women receiving two doses of intermittent preventive treatment are the number of pregnant women who receive at least two preventive treatment doses of an effective antimalarial drug during routine antenatal clinic visits. This approach has been shown to be safe, inexpensive, and effective.

Source: Data on population are from the World Bank's Development Data Platform. Data on risk of malaria, children with fever receiving antimalarial drugs, and pregnant women receiving two doses of intermittent preventive treatment are from Demographic Health Surveys, Multiple Indicator Cluster Surveys, and national statistical offices. Data on deaths due to malaria are from the United Nations Statistics Division based on World Health Organization (WHO) estimates. Data on under-five mortality are harmonized estimates of the WHO, United Nations Children's Fund, and the World Bank, based mainly on household surveys, censuses, and vital registration, supplemented by World Bank estimates based on household surveys and vital registration. Data on insecticide-treated bednet use are from Demographic and Health Surveys and Multiple Indicator Cluster Surveys.

13. Capable states and partnership

TABLE 13.1. AID AND DEBT RELIEF

Net aid from all donors is net aid from the Organisation for Economic Co-operation and Development's (OECD) Development Assistance Committee (DAC), non-DAC bilateral (Organization of Petroleum Exporting Countries [OPEC], the former Council for Mutual Economic Assistance [CMEA] countries, and China [OECD data]), and multilateral donors. OPEC countries are Algeria, Iran, Iraq, Kuwait, Libya, Nigeria, Qatar, Saudi Arabia, the United Arab Emirates, and Venezuela. The former CMEA countries are Bulgaria, Czechoslovakia, the former German Democratic Republic, Hungary, Poland, Romania, and the former Soviet Union). See box 12 for a discussion of accounting for debt forgiveness in official development assistance statistics.

Net aid from DAC donors is net aid from OECD's DAC donors, which include Australia, Austria, Belgium, Canada, Denmark, Finland, France, Germany, Italy, Japan, the Netherlands, Norway, Sweden, Switzerland, the United Kingdom, and the United States. Ireland and New Zealand have been excluded in this compilation because their aid to Africa is negligible.

Net aid from multilateral donors is net aid from multilateral sources, such as the African Development Fund, the European

A surge in debt forgiveness grants beginning in 2002 has drawn attention to their treatment in official development assistance (ODA) statistics. These grants from the Organisation for Economic Co-operation and Development's Development Assistance Committee (DAC) countries have ballooned from a modest $2.5 billion in 2001 to $25 billion in 2005 (measured in gross terms). One-half to three-quarters of these grants have been allocated to Sub-Saharan Africa, except in 2005 when large debt relief operations for Iraq amounted to nearly $14 billion. The prominence of debt relief in aid flows in recent years is evident: bilateral ODA to Africa doubled (in nominal terms) over 2000–05, and about half of the expansion represented debt relief (see table).

There are several conceptual and measurement issues with DAC debt forgiveness statistics. Depetris Chauvin and Kraay (2005, 2006) argue that the standard data do not provide a reliable estimate of the value of debt relief—that is, in present value terms. They have developed their own present value estimates of debt relief. Another problem with DAC debt relief statistics is that forgiveness of outstanding amounts, debt service flows, and arrears is treated in the same way, even though the cash flow implications for borrowers' budgets are quite different. Despite these methodological issues, DAC debt forgiveness statistics are widely used for analytical and monitoring purposes.

Debt relief from the donors' perspective—budget effort—can be quite different from that from the recipients' perspective—availability of resources. One important question that arises then is whether ODA debt forgiveness grants represent additional flows (cross-border flows) to recipients. Several advocacy groups have argued that ODA statistics are misleading because debt cancellations do not represent "genuine" aid (see ActionAid International 2005).

DAC statistical guidelines allow debt cancellation to be reported as debt forgiveness when the action on debt occurs within the "framework of a bilateral agreement and is implemented for the purpose of promoting the development or welfare of the recipient" (OECD–DAC 2000a,b). Thus, forgiveness of ODA, other official flows, and private claims—principal, interest, and arrears—is captured in DAC statistics under "Debt forgiveness grants."[1] Appropriate offsetting items (or counter entries) for principal and interest of each type of claim are reported, but not all are ODA flows—only forgiven principal on ODA loans is included under "offsetting entry for debt forgiveness" in ODA flows.[2]

Most debt forgiveness grants in DAC statistics represent forgiveness of other official flows and private claims typically under the framework of the Paris Club. The counter entries are not ODA flows, so there is concern that recent debt actions assign a large amount of flows to recipients that do not represent any new transfer of resources. This point is well illustrated by the 2002 Paris Club debt relief agreement for Democratic Republic of Congo. The country had an unbearable debt burden and under reasonable conditions was clearly unable to meet its obligations to external creditors. The Paris Club agreement restructured $8.98 billion of debt—$8.49 billion in principal and interest arrears and $490 million of future payments (Paris Club 2002). Only about $1.4 billion of the outstanding claims

Development Assistance Committee debt forgiveness grants and net official development assistance to Sub-Saharan Africa ($ billions, 2000–05)

Year	Debt forgiveness grants	Offsetting entries for debt relief	Net debt forgiveness grants	Total net official development assistance
2000	1.23	0.43	0.80	8.14
2001	1.28	0.30	0.98	8.17
2002	2.96	0.37	2.59	11.40
2003	6.48	0.39	6.10	17.24
2004	4.97	1.73	3.24	16.71
2005	9.46	1.51	7.94	22.51

Source: OECD-DAC database.

were ODA loans. The country received Naples Terms—67 percent of commercial credits were cancelled and the remaining 33 percent were rescheduled; and ODA credits were rescheduled. (In November 2003 the country received Cologne Terms from Paris Club creditors.) The resulting DAC data for ODA disbursements in 2003 (when the bulk of relief granted under the Paris Club agreement was reported in the DAC statistics) show debt forgiveness grants of $4.441 billion and offsetting entries for debt relief of only $4.9 million. Together, these two items account for $4.44 billion of net ODA flows. The country did not receive additional resources of anything close to this amount. However, the country's debt burden was substantially reduced, and it was able to normalize relations with the international community, improving its prospects for growth.

Although debt cancellation may not deliver additional flows to borrowers, it does reflect government budget effort. The extent of the budget effort will depend on the terms of government guarantees for export and commercial credits and on the timing of writeoffs for official loans—some may already have been written down (see also OECD 2007). Because of differences in practices across donors, the extent of the budget effort for a particular debt action varies across countries.

This note is adapted from box 4.1 of *Global Monitoring Report 2007: Confronting the Challenges of Gender Equality and Fragile States* (World Bank 2007). A host of debt actions are presented in Development Assistance Committee statistics; the focus here is on debt forgiveness.

1. Reorganization of other official funds and private claims within the framework of the Paris Club often involves concessionality in the form of debt reduction, debt service reduction, and capitalization of moratorium interest. The cancellation of part of the claims (or the amount equivalent to the reduction in net present value) is treated as debt forgiveness in ODA with no offsetting items in ODA flows. Amounts of other official funds and private claims that are rescheduled are not part of ODA and are included as "Rescheduling" loans under other official funds flows.

2. Forgiven other official funds principal is reported under "Offsetting entries for debt relief" in other official funds flows and forgiven private principal is accounted in "Offsetting entry for debt relief" under private flows. There are no offsets to forgiven interest in ODA, other official funds, or private flows. Instead, appropriate counter entries "Offsetting entry for forgiven interest" are to be noted in memo items—the data for which are usually incomplete. The result is that the treatment of debt cancellation in ODA statistics assigns a larger amount of net flows to recipients than amounts actually received.

Development Fund for the Commission of the European Communities, the International Development Association, the International Fund for Agricultural Development, Arab and OPEC financed multilateral agencies, and UN programs and agencies. Aid flows from the International Monetary Fund's (IMF) Trust Fund and Structural Adjustment Facility are also included. UN programs and agencies include the United Nations Technical Assistance Programme, the United Nations Development Programme, the United Nations Office of the High Commissioner for Refugees, the United Nations Children's Fund, and the World Food Programme. Arab and OPEC financed multilateral agencies include the Arab Bank for Economic Development in Africa, the Arab Fund for Economic and Social Development, the Islamic Development Bank, the OPEC Fund for International Development, the Arab Authority for Agricultural Investment and Development, the Arab Fund for Technical Assistance to African and Arab Countries, and the Islamic Solidarity Fund.

Net aid as a share of gross domestic product (GDP) is calculated by dividing the nominal total net aid from all donors by nominal GDP. For a given level of aid flows, devaluation of a recipient's currency may inflate the ratios shown in the table. Thus, trends for a given country and comparisons across countries that have implemented different exchange rate policies should be interpreted carefully.

Net aid per capita is calculated by dividing the nominal total net aid by midyear population. These ratios offer some indication of the importance of aid flows in sustaining per capita income and consumption levels, although exchange rate fluctuations, the actual rise of aid flows, and other factors vary across countries and over time.

Net aid as a share of gross capital formation is calculated by dividing the nominal total net aid by gross capital formation. These data highlight the relative importance of the indicated aid flows in maintaining and increasing investment in these economies. The same caveats mentioned above apply to their interpretation. Furthermore, aid flows do not exclusively finance investment (for example, food aid finances consumption), and the share of aid going to investment varies across countries.

Net aid as a share of imports of goods and services is calculated by dividing nominal total net aid by imports of goods and services.

Net aid as a share of central government expenditure is calculated by dividing nominal total net aid by central government expenditure.

Heavily Indebted Poor Countries (HIPC) Debt Initiative decision point is the date at which a HIPC with an established track record of good performance under adjustment programs supported by the International Monetary Fund and the World Bank commits to undertake additional reforms and to develop and implement a poverty reduction strategy.

HIPC Debt Initiative completion point is the date at which the country successfully completes the key structural reforms agreed on at the decision point, including developing and implementing its poverty reduction strategy. The country then receives the bulk of debt relief under the HIPC Initiative without further policy conditions.

Debt service relief committed is the amount of debt service relief, calculated at the decision point, that will allow the country to achieve debt sustainability at the completion point.

Source: OECD and World Bank data.

TABLE 13.2. CAPABLE STATES

Courts are the share of senior managers who ranked courts and dispute resolution systems as a major or very severe constraint.

Crime is the share of senior managers who ranked crime, theft, and disorder as a major or very severe constraint.

Number of procedures to enforce a contract is the number of independent actions, mandated by law or courts, that demand interaction between the parties of a contract or between them and the judge or court officer.

Time required to enforce a contract is the number of calendar days from the filing of the lawsuit in court until the final determination and, in appropriate cases, payment.

Cost to enforce a contract is court and attorney fees, where the use of attorneys is mandatory or common, or the cost of an administrative debt recovery procedure, expressed as a percentage of the debt value.

Protecting investors disclosure index measures the degree to which investors are protected through disclosure of ownership and financial information.

Director liability index measures a plaintiff's ability to hold directors of firms liabile for damages to the company).

Shareholder suits index measures shareholders' ability to sue officers and directors for misconduct.

Investor protection index measures the degree to which investors are protected through disclosure of ownership and financial information regulations.

Number of tax payments is the number of taxes paid by businesses, including electronic filing. The tax is counted as paid once a year even if payments are more frequent.

Time to prepare, file, and pay taxes is the number of hours it takes to prepare, file, and pay (or withhold) three major types of taxes: the corporate income tax, the value added or sales tax, and labor taxes, including payroll taxes and social security contributions.

Total tax payable is the total amount of taxes payable by the business (except for labor taxes) after accounting for deductions and exemptions as a percentage of gross profit. For further details on the method used for assessing the total tax payable, see the World Bank's *Doing Business 2006*.

Extractive Industries Transparency Initiative (EITI) Endorsed indicates whether a country has implemented or endorsed the EITI, a multistakeholder approach to increasing governance and transparency in extractive industries. It includes civil society, the private sector, and government and requires a work plan with timeline and budget to ensure sustainability, independent audit of payments and disclosure of revenues, publication of results in a publicly accessible manner, and an approach that covers all companies and government agencies. EITI supports improved governance in resource-rich countries through the verification and full publication of company payments and government revenues from oil, gas, and mining. EITI is a global initiative and the EITI Secretariat has developed an EITI Source Book that provides guidance for countries and companies wishing to implement the initiative (http://www.eitransparency.org/section/abouteiti).

EITI report produced indicates whether the country has publicly released an EITI report. Generally, a report is produced after the EITI principles are adopted.

Corruption Perceptions Index transparency index is the annual Transparency International corruption perceptions index, which ranks more than 150 countries in terms of perceived levels of corruption, as determined by expert assessments and opinion surveys.

Source: Data on investment climate constraints to firms are based on enterprise surveys conducted by the World Bank and its partners during 2001–05 (http://rru.worldbank.org/EnterpriseSurveys). Data on enforcing contracts, protecting investors, and regulation and tax administration are from the World Bank's Doing Business project (http://rru.worldbank.org/DoingBusiness/). Data on the EITI are from the EITI website, www.eitransparency.org. Data on corruption perceptions index are from Transparency International (www.transparency.org/policy_research/surveys_indices/cpi).

TABLE 13.3. GOVERNANCE AND ANTI-CORRUPTION INDICATORS

Voice and accountability measures the extent to which a country's citizens are able to participate in selecting their government and to enjoy freedom of expression, freedom of association, and a free media.

Political stability and absence of violence measures the perceptions of the likelihood that the government will be destabilized or overthrown by unconstitutional or violent means, including domestic violence or terrorism.

Government effectiveness measures the quality of public services, the quality and degree of independence from political pressures of the civil service, the quality of policy formulation and implementation, and the credibility of the government's commitment to such policies.

Regulatory quality measures the ability of the government to formulate and implement sound policies and regulations that permit and promote private sector development.

Rule of law measures the extent to which agents have confidence in and abide by the rules of society, in particular the quality of contract enforcement, the police, and the courts, as well as the likelihood of crime and violence.

Control of corruption measures the extent to which public power is exercised for private gain, including petty and grand forms of corruption, as well as "capture" of the state by elites and private interests.

Source: Data are from the World Bank Institute's Worldwide Governance Indicators database, which relies on 33 sources, including surveys of enterprises and citizens, and expert polls, gathered from 30 organizations around the world.

TABLE 13.4. COUNTRY POLICY AND INSTITUTIONAL ASSESSMENT RATINGS

The Country Policy and Institutional Assessment (CPIA) assesses the quality of a country's present policy and institutional framework. "Quality" means how conducive that framework is to fostering sustainable, poverty-reducing growth and the effective use of development assistance. The CPIA is conducted annually for all International Bank for Reconstruction and Development and International Development Association borrowers (except Liberia and Somalia), but results are reported only for International Development Association members. It has evolved into a set of criteria grouped into four clusters with 16 criteria that reflect a balance between ensuring that all key factors that foster pro-poor growth and poverty alleviation are captured, without overly burdening the evaluation process.

- Economic management
  - *Macroeconomic management* assesses the quality of the monetary, exchange rate, and aggregate demand policy framework.
  - *Fiscal policy* assesses the short- and medium-term sustainability of fiscal policy (taking into account monetary and exchange rate policy and the sustainability of the public debt) and its impact on growth.
  - *Debt policy* assesses whether the debt management strategy is conducive to minimize budgetary risks and ensure long-term debt sustainability
- Structural policies
  - *Trade* assesses how the policy framework fosters trade in goods. It covers two areas: trade regime restrictiveness—which focuses on the height of tariffs barriers, the extent to which nontariff barriers are used, and the transparency and predictability of the trade regime—and customs and trade facilitation—which includes the extent to which the customs service is free of corruption, relies on

risk management, processes duty collections and refunds promptly, and operates transparently.

  - *Financial sector* assesses the structure of the financial sector and the policies and regulations that affect it. It covers three dimensions: financial stability; the sector's efficiency, depth, and resource mobilization strength; and access to financial services.
  - *Business regulatory environment* assesses the extent to which the legal, regulatory, and policy environment helps or hinders private business in investing, creating jobs, and becoming more productive. The emphasis is on direct regulations of business activity and regulation of goods and factor markets. It measures three subcomponents: regulations affecting entry, exit, and competition; regulations of ongoing business operations; and regulations of factor markets (labor and land).
- Policies for social inclusion and equity
  - *Gender equality* assesses the extent to which the country has enacted and put in place institutions and programs to enforce laws and policies that promote equal access for men and women to human capital development and to productive and economic resources and that give men and women equal status and protection under the law.
  - *Equity of public resource use* assesses the extent to which the pattern of public expenditures and revenue collection affects the poor and is consistent with national poverty reduction priorities. The assessment of the consistency of government spending with the poverty reduction priorities takes into account the extent to which individuals, groups, or localities that are poor, vulnerable, or have unequal access to services and opportunities are identified; a national development strategy with explicit interventions to assist those individuals, groups, and localities has been adopted; and the composition and incidence of public expenditures

are tracked systematically and their results feedback into subsequent resource allocation decisions. The assessment of the revenue collection dimension takes into account the incidence of major taxes—for example, whether they are progressive or regressive—and their alignment with the poverty reduction priorities. When relevant, expenditure and revenue collection trends at the national and subnational levels should be considered. The expenditure component receives two-thirds of the weight in computing the overall rating.

- *Building human resources* assesses the national policies and public and private sector service delivery that affect access to and quality of health and nutrition services, including population and reproductive health; education, early childhood development, and training and literacy programs; and prevention and treatment of HIV/AIDS, tuberculosis, and malaria.
- *Social protection and labor* assess government policies in the area of social protection and labor market regulation, which reduce the risk of becoming poor, assist those who are poor to better manage further risks, and ensure a minimal level of welfare to all people. Interventions include social safety net programs, pension and old age savings programs, protection of basic labor standards, regulations to reduce segmentation and inequity in labor markets, active labor market programs (such as public works or job training), and community driven initiatives. In interpreting the guidelines it is important to take into account the size of the economy and its level of development.
- *Policies and institutions for environmental sustainability* assess the extent to which environmental policies foster the protection and sustainable use of natural resources and the management of pollution. Assessment of environmental sustainability requires multidimension criteria (that is, for air, water, waste, conservation management, coastal zones management, and natural resources management).

- Public sector management and institutions
  - *Property rights and rule-based governance* assess the extent to which private economic activity is facilitated by an effective legal system and rule-based governance structure in which property and contract rights are reliably respected and enforced. Three dimensions are rated separately: legal basis for secure property and contract rights; predictability, transparency, and impartiality of laws and regulations affecting economic activity, and their enforcement by the legal and judicial system; and crime and violence as an impediment to economic activity.
  - *Quality of budgetary and financial management* assesses the extent to which there is a comprehensive and credible budget, linked to policy priorities; effective financial management systems to ensure that the budget is implemented as intended in a controlled and predictable way; and timely and accurate accounting and fiscal reporting, including timely and audited public accounts and effective arrangements for follow-up.
  - *Efficiency of revenue mobilization* assesses the overall pattern of revenue mobilization—not only the tax structure as it exists on paper, but revenue from all sources as they are actually collected.
  - *Quality of public administration* assesses the extent to which civilian central government staffs (including teachers, health workers, and police) are structured to design and implement government policy and deliver services effectively. Civilian central government staffs include the central executive together with all other ministries and administrative departments, including autonomous agencies. It excludes the armed forces, state-owned enterprises, and subnational government.

- *Transparency, accountability, and corruption in the public sector* assess the extent to which the executive branch can be held accountable for its use of funds and the results of its actions by the electorate and by the legislature and judiciary, and the extent to which public employees within the executive are required to account for the use of resources, administrative decisions, and results obtained. Both levels of accountability are enhanced by transparency in decisionmaking, public audit institutions, access to relevant and timely information, and public and media scrutiny.

Source: World Bank's Country Policy and Institutional Assessment 2005.

14. Household welfare

The questions asked in household surveys vary by country. Quintiles are derived by ranking weighted sample population by area of residence (rural and urban) and per capita expenditure. Two sets of quintiles are calculated, one for rural and one for urban. Each quintile contains an equal number of people rather than households. The definition of rural and urban also vary by country. See box 13 for a discussion of the West and Central Africa Poverty Mapping Initiative, which combines census and household survey information to construct detailed poverty maps.

Sample size is the number of households surveyed in the country.

Total population is the weighted estimate of all the surveyed population in the country based on the survey—that is, it is the weighted sample population.

Age dependency ratio is the ratio of dependents—people younger than 15 or older than 64—to the working-age population—those ages 15–64.

Average household size is the average number of people in a household.

Monogamous male is a household headed by man who has no more than one spouse (wife).

Polygamous male is a household headed by a man who has more than one spouse (wife).

Single male is a household headed by a man who is widowed or divorced or who has never married.

De facto female refers to a household without a resident male head or where the male head is not present and the wife is the head by default and serves as the main decision maker in his absence or a household where the resident male head has lost most of his functions as the economic provider due to infirmity, inability to work, or the like.

De jure female refers to a household headed by a woman who is widowed, separated, or divorced or who has never been married.

Mean monthly expenditure is the average monthly expenditure on both food and non-food items. See box 14 for a discussion of using income data to inform policy.

Mean monthly share on food is total monthly food expenditure and food own consumption as a share of total household expenditure.

Mean monthly share on health is total health expenditure (consultation, medical procedure, among other) as a share of total household expenditure. Health expenditure excludes hospitalization.

Mean monthly share on education is total education expenditure (tuition, transport, and the like) as a share of total household expenditure

Primary school within 30 minutes is the share of households that live within 30 minutes of a primary school.

Net primary enrollment rate is the ratio of children of a country's official primary school age who are enrolled in primary school to the total population of the corresponding official primary school age. Primary education provides children with basic reading, writing, and mathematics skills along with an elementary understanding of such subjects as history, geography, natural science, social science, art, and music.

Net secondary enrollment rate is the ratio of children of a country's official secondary school age who are enrolled in secondary school to the total population of the corresponding official secondary school age. Secondary education completes the provision of basic education that began at the primary level and aims to lay the foundations for life-long learning and human development by offering more subject- or skill-oriented instruction using more specialized teachers.

Tertiary enrollment rate is the number of students currently in tertiary education per 10,000 people. Tertiary education, whether or not to an advanced research qualification,

There are often large regional differences in social indicators within a country. But geographic poverty profiles based on household surveys tend to be limited to broad areas because survey sample sizes prevent analysts from constructing valid estimates of poverty at the local level. At the same time policymakers often need finely disaggregated information at the neighborhood, town, or village level to implement antipoverty programs. Following a methodology developed by Elbers, Lanjouw, and Lanjouw (2003), the World Bank's Africa Region launched the West and Central Africa Poverty Mapping Initiative to combine census and household survey data to construct detailed poverty maps.

The methodology is straightforward. First, a regression of adult equivalent consumption is estimated using household survey data,

limiting the set of explanatory variables to ones common to both the survey and the latest census. Second, the coefficients from that regression are applied to the census data to predict the expenditure level of each household in the census. Third, the predicted household expenditures are used to construct a series of poverty and inequality indicators for different geographical population subgroups. Although the idea behind the methodology is simple, its proper implementation requires complex computations.

The table below lists the countries participating in the initiative, the year of the census and survey data used, and the administrative level at which poverty estimates are available. The map below—based on the data from the 1998/99 Ghana Living Standards Survey and the 2000 Housing and Population Census—shows poverty by district in Ghana.

Countries participating in the West and Central Africa Poverty Mapping Initiative

Country	Census year	Survey year	Administrative levels measured (number)
Burkina Faso	1996	1998	Region (13), Province (45), Department (383)
Cape Verde	2000	2000/01	Ilho (9), Concelho (17), Freguesi (31)
Côte d'Ivoire	1998	2002	Region (19), Department (58), Sous-prefecture (254), Secteur (444)
Gabon	2003	2005	Province (9), Department (48), Canton (219)
Gambia	2003	2003/04	Local government area (8), District (39)
Ghana	2000	1998/99	Region (10), District (138)
	2003[a]	2005/06	Region (10), District (110)
Guinea	1996	2002	Region (8), Prefecture (38), Commune (341)
Mali	1998	2001	Region (9), Cercle (49), Commune (703)
Mauritania	2000	2004	Wilaya (13), Moughata (53), Commune (216)
Niger	2001	2005	Department (8), Arrondissement (36), Canton/commune (175)
Nigeria	2006[a]	2003/04	State (37), Senatorial (109)
Rwanda	2002	2000/01	Province (5), District (30), Secteur (416)
Senegal	2001	2001/02	Region (11), Department (34), Arrondissement (133), Commune (426)
Sierra Leone	2004	2002/03	Province (4), District (14), Chiefdom (166)

a. Core Welfare Indicator Questionnaire.
Source: Coulombe and Wodon 2007.

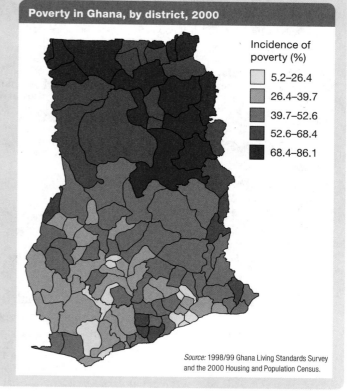

Poverty in Ghana, by district, 2000

Incidence of poverty (%)
- 5.2–26.4
- 26.4–39.7
- 39.7–52.6
- 52.6–68.4
- 68.4–86.1

Source: 1998/99 Ghana Living Standards Survey and the 2000 Housing and Population Census.

normally requires, as a minimum condition of admission, the successful completion of education at the secondary level.

Adult literacy rate is the percentage of adults ages 15 and older who can both read and write a simple sentence in any language.

Youth literacy rate is the percentage of youth ages 15–24 who can both read and write a simple sentence in any language.

Health center less than 1 hour away is the percentage of the population living less than 1 hour away from a health center.

Health center less than 5 km away is the percentage of the population living less than 5 kilometers away from a health center.

Morbidity is the percentage of the population who were sick or injured within a given number of weeks before the survey.

Health care provider consulted when sick is the percentage of sick people who took any remedial action when sick.

Type of health care provider consulted is the type of facility visited by a sick household member. *Public* includes fully government-owned

In many African countries household surveys are well designed to measure consumption and poverty as well as human development outcomes and access to basic infrastructure. But detailed information on the sources of income and the livelihoods of households and individuals are still often lacking. This is problematic because income data is essential to identify the links between growth and poverty reduction, to determine ways to improve the household well-being, and to understand the potential impacts of economic shocks.

To show how simple tabulations on income sources can inform policy debates, consider cotton. World cotton prices (as measured by the Cotlook A Index) have been declining for most of the past decade, and farmers in West Africa especially have suffered from low producer prices. Income data can first be used to identify cotton producers in household surveys. The table below provides data for the "cotton-4" countries—Benin, Burkina Faso, Chad, and Mali. It suggests that cotton producers are on average more likely to be poor than the population as a whole, except in Burkina Faso.

Data on income (and thus implicitly on production levels) can also be used to assess who would benefit from higher producer prices. The table suggests that except for Burkina Faso about two-thirds of cotton production is accounted for by households in the bottom three quintiles of per capita consumption. About two-thirds of the additional income that would be generated by higher cotton producer prices would benefit these households, which are often considered vulnerable because many are poor and those who are not are have consumption levels close to the poverty line.

Finally, although not shown in the table, the same data can be used to simulate the impact of changes in producer prices on poverty among producers and among the population as a whole. Because cotton typically accounts for only about half the total income of households producing cotton, and total income also accounts for only half the consumption of households observed in the surveys, poverty measures tend not to change dramatically with producer prices. At the same time, even small differences in income or consumption levels can make a big difference for households that have to survive on very meager resources.

Poverty among cotton producers and distribution of production, select West African countries, various years (percent)				
	Benin (2003)	Burkina Faso (2003)	Chad (2003)	Mali (2006)
Prevalence of poverty				
Whole population	39.0	46.4	55.0	47.4
Cotton producers	53.6	47.2	72.7	77.8
Share of cotton production				
Bottom population quintile	22.0	13.1[a]	24.6	23.2
Bottom two population quintiles	44.4	32.3[a]	51.7	48.6
Bottom three population quintiles	65.9	49.9[a]	67.3	71.6

a. Data are from the 1997/98 priority survey.
Source: Tsimpo and Wodon 2007.

as well as semi-public health facilities. *Private, modern medicine,* is facilities set up with profit as their main focus and includes private doctors. *Private, traditional healers* refer to health care providers whose knowledge, skills, and practices are based on the experiences indigenous to different cultures and whose services are directed toward the maintenance of health, as well as the prevention, diagnosis, and improvement of physical and mental illness. *Other* is other types of health providers that cannot be classified by the categories described above.

Birth assisted by trained staff are the percentage of deliveries attended by personnel trained to give the necessary supervision, care, and advice to women during pregnancy, labor, and the postpartum period; to conduct deliveries on their own; and to care for newborns.

Immunization coverage, 1-year-olds, is the percentage of children ages 12–23 months at the time of survey who received one dose of Bacille Calmette Guerin vaccine, three doses of polio vaccine, three doses of diphtheria, pertussis, and tetanus vaccine, and one does of measles vaccine.

Measles immunization coverage, 1-year-olds, is the percentage of children ages 12–23 months at the time of survey who received a dose of measles vaccine. A child is considered adequately immunized against measles after receiving one dose of vaccine.

Stunting is the percentage of children under age 5 whose height for age is more than two standard deviations below the median for the international reference population ages 6–59 months. The reference population, adopted by the World Health Organization in 1983, is based on children from the United States, who are assumed to be well nourished.

Wasting is the percentage of children under age 5 whose weight for height is more than two standard deviations below the median for the international reference population ages 6–59 months. The reference population, adopted by the World Health Organization in 1983, is based on children from the United States, who are assumed to be well nourished.

Underweight is the percentage of children under age 5 whose weight for age is more than two standard deviations below the median for the international reference population ages 6–59 months. The reference population, adopted by the World Health Organization in 1983, is based on children from the United States, who are assumed to be well nourished.

Water source less than 1 hour away is the percentage of the population living less than 1 hour away from a water source.

Water source less than 5 km away is the percentage of the population living less than 5 kilometers away from a water source.

Market less than 1 hour away is the percentage of the population living less than 1 hour away from a market.

Market less than 5 km away is the percentage of the population living less than 5 kilometers away from a market.

Access to improved water source refers to the percentage of the population with reasonable access to an adequate amount of water from an improved source, such as a household connection, public standpipe, borehole, protected well or spring, or rainwater collection. Unimproved sources include vendors, tanker trucks, and unprotected wells and springs. *Own tap* is a household water connection. *Other piped* is a public water connection. *Well, protected,* is a ground water source.

Traditional fuel use is the percentage of the population using traditional fuels such as firewood and charcoal as the main source of cooking fuel.

TABLE 14.1. BURKINA FASO HOUSEHOLD SURVEY, 2003

Household is the basic socioeconomic unit in which the different members—related or living in the same house or property—put together their resources and jointly meet their basic needs, including food, under the authority of one person who is recognized as the head.

Source: Burkina Faso's Institut National de la Statistique et de la Démographie carried out the Enquête Prioritaire II sur les Conditions de Vie des Ménages au Burkina. Data were collected in 2003. The project was funded by the government of Burkina Faso, the World Bank, the African Development Bank, and the United Nations through the United Nations Development Programme.

TABLE 14.2. CAMEROON HOUSEHOLD SURVEY, 2001

Household is people who live under the same roof, take their meals together or in little groups, and put some or all of their incomes together for the group's spending purposes, at the head of household's discretion.

Source: Cameroon's Bureau Central des Recensements et des Enquêtes of the Direction de la Statistique et de la Comptabilité carried out the Enquête Camerounaise auprès des Ménages in 2001.

TABLE 14.3. ETHIOPIA HOUSEHOLD SURVEY, 2000

Household is a person or a group of people who live under the same roof, share the same meals, and recognize one person as the head.

Source: The 1999/2000 Household Income, Consumption, and Expenditure Survey was carried out by the Central Statistical Office. The data collection process was carried out from June 1999 to February 2000.

TABLE 14.4. MALAWI HOUSEHOLD SURVEY, 2004

Household is a person living alone or a group of people, either related or unrelated, who live together as a single unit in the sense that they have common housekeeping arrangements (that is, share or are supported by a common budget). Someone who did not live with the household during the survey period was not counted as a current member of the household.

Literacy measures the ability to read and write a simple sentence for those who had not attended school in the past two months and was defined based on education attainment for those who had attended school in the past two months.

Source: The Malawi National Statistics Office carried out the Integrated Household Survey in 2004/5.

TABLE 14.5. NIGER HOUSEHOLD SURVEY, 2005
Household is the set of people who partly or totally shared their expenditures, had not been absent for more than 6 of the 12 months preceding the survey, and were not domestic help. For polygamous households each wife and her children were considered to be a separate household.

Literacy measures the number of people with ability to read and write in Portuguese.

Source: Direction de la Statistique et des comptes nationaux carried out the Enquete Nationale sur les Conditions de vie des Menages from April 14 to July 11, 2005.

TABLE 14.6. NIGERIA HOUSEHOLD SURVEY, 2004
Household is a group of persons who normally cook, eat, and live together. Number of months sharing in these activities was another criterion used to qualify as a household a member (minimum of three months). However, all heads of households irrespective of number of months living elsewhere were included as household members. These people may or may not be related by blood, but make common provision for food or other essentials for living, and they have one person whom they all regard as the head of the household.

Literacy measures the number of people with the ability to read and write either in English or any of the local languages.

Source: The Federal Office of Statistics, Abuja, of Nigeria carried out the Nigeria Living Standards Survey, an integrated survey. Data were collected between September 2003 and August 2004.

TABLE 14.7. SÃO TOMÉ AND PRINCIPE HOUSEHOLD SURVEY, 2000
Household is the set of people, related or not, who live together under the same roof, put their resources together, and address as a unit their primary needs, under the authority of one person whom they recognize as the head of the household.

Literacy measures the number of people with the ability to read and write a simple sentence.

Source: The Instituto Nacional de Estatistica of the Ministério de Planomento, Finanças e Cooperaçao carried out the Enquête sur les Conditions de Vie des Ménages in 2000. The project was financed by the government of São Tomé and Principe with assistance from the African Development Bank and the United Nations Development Programme. Technical assistance was provided by the International Labour Organization.

TABLE 14.8. SIERRA LEONE HOUSEHOLD SURVEY, 2002/03
Household is a group of people who normally cook, eat, and live together. Number of months sharing in these activities was another criterion used to qualify as a household a member (minimum three months). However, all heads of households irrespective of number of months living elsewhere were included as household members. These people may or may not be related by blood, but make common provision for food or other essentials for living, and they have one person whom they all regarded as the head of the household.

Literacy measures the number of people with the ability to read and write a simple sentence in either English or the local languages.

Source: The Sierra Leone Central Statistical Office carried out the Living Conditions Monitoring Survey. Data were collected between 2002 and 2003.

TABLE 14.9. UGANDA HOUSEHOLD SURVEY, 2002/03
Household is individuals who normally eat and live together.

Literacy measures the number of people who responded that they could both read and write. The level of education was also used to determine literacy.

Source: The Uganda Bureau of Statistics carried out the National Household Survey. Data collection occurred between May 2002 and April 2003. The project was funded by the government of Uganda and the World Bank. Statistics Denmark and the World Bank provided consultants for technical support.

References

ActionAid International. 2005. "Real Aid: An Agenda for Making Aid Work" Johannesburg, South Africa.

Adams, Richard, Jr., and John Page. 2003. "International Migration, Remittances, and Poverty in Developing Countries." Policy Research Working Paper 3179. World Bank, Washington, D.C.

AITE. 2005. "Consumer Money Transfers: Powering Global Remittances." Boston, Mass.

Banerjee, S., Q. Wodon, A. Diallo, T. Pushak, H. Uddin, C. Tsimpo, and V. Foster. 2007. "Access, Affordability, and Alternatives: Modern Infrastructure Services in Africa." Africa Infrastructure Country Diagnostic Study. World Bank, Washington, D.C.

CONCORDE. 2007. "Hold the Applause! EU Governments Risk Breaking Aid Promises." Brussels.

Coulibaly, Kalamogo, Kene Ezemenari, and Tembo Maburuki. 2007. "Cross Border Trade in Rwanda." Background paper to the Country Economic Memorandum. World Bank, Washington, D.C.

Coulombe, H., and Q. Wodon. 2007. "Combining Census and Household Survey Data for Better Targeting: The West and Central Africa Poverty Mapping Initiative." World Bank, Washington, D.C.

Cull, Robert, Lance E. Davis, Naomi, R. Lamoreaux, and Jean-Laurent Rosenthal. 2006. "Historical Financing of Small- and Medium-Size Enterprises." *Journal of Banking and Finance* 30 (11): 3017–42.

Da Cruz, Vincent, Wolfang Fengler, and Adam Schwartzman. 2004. "Remittance to Comoros: Volume, Trends, Impact and Implications." Africa Region Working Paper N075. World Bank, Washington, D.C.

Depetris Chuavin, Nicolas, and Aart Kraay. 2005. "What Has 100 Billion Dollars Worth of Debt Relief Done for Low-Income Countries?" Unpublished manuscript. World Bank, Washington, D.C.

———. 2006. "Who Gets Debt Relief?" Policy Research Working Paper 4000. World Bank, Washington, D.C.

Economist Intelligence Unit. 2007. "Ghana Country Economic Report." London.

Elbers, Chris, Jean Olson Lanjouw, and Peter Lanjouw. 2003. "Micro-Level Estimation of Poverty and Inequality." *Econometrica* 71 (1): 355–64.

El-Qorchi, Mohammed, Samuel Munzele Maimbo, and John Wilson. 2003. "Informal Funds Transfer Systems: An Analysis of the Informal Hawala System." IMF Occasional Paper 222. International Monetary Fund, Washington, D.C.

Freund, Caroline L., and Nikola Spatafora. 2005. "Remittances: Transaction Costs, Determinants, and Informal Flows." Policy Research Working Paper 3704. World Bank, Washington, D.C.

Genesis Analytics. 2003. "Money Transfer Services in Southern Africa." Johannesburg, South Africa.

Gundel, J. 2003. "The Migration-Development Nexus: Somalia CaseStudy." In N. Van Hear and N. Nyberg Sorensen, eds., *The Migration Development Nexus.* Geneva: International Organization for Migration.

Horst C., and N. Van Hear. 2002. "Counting the Cost: Refugees, Remittances and the War against Terrorism." *Forced Migration Review* 14: 32–34.

Hussmans, Ralf. 2004. "Measuring the Informal Economy: From Employment in the Informal Sector to Informal Employment." Working Paper 53. International Labour Organization, Policy Integration Department, Bureau of Statistics, Geneva.

ILO (International Labour Organization). 2002. "Women and Men in the Informal Economy: A Statistical Picture." Geneva.

IMF (International Monetary Fund). 2003. *Foreign Direct Investment: How Countries Measure FDI 2001.* Washington, D.C.

———. 2007. "Draft Balance of Payments and International Investment Position Manual." Washington, D.C.

IMF (International Monetary Fund) Committee on Balance of Payments Statistics. 2006. "Definitions of Remittances." Nineteenth Meeting Outcome Paper. October 23–26, Frankfurt, Germany.

Mazzucato, V., B. van den Boom, and N.N.N. Nsowah-Nuamah. 2004. "The Impact of International Remittances on Local Living Standards: Evidence for Households in Ghana." Paper presented at the United Nations Development Programme Conference on Migration and Development, 2004, Accra.

Montclos, M.A. Perouse de. 2002. "Violences xénophobes en Afrique." *Le Monde diplomatique* 62: 21–24.

Montclos, M.A.P.d., and P. Kagwanja. 2000. "Refugee Camps or Cities? The Socio-economic Dynamics of the Dadaab and Kakuma Camps I Northern Kenya." *Journal of Refugee Studies* 13 (2): 205–22.

OECD (Organisation for Economic Co-operation and Development). 2007. *Development Cooperation Report 2006.* Paris.

OECD–DAC (Organisation for Economic Co-operation and Development–Development Assistance Committee). 2000. "Handbook for Reporting Debt Reorganization on the DAC Questionnaire." Paris.

———. 2000. "DAC Statistical Reporting Directives." Paris.

Orozco, Manuel. 2005. "Conceptual Considerations, Empirical Challenges and Solutions in Measuring Remittances." Report presented at the Centro de Estudios Monetarios Latinoamericanos meeting in September 1, Mexico City.

Page, John, and S. Plaza. 2006. "Migration, Remittances and Development: A Review of Global Evidence." *Journal of African Economies* 15 (Supplement 2): 245–336.

Paris Club. 2002. "Democratic Republic of Congo." Press Release, September 13. Paris.

Sander, C, and S.M. Maimbo. 2003. "Migrant Labor Remittances in Africa: Reducing Obstacles to Development Contributions." World Bank, Washington, D.C.

Tsimpo, C., and Q. Wodon. 2007. "Poverty among Cotton Producers: Evidence from Africa." World Bank, Washington, D.C.

UNCTAD (United Nations Conference on Trade and Development). 2005. "FDI Statistics: Data Compilation and Policy Issues." Note by the UNCTAD Secretariat for Expert Meeting on Capacity Building in the Area of FDI: Data Compilation and Policy Formulation in Developing Countries, 12–14 December, Geneva.

Wodon, Q. 2007a. "Is There a Divergence between Objective and Subjective Measures of Poverty? Evidence from West Africa." World Bank, Washington, D.C.

———. 2007b. "Using Simple Cross-Country Comparisons to Guide Measurement: Poverty in the CFA Franc Zone." World Bank, Washington, D.C.

World Bank. 2006. *Global Economic Prospects 2006: Economic Implications of Remittances and Migration.* Washington, D.C.: World Bank.

———. 2007. *Global Monitoring Report 2007: Confronting the Challenges of Gender Equality and Fragile States.* Washington, D.C.

World Economic Forum. 2007. *Africa Competitiveness Report 2007.* Geneva.

User's Guide
Africa Development Indicators 2007 CD-ROM

Introduction

This CD-ROM is part of the Africa Development Indicators suite of products. It was produced by the Office of the Chief Economist for the Africa Region and the Operational Quality and Knowledge Services Group in collaboration with the Development Data Group of the Development Economics Vice Presidency. It uses the latest version of the World Bank's *STARS* data retrieval system, Win*STARS version 5.0.

The CD-ROM contains about 1,000 macroeconomic, sectoral, and social indicators, covering 53 African countries. Time series include data from 1965 to 2005.

Win*STARS 5.0 features mapping and charting and several data export formats (Access™, ASCII, dBASE™, Excel™, and SAS™). We invite you to explore it.

A note about the data

Users should note that the data for the Africa Development Indicators suite of products are drawn from the same database. The general cutoff date for data is July 2007. Data for *African Economic Outlook 2007* country analyses may differ from those for the Africa Development Indicators suite of products because of different data sources or methodologies.

Help

This guide explains how to use the main functions of the CD-ROM. For details about additional features, click *Help* on the menu bar or the *Help* icon; or call one of the hotline numbers listed in the *Help* menu and on the copyright page of this booklet.

Installation

As is usual for Windows™ products, you should make sure that other applications are closed while you install the CD-ROM.

To install the single-user version:

1. Insert the CD-ROM into your CD drive.
2. Click on *Start* and select *Run*. Type D:\SETUP.EXE (where D: is your CD-ROM drive letter), click *OK* and follow the instructions. For Windows Vista™, click the Computer icon on your desktop, navigate to your CD-ROM drive, and launch the Setup application.
3. Win*STARS 5.0 requires Microsoft Internet Explorer™ 4.0 or higher. If you do not have Internet Explorer, it may be downloaded at no charge from www. microsoft.com. It does not need to be your default browser. If you do not wish to use Internet Explorer, you have the option to install Win*STARS 4.2.

You can delete this program at any time by clicking on *Start, Settings, Control Panel, Add/Remove Programs*. To reinstall it, reboot your computer first.

Operation

To start the CD-ROM, go to the *WB Development Data* program group and click on the *Africa Development Indicators 2007* icon.

Note that standard Windows™ controls are used for most functions. For detailed instructions, refer to the on-screen *Help* menu or tool tips (on-screen explanations of buttons that are displayed when the cursor rolls over them).

Features and instructions

Win*STARS has four main functions—*Home, Query, Result,* and *Map*. Move among them at any time by clicking on the respective tabs.

Home

On the *Home* screen you can access each element of the Africa Development Indicators 2007 CD-ROM. Use the browser controls to link to the Africa Development Indicators tables, *The Little Data Book on Africa 2007,* time series database, maps, *African Economic Outlook 2007* country analyses, and other related information.

Query

1. Click on the *Query* button to start your time series selection.
2. Click on each of the *Country, Series,* and *Periods* buttons and make your selections on each screen. There are many ways to make a selection—see below, or use the *Help* menu.
3. Highlight the items you want.
4. Click on the *Select* button to move them into the *Selected* box.
5. Deselect items at any time by highlighting them and clicking on the *Remove* icon.
6. When selection is complete, click on *OK* to return to the main *Query* screen.
7. If you want to, you can display information on data availability by clicking on the *Availability* icon. You can choose to count time series or total observations.
8. Click on *View Data* to see the data on the *Result* screen.

Making selections. Countries: You can select countries from an alphabetical list, by *Classification* (region, income group, or lending category), by *Criteria* (up to two can be specified), or by *Group* (aggregates have been calculated only when there were adequate data). *Series:* You can choose from an alphabetical list or by *Category.* When selecting series by category, the subcategory buttons change with each

category. *Periods:* Select time periods from the *Periods* list box.

Creating your own country or indicator list. You can create your own group of countries, series, or periods by saving your query on the appropriate screen. You can also save all elements of the query on the *Query* screen. You can reload a saved query in a future session.

To save a query:

1. Highlight items on any of the *Countries, Series,* or *Periods* (or any two or all three) selection screens and click on *Select* to place them in the *Selected* box.
2. Click on the *Save Query* icon and follow the naming prompts.

To load a query:

1. Go to the selection screen in which your query is saved. For example, if you have saved a set of countries, go to the *Countries* selection screen.
2. Click on the *Load Query* icon, select the query you want, and click on *OK*.

To modify a saved query:

1. Load the query.
2. In the *Selected* box, highlight the items to be removed and click on the *Remove* icon.
3. Add new items if necessary.
4. Resave the query.

Result

On the *Result* screen, data are presented in a three-dimensional spreadsheet and, initially, in scientific notation. Data for the third dimension are presented on separate screens. You can change the selection displayed by clicking on the third dimension scroll box. You can also change the scale and the number of digits after the decimal. If the column is too narrow to present all the digits, they will appear as a series of ######. Double click on the column's guideline to widen it, or choose a larger scale (millions, for example). To scale series individually, click *Options* and check *Enable Series-Level Scaling.* Click the far right scroll box to view the percentage change over each selected period or to index the data.

Changing the orientation. You can view the result in six different orientations (countries down/periods across, series down/countries across, etc.). To change the orientation, click on the *Orientation* scroll box.

Charting and mapping data. On the *Result* screen, you can chart or map the data displayed. Highlight a set of cells for charting or a particular cell for mapping. Click on the *Chart* or *Map* icon on the toolbar accordingly. The charting function has many features. After you have displayed a chart, right click on the chart to open the *Chart Wizard* for more options. Mapping is described on page 8. From this screen you can choose to map all countries or only your selected countries. *Cutting, pasting, printing, and saving.* You can cut, paste, and print the result, or you can save the spreadsheet in another format. Click on the appropriate icon on the toolbar and follow the prompts. Click on Help for more details.

Map

On the *Map* screen, you can select a country and view a set of tables describing it, or you can map a series for all countries. In the upper left corner of the screen, the country name will appear as the cursor rolls slowly over the map. To zoom in for a closer look at the map, click on the *Zoom* icon.

Selecting a country or viewing country tables. To highlight a country and view any of its tables, click on the country on the map or select it in the *Locate a Country* scroll box in the upper right corner.

Mapping a series. On the *Map* screen, click on the *Series* icon. A list of key indicators will be displayed. (To show all available indicators, click on the box by *Show default series* to remove the *X.*) Highlight a series, select a period from the *Available Periods* list box (the default is the latest available) and click on *Paint Map*. The map will be colored according to the legend settings, any of which you can change. Note that as the cursor moves across the map, the series value is now also displayed in the upper left corner.

Changing the map legend and colors. The default interval range is an equal number of countries. To set an equal interval range or to map multiple periods, click on the *Recalculate* icon. Set your own intervals by editing the legend. To change map colors, double click on the legend color boxes. Press the *Remap* icon to see your changes.

Printing and saving. Click on the appropriate icon to print the map or save it as a bitmap or metafile.

License agreement

You must read and agree to the terms of this License Agreement prior to using this CD-ROM product. Use of the software and data contained on the CD-ROM is governed by the terms of this License Agreement. If you do not agree with these terms, you may return the product unused to the World Bank for a full refund of the purchase price.

1. **LICENSE.** In consideration of your payment of the required license fee, the WORLD BANK (the "Bank") hereby grants you a nonexclusive license to use the enclosed data and Win*STARS retrieval program (collectively, the "Program") subject to the terms and conditions set forth in this license agreement.

2. **OWNERSHIP.** As a licensee you own the physical media on which the Program is originally or subsequently recorded. The Bank, however, retains the title and ownership of the program recorded on the original CD-ROMs and all subsequent copies of the Program. This license is not considered to be a sale of the Program or any copy thereof.

3. **COPY RESTRICTIONS.** The Program and accompanying written materials are copyrighted. You may make one copy of the Program solely for backup purposes. Unauthorized copying of the Program or of the written materials is expressly forbidden.

4. **USE.** You may not modify, adapt, translate, reverse-engineer, decompile, or disassemble the Program. You may not modify, adapt, translate, or create derivative works based on any written materials without the prior written consent of the Bank. If you have purchased the single-user version of this product, you may use the Program only on a single laptop/desktop computer. You may not distribute copies of the Program or accompanying written materials to others. You may not use the Program on any network, including an Intranet or the Internet, without obtaining prior written permission from the Bank. If you have purchased the multiple-user version of this product, your license is valid only up to 15 users. Should you need to add additional users, please send a request, indicating the number of users you would like to add, to: World Bank Publications, Marketing and Rights, 1818 H Street, N.W., Washington, D.C. 20433, fax: 202-522-2422, email: pubrights@worldbank.org.

5. **TRANSFER RESTRICTIONS.** This Program is licensed only to you, the licensee, and may not be transferred to anyone without prior written consent of the Bank.

6. **LIMITED WARRANTY AND LIMITATIONS OF REMEDIES.** The Bank warrants that under normal use the CD-ROMs on which the Program is furnished are free from defects in materials and workmanship for a period of ninety (90) days from delivery to you, as evidenced by a copy of your receipt. The Bank's entire liability and your exclusive remedy shall be the replacement of any CD-ROMs that do not meet the Bank's limited warranty. Defective CD-ROMs should be returned within the warranty period, with a copy of your receipt, to the address specified in section 9 below. EXCEPT AS SPECIFIED ABOVE, THE PRODUCT IS PROVIDED "AS IS" WITHOUT WARRANTY OF ANY KIND, EITHER EXPRESSED OR IMPLIED, INCLUDING, BUT NOT LIMITED TO, THE IMPLIED WARRANTIES OF MERCHANTABILITY AND FITNESS FOR A PARTICULAR PURPOSE. THE BANK DOES NOT WARRANT THAT THE FUNCTIONS CONTAINED IN THE PROGRAM WILL MEET YOUR REQUIREMENTS OR THAT THE OPERATION OF THE PROGRAM WILL BE UNINTERRUPTED OR ERROR-FREE. IN NO EVENT WILL THE BANK BE LIABLE TO YOU FOR ANY DAMAGES ARISING OUT OF THE USE OF OR THE INABILITY TO USE THE PROGRAM. THE ABOVE WARRANTY GIVES YOU SPECIFIC LEGAL RIGHTS IN THE UNITED STATES THAT MAY VARY FROM STATE TO STATE. BECAUSE SOME STATES DO NOT ALLOW THE EXCLUSION OF IMPLIED WARRANTIES OR LIMITATION OF EXCLUSION OF LIABILITY FOR INCIDENTAL OR CONSEQUENTIAL DAMAGES, PARTS OF THE ABOVE LIMITATIONS AND EXCLUSIONS MAY NOT APPLY TO YOU.

7. **TERMINATION.** This license is effective from the date you open the package until the license is terminated. You may terminate it by destroying the Program and its documentation and any backup copy thereof or by returning these materials to the Bank. If any of the terms or conditions of this license are broken, the Bank may terminate the license and demand that you return the Program.

8. **GOVERNING LAW.** This license shall be governed by the laws of the District of Columbia, without reference to conflicts of law thereof.

9. **GENERAL.** If you have any questions concerning this product, you may contact the Bank by writing to World Bank Publications, CD-ROM Inquiries, The World Bank, 1818 H Street, N.W., Washington, D.C. 20433, email: data@worldbank.org. All queries on rights and licenses should be addressed to World Bank Publications, Marketing and Rights, 1818 H Street, N.W., Washington, D.C. 20433, fax: 202-522-2422, email: pubrights@worldbank.org.